Three I
Hermit Kingdom

Three Days in the Hermit Kingdom

An American Visits North Korea

EDDIE BURDICK

McFarland & Company, Inc., Publishers
Jefferson, North Carolina, and London

LIBRARY OF CONGRESS CATALOGUING-IN-PUBLICATION DATA

Burdick, Eddie, 1962–
    Three days in the hermit kingdom : an American visits
North Korea / Eddie Burdick.
        p.   cm.
    Includes bibliographical references and index.

    ISBN 978-0-7864-4898-2
    softcover : 50# alkaline paper ∞

    1. Korea (North)— Description and travel.   2. Burdick,
Eddie, 1962– — Travel— Korea (North)   I. Title.
DS932.4.B87   2010
    951.9305'1— dc22   2010011640

British Library cataloguing data are available

Front cover: International Friendship Exhibition at Mount
Myohyang

Manufactured in the United States of America

McFarland & Company, Inc., Publishers
  Box 611, Jefferson, North Carolina 28640
    www.mcfarlandpub.com

Table of Contents

Acknowledgments

Numerous individuals provided significant contributions that were of importance to this work. Primarily Dr. Wally Fredrickson was instrumental in assisting with translation from Korean and was an invaluable resource as a traveling companion, J Herman Brouwer of Wageningen offered translation of Dutch documents and articles on North Korea, while Dr. Frankie Carlton was always glorious in offer translation assistance with unusual North Korean syntax and verb use, and the curmudgeonly Mayor of Itaewon provided enlightenment, pointed out the connections, and revealed the essential 그냥 of 몰라.

Preface

American tourists in North Korea are a rare breed, but they do exist. This book chronicles a tightly controlled regime-sanctioned excursion to North Korea during just the third brief window of opportunity for US citizens to be granted North Korean tourist visas since the armistice in 1953. South of the Demilitarized Zone and across the rest of the world journalists use the mercilessly clichéd phrase "technically still at war" virtually every time either of the two Koreas is mentioned. After all it is true; an armistice was signed, but a peace treaty has yet to be formalized. The Korean War has been ongoing for more than half a century.

In North Korea, however, the war is not only finished, it was won. Through the magnificent leadership of the most brilliant military strategist ever to tread the earth the North Koreans soundly defeated the imperialist aggressor Yankee dogs and their lickspittle puppet-state allies. For a tightly scheduled and well orchestrated sixty-six hours the North Koreans allowed me in for a look. They showed their war trophies. They showed me their magnificent physical accomplishments and relentless cement monuments, they demonstrated their single-minded devotion to the President for Eternity and his infamously coiffured son, they demonstrated bizarre reasoning to justify their revisionist history, they lavished me with food and dazzled me with spectacular performances, and at night they sequestered me on a guarded island for safekeeping. Most importantly, they provided a firsthand glimpse of something very few people are allowed to see — the Democratic People's Republic of Korea in all its self-reliant, bellicose, absurd glory.

The names of all individuals I encountered, Korean or foreign, have been altered to protect their identity. All of the events actually took place as described, however. When it comes to the Korean peninsula, you can't make this stuff up.

In many aspects North Korea is frozen in the early 1950s of the Cold War when there were two Chinas; one Red and one Free. To maintain that ominously gray image it was tempting to use the pre–Pinyin Wade-Giles Romanization system to present references to the people and places of China — when Beijing was Peking, Mao Zedong was Mao Tse-tung, and Deng Xiaoping was Teng Hsiao-p'ing. However, since this book actually takes

1

place in the recent past, the current pinyin system is used to render Chinese names.

Korean names are Romanized as per the style of the individual's national origin. North Koreans are presented as they would Romanize their own name in the North with all initial letters capitalized and no hyphen anywhere to be seen — Kim Il Sung — while South Koreans are allowed the more recent trend of hyphenation and use of lowercase initial letter in the final given name — Park Chung-hee. For reasons of neutrality transliteration is generally with the McCune-Reischauer Romanization system for words originating from either of the two Koreas.

There are thousands of books on North Korea out there, many of them well researched, beautifully written, and very informative. What follows is different. I did not set out to present research, or detail technical issues, or chronicle history, nor to tackle the thorny issues of weapons of mass destruction, mass starvation of the peasant class, regime change, or the cult of personality. I set out to go have a look for myself. This is what I saw.

Introduction

Seated in a dark, muggy reception room, rivulets of sweat married my back to the shoddy vinyl love seat. I knew ultimately when I stood there would be a thunderous, juicy public proclamation as my back divorced the plastic. That was yet to come. The room was uncomfortably silent while our hosts discussed matters in the privacy of an adjacent dark and muggy room.

We had created an uncomfortable conundrum for the diplomats. Two young American graduate students showed up at the front door of the North Korean Embassy requesting a meeting to talk about enrolling for a few semesters of study in one of their universities; preferably Kim Il Sung University, and preferably Korean linguistics, but anything would do. Anything that would grant entry to an otherwise closed and mysterious world. Being on the receiving end of a Study Abroad Program was not something familiar to North Korean academics, much less North Korean diplomats, and large young American men making such unfamiliar requests in Korean was an oddity beyond belief. They had sat with us on the lurid vinyl sofas in the gloom and listened politely as we stated our case and sought their wise council. They had both sucked air loudly through their teeth, sometimes alone, sometimes in unison, as they sat and confronted this utterly bizarre request.

Remnants of Confucian hierarchy are still scattered about the North Korean psyche, and like Confucians of old were fundamentally aware there is a correct path on which all are destined to trod, modern residents of the peninsula gravitate towards the mean. Maintaining the proper balance in society depends on each individual remaining on the well-trod path. There is no room for exploration, nor for creative independence. One does what is supposed to be done and then the dynamic is as it is supposed to be. One does not go out on a limb and do the unexpected because that is not supposed to be done. Posta'/not posta'; it's a binary system that has served the peninsula well for almost five thousand years.

Deputy Chief of Mission Mr. Lee and the First Political Officer (also) Mr. Lee welcomed us at the front door of what had previously been just another house in a working class Bangkok neighborhood. On instructions from Pyongyang they had upgraded a trade mission to a full-fledged embassy only days before our unexpected arrival. The room was completely bare except for the gaudy vinyl sofas. They hadn't yet had the electricity turned on.

I had only been studying Korean for a few months and was capable of doing little more than quietly struggling to understand as my friend who was already fluent in the language explained our motives. No, we were not spies. No, we were not joking, we really weren't spies. Yes, we could speak Korean, wasn't this conversation evidence? (It was at that point that one or both Mr. Lees knowingly glanced at me, the silent one). Yes, it was really true, we were both Americans. Yes, we understood that North Korea and the United States did not maintain diplomatic relations.

The long string of probing questions never appeared to penetrate the cloud of confusion hanging over the diplomats and that required lots of air to be sucked through clenched teeth. A tray of warm Coca-Cola was produced and small tumblers were filled and passed around. The North Koreans didn't touch theirs.

They probed until the Alpha Lee decided they had enough to go on and he excused the two of them. They quietly withdrew into an even darker portion of the house as we sat glued to the plastic furniture. It felt like a quarter of an hour slowly passed before they eventually returned.

After a few moments they did return and even in the dim light through grimy windows I could immediately see that while out of the room both of them had removed their requisite Kim Il Sung lapel pins. Alpha Lee caught my eye and knew instantly that I had noticed the missing accoutrements. A North Korean without a lapel pin is like an American without credit card debt ... statistically possible but fundamentally wrong.

As I sat gazing at the empty lapels, Alpha Lee stood to indicate our meeting was finished. He suggested as US citizens we take our request to the North Korean diplomatic mission to the United Nations in New York because in Bangkok they had no facility for dealing with such requests, but they assured us they would put in a good word. Promise. Of course their colleagues in New York had no facility for dealing with such requests either. A loud flatulent sound echoed through the empty house and into the courtyard as I struggled out of the vinyl sofa.

We stepped around their three gleaming Mercedes-Benz sedans, each with diplomatic plates. Stretched above the length of the compound's small parking area was a clothesline with graying diplomatic undergarments hanging languidly as if there was absolutely nothing abnormal about walking across an embassy compound and glancing up to see the Ambassador's threadbare skivvies waving in the breeze. In fact, it could have been the Ambassador's as well as the Deputy Chief of Mission's, the First Political Officer's, Chargé d'affaires', and Defense Attachée's — there were a lot of North Korean under-things up there drying on the line.

The guard silently shut the little gate behind us as we stepped off North Korean soil and back in to the steady buzz of capitalistic Thailand. I stood in the tranquil little lane dazed by the heat and stunned after my first face-to-face encounter with North Koreans. I wouldn't have been any less stunned if I had just been beamed back down from the mother ship after a complete and thorough cavity probe by inquisitive interstellar aliens. (The freaky silent gray aliens, not the big slimy ones with fangs.) The North Koreans had been completely odd in every aspect of the encounter, every nuance, every glance, every subtle flick at unseen flakes of dandruff. We had just been entertained by the sideshow freaks of the Bangkok diplomatic corps.

Most North Korean embassies are behind a wall. Into that wall is usu-ally fitted a glass-fronted display case into which photographs from North Korea, of North Koreans, and specifically portraits of North Korea's magnan-imous twin leaders are displayed. Still numb from my thorough cavity probe, I turned towards the wall and noticed one of these display cases. There, pinned to the corkboard behind the locked glass front, were two dozen glossy pho-tographs of all the best that North Korea had to offer: huge cement stadiums, avenues of Soviet-style cement apartment blocks, sweeping cement monu-ments against the dramatic cement skyline. Lots of lovely cement in three dozen different shades of socialist gray. Also featured were glossy photographs of happy members of the proletariat reaping bumper harvests, tightening bolts on sparkling new machinery, and sweeping the pavement clean of dust. The sweepers were maniacally, deliriously happy to be privileged enough to reside in the Worker's Paradise; members of the Lumpenproletariat so psychotically bounding with euphoria that it was obvious their facial muscles were perma-nently stuck on the grin setting.

Then there were the photographs of the twins. Actually not twins ... actually father and son but always presented as being equal in their gleeful wonderfulness. These weren't any ordinary national leaders. These were the Kims. Kim Il Sung and Kim Jong Il — a father-and-son political tag team com-bination so far out on the fringe of the communist world that even the Alba-nians were standoffish towards them.

I stood there in the hot Bangkok morning, sweat dripping down my neck, peering into the display case to see one of the Kims standing in a wheat field explaining to the agricultural experts how they could alter practices to increase yields, or standing over the catch recently brought ashore by deep-sea fishermen expertly explaining to them that if they would revise their angling methods they would increase the bulk of their daily take, or if the hydroelectric technicians would re-sequence their transformer array, or if the cooks in the kitchen would just use a slightly different temperature for the steaming of rice, or if the mathematicians would just carry the equation out three more decimal places, or if the mine engineers would just recalibrate the drill bits...

Looking at the photographs it was obvious that the Kims, especially father Kim Il Sung, but also the wunderkind Kim Jong Il, were intellectual giants among a world of air sucking morons. True renaissance men, experts in every field, gifted in all topics. No wonder they had bubbled to the top of their society and were the beloved leaders. The people not only idolized them, the nation absolutely needed their patented on the spot guidance.

All the furmurs in the photographs had it wrong — it took the Kims to set them right. All the biochemical engineers had been almost, but not quite, on track — it took Kim Il Sung to show them the precise way forward. Each and every one of the textile factory workers from top management down to the lowest level manual laborer had missed the point entirely until Kim Jong Il came along and provided that on-the-spot guidance for which he was so valued. The thick-skulled train engineers, even after 30 years of work, needed one (or both) of the Kims to come along and explain the fundamentals of their job to them. As obvious as it might be to others, it never occurred to North Korean cement factory workers that there was a better way to shovel.

The photos always caught the Kims mid-gesticulation. Their arms were always outstretched and their hands were always turned slightly upwards as they emphasized a salient point to the obtuse air-sucking masses. Their expressions were always benevolent and intense, their eyes fixed on the near horizon — just outside the range of the photograph. The gormless citizenry, in every last photo, stood at the feet of one or both Kims and listened with slack-jawed, concentrated fascination. Usually it had dawned on one or two of the brighter of the minions that this on-the-spot guidance stuff was pretty stinking valuable and they had whipped out a notepad and were hurriedly capturing the exact quote. Thankfully it had dawned on the photographer to take the lens cap off and capture the historic moment. Fortunately for North Koreans every word ever spoken by either Kim was recorded and archived for future air-sucking generations.

The photos were an odd testament to the adulation of the two Kims, but at the same time an admission that the hoi polloi were complete and utter idiots. Even the highly trained technical experts in white smocks were morons. The photographs announced it to the world. While I stood pondering the implications of this photographic admission, I suddenly realized that to each and every one of the glossy photographs someone had taken a straight pin and very carefully poked out the pupils in each eye. The holes in the photograph were from behind and each little photographic eye had a tiny erupting ridge of torn paper where the straight pin had been carefully punched through.

From one end of the display case to the other, every single eye in every photograph had been delicately blinded. It was obviously an inside job. Your average Bangkok vandal doesn't take the time to unlock a display case in the exterior wall of the new North Korean Embassy and remove each photo from the corkboard so as to delicately push a straight pin through the back side of each pupil in each photograph, then remount the photos on the corkboard, lock up the case, and scamper away to vandalize the display case at the next embassy up the lane.

No, this was fairly obviously an inside job carried out by somebody on the other side of the wall. I stood in the street riveted in place by the weird vandalism, by the dingy underwear hanging overhead on the ambassadorial laundry line, by the now-you-see-me-now-you-don't Kim Il Sung lapel pins, by the whole peculiar affair with the freaky communist envoys and their warm Coca-Cola, and I made a vow to myself right then and there that someday I would find a way of visiting North Korea.

I had no way of knowing at the time, but almost the entire communist world was about to come apart at the seams. For years we had postulated the Cold War domino theory — but nobody ever anticipated the domino theory playing out in reverse. As communist regimes stumbled and died in quick succession, North Korea's domino remained defiantly upright. The bizarre little nation with the god-like leader and the air-sucking populace beckoned.

Arrival and Day One

Saturday, 28 April 2007

As the Air *Koryo* Ilyushin Il 62 strained through the airspace above the Yalu River, the indistinguishable mountains on one side belonging to the people of the People's Republic of China and the indistinguishable mountains on the other side belonging to the people of the Democratic People's Republic of Korea, a uniformed North Korean woman picked up the receiver on an old Soviet-made black rotary telephone and started speaking in heavily accented Korean. The phone wasn't mounted on the cabin wall, it was as if it had been pilfered from a desk in an office in Moscow in late 1953 and recycled for use in the airplane. It utilized not screws, but the advanced science of gravity to keep it firmly on a shelf in the galley. When it rang it sounded like an old back Soviet telephone on an office desk in Moscow in 1953 was supposed to sound ... communist.

It was as if the entire plane full of travelers had gone back in time to the height of the Cold War. Free China sat across the straight from Red China, Mao was still Tse-tung, and the streets of Peking were teeming with ChiComs. Across the Yalu River Red China's dutiful comrades, the Norks, as they were known by the cigarette-sucking uniformed defenders of the American way, were pulling their weight in the Comintern by remaining belligerent and enigmatic while hiding behind a cloak of secrecy.

She wore a snug red pinafore over a blue and white uniform of the finest *vinalon*.[1] Affixed to her lapel was a small pin featuring the image of Kim Il Sung. Her presence exuded regime-appointed authority and within the realm of the passenger portion of the fuselage she not only passed out reading material, drinks, and food: she ruled. She gave off vibrations that pre-dated flight attendants. She pre-dated stewardesses. She was a North Korean Sky Comrade. She was a Sky Comrade with a countenance, and poise, and a set of rehearsed announcements that were a throwback to the dark days of the Cold War. She wasn't there to assist one to have a safe and pleasant travel experience as much as she was there to act as her nation's first line of defense against foreign visitors. It is rumored that North Korean Sky Comrades are routinely issued sidearms and she carried herself with the assurance that comes with having a PK39 tucked in one's waistband. At least that's the rumor.

Her delivery was so packed with emotion that it was obvious she was on the verge of tears. It was painfully apparent she was overcome with such strong remorse that it was taking every bit of her self control to keep from breaking down and weeping right there in front of all the passengers. The other passengers gazed intently in to seatbacks as they concentrated on her every word. They all looked as concerned as she did. None of them looked as if their tears were just about to start flowing. She was using "the voice."

After a few moments she paused, drew a deep breath, and repeated the entire presentation in stilted English. I had understood enough of the Korean announcement to know that she was delivering the same basic jingoistic history lesson. Unlike the first version, when she said it in English, she displayed all the emotion of an amusement park ride operator telling patrons to remain seated until the ride comes to a complete stop. She informed the tightly packed plane that we were honored to be crossing from the People's Republic of China to the Democratic People's Republic of Korea above the very border that the Great Leader General Kim Il Sung had crossed at the explicit invitation of the Chinese to marshal forces among the displaced Korean community of patriots longing to see their beloved homeland saved from imperialistic tyranny and then later return to the fatherland and lead the noble people to glorious victory in the Fatherland Liberation War. She said all that without taking a breath. I glanced out the window. It all looked the same to me. From that altitude it was just indistinguishably remote mountainous terrain, but the swelling of emotion in the collective breast of the North Koreans was audible. You could hear the vinalon being stretched as their chests puffed up.

The plane was endlessly fascinating. It isn't often that one jumps into a North Korean passenger jet and zips off to Pyongyang for a long weekend, but there I was in a middle seat at the front of the economy-class section where I could peer into the galley and see the North Korean Sky Comrade and her solid black rotary phone. I could see the Cyrillic signage all over the galley. I could see the frayed 1960s style design of the interior. I couldn't see much else.

The interior of the plane smelled mildly of rancid meat and as soon as I had boarded in Beijing, I had one of those olfactory-triggered memories anosmatic tourists are never allowed to enjoy. I was suddenly transported back to a Yugoslavian ski resort perched on a ridge of mountains between Macedonia and Kosovo where the main chalet featured an aromatic bouquet of meat products well past their use by dates. The smell was so strong that even through the requisite haze of Eastern European cigarette smoke one could still discern moldy pork butts and rotting beef tongue. The plane featured a little of that same rancid abattoir aroma.

My fellow passengers were almost exclusively North Korean. North Koreans were identifiable by their Kim Il Sung lapel pin, by their dark somber attire, and by their strikingly bad haircuts. Men and women, young and old; it was apparent that while outside the fatherland they had all saved on expenses by not expanding their wardrobes, and they had all taken a stab at using sewing scissors and hand mirrors to cut back on the personal grooming line item. Some of them had taken many stabs.

They had come with two or three times their allotment of baggage and anything that couldn't be checked at the counter instantly became carry-on luggage. Carry it on they did. The Il 62 doesn't feature overhead compartments, it features an overhead shelf. The shelf runs from the first row to the last and is one uninterrupted surface above the heads of passengers. There are no doors (that would make it a compartment), there is no strap (that would provide a degree of safety), and there is no helpful sign telling passengers to be careful because things on the shelf might fall down during the flight. That would make too much sense. There's just a shelf. Onto that shelf carry-on luggage is placed and, assuming a calm flight completely devoid of turbulence, the carry-on items use the same advanced gravitational technology as the big black Soviet phone and simply lie there. If, however, turbulence is encountered, then the contents of the shelf would probably come raining down on the heads of the passengers below. We never found out — not because we avoided all turbulence, but because the North Koreans packed that shelf so tightly with carry-on items that if the pilot decided to do a celebratory barrel roll as he approached Pyongyang the contents of that shelf would have remained firmly in place. Likewise, the North Korean passengers could have gone through the barrel roll without the aid of a seatbelt because the carry-on items stowed around their feet were sufficiently numerous to lock them firmly into place for the duration of the flight.

The Sky Comrade picked up the telephone, still firmly held in place by gravity alone, and announced first in Korean, then in English, that drinks would be served thanks to Kim Jong Il and for the sake of the people. I'm not making this up, she really said that. But first, she said, there would be a series of safety announcements we were encouraged to watch.

Using the big black Soviet telephone like a microphone, Sky Comrade Number One stood behind a curtain and read words that were incomprehen-

sible in Korean or English. As she spoke into the phone her voice was broadcast throughout the cabin. Standing at intervals within the cabin other uniformed (and potentially armed) Sky Comrades acted out the unintelligible
dialogue. In unison they would jump out from behind a curtain in to the
center of the aisle and pantomime the words being read through the speakers. Then, as Sky Comrade #1 paused before going to the next topic, the other
Sky Comrades would jump back behind the curtain to retrieve the next prop
to be used in the pantomime. In unison they jumped out and played with a
demonstration safety belt, then jumped back out of sight. Then In unison
they all jumped out again and fumbled with life vests with straps and buck-
les and cranks and complex over-under cantilevered supports, then as if a single being, they jumped out of sight behind the curtain. The jumping in and
out and the stilted fumbling with props captured the attention of the cabin
and unlike a flight on a commercial airliner anywhere in the capitalist world;
the passengers were actually paying close attention to the demonstration/spec-
tacle. It was like a grand puppet show at cruising altitude and the audience
was riveted. The Sky Comrades had our complete and undivided attention.
At that very moment if there had been some tragic mishap that forced the
Sky Comrades to actually start giving commands for emergency procedures
not a single passenger would have moved a millimeter or lifted a finger. This
is due mainly to the fact that the voice coming over the PA system was speaking both Korean and English so horrendously accented and through such
static-filled speakers that not a soul within earshot had a clear understanding of what she was attempting to say, but since we were mesmerized by the
bizarre puppet show/safety demonstration and in utter amazement, we all
held our breath to see a young, well manicured, reasonably intelligent looking North Korean woman in uniform jump out from behind a curtain to
pantomime the next crucial bit of life-saving information. Well after the
demonstration had ended we were all still silently peering forward in anticipation of another uniformed body springing forth from behind a curtain.

   As soon as the puppet show ended, the work commenced. From behind
the curtain appeared one of the puppets. She worked her way through the
cabin dispensing the glossy *Korea Today,* and *The Pyongyang Times,* as well as
various North Korean trade journals. I requested a copy of each and also the
latest edition of *Foreign Trade.* Air *Koryo* is, without a doubt, the one and
only airline in the world that does not feature an "award winning" in-flight
magazine. Every other airline in existence, no matter how mediocre other
aspects of their service might be, has managed to produce an in-flight magazine on the leading journalistic edge and has racked up awards to show for
it. Even charter airlines that fly seasonal passengers to frayed and tattered

resorts on the Black Sea boast an "award winning" in-flight magazine. Air *Koryo* is the exception. No "award winning" in-flight magazine, no frequent flier program, no business class lounges, and no authorization to fly through the air space of most of the world's nations.

The reading material was strictly state sanctioned. The edition of *The Pyongyang Times* being distributed on that flight (No.16 [2,426], 21 April, *Juche* 96) featured headlines such as: NATION MARKS KIM IL SUNG'S BIRTH-DAY, LED BY BRILLIANT COMMANDER, IN LOVING MEMORY OF NATION'S FATHER, and on and on in the same style and with the same haphazard capitalization. The articles were repetitious exaltations of the party line with a predictable frequency of words such as glorious, reactionary, and imperialist-aggressors. The glossy *Korea Today* (No. 610, *Juche* 96 #4) was a bit easier to digest because it featured big photographs with each article (the big photographs of heroic socialist accomplishments were easier to look at than the accompanying text which painstakingly described those heroic socialist accomplishments). For example, the piece titled "Innovation in Production Excavators" featured six colorful photographs of production excavators and the dutiful workers who produce them. The piece called "For The Production of More Iron and Steel" featured dazzling photographs of iron and steel production, and the piece they opted to call "Power Production at Thaechon Youth Power Station No. 4" featured large photographs of said power station producing said power (I was quietly disappointed when I did not encounter photographs of scores of teenagers strapped to treadmills).

Despite the wacky capitalization in headlines, it is obvious that the North Koreans are slightly more proficient at copyediting and proofreading English than their South Korean counterparts. In the twenty-first century there aren't many areas in which the North Koreans excel beyond the South Koreans, but in the public display of locally produced English text the North Koreans are pumping out grammatically correct and perfectly spelled dogma while the South Koreans sprinkle their newspapers, books, billboards, and packaging with gibberish known locally as "Konglish." Both Koreas use native speaking editors to help them polish what is churned out, but in the North it appears that the native speakers of English are taken seriously, while in the South their input may or may not be ignored.[2]

When the written refreshments had been dispatched, the Sky Comrades started handing out liquid refreshments. They used an old Aeroflot cart that didn't have any brakes. As they stopped to serve drinks, one would wedge her shoe against the wheel on the aft side, while the other wedged her shoe against the wheel on the fore side. It wasn't that the brake function of the cart was broken — it was that there had never been brakes. It was a tray loaded with bottles. Below the tray four spindly legs reached the floor. At the end of each spindly leg was a simple wheel. No gears, no brake, no unnecessary adornment ... just a wheel. The safety implications were no more or less significant than an airplane featuring an open overhead shelf on which unsecured luggage is stowed for the duration of a flight. The safety implications were no more or less significant than those for the big, black, solid Russian telephone being held down on the counter in the galley with nothing more than gravity.

Basically, drinks were a choice of bottled water, tinned fruit juice, beer, or *soju*.[3] I had long heard of the surprising quality of North Korean beer and decided to commence my thorough evaluation seated right there on the plane. I looked at the Sky Comrade and said, "I'll have a beer, please." And she looked right back at my eyes and said, not so much as confirmation but rather as instruction, "You will have beer." I didn't argue; I took the beer.

Years earlier I had sampled the beers of South Korea and was well aware of the painfully limited range available there. In essence there had been one beer in South Korea and it was produced by three competing breweries. They all ended up bottling what was in essence the same product. The bottles and labels were different, but the thin uneventful pissy lager that came out of the bottle was universal. Rumor has it that those days are gone and it is now possible to find a bit more variety at a South Korean watering hole, but I was braced for the same foul waste of perfectly good barley that I had known in the South. To my amazement, the bottle of *Ryongsong* Beer I was served tasted not a bit like the swill I expected. No rat hairs or rodent excrement seen floating on the surface, no flat formaldehyde aftertaste, no lingering disappointment after the first sip. The beer was actually very good. In fact, it was good enough that I believe they could compete in the international market. Of course, they'd have to come up with an alternate name that Westerners could say time and again as they ordered rounds deep into a night of drinking. The name *Ryongsong* is difficult for the non–Korean to say before the first bottle, much less after the eighth.

As soon as the drinks were disbursed, the meal cart came rocketing down the aisle. The distribution of meals was considerably quicker than the distribution of reading material and drinks because the Sky Comrades didn't need to bother asking about choice. There was one choice to be made — one took the mystery meal box, or one did not. There was no option behind curtain number two, and the lovely Carol Merrill was nowhere to be found.

It was as if the pair of Sky Comrades had been cut in half to create a team of four. The dividing line was at the waist. A little imaginary dotted line was drawn around their trim waists, and then an imaginary surgical laser sliced them painlessly in half to create a team of four. The two upper bodies busied themselves with meal distribution, while the two lower bodies (quite independently) oversaw the tricky task of getting the rickety meal cart moved down the aisle without the aid of brakes.

There was a beautiful dance-step rhythm and as they walked their cart down the aisle with their feet. They did not need to communicate between each other to know precisely when to apply their shoe-brake, or exactly when to release their shoe-brake. The feet knew, and they worked in consort without the need to discuss the particulars of timing. The cart just drifted forward as needed. Their toes silently stepping on the wheels to stop them, then without any perceptible signal the toes released the cart and it drifted forward again.

While the lower team members were moving the cart down the aisle, the upper team members were delivering boxed meals to curious passengers. Quick eye contact between Sky Comrade and passenger was the only communication. If, during that brief moment when eyes were locked, the passenger vocalized opposition to receiving the meal, then (in theory) the meal would have been withheld. This was only theoretical because nobody refused the mysterious box. The Sky Comrade would look into the eyes of the passenger and if in that seven milliseconds of contact there was no obvious indication of refusal, then with the flick of a wrist the meal was sent sailing deftly to the passenger's fold-down tray. Thump.

The meal was uneventful. In the center of the molded aluminum meal tray was an odd sheet of compressed meat-like substance that was a sickly shade of gray, a roll of sweet bread, a tiny jar of Austrian jam, a single wilted lettuce leaf, a wad of cutlery, paper napkins, and condiments sealed in a plastic bag. I carefully extracted my camera and made one quiet bird's-eye-view photograph. I expected to be reprimanded for the unauthorized photograph, but as I stealthily slipped the camera away I glanced up to see several other passengers making the same photograph of the same sheet of gray meatish material on their tray.

I took one cautious nibble of the gray stuff and decided to leave well enough alone. I had read my Upton Sinclair, I knew the score. I finished the glass of *Ryongsong* beer and went back to reading about increased production of excavators and the happy factory workers who were determined to crush the imperialist obstacles placed in the path of the advancing Korean people. Through the peerless guidance of the Great *Songun*[4] General Kim Jong Il, they would create the world's best excavators and most delicious Soylent Gray and they would realize the dream of a Worker's Paradise in which excavators are free for all, and Soylent Gray is in never-ending lip-smacking abundance.

As quickly as the brace of Sky Comrades had divided themselves like flat-worms and doubled the speed with which they distributed the food, they repeated the process in reverse and collected the remnants. Most of the trays of food went uneaten. The Soylent Gray had not been a hit.

Despite the fact that anyone close enough to start a descent into Pyongyang's *Sunan* Airport had already been vetted thoroughly by the author-ities, there were still immigration and customs declarations with which to deal. The straining IL 62 gasped in near-exhaustion, crested the apogee, and arced in to a downhill slide towards Pyongyang that was so much less taxing on the engines that the cabin noise level was suddenly and quite pleasantly reduced to a tolerable level. The Sky Comrades appeared and passed out the required documents knowing full well that every single passenger on the air-plane, apogee or no, had already been thoroughly scrutinized and subse-quently cleared for entry into North Korea. This took place in a dark little Beijing office long before anyone was allowed onto the plane, so the pieces of paper being passed out to passengers were ultimately meaningless. In a place like North Korea it is best not to belittle the bureaucracy.

The customs declaration was printed on recycled paper. There were artis-tic bits and chunks suspended in it like the handmade paper sold in craft shops. The form required passengers to confirm the possession of "GPS or Navigator" and "publishings of all kind" and any "killing device." While I would normally have focused on the killing device and wondered what sorts of killing devices the North Koreans have confiscated from forgetful passen-gers on previous flights, or if the publishings of any kind included the mag-azines and newspapers the Sky Comrades just distributed, or if they were thinking more in terms of salacious and prurient material such as *Jugs*, the *Sydney Morning Herald*, or *Animal Farm*, I was preoccupied. The mention of "GPS or Navigator" had me thinking of 39°00'00" North and 126°00'00" East.

On the internet there is a group of people obsessed with taking photo-graphs at points on the globe where longitude and latitude lines converge. Their fanatical obsession rivals that of the members of the Southwest England Cheese Label Collector's Guild. They are rabid freaks with hand-held global positioning system devices and digital cameras who travel the globe in a race to see who can snap a picture at the most obscure and difficult to reach con-vergence point. They have a creed, and rules, and strict guidelines for snap-ping the picture and, for all I know, a secret handshake.

I was transfixed by the web page presenting their trophy pictures and tales of horrific ordeals and hardship to get to a precise location and record the spot according to explicit rules, then e-mail the report and photographs back to Cheese Label Central for thumbtacking to the electronic corkboard. When I stumbled across the web page featuring the obsessive accounts and meticulously presented photographs, I was captivated. Some of them spent significant time and money to transport themselves, their GPS reader, and their digital camera to some snake-infested knoll in the middle of an inhospitable third world country just so they could claim the honor of being the first.

All the easy spots were bagged long, long ago. These geographic Cheese Label fanatics have been at it for a while and though there are tens of thousands of points of convergence to be documented and photographed, rest assured that the convenient spots are all logged. It is the incredibly inconvenient and inhospitable that remains empty and unvisited on their progress map. It appears that the fanatics are drawn to the difficult spots and the dispatches they send back after conquering one of those tricky locations are more and more intricate in gleeful description of the hardships and complexity.

Virtually all of Western Europe was long ago conquered. The hospitable bits of North America (i.e. all of the lower 48 of the United States, and everything within easy driving range of Toronto in Canada) were chalked up some time back. Each spot in or near the populated fringe of Australia is dutifully ticked off with photos submitted and narrative posted. South Africa and Southeast Asia are quickly running out of spots that have not been visited. The popularity of visiting these meaningless spots on the globe is so rapidly growing that now there are multiple visits with photographs and narratives describing the place from year to year as different individuals and groups struggle through thickets and into jungles and hop fences and wade through rice paddies up to their pudendums to use their hand-held gizmo to find the precise location of the convergence of a north-south line and an east-west line that are, in truth, not really there.

The remaining unvisited spots are, as one might expect, in locations difficult to access; in the middle of Brazilian jungles, on the northern tip of Siberia, in the middle of a Central Asian desert, in a desolate wasteland well beyond the last watering hole, on little specks of land in the middle of an ocean. The fanatics look at the map and see the steady progression of unvisited spots being rhythmically ticked off as day after day more and more locations become cataloged and photographed and relegated to the list of places where human feet have already trampled and digital cameras have already recorded, and GPS devices have already triangulated, checked, double-checked, and triple-checked.

As more and more people discover this potentially expensive pastime, the exhaustive list of convergence points dwindles down to squat. Those unvisited spots that remain are more and more difficult to access. The narratives for recent acquisitions more and more often mention support crews, and refueling ships, mosquito netting, and native porters. It used to be that a person with a modicum of interest in cartography would discover the hobby on Tuesday and by Saturday go down to the local gadget shop and buy an inexpensive GPS device, then on Sunday take the kids out for an afternoon drive and bag a documented visit to a convergence spot. They were back home in time to wash, feed, and stable the kids then grab a cup of coffee and upload the documentation to lay claim as the first Cheese Label Collector at that spot. Now when someone discovers the hobby for the first time, they must consider inoculations, passports and visas, air tickets, traveler's checks, and phrase books in native dialects if they plan on journeying to one of the remaining virgin spots.

A great deal of the expansive wastelands of the Middle East remain full of unvisited spots. Much of the interior of Africa and Australia are yet to be documented. Antarctica and Greenland are pretty much up for grabs. And then there are the places where politics frown on such things as bands of merry foreign tourists wandering around with hand held GPS devices, cameras, and notebooks — places such as North Korea.

According to the Cheese Label Collector's Guild there are 18 points of convergence within the sovereign territory of the Democratic People's Republic of Korea.[5] As would be expected, none are yet logged as having been visited. Some of the spots are in remote mountainous areas or in areas so close to sensitive military targets that it is inconceivable the North Koreans would ever allow anyone to get close. However, there happens to be one particular point of convergence (39°00'00" North and 126°00'00" East) just beyond the Eastern suburbs of Pyongyang. In fact, it is only 22 kilometers (as the proletariat's crow flies) from Kim Il Sung Square! From the very heart of Pyongyang a twenty-minute taxi ride to the east would place one at the foot of a gentle hill. A short hike up a trail on the hill would take the visitor to a small clearing. On one side of that little clearing is the point of convergence. I know because I have studied the satellite images and measured the distance and considered the contour of the land and the convenient proximity to that nation's best hotels and the general ease, comparatively speaking, with which one might bag this particular point of convergence.

I have no real desire to visit that spot myself. I am not motivated to exert energy going to a particular location on the globe that has no other significance than the fact that cartographers agree there are two invisible lines that meet there. Two invisible lines meet on the sofa in my den too. In fact, invisible lines dissect all sorts of comfortable and convenient places. There are invisible lines cutting right across my easy chair, other lines meet right in front of my refrigerator, there are lines conveniently located throughout my neighborhood book shop, my favorite restaurant, and in all sorts of air conditioned locales with refreshments for sale. I don't need to go out among the thorns, snakes, and disease-laden vermin to stand on a spot where two invisible lines meet. I'm simply not interested. I would, however, look very favorably on organizing a tour of those obsessive individuals for two succinct reasons: rabidly fanatical people can be quite entertaining if they stand far enough away as to not spill their drink on you, and rabidly fanatical people have no reservations about spending inordinate amounts of money.

I could easily see organizing a tour of a dozen Cheese Label Collectors interested in spending a pile of cash to make sure they were able to walk up a hill on the outskirts of Pyongyang, double-check their GPS readings, make a couple dozen digital photos, and spend the remainder of the day caressing the goose bumps on their arms for having accomplished something so spectacularly noteworthy. I'm not interested in pursuing a tour company designed to organize visits to points of convergence in exotic and difficult to access locations, though I know that idea would make millions (feel free to take it and run with it), but a one-off trip to North Korea under certain lucrative circumstances would be a hoot. Now and again I imagined the possibility of arranging this group of wealthy eccentrics to fly all the way to Pyongyang to cross one more convergence of invisible lines off their list, but as we descended in to Pyongyang and I realized the customs officials were intent on confirming the possession of "GPS or Navigator," I could probably kiss my get-rich-quick North Korean points of convergence tour for cheese label fanatics goodbye. I would probably have equal chances of being granted permission for a tourism scheme based on "killing devices."

As the plane descended in to *Sunan* Airport we were low enough that I could make out farms and roads and houses. We dropped closer still and I could see farmers working in the fields, and count the number of people squatting beside the mud brick huts. Here and there among the mud houses were large red boards onto which a Korean character was painted. They were set in order along the edge of fields and along paths and spelled things such as LONG LIVE THE GLORIOUS *JUCHE* IDEOLOGY! and WE ARE ONE!

The Sky Comrade appeared in the galley and picked up the old Soviet phone and started speaking. First in Korean, and then in English, she didn't bother to tell us to put our seatbacks and tray tables in the upright and locked position, nor did she tell us to stow anything we might have removed from the overhead shelf. She didn't provide a single reminder about safety regulations. She didn't tell us to return to our seats. She didn't tell us to close our window shades so we wouldn't know what the runways looked like from above (like the South Koreans used to). She picked up the big black Soviet telephone and proudly announced that we were descending to Pyongyang, "where the Great Leader Kim Il Sung lies in state and the Dear Leader Kim Jong Il carries out the duties of leading the nation." Silence fell on the cabin as 186 passengers pondered this revelation.

The entire cabin of passengers remained silent as the plane turned off the runway and slowly rolled toward a barren expanse of tarmac near a smart line of IL-62s and two bulking Il-72s and Tu-154s. Though clean and appar-

Built in the Soviet Union in 1979, this Ilyushin IL-62-M regularly flies between Beijing and Pyongyang. Though Air Koryo has a handful of international routes around East Asia approved for use, in reality the only regular service is to Beijing and back. Several Tupolev and Ilyushin passenger jets are neatly displayed on the tarmac at Sunan Airport, but their flight-worthy status is doubtful. Banned from operating in European Union airspace, Air Koryo is rumored to have started the process of replacing its ancient fleet with newer Russian-made passenger jets.

ently ready to fly, looking at the planes proudly parked on the tarmac made one wonder how long it had been since they were actually up in the air. When the entire nation needs little more than regular service between Beijing and Pyongyang, why maintain a fleet of costly old airplanes from the Soviet era? In fact, Air *Koryo* is banned from flying to any location in the European Union,[6] not that there is much need to go these days. At the peak of the Cold War, Air *Koryo* used to have regularly scheduled long haul flights to Moscow, and then on to Sofia. Those would have been long, grueling flights in uncomfortable seats, the monotony broken only by the Sky Comrades doing their flatworm division at meal time. The Ilyushin Design Bureau never got around to fitting their aircraft with entertainment systems (public or private) and one can only imagine the monotony of a 22-hour flight to Sofia with nothing but *The Pyongyang Times* and *Korea Today* for light reading. After all, Air *Koryo* does *NOT* feature an "award winning" in-flight magazine. Like so much of what I would see in North Korea, I couldn't help but wonder if these once operational passenger jets parked on the tarmac were now just maintained as props in yet another *Juche*[7] Studio back lot.

The passengers did not react like passengers arriving in South Korea, where the throngs traditionally elbowed to the front of the line before the door of the plane is opened. There was a measured calmness about the way people stood, looked around at the cabin, gathered their things, and then knowingly, almost reluctantly, made their way towards the door. Everybody knew what awaited them outside the plane and nobody was in any particular rush to go encounter it.

It was a sunny April afternoon when I eventually stood up to meet my fate. I stepped out and walked down the stairs to the tarmac below. Though it would have been a lot quicker and more efficient for the passengers to have just walked over to the terminal building, a group of buses pulled up and passengers slowly got on and found seats. The buses made wide, slow arcs around to the terminal building at a speed just a bit slower than walking. I know because the uniformed staff walked past the bus towards the terminal building. As we pulled up, the same support staff that assisted passengers to get on the buses opened the bus doors and assisted the same passengers off the bus.

A large portrait of Kim Il Sung was positioned at the top of the terminal building and his benevolent face peered out across the open expanse of the airport. The portrait was positioned in just the right angle so that the eyes mysteriously followed each plane as it landed, and then followed it again when it taxied down to the end of the runway and took off.

As a boy growing up in Texas, I had been dutifully taken to all the historic sites across the state and was patiently shown time and again why Texans are better than run-of-the-mill regular Americans. The volunteer tour guides made a point of instilling in each and every child an understanding of the peerless virtues emanating out of Texas. It was while in the museum section of the San Jacinto Monument that one of those well-meaning jingoistic guides pointed to the framed portrait of General Sam Houston, Father of the Nation, most virtuous of all Texans, and made sure my entire class of fellow 7-year-olds saw his gaze and realized that as we walked around the room his eyes would follow. After all, the eyes of Texas really are upon you. This tidbit of information did much to seriously unnerve 32 otherwise rambunctious 7-year-olds and we spent the remainder of the tour very quietly moving back and forth across the museum to see the General's eyes following us. I still recall the hair on the back of my neck standing at attention the entire time I remained within his spooky gaze. There were probably quite a few nightmares and wet beds that night.

It was only reluctantly as a teen that I accepted a portrait's moving eyes as a simple optical illusion. It was a letdown kind of like the whole Santa Claus–Easter Bunny–Tooth Fairy sham. Looking up at the huge portrait of Kim Il Sung and his beatific eyes I wasn't quite sure whether or not this particular portrait might have been an exception to the rule. There was something very unnervingly mysterious about that portrait.

Below the portrait was the second-story observation deck and behind a huge window wobbled a throng of family members there to welcome their loved ones back to North Korea. They wobbled because they were all either really old, or really young; old creased women and hunchbacked men in traditional Korean garb, and a lot of toddlers with blank expressions. There were a few representatives of other demographic groups — one or two young mothers, a couple of middle-aged men — but mainly it was the very old and the very young. They wobbled and hopped and waved and silently mouthed things through the thick glass. I looked around at my fellow passengers and didn't notice a single person acknowledging the glee coming from the observation deck above. The people behind the glass were teary-eyed with joy, and the people on the ground below were ignoring them even though it was obvious by the banging on the glass, the eye contact, and frantic hand signals that the people upstairs recognized the people down below.

As a group we took a half step forward, then paused, then took another half step forward and paused. While we waited I overheard the telltale nasal twang of a Seoul accent coming from several directions. No longer was it absolutely impossible for South Koreans to visit their Northern cousins. In a very cement-gray North Korea I was surrounded by checked, plaid, striped, and polka-dotted South Koreans about to enter the country, something unimaginable not too long ago.

The immigration desks were placed just inside the door and the entire planeload of passengers disgorged and met up again at this inconveniently positioned logjam. The North Korean officials already knew exactly who each and every passenger was, they had already done a thorough screening of all application papers the day before the plane's departure, they had vetted each and every one of us and already had a photocopy of our passports and entry documents. I know because I had to submit mine to them a day and a half in advance. However, they insisted on one last opportunity to scrutinize and intimidate.

The desks were reminiscent of those in Moscow: a countertop so high that the average person could see nothing more than the squinty little eyes of the uniformed official seated in the closed cubicle. Most of the time those eyes were cast downward where the official scrutinized the paperwork. They squinted their eyes because of the poor lighting — I'm sure all of them, though in their twenties, had vision problems. It was the myopic squint of someone who accidentally left their reading glasses at home, and they all had it.

When it was finally my turn, I walked up to the desk and presented my passport and documents to the squinty little eyes. They blinked, then a hand shot up from the darkness and my passport and papers were gone. Then all I saw was the top of the immigration official's big Soviet-style hat. The hat moved as the official moved down in the dimness below me. I leaned forward as far as possible in an effort to see beyond the edge of the counter, but all I could make out was the gently swaying hat in the dimness. Without any fanfare, I heard the sound of papers being stamped, then the squinty little eyes peered up and the hand shot out of the dimness and deposited my passport with a North Korean entry stamp on a new temporary special-class running-dog imperialist insert page.[8]

Contrary to popular belief, the United States government does not prohibit citizens from going to North Korea as tourists. If an American is loopy enough to go, then the US government stands aside and chuckles as they depart. The problem is getting the North Koreans to allow the American citizen in. It doesn't happen very often. North Korean Immigration officials don't chuckle. I squeaked by and got into North Korea through a window of opportunity that had, up until then, been opened on only two occasions since the signing of the armistice in 1953. In 54 years the North Koreans had issued tourist visas to Americans only three times. I was entering the Worker's Paradise during a very rare sixty-six-hour window of opportunity. Looking around at the people who entered North Korea from our flight, it was obvious that either word had not gotten out about Yankee imperialists being admitted as tourists, or the Americans were staying away in droves. Either way, the vast majority of people passing through Immigrations that afternoon were not holding a US passport.

In fact, there were only three other US passport holders I was aware of and they were whom I was searching for. We four comprised a tour group put together by an American-based tour operator and we four would spend the next (exactly) sixty-six hours in the Worker's Paradise. I stood just beyond the immigration desk with passport and special-class running-dog imperialist insert page in hand while I scanned the crowd for three familiar faces when a hand gently took my arm and led me towards the three other Americans. I looked down to see a wiry little Korean man in dark jacket and tie shepherding me through the crowd in a way that would become very familiar over the next sixty-six hours. He took me to Charles, the tour operator who had put this four-person sixty-six hour whirlwind visit together. Charles had the distinction of having had led numerous tour groups to North Korea in the past, but more significantly he is probably the only private US citizen since the final days of the Korean War who can legitimately claim to have driven a car in North Korea. Beside Charles was Alice, an intrepid orange-haired world traveler who worked in the marketing department of a Midwestern university and made it her life's mission to see as much of the planet with her own eyes as possible, and my old friend Wally. Since we had first visited the North Korean Embassy in Bangkok 16 years previous, Wally had finished his PhD and gone to work for a think tank where he did a great deal of thinking about North Korean nuclear bombs. It had been a long time since we had knocked on the gate of the North Korean Embassy in Bangkok, but here we were. If one plans to visit North Korea it should be in the company of fellow travelers prepared to appreciate the absurd.

The four of us were instructed in English by the stern little Korean man to hand over any mobile telephone we might have, and he went so far as to suggest places one might double check to see if there might happen to be an unexpected mobile telephone tucked away unexpectedly. Oddly he never asked about GPS or Navigator, killing devices, or publishings of any kind. It appeared that if I had been able to get my killing device that far, I would have been home free and could have commenced the spree at any point in our visit.

For the next (exactly) sixty-six hours virtually all conversations were in English even though our hosts would quickly learn that two of us could communicate in Korean. The stern little Korean then shepherded us out the front

door and into the parking lot where numerous Japanese-made minivans waited
with drivers slumped over the latest copy of *Rodong Shinbun,*[9] or standing
beside the minivan sucking on a foul-smelling cigarette. Our driver was not
the sucking kind, at least not in public, and he was dutifully slumped over a
copy of *Rodong Shinbun* mouthing the words as he read. The little Korean
shepherd introduced himself as Mr. Kim, his older companion and fellow tour
guide and minder was also Mr. Kim. Though they provided their given names,
for the remaining sixty-five hours and thirty minutes they would be Kim the
Younger, and Kim the Elder. The driver, who by now had stilled his lips and
put away the official organ, was introduced as Mr. Bae. In a society where a
quarter of the people have the family name Kim, it isn't surprising that two
out of the three of them were Kims. Mr. Bae started loading our bags into
the minivan while we four Americans spread out across a space designed for
sixteen Japanese. Mr. Bae slipped on his big, mirrored aviator sunglasses and
the seven of us rolled out of the small parking lot in the direction of the city.

Pyongyang doesn't fade from city center to suburb to outskirts to rural
setting; Pyongyang comes to an abrupt halt. It's as if the Central Planning
Committee took out a map and drew a line and decided the area to one side
would be urban, and to the other side it would be forest and open fields. *Sunan*
Airport is just twenty kilometers from the center of Pyongyang, but the largely
vacant countryside around the airport would suggest it is out in the middle
of nowhere. Behind his aviator glasses Mr. Bae drove at a steady fifty kilometers per hour even though the road was posted at eighty.

A printed itinerary was distributed by Mr. Kim the Elder while Mr. Kim
the Younger gave a quick rundown of the various sites we would be shown
during our stay in the capital. A rapid scan of the list revealed several highlights had been omitted and I quickly glanced at Wally who looked up and
disappointedly shook his head. We were not scheduled to visit the USS *Pueblo*,
we were not scheduled to visit Kim Il Sung's mausoleum at the *Kumsusan*
Memorial Palace, nor the International Friendship Exhibition at Mount
Myohyang— the official underground treasure house of state gifts. These were
all significant for me: the *Pueblo* because it was the biggest war trophy ever
taken from the United States, *Kumsusan* Memorial Palace because in true
communist fashion the creepy mummified remains of Kim Il Sung were on
display there, and the International Friendship Exhibition because it was
alleged that in the collection of elaborate jewel-encrusted, gold-plated, dia-
mond-tipped gifts presented to Kim Jong Il was an off-the-shelf suburban-
sporting-goods-store-variety basketball presented by US Secretary of State
Madeleine Albright. When presented, the basketball had reportedly caused

ruffled feathers and a cool reception. That simple run-of-the-mill basketball had captivated my imagination since the Clinton Administration had nonchalantly released news of its presentation in October 2000. Alas, we would have to make do instead with the Children's Circus and a banquet on a boat permanently moored on the *Taedong* River.

Through the trees we could see open fields being prepared for planting in the next week or two. All along the edges of the open fields, at regular intervals, were square wooden blocks with individual Korean characters painted on them. They intoned such warm and welcoming sentiments as "collectively stamping out the Imperialists" or crushing the aggressors through collective labor." Koreans on both sides of the DMZ sometimes cling to the belief that their language is secret and nobody but them can unravel its mysterious meaning. That might explain why Koreans on each end of the peninsula sometimes post signs that would otherwise be socially awkward. For many years the backs of stall doors in the public toilets of Seoul's *Kimpo* Airport were festooned with a sign that stated (in Korean only), "We are a cultured people — Let's maintain public morals: Use toilet paper sparingly, After using the toilet, do not fail to depress the lever behind it..." Obviously non-Koreans would never decipher the mysterious text, so there was no need to feel embarrassed about the marvelous irony of a cultured people instructing each other about wiping and flushing.

Mr. Bae kept us at a steady fifty kilometers per hour and we rounded a bend to see one of Pyongyang's noteworthy billboards. Very recently photographs of a billboard in Pyongyang started showing up in news articles about the novelty of a nation's very first hoarding. Soon the billboards were the talk of DPRK aficionados and Koreaphiles. What made the billboards even more interesting is that they advertised the *Hwiparam*[10] — North Korea's first locally assembled passenger car. In a nation where the average citizen needs to save their entire paycheck for a total of 376 years in order to buy a new flat screen television from one of the consumer electronics firms on the southern end of the peninsula, how many lifetimes might it take that citizen to save up to purchase an automobile? I guess that wasn't the point, the point was North Korea had joined the ranks of car-producing nations and they were quite proud of this fact. They were proud enough that they built a billboard so they could advertise ... a rather odd capitalistic pursuit in a place where marketing isn't required because the Dear Leader instructs the people in what they desire and what they don't desire.

The other fascinating thing about the *Hwiparam* is that it is the product of *Pyonghwa* Motors, a joint venture company 30 percent owned by *Ryonbong* General Corporation — one of many state owned businesses that is

Looking over the shoulder of a state-appointed driver, through the windshield can be seen one of the few billboards in North Korea that does not proclaim regime-sanctioned propaganda. This one promotes the *Hwiparam* or "Whistle Car," a locally assembled Fiat produced by *Pyonghwa* Motors, a joint venture company 30 percent owned by North Korea's *Ryonbong* General Corporation and 70 percent is owned by *Pyonghwa* Motors of Seoul — a front company for the Unification Church.

basically a front for the Kim Jong Il regime. The other 70 percent is owned by *Pyonghwa* Motors of Seoul — a front company for none other than the reverend Moon Sun Myung's Unification Church. A Moonie Mobile.

As the van closed on Pyongyang I pulled my digital camera out to start taking pictures, but stopped short when I realized that when in North Korea it is probably wise to run any plan by one's minder before putting said plan into action. I turned to Mr. Kim the Younger, for he appeared to be the designated leader, and asked under what circumstances should I refrain from taking photographs. I expected a stern explanation with specific guidelines and the eventual suggestion that each time I think I might like to take a photograph I pause, find him, and seek his firm input. I raised my voice in hopes that if I were to break the ice and ask in such a way that everyone heard me asking, and if everyone heard Mr. Kim's instructions, we could avoid having to repeat the instruction process again at any point during the stay.

I said, "Mr. Kim, do you have any instructions about taking photographs?" Then I braced myself for an unyielding sermon that would be not so much demeaning as belittling.

Above the engine noise Mr. Kim the Younger raised his voice so all in the van could hear, then replied in a cheerful voice, "Feel free to take a photo of anything at all, but don't take a photo of soldiers because they will get very angry." Then he laughed and went back to his conversation with Charles

I figured as blood-sucking capitalist leech war mongers we would not be allowed anywhere near a military installation so the chance of being within range to take a photo of a soldier with a $320 digital camera from a duty-free counter in the old Bangkok Airport was probably slim. However, that set the mood and I had it in my mind to be extra careful to check that there were no uniformed soldiers in the viewfinder before I pushed the button on said unimpressive camera.

Other visitors had come back from North Korea with tales of stern minders forbidding any photos taken from a moving vehicle, any photos of the dilapidated trains, trams, and buses, or photos of buildings that weren't designed to be admired by foreigners. They told stories of irate minders examining entire memory sticks of digital photos then singling out specific shots as offensive and therefore in need of being digitally erased. I had no desire to confront an incensed minder with a stash of incriminating photos on my memory stick; it was clear I was going to have to be very careful when I took the incriminating photos.

The surroundings started looking a little less desolate with collections of low-level houses appearing more and more often. People could be seen along the roadsides more frequently — working the fields, or riding bicycles on the shoulder, or walking on the pavement adjacent to the road.

It quickly became obvious that the visual landscape of North Korea is lacking familiar shapes and colors of the corporate logos of multinational corporations. There are no familiar golden arches around any bends in any roads, there are no red Coke logos nor the trademarked "ribbon device" over the entrance to any shops, no roadside stations selling gasoline under patterned displays of simple primary colors that would be recognized as a particular corporate logo anywhere on the globe. There simply are no corporate logos. The visual landscape was lacking in primary colors. As I gazed out the window of the van and we drove closer and closer to Pyongyang, I was more and more aware that I wasn't seeing any primary colors with the exception of red. There were red banners and tablets with red characters spaced along the horizon, there were red kerchiefs around the necks of children, but hard as I looked I saw virtually no other primary colors. Not many secondary colors either.

The landscape was earth tones and greens and cement-gray. The fields were a bare-earth-brown with clumps of green along the edges. The clusters of houses were devoid of color other than a variety of hues drawn from low grade cement. The garments on the people were routinely dark and the whole scene was subtly somber. Not unhappy, just somber in a no nonsense kind of way as if the Worker's Paradise does not have time for the frivolity of primary colors. It certainly doesn't have time to mess around with secondary colors.

Without fanfare, from a gap in the tree line, emerged the silhouette of an image I knew well. All Koreaphiles know it well. The 105-storey *Ryugyong* Hotel could be seen long before any other building in Pyongyang. While we were still driving through countryside, off in the distance loomed that mas-

A typical street scene in central Pyongyang: artificial, sterile, and dedicated to the display of monuments to the Kims and propaganda slogans. Atop the building on the left, the sign proclaims, "Long Live the Military-First Revolutionary Ideology!" Mounted on the lower building to the right is a sign that states, "The Great Kim Jong Il of the 21st Century."

A North Korean electric trolley bus plies the streets of Pyongyang through the willow trees in the shadow of the 105-story unfinished *Ryugyong* Hotel. Pyongyang has long been nicknamed "the city of willows" and, in fact, that is the English translation of the word "ryugyong." Shortly after this photo was made crews started the process of covering the cement pyramid with a glass veneer.

sive pyramid of totalitarian aesthetics, a vertical monument to low-grade cement.

As is the case with much of North Korea, there is a variety of opinion about the *Ryugyong* Hotel and the reasons for commencing construction, the reasons for halting construction, the architectural issues, the plans for the future, etc. In my experience the people with the thinnest credentials usually make the most assured sweeping statements about the *Ryugyong*. The anonymity of the Internet provides a curtain from behind which the most absurd claims often come.

It is said to be 105 stories tall, but judging building height is often tricky on the Korean peninsula. One has to take into consideration that buildings are frequently devoid of a fourth floor due to Oriental superstition. Some buildings eliminate any floor containing the numeral four, so a Korean building claimed to be fifteen stories tall might have only twelve elevator options. Still other buildings are devoid of the thirteenth floor due to Occidental superstition. Sometimes the superstitions are combined to create confusing sequential oddities in floor numbering. A popular building in Seoul is known as the "63 Building," yet the highest floor is the sixtieth. The sixty-first through sixty-third simply don't exist.

I never discovered if the North Koreans have the same floor numbering issues that their Southern cousins have when it comes to tall buildings, but eventually I got close enough to confirm that the *Ryugyong* Hotel is in fact a cement shell devoid of any finishing touches. Both Mr. Kim the Younger and Mr. Kim the Elder casually referred to it as "still under construction." It was fairly obvious that it had not been "under construction" in many years. Contrary to what I had heard previously, no effort was made to hide the ominous *Ryugyong* Hotel from us, or to deny that it existed. We were not stopped when cameras were aimed at it and each and every time someone in our tour group brought it up, one of the Kims would freely discuss it as being "unfinished" or "under construction," then would move on to the next topic.

Looming over the skyline, it remains a permanent marker of grandiose folly, but contrary to what the punters say, it was in no way sinister. It has been common for journalists to point out how menacing the silhouette of the *Ryugyong* is as it hangs above everything else in the city. On the contrary, I didn't find it menacing at all. True, it looked like there was probably a lack of logistical planning and some shoddy design and construction work, but the basic shape of the giant pyramid was more than just interesting — it was appealing. Again and again from all over the city I found myself turning to gaze at the outline of the unfinished *Ryugyong* in fascination — not disdain.

The trees came and went and our view of the edifice was obscured until we rounded a small bend in the road and again I took in the huge, thin gray pyramid and marveled at the odd beauty. That's the thing, I realized; it isn't ominous or sinister or menacing in the least. The *Ryugyong* Hotel is beautiful, even in its unfinished shoddy state. It stands in the middle of the Pyongyang skyline, unique in its gravity-defying angles and oddly balanced symmetry. The unfinished edifice will inevitably always remain unfinished and the quality of construction is below standard — even to a layman's eyes as he drives past in a van — but to toe the line and mimic the disparagement many others have written would be mindless. It would be akin to claiming that in 1940, under Phillippe Petain's Vichy France, the previously elegant Eiffel Tower was evil and depressing and took on menacing aspects of spineless collaboration until suddenly in 1944 when the region was pushed out — then it was acceptable to admit that the Eiffel Tower is actually kind of attractive, but for four years it had been unanimously agreed that it was uniformly ugly.

The *Ryugyong* Hotel is a testament to the stupidity of centralized planning, the irrational decisions made when caught in a game of one-upmanship, the vanity of the Kim Dynasty being fed at the cost of the Korean people, and labor used to construct the hotel may have even been slave labor. That doesn't alter the fact that the lines remain beautiful and the delicate wings of the pyramid almost defy gravity.

The looming gray behemoth, streaked with rust stains slowly creeping down from the derelict construction crane bolted to the pinnacle, looked forever abandoned as a colossal mistake, but a year later the North Koreans would quietly announce that after a twenty-year hiatus, construction was to resume.

Without warning, Pyongyang's outer neighborhoods were suddenly around us. The fields abruptly gave way to cement-colored structures on either side of the road and as we approached the city they gradually became taller. Mr. Bae drove the van around a bend in the road and then we made a turn onto a street that ran along the bank of the *Potong* River.

On a knoll beside the road was what appeared, at first glance, to be a billboard, but of a more permanent nature. It was approximately the same size as a billboard, but fabricated completely out of cement. Rather than advertising a product it featured a huge beautifully rendered mosaic. The illustration was of a younger, smiling, vigorous Kim Il Sung providing his renowned on-the-spot guidance to a group of peasants happily trundling through the mud with buckets and shovels as they constructed a flood-control canal. Mr. Kim the Younger explained that after the Fatherland Liberation War, Kim Il Sung had provided brilliant guidance in reconstructing the

A propaganda billboard in central Pyongyang during the evening commute. Other than the single exception of a few advertisements for a locally assembled automobile, all billboards in North Korea are for propaganda of one form or another. The flag proclaims, "Our type of Socialism..." and below is written, "...is unfailingly invincible." The figure holds aloft the writings of the Great Leader.

city of Pyongyang. It had been virtually flattened by imperialistic American bombs and within a very brief period Kim guided the North Korean people to crawl out from under the rubble and slap together the single most glorious conurbation the world had ever known. Part of that brilliant master plan had been Kim Il Sung's realization that the flooding along the *Potong* River had to be brought under control so he gathered the righteous citizens and led them in hand-digging a brilliantly designed canal that would divert the floodwaters and alleviate that part of Pyongyang from the annual floods that had been so devastating in the past. Brilliant.

Apparently the Japanese imperialists had recognized the problem and started working on the task of rerouting the *Potong* but failed to finish the work before being flung marched back to Japan at liberation. As soon as he was finished ushering them out, Kim Il Sung stepped in and corrected all the innumerable Japanese engineering mistakes, truncated the log frames and Gantt charts, and with nothing more than a gaggle of happy Koreans and some spades, accomplished the engineering marvel in a mere 55 days. As soon as the happy peasants wrapped up work on the *Potong* River Improvement Project they concurred that some sort of monument was required, so they decided that on top of the nearby *Ponghwa* Hill; The Monument to the *Potong* River Improvement Project should be erected. For twenty-five years North Koreans were preoccupied with other more pressing matters, but in the early seventies a great wave of nationalistic monument construction spread across North Korea and suddenly constructing giant cement tributes was again high on the nation's agenda. There were hundreds and hundreds of cement tributes built so they didn't actually get around to the monument commemorating the *Potong* River Improvement Project for a quarter of a century. I could just catch glimpses of the monumental tower as we passed on the road at the foot of the hill.

Lower down near the base of the hill the colorful mural showed yet again that even the combined intellect of a few thousand average citizens could do little more than create idiotic municipal planning schemes that resulted in flooding year after year. It took Kim's laser-like focus to see through the fog of confusion and come up with just the right technique to dig through the mud and send the deluge on its way — never to trouble the contented masses again.[11]

As we drove by the mural Mr. Kim the Younger told us the glorious story of the *Potong* River Improvement Project. As he recounted the fabled exploits, Mr. Kim the Elder looked on from the back of the van and listened, not so much to make sure the content adhered to the party line, as much as it appeared he simply enjoyed hearing the stories about the Great Leader. His

eyes often grew misty as the other Mr. Kim revealed the heroic and munifi-
cent feats that not only the leaders accomplished, but also the ordinary people. Both of our tour guides appeared to be just as awestruck by North Korea
as we were.

Views of the *Ryugyong* Hotel came and went behind buildings and trees
as we drove. Newer articulated buses moved up and down the roads, along
with very old Chinese buses that looked as if they might have very well been
part of the first shipment of fraternal aid to the North Koreans after the fatherland was liberated. The bodywork on many of the local buses suggested it
had originally been done by hand — with hammers. All the buses were filled
to capacity with dark-clad evening commuters on their way home after a productive day of toiling with the collective masses.

Here and there people walked along the sidewalks in somber garments.

Contrary to lingering rumors, bicycles exist and are used in Pyongyang. The
Tianjin Digital Bicycle Plant in Pyongyang produces 40 different models and
churns out tens of thousands per year. Here a lone cyclist rides past the
Pyongyang Grand Theatre — built in 1960, it was one of the first Pyongyang
buildings to be erected after Kim Il Sung demanded the North Koreans stop
mimicking the architectural style of the Soviets.

Occasionally there were bicycles[12] and frequently they were being pushed to allow the rider to dismount and chat with a fellow pedestrian as they walked along. Every pedestrian was somber even though it was closing time and the weekend was upon them.

Without warning, Mr. Bae turned the van into a gentle curve and we unexpectedly pulled to a stop in front of a guardhouse and gate at the entrance of a complex. The sign on the wall announced in Korean that it was the Korean Feature Film Studio — not one of the stops scheduled for our tour. This was a surprise because we had been warned that the itinerary was rigid and our guides had no authority to create flexibility. Despite the expectation that the guides had no choice but to keep on goose-stepping according to schedule, our entire visit ended up being filled with impromptu itinerary changes and surprise visits to previously undiscussed stops. We had just settled into our seats and we were already at our first stop of the tour.

Mr. Kim the Younger stepped out of the van and had a quick word with the lone soldier in the guardhouse. The entire complex was openly patrolled by uniformed and armed soldiers. Virtually everything in North Korea is openly patrolled by uniformed and armed soldiers, so that didn't necessarily indicate any extra significance to the studio. Other openly uniformed and armed soldiers joined him in the guardhouse for quiet consultation. They all looked very serious.

Mr. Kim disappeared inside and it became quiet and still as we waited to find out what he was doing. It was the end of the workday and even as we sat at the entrance inside the van, the staff from the movie studio trudged out through the front gate in groups. They glanced at the foreign faces in the van with little interest — it was obvious that they had seen vanloads of foreign visitors pull in to the complex before.

As we waited on Mr. Kim it dawned on me that this was probably the studio in which South Korean film director Shin Sang-ok and his South Korean actress wife Choe Un-hui worked in the seventies and eighties.[13] The story of how, recently divorced from him, she was abducted while visiting Hong Kong and trundled off to North Korea where she was kept under house arrest, and of how he, despite the divorce, raced off to Hong Kong to track her down and was similarly abducted by North Korean agents, and of how after four years of separate imprisonment they were reunited at a Pyongyang dinner party, and of how Kim Jong Il himself played matchmaker and got the couple to re-marry, and of how the couple then made propaganda movies for the regime is reminiscent of some wonderfully tawdry B movie script with smarmy twists and turns on a manipulative emotional rollercoaster. The only

Near the corner of Sosong Street and Haebangsan Street in central Pyongyang, workers pause to squat in the dust before starting the Saturday evening commute home to enjoy their one-day weekend. Virtually everyone in Pyongyang either walks or uses public transportation to move between home and work. Private cars reportedly exist, but are increasingly rare because the average North Korean would not amass sufficient funds to acquire a car during a lifetime of labor. The sign proclaims, "You and I, together let's move forward to build a rich and powerful fatherland."

difference here — this story is true. Though the devious plan was for Shin to make regime-friendly films that would sway worldwide opinion towards Kim Il Sung, in the end the only memorable product was a 1985 Godzilla-knock-off called *Pulgasari*, and the only truly memorable thing about *Pulgasari* is that the North Koreans managed to get the very same suit actor who wore the rubber Godzilla suit in Tokyo to fly over and don the *Pulgasari* suit for filming in Pyongyang.[14]

Somehow Shin and Choe talked Kim Jong Il into unlocking the golden cage and allowing them to fly to Vienna for a movie-related business meeting. Once in Vienna they went directly to the US Embassy and sought political asylum. They were quietly sent to an undisclosed location in the US and only returned reluctantly to South Korea years later. When they did return to South Korea they did so in possession of secretly recorded conversations with Kim Jong Il tucked away in their carry-on bags and, word on the street in Seoul had it, the recordings proved once and for all that the reason nobody had ever heard Kim Jong Il speak in public was because of a horrible speech impediment.

Until 1992 there was no known recording of Kim Jong Il's voice in the outside world, and then one day a snippet of official North Korean video found its way out and showed Kim shouting in staccato Korean, "Glory to the officers and men of the heroic Korean People's Army!" That was it. That's all anybody had ever heard to that point. In fact, even after that, most people who knew of the quote had read about it, but had never actually heard the recording.

The North Korea watchers who had previously sworn Kim was mad, or mute, or stammered, or lisped, now claimed that he had been coached in saying those few words and when he spat them into the microphone he was saying as much as he could say without revealing ... it. The "it" was whichever of the defects to which one subscribed. Then the director and actress returned to South Korea and with them came the tapes and, word on the street had it, the revelation wasn't that he stammered, or lisped, but that he spoke in a voice that sounded like he had just inhaled the contents of a couple of helium balloons. He sounded like Mickey Mouse! Apparently when he shouted out, "Glory to the officers and men of the heroic Korean People's Army!" in the video he had been faking it to cover up the helium breath.

Mr. Kim the Younger returned from the guard post to reveal splendid news: though we had arrived at closing time, the committed and enthusiastic staff of the film studio were thrilled to be able to show us the facilities from which the cream of North Korea's cinematographic crop comes. In tow was a dark-suited Mr. Lee, an official from the studio who, despite being caught at the gate as he was trying to go home after a six-day work week, was thrilled to spend an unexpected hour or two going back to work on a Saturday evening. His Kim Il Sung lapel pin sparkled in the light of the quickly setting sun. So did his gold tooth.

Mr. Lee jumped into the van and instructed Mr. Bae where to drive. We went about 100 meters and stopped so Mr. Lee could explain where we were and what we were doing. He started rattling away in well rehearsed, albeit accented, English. He gave the facts and figures that demonstrated how this modest studio fifteen minutes outside Pyongyang was actually one of the most productive, and certainly most innovative studios in the world. Both Hollywood and Bollywood paled in comparison because what those two places had in quantity, this studio made up in thematic quality.

It was while we were stopped that Wally looked out the window and saw a long rectangular sign mounted in the garden in front of one of the studio buildings. He smiled and silently motioned for me to look. While Mr. Lee continued to extol the virtues of the studio and the honorable work that goes on there, I turned to see a bold red background festooned with big white

Just inside the compound of the Korea Feature Film Studio, this billboard is positioned to be seen by anyone passing through the gates. It proudly proclaims, "Long live the peerless Commander General Kim Jong Il who has established our country as one of the world's nuclear states!" The Korean guides made no effort to bring the sign to the attention of foreign visitors, nor to translate the Korean text.

Korean characters that stated, "Long live the peerless commander General Kim Jong Il who has established our country as one of the world's nuclear states!"

Mr. Lee continued his well-scripted presentation, the two Mr. Kims sat quietly listening along with Charles and Alice, but Wally and I gazed bug-eyed and grinning at the sign in the garden. North Korea had publicly joined the nuclear club only six months before when they proudly detonated a modest nuclear device down at the bottom of a mine shaft. They joined the club with a bang.

Mr. Lee came to a natural breaking point in the presentation and it was clear that the intent was to drive a bit deeper into the studio and listen to the next installment of rehearsed presentation. Before anything could happen, Wally caught Mr. Kim the Elder's eye and said, "Would it be OK if I stepped out and took a picture of that sign?" Mr. Kim hesitated and Wally said in fluent, albeit Seoul-accented, Korean, "I just want to step out and take a picture of that sign ... is it OK?"

Mr. Kim the Elder didn't appear to notice that the request had been repeated in Korean. He said, in English, "Yes it will be no problem to take photographs of the sign." So we all bounded off the van and snapped photos of the ominously boastful sign, then turned and quickly got back in the van. Even as we moved on into the studio, heads turned to look back at the menacing words until they were out of sight.

The van moved forward towards the next stop in the studio tour and Mr. Kim the Elder said to Wally in a serene voice, "You speak Korean very well ... with a good accent." That was the extent of his surprise and he revealed no alarm or distress as might have once been common in South Korea when a foreigner masters the language to such a degree. For the duration of our visit both guides predominately used English, but showed no sign of hesitation to shift into Korean when speaking with Wally. Over the years, in South Korea, time and again I had seen Wally's mastery of the language cause much air to be sucked through many teeth. What unnerved their cousins in the South didn't appear to be an issue in the North.

The van stopped deeper inside the studio and we all stepped out. Groups of studio staff members streamed out towards the gate we had just entered as Mr. Lee continued to deliver his scripted narrative.

We stood across from a huge bronze statue of Kim Il Sung providing on-the-spot guidance to the cast of *Flower Girl*, one of North Korea's greatest cinematographic achievements (according to the North Koreans ... nobody else appears to have seen it). As we stood, Mr. Lee lovingly revealed that Kim Il Sung himself had, since the studio's founding in 1947, provided on-the-spot guidance thirty times. That means the Great Leader himself, the Comrade of the People, the Lodestar, the Peerless Diplomat, took time away from running the state to zip up to the studio to give the directors, producers, actors and actresses, and even the set designers his personal input and involvement on the smallest of details. It must be understood that in North Korea films are not seen as entertainment vehicles for generating financial profits, they are tools for educating the masses in the correct path. Therefore Kim Il Sung recognized how much was at stake with these new-fangled moving pictures. One misstep in dialogue or direction and you might have a cinema full of laughing minions rather than masses being educated in the correct revolutionary spirit. The occasional visit to the studio appears to have acted as a steady reminder that this movie making stuff was serious business. It was clear that Mr. Lee didn't see his job as fun or glamorous, he was helping the Dear Leader educate the masses through film. It was serious business.

The Great Leader is one thing, but the Dear Leader is quite another. Kim Jong Il is so frequently reported in the Western press as being a movie buff that substantiation is no longer required. Somehow we just know. We know that his reported collection of tens of thousands of Hollywood movies is true because media outlets have repeated it so much that it has to be true. Much of what I had heard about him had been presented in such a matter-of-fact way that it sounded plausible, but in reality nobody has ever actually substantiated the claim about the obsessive penchant for Hollywood movies.[15] Mr. Lee very proudly informed us that Dear Leader Kim Jong Il had visited the studio a whopping 590 times to provide his invaluable on the spot guidance.[16]

As we stood and listened to Mr. Lee provide more detail and trivia about the studio and visits by the Kims, I was consumed by the realization that while in North Korea it might be possible to obtain a copy of Kim Jong Il's coveted book, *On the Art of the Cinema*.

In 1973, when Kim Jong Il was just 31 years old, he published a book titled *On the Art of the Cinema*—treasured among DPRK aficionados as a "must have" addition to any collection. Though unknown in Hollywood, according to the North Koreans this is the single most insightful and revealing reference on cinema ever produced. I had long known of the book and, like most people on the planet, had no way of seeing a copy, much less finding one in a book shop and making the trip from cut-out bin to the cash register. Years earlier I had been in Southeast Asia and made a point of finding the state book shop in Hanoi, and again in Vientiane, with the expectation that if North Korean texts were going to be available outside North Korea, then the state book shop in one of the last remaining communist nations would stock them. They didn't. In fact in Hanoi the shopkeeper had never heard of Kim Il Sung or Kim Jong Il despite the fact that they are both astonishingly prolific writers. On a different trip a pair of shopkeepers in Vientiane had trouble keeping their eyelids up on a sweltering afternoon and couldn't be bothered with my silly questions.[17]

Over the years I had heard of *On the Art of the Cinema*, usually in mocking terms, because of Kim's lack of credentials in the movie-making industry. But as the Western media repeated again and again the allegation that not only was Kim a big fan of film, but that he had a collection of 10,000 or 20,000 or 150,000 or 250,000 videos (the number seems to grow with each recitation of the claim), the mockery abated. After all, if Quentin Tarantino can come out of nowhere and be taken seriously as a film guy, then why not Kim Jong Il?

Mr. Lee ushered us back into the van and we drove deeper still into the

studio compound. We passed a pair of gigantic mosaic murals and I immediately recognized the colorful images of various film-related occupations in
action. I knew them from photographs previous non–American visitors had
taken from the same location on their visit to the world's most significant studio. The murals depicted Directors directing, and Actors acting, and Producers producing, and Gaffers gaffing, while Key Grips gripped, and Best
Boys did what Best Boys do. They were all depicted as being very busy and
very determined. Other than the elaborate murals, we could have been driving slowly in to a university campus because the buildings smacked of 1960s
regional junior college. Until we rounded the bend and entered the back lots.

We were instantly transported 500 years into Korea's past and found ourselves in the middle of the medieval Korea set. It wasn't very convincing with
the *Ryungyong* Hotel's giant gray silhouette on the horizon, but I could see
how Kim Jong Il or Quentin Tarantino would be able to position cameras in
such a way as to avoid capturing the towering pyramid in the critical shots.
I assume that is what a lot of the on-the-spot guidance ends up being — pointing out such *faux pas* and explaining how to correct them to the thick-skulled
groundlings.

We gathered in a mock *Choson* Dynasty courtyard. During our slow
meander deep into the studio complex there had been a continuous exodus
of weary-looking, somber staff members. They quietly moved towards the
front gate and we quietly moved towards the back lots. Now the streets and
walkways and sets were all still, silent, and empty and Mr. Lee looked a little flustered that he was going to have to conduct the entire tour without the
option of dragging colleagues in to share the chore. Then, just as he was starting to explain details about the *Choson* Era set, he heard movement within
one of the false-front buildings. He excused himself and scurried across the
courtyard and spoke at a crack in the wooden wall. From within came a
muffled voice in response and Mr. Lee was visibly relieved.

She was Miss Yoon and she had been inside wrapping things up as quickly
as possible in order to go home. Mr. Lee requested she stick around and help
with the foreign guests and her mouth said she would be delighted while her
eyes said, "Damn it, Chul Su! I was thirty seconds from the door. You always
do this to me on Saturdays. Never Tuesday. Never Thursday. No. You have
to pick Saturdays. Thanks a lot, kimchi-breath." Like many of the people I
would see during my brief stay, Miss Yoon was obviously fatigued. She was
poised and well groomed, but her eyes gave away the fact that she really could
have used a good feed and a long nap.

She briskly opened all the doors and cabinets she had just been closing.
It was the *Choson* Era wardrobe department and it was conveniently tucked

away within one of the false front structures right in the middle of the court-yard set. The costumes were shoddy and frayed and wouldn't stand up in a close-up shot. Kim Jong Il and Quentin Tarantino probably knew of some camera technique for getting around that conundrum ... maybe polarized filters, or back lighting, or reverse angles or something.

Mr. Lee asked Miss Yoon in Korean if she would mind allowing the vis-itors to go through the routine. She nodded agreement without looking up and Mr. Lee turned to us and said in English, "Miss Yoon invites you to try on the costumes, pose for photographs in the costumes, please..." and with that he made a sweeping gesture towards the racks of shoddy costumes and smiled.

Miss Yoon hauled out a faux *Choson* Era stool and placed it in the mid-dle of the courtyard set. At the firm insistence of both Kim the Younger and Elder we hurriedly donned ill-fitting costumes, placed papier-mâché helmets on our heads, gripped wooden swords, and smiled for the camera right there in the middle of the packed dirt courtyard where so many North Korean epics had been filmed — epics that will forever remain unknown and unwatched outside of North Korea.

I inspected the resulting photos long after that afternoon and discovered well-fed beefy men giggling like schoolgirls from within terribly undersized costumes that appeared to have been strung together for a low-budget sub-urban high school musical.

As we disrobed and placed the threadbare martial costumes on hangers back among all the others and sat our papier-mâché accoutrements on the appropriate shelves, I turned to Miss Yoon and asked, "How much?"

She looked at me in bewilderment. I turned to Mr. Lee and started to repeat the question in English but before the words were out of my mouth I realized my mistake.

In the Worker's Paradise a concept such as charging tourists to take pho-tographs is alien. Neither Mr. Lee, nor Miss Yoon, nor either of our minders could conceive of the expectation that there would be a small remuneration in exchange for the brief use of the studio's costumes.

At tourist spots all across the planet there are people sitting in the shade with headdresses or cloaks, or funny hats, or kitted out in local ethnic minor-ity costume, or they have an animal on a leash, and when the sweating, pink tourists lumber down out of the bus, those people emerge from the shade and generate a small profit. The goofy tourists simply must have a photograph wearing the funny hat, or stand beside the person in local costume, or stroke the animal on a leash. This is a tried and true mechanism for generating cash and is a noble profession with a long history. Since the dawn of the instamatic camera tourists have been handing these people wads of colorful, crumpled local currency in exchange for a few moments under the headdress. Some of these people are even unionized.

The North Koreans were oblivious. Like many other things I would discover during my visit, what appeared to be a logical expectation was completely alien to the Koreans. Setting a small price for the photo opportunity would have been completely within the parameters of normal tourism expectations, but the Korean Feature Film Studio is a particularly long way off the well-beaten tourist track and well outside the realm of the normal.

Back in street clothes, and back in the van, Mr. Bae followed Mr. Lee's instructions and slowly drove deeper in to the silent studio grounds. Beyond the *Choson* Era set was a Seoul set. After having lived in Seoul for many years, I was struck by just how much the set did not resemble that city. It looked as if it had been constructed from plans based on photographs taken in the pre-war 1940s. It featured false front brothels and bars and gambling dens for the imperialistic degenerate American G.I.s. It was obvious that these places of vice were for the Americans because the movie set signage was all in English. Each building was ingeniously designed in such a way that the exteriors had a variety of appearances, thus multiplying the options a skilled director (such as Kim Jong Il or Quentin Tarantino) would have when selecting the background for a particular shot. Obviously the North Koreans are not interested in making movies about modern Seoul, they are still preoccupied by the Seoul of half a century ago and the events that happened then — thus the anachronistic appearance.

The van meandered around a corner and we were transported to colonial Korea with tell-tale signs of Japanese occupation. That street looked very much like it had been picked up from one of Korea's modest towns in 1920 and gently placed between the *Choson* Era royal courtyard and 1950s Seoul.

Around another bend in the road was a little European enclave with single-occupant chalets and villas surrounded by manicured lawns and shrubbery. Just through the shrubbery was the 1950s brothel, and behind the hedge was the side of the Japanese colonial post office/fishmonger (depending on one's vantage point). It was all very compact and painstakingly positioned.

Beyond all the sets and false fronts, against a small hill at the back was a vast cement structure.

"What is that?" I asked in touristic bewilderment.

"That is a tank for filming underwater scenes," Mr. Kim the Younger replied matter-of-factly.

I have never actually seen a North Korean film. I don't have anything on which to base my opinion, but I would guess that not many underwater scenes are scripted into their films. With a steady output focusing on the bitter injustice of the Japanese colonial period, and the bitter injustice of the American imperialist aggressors, and the bitter injustice of the South Korean special class stooge toadies and their puppet-clique regime — when would they need to film anything underwater?

The van slowly moved by the old, bleached cement tank and I could see that indeed if there were water inside it would be a considerable volume. I had a very difficult time visualizing a North Korean film crew donning scuba gear and getting into the tank with waterproofed film equipment. Mr. Bae turned the van and we turned to retrace our path through the complex.

We wound our way back towards the front gate and Mr. Lee stood in the front of the van in silence. He was finished and had no more to say. Like his colleagues, he had put in a long hard week and he was ready for a break. We had arrived unexpectedly at the end of the day and he had been very gracious in his willingness to delay his departure for home by an hour to allow us to see what most people are never shown.

He accepted the thanks of both Kim the Younger and Kim the Elder and smiled graciously, but just like all the rest, it was his weary eyes that gave him away. He stepped off the bus looking haggard and ready for his thirty-six-hour weekend.

The sun was low on the horizon as we left the studio and turned left into the roadway, and the streams of rush hour commuters continued to make progress towards home and the brief weekend. The limited range of colors and styles of garments was striking. Everyone was similarly attired in moderately formal (if not completely formal) business dress. Black, navy, and charcoal gray were the most common colors, interspersed occasionally with the olives and khakis of military uniforms.

The commute in Pyongyang doesn't involve personal cars. The people were walking, or in buses, or electric trams. A few congregated at tram and bus stops waiting for a ride, but many more hoofed it. By removing personal cars from the social equation the Great Leader added a degree of control over the urban populace while also increasing the artificial amusement park ambiance of the city.

We passed one cluster of pedestrians after another. They were all in somber garments, with no exceptions. There were no displays of midriffs, nor undergarments stylishly exposed. There were no young men bustin' a sag, no young women exposing bare skin between navel and waistline. Nobody wore athletic shoes. Nobody wore a baseball cap frontward or backwards ... there

The evening commute in Pyongyang features a metro system, trams, pedestrians, and a fleet of electric trolley buses. Many of the buses appear to be thirty to forty years old and of Chinese origin, despite North Korean claims that all systems of transport in North Korea are designed and fabricated by the people under the brilliant guidance of the Dear Leader.

were no baseball caps. No names of sports teams screen-printed across chests, no corporate logos, no university names, no polo ponies, penguins, or crocodiles. There was nothing to distinguish the attire of a young man of twenty-five from a middle-aged man of forty-five, or an older man of sixty-five. They were all smartly outfitted in state-produced and state-approved fashion.

Individually a resident of Pyongyang could be picked up and transported to any city in the world and inserted in to a crowd of pedestrians and nobody would take a second look. Collectively, however, they were striking in the solemnity of their appearance — as if the entire city had just departed a funeral.

Through the *Mankyongdae* section of the city we traveled along the tree-lined *Potong* River Improvement Project canal on a road that, despite the fact that it was the evening rush hour, was almost devoid of vehicles.

Ahead and to the side I saw through the trees what appeared to possibly be a church. Mr. Bae kept the van steadily moving along and as we got closer it appeared more and more that it really was a church. There was no cross, nor any name screwed into the building's exterior wall. There was no public proclamation on or anywhere near the building. I just knew.

I was raised a three-times-a-week Baptist on the Texas Gulf Coast where three times a week is the bare minimum. After an upbringing of revivals and camp meetings and dinners on the ground and weeklong extra curricular evangelical obligations, I pretty much know a church when I see one. Doesn't matter what brand, doesn't need to be a cross, doesn't need to be a sign or any iconography or visible symbolism—there is something about a church building that announces that it is a church building just by sitting there in the community quietly being a church.

There was light scaffolding around the building I was looking at and obviously there was work going on. Despite that, the architecture clearly suggested "church."

I turned to Mr. Kim the Younger and innocently asked, "Is that a ... church?"

Sitting trapped inside a godless heathen atheistic communist stronghold logic suggested the building should be anything but a church.

As if he had been waiting in anticipation of one of the foreign guests to notice and ask, he nonchalantly said, "Of course, that is one of Pyongyang's churches. There are many," and without prompting, he added proudly, "In North Korea we have freedom of religion."

I didn't think to ask if freedom of religion in North Korea implied that he and his neighbors could go sit in the pews without being observed and reported, or if the person in the pulpit was appointed by the state, and if the parishioners could get their hands on a Bible should they desire a copy ... and if any such Bible would be bowdlerized. I didn't think of those questions at the time. At the time, I sat in silent awe as we passed.

I was looking at the *Pongsu* Church. It had been built in the late 1980s in apparent anticipation of the flood of foreign guests attending the 1989 13th World Festival of Youth and Students. The assumption is that North Korea wanted to demonstrate to the world that Christianity was free to exist in the Worker's Paradise despite what we might have heard otherwise.

Eventually more than 22,000 students went to Pyongyang to participate in the festival. They traveled from more than 170 nations[18] and represented their local chapter of the World Federation of Democratic Youth, or their affiliate of the International Union of Students, or the Young Fabians, or some similarly leftist organization. I have a difficult time imagining that among 22,000 students of the socialist or Marxist persuasion there would have been a single one interested in getting up on a Sunday morning to seek out a service in the local house of worship. These were partying twenty-somethings in the prime of life on their summer holiday in an exotic location surrounded by thousands of university students of the opposite sex. These kids traveled all the way to Pyongyang because they were the type of students who get excited at the thought of attending an organized anti-imperialist rally. These were the kind of young people who wear one of those hackneyed T-shirts with a Che Guevara silhouette and actually know who the silhouette is. They can sometimes even go as far as to tell you that Alberto Korda took the photo used for the silhouette on all those clichéd shirts. They were busy discovering the joys of Korea's favorite social lubricant —*soju*. It was summertime and they were hot, horny, and lovestruck and I'm sure not a single one of them made a pilgrimage to the *Pongsu* church.

But *Pongsu* church was there in case they did want to worship. So was the *Changchung* Catholic Cathedral. Since then the *Chilgol* Protestant Church opened nearby, and the Russian Orthodox Church of Life-Giving Trinity in the *Chonbek* district followed. It is obvious that the North Koreans are concerned about their image and want to make sure the world sees just how tolerant they are of Christianity.

In 1794 Catholicism arrived on the peninsula and the first Protestant missionaries showed up ninety years later. In the following hundred years Christianity exploded in growth. South Korea is now second only to the United States in the number of Christian missionaries sent around the world to deliver the gospel and the nation boasts several of the world's largest Protestant congregations. Depending on who is presenting the statistics, Christianity may have already surpassed Buddhism in number of South Korean adherents. But it wasn't always so. In the early years of the 20th century it was North Korea that was the hothouse of Bible-thumping Christianity on the peninsula.

Pyongyang was known by some as "the Jerusalem of the East" because of the significance Christianity played in scope and impact, not to mention numbers of converts.

Kim Il Sung's family are reported to have been converts and there are even accounts of little Kim Song Ju,[19] as he was named at birth, attending Protestant services in Pyongyang with is mother.

Our visit to Pyongyang was just a few short weeks after the 100th anniversary of the Great 1907 Pyongyang Revival — to this day one of the most significant events in the history of the church in East Asia. Inasmuch as Christianity has altered the course of South Korean history in the second half of the last century, the Great 1907 Pyongyang Revival altered the course of the first half of the last century in the northern part of the peninsula. South Korea's modern evangelical boom can be linked directly to Pyongyang. Now largely forgotten, the revival started on 14 January 1907 when in Pastor Samuel A. Moffett's First Church of Pyongyang an impromptu gathering of Korean believers started a spontaneous spiritual awakening much akin to the Great Welsh Revival that had taken place three years prior. In fact news of the Great Welsh Revival had reached Pyongyang and probably influenced adherents there. Pyongyang quickly became a vibrant center for the local church and for missionary work. That reputation lasted for decades and by 1933 there were so many missionaries in the region that the Pyon Yang Foreign School operated in Pyongyang. The children of missionaries across Northeast Asia were shipped off to Pyongyang in order to enroll. In that year young Ruth McCue Bell enrolled as a freshman and would spend three years attending high school there before returning with her parents for a furlough in the United States. Through marriage she would later take the name Mrs. Billy Graham.

While a few Koreans south of the DMZ gathered to mark the anniversary of the event, it passed without notice in Pyongyang. Since 1974 the state has managed Christianity through the Korean Christian Association and spokesmen for the association made no announcements nor any public display that would suggest they understood how historically significant the anniversary was to the religion they represent.

It appears that the real function of the association is to provide a convenient organ through which eager Christians south of the DMZ can channel funds and assistance. It is assumed that the pastors and priests of the few churches in Pyongyang are actually appointed by the KCA and are about as "Christian" as any other North Korean state-appointee.

For several years churches and Christian organizations in South Korea and other nations have channeled money through the KCA to support the *Pongsu* Church. Thanks to that support the church now has a small noodle factory in the basement. In follow-up visits supporters have been shown the noodle production, but when they arrive for Sunday morning services either the building is locked up tight and vacant, or there is an organized service with "parishioners" in the pews and a "pastor" delivering a speech that is more political indoctrination than Biblical homilies.

Over the years defectors and escapees have claimed that there are numerous underground churches across North Korea. Other than that, it appears the Kims have succeeded in bottling Christianity up and using it as a much needed conduit for attracting hard currency. Though we passed too quickly to make it out at the time, later I read news reports that a South Korean group had donated millions of dollars for the expansion of the *Pongsu* Church sanctuary. The scaffolding may have been due to that expansion. It would be interesting to discover where the anticipated new parishioners will come from.

The *Ryugyong* Hotel appeared and disappeared behind buildings and trees and as we drew closer it loomed larger. I gazed at the cement outline in an attempt to see what critics in the West saw that was so disturbing. In various places the unfinished building has been called a variety of deprecating things. The comments usually feature words like "menacing" or "unnerving" or some superlative like "the most disturbing building on the planet." The silhouette is startlingly unusual and calls out to be inspected, but I couldn't make out anything particularly unsettling about it as it disappeared behind a cement-hued apartment block.

Evening rush hour continued and moving through the city we encountered Czechoslovakian-made Tatra KT8 electric trams packed with serious-looking people. Now and then a grin could be seen through a tram window, but mostly the people just looked weary and looked away.

The Tatra trams moved slowly but steadily up and down tracks set into the cement roadways. From time to time one of the elongated trams would pass over a spot where the cement surface under the rails had disintegrated and would be forced to a crawl. As the trams passed those spots the steel rail above the hole would sag and flex. As soon as the tram was clear of that pothole it would speed up the tracks only to slow down again for the next.

Among the trams of Pyongyang are also electric trolley buses. Judging by body design they were either a gift of the fraternal comrades next door in China, or were fabricated in the Worker's Paradise on a Chinese design. North Koreans have long been noted for their penchant for reverse engineering and it wouldn't be surprising if they had accepted a donation of Chinese electric buses and quietly kept one or two aside to dismantle and copy piece by piece.

The buses were just as full as the trams with dark-suited somber masses commuting home for their Worker's Paradise 36-hour "weekend." The commuters looked fatigued. Keeping the revolution going after all these years was hard work and it showed on the creased and lined faces of the masses.

Among all the commuters there were few bicycles and no motorcycles. Official cars passed now and again, usually dark-tinted Mercedes-Benz sedans, and each one appeared very official as it sped down the middle of the boulevards paying no heed to intersections or traffic signs.

At intervals we passed uniformed traffic wardens stationed in mid-intersection. The traffic wardens are the stuff of Western journalist fantasy. According to which report one reads, they are all winners of beauty contests, they are all former Miss North Koreas, they are all hand picked by the licentious Dear Leader himself, they are all the most beautiful girls in all of Korea and are granted the honor of being a traffic warden as a reward for something ... maybe as a reward for simply being beautiful. I find it difficult to believe that North Koreans would spend time and energy on something as profligate as a beauty contest, but the cloak of secrecy hanging over Pyongyang is big enough to hide many surprising enigmas. Journalists have painted them, at times, as succubi standing at the major crossroads of the capital city of the most evil of places. After hearing about them for many years, I can attest to the fact that the traffic wardens of Pyongyang are indeed soft on the eye.

However, no matter how nymph-like they appeared from a distance, as we drew close and got a better look, each and every one of them had an unwavering stone-faced countenance. They looked like they should have been at a suburban shopping mall shrieking and giggling with friends over a deep-fried sugar-coated morsel in the food court. But they stood in the intersections of Pyongyang and glared at pedestrians, cyclists, and drivers of buses and trams. They gave every appearance of being completely unwilling to put

The Traffic Wardens of Pyongyang have a reputation for being the most beautiful young women in North Korea. They stand within white circles painted in the middle of intersections and conduct a syncopated ballet of movements and gestures to control the non-existent flow of urban traffic. Despite reports to the contrary, traffic lights do exist in Pyongyang, but they remain switched off in preference to the Traffic Wardens.

up with even the slightest infraction of the traffic rules and their collective glare announced that should anyone care to infract they were prepared to respond.

These women were out there to do a job and because there is so little traffic on the streets of Pyongyang they can devote full and undivided attention to each vehicle as it passes into and out of their zone of authority. It appeared that they were scrutinizing each and every move made by each and every vehicle, dark-tinted or not.

They stood in form-fitting military style uniforms of blue with pristine white military hats, pristine white gloves, and pristine white socks. Gold-colored epaulettes, coupled with the requisite Kim Il Sung lapel pin, provided an air of authority despite their obvious youth. They all wore simple black leather shoes with a moderate heel that, among three-times-a-week Baptists, are known as "sensible shoes." They all held a baton ostensibly designed to aid in the direction of passing vehicles, but there would have been a tacit understanding among drivers that she could probably hurt people pretty good with it if they opted to ignore her directives.

Each of them stood on a spot that was the precise middle of the intersection of two broad and empty boulevards. Around the spot on which the warden stood was painted a meticulous white circle, just as pristine as the gloves and socks. Right there in the middle of the intersection, perfectly proportioned around their petite feet in paint inevitably supplied by the Korea Paint Exchange Centre[20] which I had seen advertised in a publication on the flight in, they stood on duty to control vehicular movement across the capital.

They stand frozen at attention in the center of their pristine white circle and gaze off in the distance, then as if instructed by some unseen signal from stage left, they snap into action and go through a mechanical routine of contorting arms and legs, and flicking wrists, then snapping heads to one side and twisting then freezing, baton pointing up this boulevard then down that one, then moving again, in an orchestrated ballet of robotic precision designed not so much to direct traffic as much as to announce that the state has appointed her to direct it. They twirl and freeze, snap and turn, point and glare, then turn 90 degrees and go through another set of choreographed motions that have no palpable meaning. The entire routine is conducted atop those black "sensible shoes" that are dragged and shuffled as she pivots and kicks and turns. It was only after driving past several that it became apparent that within the pristine white circle and under the black "sensible shoes" into the roadbed had been placed a steel plate flush with the surface of the street. It is on that square steel plate that she does her traffic boogie and thus any leather soles are spared a quick death.

There is a familiarity in the routine because it is reminiscent of the goose-stepping soldiers captured on film auto-frog marching through Kim Il Sung Square and broadcast on television behind any Western talking head saying anything about North Korea anytime there is anything to say about North Korea. They also use that footage when they don't really have anything to say but need something North Korean behind the talking head. Those soldiers exert so much energy kicking their legs up in steps that commence above head height, while at the same time keeping the rest of their body rigid and unchanged, that maintaining that march across the square under the viewing platform is a physical endurance test. I suspect many soldiers are gasping for breath as soon as they are out of Kim Jong Il's line of sight. The traffic wardens go through similarly ridiculous acts of motion, but in a more feminine way. It is gracefully robotic and completely mesmerizing.[21]

We all slipped our cameras out and snapped blurred photos of the wardens as the van rolled by. Previous groups of foreigners had been allowed to stop, get out of the vehicle, and take photos of the wardens from the sidewalk but we were on a tight schedule and were racing the setting sun, so the Kims made no provision for warden watching that evening.

One of the many North Korean fallacies repeated again and again is that Pyongyang has no traffic lights. Sometimes pundits go as far as to state that the winsome wardens are there in place of traffic lights. At many of the Pyongyang intersections where the traffic wardens pirouette within the white circle, there were indeed traffic lights. They just weren't turned on. Maybe they aren't turned on because there is no electricity, or maybe it is a cognizant decision to turn the lights off in order to generate more jobs, or maybe the cost of outfitting a warden is lower than the cost of replacement bulbs. Whatever the reason, the traffic signals were inoperable — but they do exist.

On instruction from Mr. Kim the Elder, Mr. Bae turned a corner and pulled the van up against the curb and we were allowed to step out on to the wide sidewalk. All around us there were somber people walking home, or pausing to speak with friends, or quietly smoking.

There was no casual attire. Not only did my eye miss primary colors and the familiar shape of international corporate logos, it missed baseball caps and low rise jeans and bulging midriffs and pierced anything. It missed skirts above the calf. It missed gum chewing, and yammering in a mobile phone at an inappropriate volume, and eating junk food while walking, and little wires leading up to tiny little speakers in ears, and the familiar things one would see being carried in the city — like shopping bags, and books, and newspapers, and parcels. My eye missed fat people.

It was eerily similar to the movie set we had just departed. At first glance it was convincing, but it wouldn't stand up to close inspection. All around us the extras who were making their way home had no concept of how thin the veneer appeared.

Charles pulled out his camera and started taking photos and when the rest of us saw that neither of the Kims were going to offer objection, we started taking photos too.

We were below the twin pink towers of the *Koryo* Hotel, both 45 stories topped with matching revolving restaurants. The *Koryo* Hotel is distinct for several reasons, but on first sight the thing that sticks out is its pinkness. In keeping with the trend away from primary colors, the *Koryo* towers are a resplendently odd shade of pink. In a big stark city dominated by three dozen shades of gray, a pair of pink towers tend to stand out.

For the first of many occasions I was struck with a tingly sense of wonder that verged on déjà vu. After many years of poring over photographs of Pyongyang I knew all the buildings and monuments by sight. It was akin to the feeling one gets when, after a lifetime of seeing only photographs, for the first time the Eiffel Tower, or Houses of Parliament, or Sydney Opera House is viewed in person. Except this was not one monument, but a cityscape full of them. Everywhere I looked there was a familiar structure. I was seeing it for the first time, but I knew the shape and color and setting already.

Wally walked over to take a photograph of an immense jingoistic propaganda poster while Charles and Alice took photos of the people, buildings, and trams. Another common Koreaphile fallacy was proven wrong as they snapped away in all directions. In the beginning we requested permission to take photos, but soon that evolved in to a simple silent glance at one of the Kims. When, after a while, it became apparent that they weren't going to offer any resistance, we simply took photos of anything and everything.

Of course, we had freedom to take photos of anything and everything because we were carefully herded to locations deemed acceptable for foreigners to visit. The path by which we got there was deemed acceptable for foreigners to travel. The people we saw on the streets were, by the very fact that they were in Pyongyang, deemed acceptable and trustworthy and sufficiently loyal to not fall prey to any prurient temptations we might toss in front of them, therefore we were allowed to photograph them at will. Everything we could place within a viewfinder during the entire sixty-six hour visit had been vetted and found acceptable for us to photograph.

Like visitors to an amusement park, who are never given access to the backsides of the buildings where the garbage cans are stored, we were shown the false fronts in the film studio, then taken out in to downtown Pyongyang and shown the false fronts there as well. The people walking down the street

The twin towers of the of the 45-story *Koryo* Hotel feature rooftop revolving restaurants that reportedly have not functioned in years. The *Koryo* Hotel was the site of the first inter–Korean family reunions in 1985. Arranged by the respective Red Cross offices on each side of the DMZ, some of the South Koreans who traveled to the *Koryo* Hotel in anticipation of seeing immediate relatives for the first time in many decades were led into the waiting room and then, at the last possible moment, informed that their relatives inexplicably declined to meet them. In the parking lot in the foreground is a Soviet-made Lada Niva.

or commuting home in a Czechoslovakian tram were bit actors playing a significant role in the stage production we were photographing.

While it may have been that we had the good fortune of drawing two guides not particularly concerned with where we pointed our cameras, they were also very deliberate in where they took us and what we were allowed to see. What came across as being indifference may have actually been very subtle manipulation.

We did not pause long at that spot. We stood in the shadow of the *Koryo* Hotel long enough to take a few photos and ask a few questions about our surroundings before being ushered on to the next item on the itinerary. In the few moments we stood there on the corner and took in the surrealistic atmosphere, I noted stark and dramatic differences between that corner and any similar corner in Seoul. South of the border there would have been ubiquitous mobile street restaurants known in the local language as *pojangmacha*, or "covered horse carts," already out selling their food and drink to customers perched on stools. There would have been a visual cacophony of advertising anywhere the eye paused with innumerable backlit signs plastered across the exterior walls of buildings. The visual landscape would have been busy with flashing neon and rotating banners and everything would have been accompanied by insipid local pop music blasting through low-quality speakers that guarantee distorted sound.

In contrast, the Pyongyang sidewalk was free of mobile noodle merchants and this visual landscape featured large expanses of unbroken planes of cement-colored cement. There was no pop music, insipid or not. In fact, other than the noise of a passing bus or tram, the loudest sound was conversation as people walked past and those conversations were between people — not between a shouting pedestrian and a mobile telephone. It was mildly unsettling.

Mr. Kim the Elder directed us a few meters away and we started descending into the pride of North Korean tour guides and tunneling engineers — the Pyongyang Metro System.

We were at *Puhung* Station at the southern end of the *Chollima* Line. The station we entered had been built when the line was extended in 1987, but it appeared as if it was much older. The *Chollima* Line runs under *Podunamu*, *Kaeson*, *Sungni* and *Yonggwang* streets along the river through some of the most densely populated sections of the city. Over the years I had heard bizarre and fantastic tales about the Pyongyang Metro. Many claimed that like so many things in the country, it was fake; a Potemkin Metro designed to do nothing more but impress visitors. They claimed that the lack of electricity means the carriages only move when visitors are scheduled to be in the system, that there are actually only two stations (*Puhung* and *Yonggwang*), that the same North Koreans can be seen getting on and off the carriages again and again — thus proving the entire thing is a sham.

Granted, every account of foreign visitors being shown the Pyongyang Metro involves travel between the same two stations. The visitors are taken into one station, allowed to loiter and examine the extravagant decorations of the vaulted platform area, ushered into a carriage and allowed to ride to the next station where they are ushered off and allowed to loiter and examine the grandiose decorations of that vaulted platform area. Then the visitors are put on the escalator and sent back up to street level. In all recent accounts of visits to Pyongyang the only two stations accessible to tourists are *Puhung* and *Yonggwang* — the two we were shown. I suspect this is just good management. The North Korean officials strictly limit the stations to which foreigners have access simply to minimize the opportunities for foreigners to intermingle with locals.

As for the lack of electricity — I had been watching electric trams and trolley buses running up and down the streets of Pyongyang for a couple of hours and accepted that as evidence that the officials were capable of generating at least sufficient electricity to do that. Why couldn't they also opt to power a subterranean metro system?

In North Korean mythology a twenty-four-year-old Kim Jong Il visited Peking (now known as Beijing) in 1966 and was inspired by the construction of the new Beijing subway there. On his return to North Korea he single-handedly guided the nation in building the world's deepest public transport system. After a single inspection tour in Red China his penetrating observations were sufficient for him to return home and expertly guide the engineers, technicians, and laborers through the entire process.

Like much of the national myth, it appears that this retrofitted account was created by the Ministry of Love to enforce the double plus good admiration for the peerless wisdom of the Dear Leader. In reality, it was probably Kim Il Sung who prompted the construction that started in 1968 and much of the enthusiasm would have been for the creation of a dual-purpose metro and underground fallout shelter, as was the style in Moscow and Peking during the Cold War.

There is much speculation and little substantiation when it comes to the Pyongyang Metro. It remains one of the mystifying portions of that urban landscape. There is speculation about the existence of additional secret lines crisscrossing the city that are used only by high officials, there is speculation that the military has a secret line crossing under the river, there is speculation that hundreds were killed during construction, there is speculation that the Chinese postponed finishing the Beijing Metro in order to send their subway construction crews to North Korea to lend a collectivist hand. Outside of the Kim clique, nobody really knows. It's all speculation.

We stood in the covered street-level entrance and looked at a much-photographed system map mounted on the wall. It shows up in all the tourist accounts. It is one of those kitschy maps where the hapless potential rider can push a button next to the name of the station and up on the map a corresponding light appears. This type of map was previously used in the extensive Tokyo Metro system where the knot of lines looks like a bowl of udon noodles and one often needs serious help due to the sheer complexity of it all. With a dozen lines, nearly 300 stations, and almost eight million passengers a day crisscrossing the Tokyo system, one of those maps with blinking lights would be quite useful.

In Pyongyang there are only two lines; one has eight stations and the other has nine. Nobody outside the regime knows how many passengers use the Pyongyang Metro each day, but it is a tiny number compared to Tokyo. They don't need the map with the blinking lights — they know exactly where they are going. Tourists don't need the blinking light map because they are never going to enter the subway without being escorted by minders who know the way. It is unclear why the blinking light map exists. What purpose does it serve other than to illustrate to the world that the North Koreans can produce a blinking light map just as good as the ones in Bulgaria, East Germany, or the Soviet Union?

We stood against the wall and looked at the blinking light map with an appropriate amount of appreciation. We assured our hosts that as blinking light maps go, this indeed was a prime example of one. It had, after all, blinking lights all over the map which confirmed its qualification as a blinking light map. We all stood and admired the map in reverential silence, the North Korean minders standing in silent admiration just a little longer than was socially comfortable.

The rush-hour commuters continued past in a steady stream as they made their way towards the escalators that would take them down to the platform. Mr. Kim the Younger announced that he would secure our tickets and stepped away to converse with a uniformed official behind a booth. I looked back at the map (which Mr. Kim the Elder was still silently admiring) and noticed that each of the stations on each of the two lines were indicated in Korean, and beside the name was a socket into which the bulb was screwed. Two things were readily impressive: each and every bulb was working, and each line on the map already had two extra sockets to allow for future expansion. In the twenty years since that station had been built there hadn't been any expansion work on the publicly accessible portion of the Pyongyang Metro, but the blinking light map was ready to accommodate a pair of new stations whenever they got around to it. During the same twenty-year period, Seoul had increased its metro system by more than a hundred new stations.

Mr. Kim returned and indicated we should follow him down the escalator. As we followed, Alice enquired about the tickets, while Charles asked how much the fare was and if foreigners pay the same as locals. Mr. Kim gave a mumbled response but it was clear through body language that he was uncomfortable speaking while on the escalator. We never saw tickets or tokens and we were never asked for money. We simply followed a silent Mr. Kim the Younger, while Mr. Kim the Elder brought up the rear."

There was a single downward moving escalator, and a single upward-moving escalator. In Seoul, officials used to go to the trouble of buying and installing escalators in new subway stations, then, after installation was com-

Descending the escalator into *Puhung* Metro Station in Pyongyang. Now surpassed, at one time *Puhung* was claimed to be among the deepest metro stations in the world. Martial music is piped in for the enjoyment of commuters who tend to refrain from speaking in the presence of non–Koreans while on the escalator. Tickets cost the equivalent of 3.5¢.

plete, turn the escalators off to save on the cost of electricity. In the end they had what amounts to extraordinarily expensive stairs. Unlike Seoul, the escalators in Pyongyang were allowed to operate. The Pyongyang Metro is purported to be the deepest in the world at more than 100 meters below the surface. Looking down the shaft through which the escalator was steadily moving it appeared to easily have been 100 meters or more. The escalators moved at a steady clip, but it still took a very long time to reach the bottom. Doubling the speed by walking up or down the moving escalator is simply not tolerated and all commuters stood stock-still and quietly gazed forward during their silent trip. Posta.

As we descended deeper I recognized an odor that was very reminiscent of the peculiar aroma in the bowels of the Moscow Metro system. I'm not sure what the smell is. It certainly isn't objectionable and not necessarily unpleasant, just distinct. Maybe old communist subway systems just have an idiosyncratic smell. It wasn't at all like the peculiar abattoir smell of the airplane — this was a metro smell.

We descended into the shaft as very stern martial music played through hidden speakers. Recessed and hidden lighting created a pale, eerie glow on the walls. We were on the inside of a perfectly smooth cylinder that had been painstakingly plastered to such an extent that it appeared we were moving down through a gigantic drinking straw. As we descended deeper into the shaft the quiet conversations that had been mumbled among the foreigners drifted away until, like the Koreans, we stood in total silence and looked forward. Already we were being assimilated into the system.

On reaching the foot of the escalator our group followed Mr. Kim the younger deeper into the underground station. The infamous triple steel blast doors were there set into the wall and on tracks that would allow them to be drawn across the entry to create a fallout shelter within the confines of the platform.

Entering the platform area was impressive in the Moscow sense of the word. Expansive mosaic murals and elaborate light fixtures and vaulted ceilings over beautifully finished flooring were all evidence that Kim Il Sung's command to make metro stations cathedrals of the people had been carried out in earnest. It really was cathedralesque. Except for the carriages that kept rattling to a stop right in the middle of the cathedral and disgorging passengers ... other than that it really was cathedralesque.

At the end of the platform was a huge mural[23] of grinning Kim Il Sung striding forth under high voltage wires and smokestacks and surrounded by similarly happy technicians and workers garbed in attire appropriate to their jobs, but not specific enough to put a finger on exactly what it is they were supposed to be doing. The entire mural was done in a yellow motif that brightened that end of the platform. Like the many monuments of Pyongyang that gave me a sense of déjà vu, over the years I had seen photographs of this cheerfully yellow mural time and again.

Parallel to the tracks were more large mosaics, one on each opposing wall stretching at least 200 meters down the length of the platform, depicting the ubiquitous happy North Korean citizen-workers beaming with pride at their accomplishments. The mosaic proletariat had happily electrified villages, and fabricated locomotives with wrenches, and irrigated previously unproductive tracts of land with shovels and trowels, while simultaneously cheerfully standing guard against Imperialist hegemony at the frontier. Each mosaic man and woman beamed with the pride of accomplishment.

Alice turned to Mr. Kim the Elder and asked if the murals were named. Mr. Kim glanced at the nearest mural and, after a moment of pause, turned back to her and said, "This one is called *Innovation Morning*." I looked at the deliriously contented workers depicted in the mural and noticed low in one corner was the Korean title: *Three Revolutions*.[24] Either he took considerable liberty in his translation, or she had caught him flat footed. Time and again during our stay it was unclear if the guides were taking liberties with their presentations or if I was missing some crucial fact. The catchphrases of the regime quickly become tautological as they reappeared again and again and again. One of the catchiest of catch phrases in North Korea is "Three Revolutions" and it can be seen spewed across the visual landscape on posters and signs and murals. The Three Revolutions are ideological, technical, and cultural and have been used as jingoistic motivators since the early 60s. It was as if the regime came up with a campaign slogan that was so stinking good that even after they secured control of their half of the peninsula they decided to keep the slogan around and now, decades later; it was still on the tip of every tongue. It wasn't obvious if the hackneyed "Three Revolutions" was the name of the mural or not, but those words had been carefully worked into the mosaic in little red tiles.

The rolling stock in the Pyongyang Metro is completely North Korean. From design to fabrication, everything was accomplished by the self-sufficient North Koreans — probably after plenty of on-the-spot guidance from an appropriate authority on the subject. At least with self-confidence that suggested he knew what he was talking about, Mr. Kim the Younger assured me that the carriages were all completely North Korean. On the contrary, the Red Chinese report having provided the original Metro carriages, and subsequently the Germans (both East and West) claim to have supplied used carriages from both sides of divided Berlin. These days subterranean Pyongyang appears to be dominated by refurbished German rolling stock. It is quite possible that Mr. Kim sincerely believed what he said, even though subway enthusiasts from around the world would have been able to glance at the carriages and immediately identify them as being from Berlin.

The rattling cars were free from even the slightest bit of graffiti. No spray-painted tags, no cryptic marks scrawled in indelible ink, no initials chiseled into unsuspecting surfaces. The paint was clean and unmarred, the windows were crystal clear, and there was not a scrap of litter to be seen. The Pyongyang Metro felt just like an amusement park monorail ... and not at all like a transport system in a public place.

Eventually both Mr. Kims grew weary of the four of us gawking at what they had seen time and again, and on the next set of carriages pulled up at the platform we were instructed to step inside.

The doors were opened and we were ushered in through the last door of the last carriage, a safe distance from the majority of people getting on to the train. Despite it being evening rush hour and time for everyone to be commuting home, the carriage was not full. In fact, there were empty seats here and there we could have taken had not both Mr. Kims been eager to keep us corralled as a small herd in the extreme rear of the carriage. Sheep-like we huddled together pressed into a shadowy corner.

Our fellow passengers were all smartly attired, just like everyone I had seen up on the surface. Dark jackets, ties, skirts well below the knee and the omnipresent Kim Il Sung lapel pins. They didn't gawk at the corpulent visitors. In any of the metro systems in South Korea it would have been expected that a few of our fellow passengers would openly and unabashedly gawk with laser-like unblinking obsession. South Korean gawkers can ride between stations without breaking their stare or blinking. Under the streets of Pyongyang eyes were silently and automatically averted. The embodiment of unfettered, unadulterated capitalism unleashed and roaming about the Worker's Paradise is not to be gazed on directly. We corpulent visitors were shown Medusa-like difference.

At the far end of the dimly lit carriage, up above the doorway where the German manufacturer's plaque would have been, there were two small portraits of father and son — their expressions of pleasant contentment evidence that the commuters had all been diligent at their tasks and could rest assured that both the late Great Leader, as well as the Dear Leader were satisfied with their efforts. Kim Il Sung's eyes followed us as we rocked back and forth in the moving carriage. I glanced down at Mr. Kim the Elder's lapel pin and for the first time was able to get a close look. The lapel pin and portrait in the carriage were identical representations of Kim Il Sung. They featured the same beatific expression on the same prudent-yet-compassionate face. The tiny eyes on the lapel pin, like the eyes in the portrait at the end of the carriage, were moving as they watched me.

Maybe the entire Pyongyang metro system *is* actually a farce, maybe it is used as a showpiece to impress foreign visitors; a subterranean Potemkin village on wheels. After all, the only two stations any outsider is ever shown are *Puhung* and *Yonggwang*.[25] All the commuters in this theatrical production are supposedly dutiful party members selected to ride the escalators and trains in never-ending circles simply to provide a convincing backdrop of commuters. The trains are purportedly timed to arrive and depart during the hour approved for observation by foreign guests, then when visiting hours have ended, the entire system is switched off, the trains are parked at the platform, the electrical currents to the chandeliers are disconnected, the last of the bogus commuters rides the escalator up to the surface, the power is cut, the curtain comes down and the show concludes until the next batch of foreigners is in town. Maybe it's true.

While rattling along the tracks towards the next station, I looked at the Koreans seated in the carriage and pondered the possibility that they were not really going home — they were fulfilling their obligation as background commuter for the afternoon. Maybe they were the ones who had drawn the short straw, so they had to go out of their way at the end of a long work week to go down and get on a subway train heading in the opposite direction of home and pretend to be a contented citizen just for the sake of the curious lumpy foreigners. Maybe.

To me they looked like nothing more than weary workers heading home. They looked completely convincing in the drudgery of an afternoon commute and I had no doubt that the exhaustion in their eyes was not an act. If the entire thing was a sham, then it was an amazingly convincing sham.

We traveled about 1,500 meters beneath the streets of Pyongyang. At the next stop, *Yonggwang* Station, Mr. Kim the Younger instructed us to follow him as he alighted from the carriage. Just like that our obligatory one-stop ride was finished. It had been completed in the same manner as the one-stop-ride U.S. Secretary of State Madeleine Albright and her entourage reportedly took, same as the one former U.S. President Jimmy Carter and his entourage reportedly took, and the same for Billy Graham, the same for the Reverend Moon, and the same as the short ride all the other visiting foreigners and their entourages took over the years. It was a well rehearsed itinerary designed to simultaneously showcase the best Pyongyang had on offer while eliminating the opportunity for any unexpected surprises. *Puhung* to *Yonggwang*. No deviation, no alteration, no opportunity for improvisation; get on, get off, all finished. Posta.

Like *Puhung* station, *Yonggwang* station was extravagant in decoration. It featured murals and bas-relief sculpture, as well as lighting fixtures that would have been more appropriate in an amusement park. Mr. Kim the Elder caught me admiring the gaudy light fixtures that crawled up the supporting columns and terminated with a spray of colored lights along the vaulted ceiling. He marveled with me for a few moments then said, "The lights are said to resemble fireworks over Pyongyang," and indeed I could make out the resemblance of a projectile crawling out of the top of the mock solomonic column, then the explosion of light up in the vault. It was all terribly kitschy.

I smiled and said, "Ah yes, I can see the fireworks," then in Korean added, "very colorful ... very festive." The subtleties of sarcasm do not translate into the North Korean collective psyche.

Apparently that was the correct reaction. He either liked my tone, or he liked my admiration, or he liked the fact that I had spoken Korean because from that point forward Mr. Kim the Elder and I maintained an unspoken camaraderie. He gently took my arm and in Korean said, "Come," and we strolled to the platform's edge.

Together we admired the mural across the tracks on the opposite wall. It depicted the riverside in Pyongyang and the city behind it. He pointed out famous structures in the mosaic skyline between the arrival and departure of trains.

Eventually he turned to me and said, "We must go, the others have left," and as I looked up it was apparent that Mr. Kim and I had been the last on the platform as the others had already made their way to the long escalator and were preparing to return to the street. Looking over my shoulder one last time as we ascended, I saw yet another train pull up to the platform and expel passengers, then move on. The number of passengers using the metro system felt inadequate for the population of Pyongyang. If it was a Potemkin subway operated only for visitors, then somewhere a short distance away there were a number of trains being surreptitiously parked. During the time we loitered in the two stations, at least a half dozen trains had come in and gone out. If the whole thing was a sham, then just a short distance down the tunnel the parked trains were starting to build up. Something was not adding up, but in North Korea nothing ever tallies completely.

The tortuously long escalator ride to the surface provided plenty of opportunity for the descending commuters on our left to gawk, but the more I looked the more I saw them all consistently averting their eyes. They tended to stare directly ahead in expressionless patience or gaze at their shoes in quiet contemplation. Maybe they were recounting the events of the day, or maybe it was something else. Maybe they were preoccupied with the playing of their part as a "normal" commuter in the grand public transport charade. Maybe.

When we reemerged at street level Mr. Bae had the van waiting at the curb directly in front of the station entrance, so we took only a minimum of steps across the pavement, entered the van, and then efficiently pulled away. I glanced back at *Yonggwang* station one last time in hopes of catching some evidence of a charade, but alas I saw not a single familiar-looking face entering or exiting as we drove out of sight. Maybe it was a real metro system with real commuters. Maybe.

The van went up *Chollima* Street past numerous buildings well known to aficionados of North Korea. The sun sank lower into the tree line on the horizon as we passed a stretch of the *Potong* River lined with numerous willows and blooming golden bell.

There were a few retail shops on the ground floor of the apartment blocks and office buildings we passed. They were dim or dark, and appeared to already be closed for the day. Through the windows one could make out lots of shelves, but not much on them. The shop fronts were uncluttered and the windows untouched by the sign writer's brush. There was no advertisement, no neon lights, and no stickers announcing that credit cards were accepted there. Like the rest of the city, the motif was variations on cement gray.

Time and again I was struck by color choices. Color was not as abundant in the visual landscape, but when it appeared, it was consistently an

Sunset over Pyongyang's *Taedong* River. The Grand People's Study house sits in the gathering gloom above Kim Il Sung Square and in the background, towering above the entire cityscape, is the unfinished 105-storey *Ryugyong* Hotel. Shortly after this photo was made, crews started the process of covering the cement pyramid with a glass veneer. As the darkness descends, the city is bathed in gloom, except for select monuments and propaganda billboards.

unexpected tertiary color or a shade that wouldn't have been an obvious choice in the West. Rather than red, blue, and yellow there was burnt coral, majestic puce, and creamy ochre. Even red, the most important color on the communist palate, always appeared just a little orangey, or a little towards pink, or it was ever so slightly fluorescent. It was never fire engine red — never Kremlin red.

Above a darkened cement-gray shop would be a single sign with a single word indicating what was on offer inside. The signs were consistently of odd colors. It was as if the People's Sign Making Cooperative had gone to the local art supply shop and discovered the cut price bin where all the unpopular colors were gathered in the hope that somebody needing midnight mauve or toasted russet would come along and requisition them. It appears that there is a major disconnect between the Korea Paint Exchange Centre and the People's Sign Making Cooperative.

Mr. Bae drove us past the famed *Chollima* statue, and then we turned in to the *Kungryong* tunnel. As the van passed through the tunnel, Mr. Kim the Younger, resplendent in his jacket and tie, perched against the seat in the front of the van, looked back at the four foreigners and said, "This is one of Pyongyang's tunnels."

As if on cue, the four of us turned to look out our respective windows at the dimly lit tunnel walls passing by in a blur. Indeed, it was a tunnel. We could see evidence as we drove past. It was a tunnel in every sense of the word. We looked back to Mr. Kim awaiting the next sentence that would explain the significance of his observation, but it never came. He was simply pointing out that this was a tunnel. So it was.

We emerged abruptly from the tunnel and Mr. Bae slowed to turn as we entered what appeared to be a park. Gone were the gray buildings with taupe signs. We were surrounded by greenery and in the near distance the *Taedong* River. The sun was below a horizon that was quickly going from blue to purple. If the People's Sign Making Cooperative had been in charge of sunsets, it would have been murky indigo to gloomy plum.

Mr. Kim the Younger then smiled and said what would be a common theme for the rest of our visit, "There has been a change of plans...." The printed itinerary he had distributed just a couple of hours before was already inaccurate. We were scheduled to view the *Arirang* Mass Games the following night, but as he made the surprise announcement the van cleared a copse of willows and there looming before us in the pitch-lavender of the Pyongyang gloaming stood the largest stadium in the world. We were unexpectedly to see North Korea's famed mass games twenty-four hours earlier than scheduled.

May Day Stadium[26] sits on *Rungna* Island in the *Taedong* River. It is so large that perspective is lost when one stands at its base and gazes up. Mr. Kim, Younger or Elder, may have been rattling off facts as we got out of the van and walked a short distance to the entrance, I don't recall. I was too busy marveling at the colossal proportions and grandiose design. It has often been repeated that the stadium was designed to resemble a magnolia blossom, but that sounds to me like one of those hackneyed bits of lore that are created long after the stadium was completed and somebody looked at it and said, "Hey ... that sort of looks like a magnolia blossom if you squint and tilt your head."

I didn't see a magnolia blossom when I stood there gazing at the towering cement arches and massive support structure. I saw lots and lots of cement hanging in the air above my head, and I didn't have to squint to make it out.

If May Day Stadium had been constructed in the United States, they would have first cut down all the trees. It would be surrounded by huge tracts of paved land appropriately sectioned and painted to allow for each individual fan to drive his or her individual inefficient vehicle as close as possible to the stadium. Each vehicle would then be left among tens of thousands of other individual inefficient vehicles for three or four hours, then after the sporting event or concert, each individual vehicle would crawl in the queue to creep towards the clogged roadways that would lead to individual homes in the suburbs.

Comparatively little of *Rungna* Island had to be denuded and paved in order to get the world's largest stadium built. As we approached the stadium entrance, we were joined by thousands of Koreans approaching on foot. Therein was the secret — virtually nobody arrived by car. There were no more than two dozen vehicles, including buses and limousines, in sight. Unless the bulk of vehicles were parked around on the backside of the stadium, most people appeared to have walked onto the island and into the stadium.

We passed a number of Mercedes-Benz limousines positioned in front of the stadium entrances. They all had dark-suited, serious-looking North Koreans seated behind the wheel — usually enveloped in a cloud of cigarette smoke. Also walking towards the stadium were throngs of costumed children preparing to take part in that evening's performance. The nicotine-coated drivers sat silently with stone-faced disinterest as the giggling performers filed past.

Mr. Kim the Younger excused himself and ran ahead to secure our tickets at the will-call window. Actually it was a stand-alone wooden booth with a stern woman peering out through the window. She obviously did not enjoy what she was doing and wasn't looking to interact with anyone she didn't have to interact with. She snarled as he approached. I decided it was best if Mr. Kim dealt with that one.

A few hundred fortunate citizens mill around before being allowed in to May Day Stadium to witness a performance during the Arirang Festival. The red neon lights on the stadium will state simply "Arirang", an onomatopoeic Korean word used as the title of the most popular Korean folk song for both Koreas, and with meaning very much dependent on whom one asks: a regretful love song about a woman, a song about a man with unrequited love who kills the woman, a song about a stupid woman in love with a useless man who decides to take an arduous journey through a treacherous mountain pass, mountain gorge, or over a mountain, etc.

We mounted the steps and ascended towards the spacious entryway. Mr. Kim the Elder kindly fed information to me in a hushed tone as I snapped digital photographs. He said matter-of-factly, "There are 87 entrances ... and it can seat 150,000 people ... but it can hold much more than that."

I stopped taking photographs and admired the sheer immenseness. Seeking superlatives in our creations is something that communists have in common with Texans. The most significant, of course, is "world's largest." World's longest, world's heaviest, and world's tallest are all good, but world's largest is the superlative of choice for both North Koreans and Texans. He watched a clutch of well-heeled Koreans entering the stadium and said, "despite the size the stadium can be completely emptied in just fifteen minutes."

The four of us were shepherded through the VIP entrance where a woman in flowing traditional garb stood taking tickets while she chatted nonchalantly with a man in military uniform beside her. Earlier in the day Wally had run down a list of Korean vocabulary that is markedly different on each side of the DMZ. Words as simple as "cow" take on a political undertone. By a deliberate effort to make a political statement through the pronunciation of otherwise apolitical words such as cow, blouse, and toilet, the two Koreas have spent half a century linguistically drifting apart. I had listened in the van as the two Kims chuckled on hearing the Southern name for cow, and necktie, and helicopter, and the name used for traditional dress worn by Korean women. In turn they would tell Wally the northern word and he would grin and repeat it, shaking his head. It all sounded so alien to ears used to the Southern form of the language. As we approached the ticket taker in her elaborate traditional costume, I had already forgotten the Northern name for her attire.[27]

All four of us scampered to the toilets in anticipation of being trapped in our seats for the duration of the performance. A colleague in Seoul had attended a 1995 sports festival in May Day Stadium and, midway through an excruciatingly long performance, got up and excused her way down the aisle in hopes of ducking into the toilets. When she finally made it to the end of the aisle, a stern uniformed Korean man was blocking her path.

"Where are you going?" he demanded in heavily accented English.

"I need to use the toilet," she sheepishly confessed.

"No!" he shouted. His outstretched hand pointed at her empty seat and he screamed over the sound of the event. "You must sit down now. The time for going to the toilet has passed. Now is the time for observing the performance!" With that she excused her way back to her seat.

As we three hulking Americans addressed the porcelain receptacles lining one wall of the spacious room, a pair of jacketed-and-tied North Koreans near the sinks strained to steal glances without being obvious, but thanks to strategically placed mirrors their inquisitive looks were quite obvious. We were inevitably the only Americans they would ever actually see in the flesh and this was their one and only opportunity to confirm the rumor about American men being retromingent. They weren't gong to pass up this opportunity for first-hand confirmation.

Our seats were perfect, smack dab in the middle of the VIP level with an unobstructed view of the entire stadium. We were ushered to large formal wooden chairs that looked as if they had been temporarily borrowed from a conference room. We were seated at a long table covered with a green felt cloth. Below us were less impressive seats with more wide-bottom foreigners already sitting and taking photos of the mammoth stadium. Behind us were Koreans in much less regal cramped seating.

Charles had arranged the tickets in advance and, thanks to his good judgment, we opted for the most expensive choice, the $150 a seat "special class" ticket. For the 90-minute *Arirang* Spectacular I had spent the equivalent of the average North Korean's earnings for six months.

In the half hour before the performance commenced we were afforded plenty of time to get a thorough look at the stadium and study the preparations for the evening. It is truly gargantuan in proportion. Seoul's 1988 Olympic stadium could be picked up and placed within May Day Stadium and there would still be room for a hundred thousand to sit down.

From floor to the highest point the stadium is sixty meters, or the equivalent of an eight-story building. Tens of thousands of chairs went empty. Entire sections of the massive stadium were solid patches of empty teal green seats. Like an American nuclear family gathered to watch *I Love Lucy* in front of the television in 1959, on the evening of our performance the entire crowd of spectators were huddled together in the best seats — front center, directly across from the card show.

The stadium was reportedly built in a desperate attempt to have the International Olympic Committee award part of the 1988 Seoul Summer Olympics to North Korea. In the lead-up to the Games, when South Korea was going full steam ahead in what they saw as their international coming-out party, North Korea first tried to play the spoiler by attempting to make sure South Korea didn't pull it off. Then when it was obvious that the Games would go forward, the North Koreans started wrangling for a piece of the action. The squabbling went back and forth for months with suggestions that maybe part of the events could be staged in Pyongyang. For a while it looked like the two Koreas might actually try to strike some sort of deal and in anticipation of coming to an agreement, the Northerners raced to have stadiums and facilities in place. If the South Koreans were going to give part of the Games to North Korea, then North Korea wanted to be ready.

The result is a city festooned with numerous sporting facilities that are much more substantial than the population would otherwise justify. Calling them white elephants is letting the North Koreans off too easily. With an economy in shambles and a population largely unable to consistently meet basic needs, throwing resources behind enormous stadiums, and futuristic ice rinks, and sprawling gymnasiums is absurd.

During the 80s when the unofficial back and forth was going on between the two Koreas it appears to have escaped both that the IOC does not award the Summer Games to a nation, but rather to a city. The North Koreans flip-flopped on the issue and went from opposing the games to supporting them and wanting a piece back to opposing them. Their stance appeared to change with the season. May Day Stadium went up during one of the periods when the North Koreans were supporting the Olympics and demanding a piece of the action. Later their stance would change. Ten months before the Opening Ceremony in Seoul, reportedly by direct order from Kim Jong Il himself, the North Koreans blew up Korean Air flight 858 as it flew above the Burmese coast. Somehow the North Koreans reasoned that killing 115 passengers and crew would result in the Seoul Olympics being canceled. In fact the games went on — but with even tighter security. One of two North Korean saboteurs was captured alive and sent to South Korea for trial and eventual execution. It turned out that she was an attractive young woman who somehow wrangled a pardon from the South Korean president.[28]

When it was apparent that the North Koreans were not going to secure any part of the Seoul Games, they took two immediate steps: they organized a boycott[29] then they sought and won the right to host the 13th World Festival of Youth and Students.[30] When the 1988 Summer Games rolled around it had been twelve years since many Cold War foes had faced each other in the sporting arena and the eyes of the world were on the revived rivalry. Nobody really cared that the North Koreans and their friends were staying home. A year later when the festival of leftist student organizations took place, nobody cared either. Except the North Koreans. To them it was the pinnacle of international recognition and they were able to showcase their achievements to an international audience ... no matter that the majority of that audience was probably comprised of horny, hung-over university students.

Sitting in that enormous stadium looking at the immense size of the playing field, I asked Mr. Kim the Younger what sports were normally held there.

"Football, of course, and the Mass Games. These days that's all," he admitted.

I asked him if baseball was ever played in the stadium, or for that matter, in North Korea.

He chuckled and said, "No, baseball is not known in North Korea. That is an American sport we don't enjoy."

But I knew otherwise. Fewer than 800 meters from where we were sitting had been the home plate to a little-known baseball diamond on the northeast corner of the island. I know because I had studied the old satellite images. In fact, according to the satellites there are several diamonds around Pyongyang.

Baseball was played all over the peninsula until the war, and then the Northerners decided that baseball was too American, and thus too imperialistic, so it was abolished. Recently there seems to be a resurgence. Apparently if their comrades the Cubans can attain Olympic glory on the baseball diamond, and as long as North Koreans can secure the needed equipment from their Communist neighbors, then it appears to be once again acceptable.

North Korea is a member of the International Baseball Federation and fields a team of North Korean players for international tournaments. Indeed, baseball is alive and well in North Korea, even if our guides were ignorant of the fact. North Koreans might not be able to recite anything from Thayer's *Casey at the Bat*, or hum a bar from Norworth and Tilzer's *Take Me Out to the Ball Game*, but they are playing the great American pastime.

As we sprawled out in the prime seats on the west side of the enormous stadium, 200 meters away, directly in front of us, sat tens of thousands of schoolchildren. They were so closely packed that no space could be seen between any two of them. They were wedged in shoulder to shoulder, hip to hip, and knees planted in the back of the head of the student in the next row. If ever there was a great Communist leveler of the masses, this was it. A hundred thousand schoolkids spatula'd in so tightly that emergency trips to the toilet were absolutely out of the question. Forty-five minutes into a performance, if fifteen thousand sphincters into the crowd, one feeble sphincter decides that resistance is no longer possible and the floodgates are about to send forth a deluge of effluvium — too bad. There were no escape routes, no exit rows, no solution for a hundred thousand students to make a hasty exit should they need to. The blueprints for May Day Stadium were obviously never reviewed by the local fire marshal. As we sat the students were steadily taking their seats and preparing for their part in the performance.

"How many students are we looking at?" I asked Kim the Younger.

He smiled and said in a confident tone, "There are a hundred thousand students seated over there. Very impressive, isn't it?"

Like so many things we would be told in North Korea, the numbers simply didn't add up. If May Day Stadium seats 150,000 people and two thirds of that number is comprised of the students seated across the stadium from us, then only 50,000 more people could squeeze in. As I looked around at the mostly empty stadium, the size was so immense that I couldn't begin to guess at a capacity ... but the students weren't taking up two thirds of the stadium. There were a lot of them and they formed a solid squirming mass from the floor up to the top rim, but surely there weren't actually a hundred thousand over there gazing back at me.

Before any more thought could be given to the mathematical conundrum, some unseen signal altered the thousands of students to pick up their flip cards and get ready for a warm up session. With twenty minutes to go before the performance was scheduled to start, the mass of children across the stadium pulled out large stacks of colored cards and placed them in their laps.

Peeking over the upper edge of the square of color, each individual student watched for the visual cue that would tell him or her what to do next. Some of them were instructed to hold up a black square, some held up yellow, and others sat motionless and maintained their white square. Individually they were holding up nothing more than a square of colored cardboard. Then, as if to pay homage to the television they were emulating, a hundred thousand students used their colored cards to create a test pattern reminiscent of the test patterns one used to see back when studio technicians used to shut things down and go home for the night. On instruction from the unseen conductor, the students played with the test pattern. Bands of color would change then drift across the sea of cards, then everything would go black, then suddenly white, then almost instantly the test pattern was back but this time rather than being horizontal it was vertical.

Close up it would have been unimpressive, but from across the stadium, where each individual student was little more than a speck, it was remarkable. Each cardboard square became a manually controlled pixel in the world's biggest television screen. The television had one channel and it was commercial-free and state-run to the glory of the Kims.

Test patterns are of interest to the adolescent mind for only a limited period, and then they need additional stimulation. The conductor knew this and from some hidden vantage point flashed an instruction unseen by the guests and countless thousands of students shouted in unison as they flipped cards.

With that one stadium-filling shout the test pattern was gone and there were gigantic Korean characters strewn across the sea of cards. From the top of the stadium down to the floor, entire sections of students would flip over their cards and create a series of huge characters spelling out their school's name. At any given time a dozen different schools would be named across huge tracts of students.

In all those tens of thousands of human-powered pixels it would have been easy to spot the lone kid who mistakenly held up the incorrect color, or flipped the card too fast or too slow, or dropped his stack of cards as his buddy Chul Su gave him a wedgie or wet willie from the row behind. But through the entire performance I never once saw a single mistake. Not even the hint of a mistake. Not one pixel off from a picture of thousands of pixels high and thousands of pixels across. They had drilled to the point of perfection and could now participate in the crowning jewel in North Korea's gift to performance art — the Mass Games.

The May Day Stadium, despite being one of the largest stadiums in the world, hasn't had many opportunities to host significant events other than the infamous card shows. Besides the 13th World Festival of Youth and Students, the stadium's only other notable use was for the three-day Pyongyang International Sports and Culture Festival for Peace in April of 1995. Through a weird and wonderful series of coincidences the North Koreans managed to get a bunch of professional wrestlers from Japan, the United States, and Canada to conduct two nights of orchestrated pandemonium and testosterone-laced mayhem in a ring set up on the stadium floor.

Officials stopped counting when 160,000 people crowded into the stadium.

They were squeezed in like greased sardines because opportunities like that come once in a lifetime for Pyongyangers. The crowd was so large that Western Koreaphiles now sometimes set the attendance at 190,000. After all, Muhammad Ali was the guest of honor. How often does a fan in North Korea get to sneak a peak at Muhammad Ali? The show on Saturday 29 April 1995 is still recognized as the all-time record attendance for a professional wrestling match. During the second night, the stadium overflowing with giddy fans, the immortal Ric Flair, Nature Boy himself, took on the Japanese legend Antonio Inoki." During that match, which had 160,000 screaming devotees on their feet in delirious glee, Flair climbed atop the uppermost rope, stood fully erect, and before he could launch himself into Inoki's chunky torso, Inoki grabbed him by the waistband and tossed him back into the ring like a rag doll.

At the very moment Flair's depilated body spun into a midair summersault — head down, feet up, bleached hair trailing in the wind, muscular arms outstretched and ready for battle to the death — a North Korean photographer snapped a picture. That picture was featured on a propaganda leaflet that filled the skies over Seoul in the autumn of 1995. For propaganda leaflet collectors, it became known as "the Flair," and that coveted little piece of glossy propaganda continues to command a very high trade value.

Just like the fall of the Soviet Empire, when the DPRK inevitably crumbles there will be long queues of people standing up to take credit. Many of them will be social charlatans with flimsy credentials, but among them will be Ric "The Nature Boy" Flair who brought credibility and notoriety to the 1995 Pyongyang International Sports and Culture Festival for Peace. The Sunshine Policy went only so far ... but Flair's signature shin breaker coupled with his patented figure-four leglock will someday be rightfully acknowledged as what started the long process of bringing down the regime in the Democratic People's Republic of Korea.

At precisely 8:00 P.M. the stadium lights dimmed, the students lifted their cards in silence, the speakers pumped the opening notes of *Arirang*[32] in to the air, and streams of costumed performers flooded the floor of the stadium.

My $150 ticket proclaimed in English, "Mass Gymnastic and Artistic Performance" but that failed to capture the diversity of what happens inside the May Day Stadium during the hour-and-a-half performance. It is part history lesson, part Marxist world view, part adulation ceremony for the Kims, and part Bollywood musical. Add to that the need to visually state again and again that the Japanese colonized the peninsula and enslaved the Korean peo-

A North Korean propaganda leaflet featuring Japanese professional wrestler (and later Japanese politician) Antonio Inoki tossing American wrestler Ric Flair into the ring during the last bout of the final night of the 1995 Pyongyang International Sports and Cultural Festival for Peace. Though Western sources claim up to 190,000 people were crammed into May Day Stadium for the event, this propaganda leaflet indicates only a modest 160,000 spectators were there. Inoki eventually pinned Flair after a grueling 14:52. In reference to the wrestling bout, on the left the leaflet states, "Highlight — Japanese Inoki confronts American Ric Flair." In the middle the caption states that 160,000 people attended the festival. The photograph on the right states, "That day's photojournalists — Festival participants came from five continents." Subsequent agreements between the two Koreas halted government-sponsored propaganda leaflet drops but in the mid–90s North Korean tracts such as this one were frequently disbursed from balloons over the skies of South Korea.

ple, and the imperialistic Americans divided the peninsula in order to carry out their malicious designs, and despite these obstacles, the peerless guidance of Kim Il Sung and Kim Jong Il have elevated the downtrodden nation to the point where North Korea is clearly the envy of the world. All of that is presented in front of the backdrop of "a hundred thousand kids" manipulating cards to form patriotic images and aggressive and jingoistic slogans and illustrations that drive home the point that North Korea is a most fortunate nation overflowing with the abundance created by the collective obediently following the judicious directives of the Leaders — both Great and Dear.

As thousands of costumed performers poured onto the floor of the stadium, the school kids flipped open cards that created an amazingly intricate alpine backdrop resplendent with glowing sky and unsullied mountainscapes. The performers overtook the entire floor of the stadium and acted out the heartbreaking enslavement (complete with shackle, chain, and manacle props) the wicked Japanese forced on them. This seamlessly blended into the next movement of the production in which the evil Americans savagely ripped

During a performance of the Arirang Festival in April 2007, hundreds of child acrobats perform on the floor of the May Day Stadium while tens of thousands of children in the stands use colored cards to create a mural depicting "normal" North Korean children. To the right of the mural is 2007 — the date of the performance — and to the left of the mural is 1932 — the date North Koreans now claim the Korean People's Army was founded. Non-Korean historians cite 1947 as the creation of the KPA. The expansive stadium is virtually empty, except for the performers and a few hundred spectators seated directly opposite the cards.

apart not only the entire peninsula but individual families. The suffering and anguish needed to be displayed first in order to set the stage for the amazing perseverance and eventual triumph over adversity that would be acted out by a cast of a hundred thousand through the next hour and a half.

In the meantime the maudlin music continued to wail through the speakers and the performers, just close enough to be seen as individuals only when viewed through a camera's telescopic lens, looked as if even though they had been through this a million times before, they were still on the verge of tears and it was due only to the strength of the Magnificent General Kim Jong Il that they even made it through this performance without collapsing on the artificial turf in a crumpled heap of emotional ruin.

The performance shifted focus and there appeared black-suited cadres spreading the good news of *Juche* and urging the people to save themselves by submitting to the will of the masses, yet despite this the heartache and anguish persisted due to the imperialist marauders and their meddling ways. At one point early in the performance, a family was dramatically torn asunder and the men were pulled in one direction and the women were pulled in the other and in the gap between them the gulf of the DMZ emerged and created a permanent barrier. A spotlight from high atop the stadium shined down on the traditionally clad girl to make sure everyone in attendance under-

stood the message. To the stirring sounds of a mawkish melody the girl pan-
tomimed tears so clearly that even those unfortunate souls in the cheap seats
would understand that the brutish Americans had made the adorable little
girl cry tears of unimaginable heartbreak. They had torn her family in half
and left her fatherless.

The stadium exploded in crescendo as the mood abruptly changed. The
lighting was altered, the performers on the floor manipulated fans and bolts
of colorful *vinalon*, and a hundred thousand kids flipped their cards in unison to reveal Mount *Paekdu* with its distinguishing crater lake and virgin
forests. To the stirring sounds of melodramatic music the cards flipped again
to reveal that we were witnessing a re-enactment of the events of pre-dawn
16 February 1942 when North Korean mythology states that the Dear Leader
was born in a log cabin on the forested slopes of Mount *Paekdu*. The North
Koreans have documented the fact that to herald the glorious occasion a dove
descended from heaven while a new star appeared in the sky over the log
cabin and despite being in pre-dawn darkness in the middle of a bitter North
Korean winter, somehow not one but two rainbows appeared to mark the
occasion. It is easy to postulate the Biblical allusions are the result of Christianity having such deep roots in North Korea, but the self-illuminating noc-
turnal double rainbow and avian visitation in the middle of a deep winter is
pure North Korean indigenous pizzazz.[33]

The performance progressed and we were treated to yet more martial
music and card tricks and performers in such vast quantity that not a square
centimeter of Astroturf could be seen. North Korean card tricks are the most
spectacular on the planet. Through official government-to-government cooperative agreements in the past, the North Koreans have exported their card
trick skills to odd places like Zimbabwe and Guyana, but the results have never
been anything to compare to what happens in Pyongyang. Photos from South
America and Africa show embarrassingly pathetic attempts at emulating the
masters. Only the North Koreans have the man-hours to invest. Only the
North Koreans have the non-primary color paint in such abundance. Only
the North Koreans can achieve the pixel ratio that comes from a generation
and a half of stunted growth and collective emaciation. As extravagant as the
card tricks are it is incredible to stop and think that they are orchestrated primarily for a domestic audience. Through the entire performance, which
included more than a hundred elaborate displays of thousands of cards, whenever a message was written across the mosaic — it was done so only in Korean.

The music soared, the cards flipped, and women in very feminine flowing
costumes were replaced by faux military uniforms on thousands of strutting
young people, both male and female, who went through a fabulously intri-

cate routine on the stadium floor while their companions in the stands quickly flipped.

Only through binoculars was it apparent that the uniformed band members on the floor of the stadium weren't playing the instruments they carried. We listened to a crisp recording of a band performing what sounded like either "The Ballad of the November 8th Pig Iron Foundry Workers Collective," or possibly "The March of Mechanization is Rapidly Passing Through Our Village," yet the performers had nothing to do with what we heard. The reeds of the clarinets were bone dry and a long way from any moist lips, the drum sticks were held rigid above the drums, the tubas didn't even have mouthpieces. But the choreography was spectacular and the complex swirling formations of the pantomiming marching band appeared to happen effortlessly.

During a performance of the Arirang Festival in April 2007, hundreds of performers in faux military attire create intricate patterns on the floor of May Day Stadium. The performers carried musical instruments as props, but the music the audience heard was pre-recorded. Tens of thousands of children in the stands used huge colored cards to create a mural depicting the Great Leader, Kim Il Sung. The design created by performers on the stadium floor is a representation of the crest of the Korean People's Army.

It was impossible to take it all in. Too many things happened at once and in too many different places in one's field of vision. As the schoolkids flipped open yet another set of cards to display a massive hydroelectric dam with rushing water that appeared to actually rush across the stadium, the performers on the floor engaged in something equally as intricate and dazzling — but it was impossible to take in both. It was always a choice in *Arirang*, if one focused on the card trick showing the People's Tractor Factory Number Seven complete with moving wheels and waving tractor driver, then one had to forfeit looking down at the throngs of young women busily explaining self reliance through interpretive dance. If one followed the interpretive dance, then one missed looking up at the high wire act where valiant young comrades conducted quintuple somersaults in midair to illustrate the collective disdain for imperialism.

Through a night full of choreographed splendor involving thousands upon thousands of participants who had their routines drilled in so deeply that they could have pulled the entire show off while completely on autopilot, a night in which any number of complex giant moving props could have malfunctioned, when the lights might have blinked off, when the speakers might have been fuzzy and distorted, when the rest of the city was bathed in darkness so we could watch megawatts of power get pumped through countless spotlights, on a night when just a couple hundred kids in the card brigade could have thrown each other off and completely ruined their magnificent mosaic illustrations, nothing had gone wrong. Things were so meticulously carried out that even the slightest error would have been obvious for the entire stadium to see.

Then, just as I was realizing how flawless the performance had been, one young boy, among thousands of young boys who were decked out in the exact same costume doing the exact same high kick, kicked in just the right way and with just the right amount of strength to launch his shoe in flight across the stadium.

There was so much going on simultaneously that unless one had been looking right at that portion of the pulsating crowd of performers, it would have gone unnoticed. But I had seen it and I was riveted as I watched to see what might happen next. The North Koreans are known for draconian reaction to anyone stepping out of line. The one-shoed lad may have been risking severe punishment.

The high kicking performers soon completed their routine and in a well-choreographed sweep to the side, they dissolved in to a group of previously hidden young women rushing out *en masse* for the next choreographed act. I could see in my peripheral vision that there were intricate card tricks unfolding up in the stands and the spotlights were focused on a different portion of the stadium where some other part of the show was supposed to be the center of attention, but my eyes were glued to the lonely white canvas shoe on the stadium floor.

It was trampled, then kicked to the side, and then kicked again as performers unknowingly passed over it as they carried out their routines. Another wave of dancers came rushing out in long flowing skirts and billowing sleeves and when they commenced dancing they filled the entire floor with twirling, billowing, fluttering *vinalon* splendor. Somewhere under the flowing *vinalon* costumes the shoe was either kicked completely out of the way, or surreptitiously snapped up and spirited away under a ruffle or a billow or a pleat. Since that day I have often pondered the fate of the one shoed boy as he returned to the dressing room to face the potential wrath of a stern choreographer. North Korean choreographers have long been rumored to utilize small arms to assist with discipline.

The card tricks increased in complexity and we were treated to enormous bulldozers moving to and fro as they carried out construction work on behalf of the proletariat, of expansive farms filled to capacity with cows and goats, but especially fecund three-story rabbits[34] which hopped across the wall of cards in great quantity.

The performance neared a crescendo and the stadium floor was quickly emptied of dainty and graceful dancers and replaced with white-clad boys outfitted for martial arts. Sitting in Pyongyang watching thousands of stern young men prepare to demonstrate the finer aspects of *Taekwondo*, I was transported back to the Opening Ceremony of the 1988 Summer Games in Seoul where, sitting in a stadium in a section of Seoul called "Silkworm Room,"[35] a group of similarly clad young men gathered on the stadium floor and did precisely the same thing: yell in unison, break boards with an extended foot, jump over partners and break boards with an extended foot, stand on something tall and then jump over an ever larger number of partners and break boards with an extended foot, then quickly gather up all the new kindling wood and scamper off to the wings so some other group could come out and perform the next routine. It was exactly the same.

As the North Korean lads cleaned the stadium floor someone behind the scenes flipped a switch and the boogie fog disco machine started pumping out dry ice fog. Within moments the stadium floor was covered in swirling mist and all eyes turned upwards where, in the glow of the spotlight a motorcycle was perched precariously on a cable that ran from the lip of the stadium on the north to the lip of the stadium on the south. Hanging from a tether

Near the finale of a performance of the Arirang Festival in April 2007, thousands of dancers perform around a globe on the floor of the May Day Stadium while tens of thousands of children in the stands use huge colored cards to create a mural depicting doves of peace. This mural came moments after the same children had used the same cards to create the image of menacing North Korean missiles streaking through the skies. To the right of the mural is 2007 — the date of the performance — and to the left of the mural is 1932 — the date North Koreans now claim the Korean People's Army was founded. Non-Korean historians cite 1947 as the creation of the KPA, but the Kim Dynasty required a different back story to substantiate the national foundation myth, so their official history was altered.

below the motorcycle was an aerial acrobat who proceeded to strut his or her stuff as the motorcycle crossed the stadium eight stories above the floor. As if that was not sufficient enough to impress, more traffic joined the motorcycle and started crisscrossing cables suspended across the bowl of the stadium with additional acrobats suspended on tethers. There were more motorcycles balanced on cables above the stadium than we would see on the streets of Pyongyang through the remainder of our visit.

When the motorcycles were out of the way, the bungee boys appeared. From the floor of the stadium groups of brightly costumed performers pulled taut a series of gigantic bungee cords suspended from above. Without warning the cords were released and acrobats were hurtled five, six, seven stories in to the air, then they gracefully arced across the stadium before surrendering to gravity. Fortunately for them their colleagues quickly arranged nets that were conveniently placed in such a way as to prohibit the soaring acrobats from lodging themselves into the floor of the stadium at the terminal of their arc.

The performance came to a climax with the floor of the stadium being re-filled with a sea of women in traditional garb. They created the effect of ocean waves by waving long bolts of *vinalon* under blue lights. They looked very much like a tempestuous ocean with giant waves of arms and sleeves and bolts of cloth lapping at the front row seats. Then, in a hauntingly beautiful sleight of hand, from the floor of the sea rose the silhouette of the Korean Peninsula. Thousands of performers who had previously been just drops in the blue ocean turned garments inside out to reveal flowing white dresses with flowing sleeves. The blue-clad women around them continued to create their waves of billowing *vinalon*, but the women in white stood stock still as the stadium erupted in applause at the sight of the Korean peninsula with

On the floor of the gigantic May Day Stadium during a performance of the Arirang Spectacular, thousands of costumed dancers create the image of an undivided Korean peninsula as well as the islands of Quelpart, Dagelet, and the Liancourt Rocks. Perpetually preoccupied with the division of the peninsula, tens of thousands of students hold up cards that state simply: "one."

no dividing line across the middle. The *vinalon* waves lapped at the shore of the unified nation and the crowd cheered wildly.

Hundreds of performers in white gazed up at the audience and it was obvious that many were just managing to hold back the flood of tears. They had practiced for countless weeks and through innumerable dress rehearsals had heard the maudlin music and seen the schmaltzy symbolism repeated again and again. Surely they were completely numb and beyond susceptibility to the emotive manipulation directed at the audience. But when it came to the point of creating the silhouette of the Korean peninsula on the floor of the stadium, along with the teary-eyed audience, their emotions were ripped open and left bare.

From the Yalu[36] River down to the southern coast of Quelpart,[37] they stood there in brilliant spotlit white and gazed up at the audience and choked back the flood of tears. Just to make sure everyone understood that the North Koreans are in absolute agreement with the South Koreans about who owns which specks of land in the Sea of Japan, off to the right there were even little islands of three or four white-clad performers surrounded by a sea of women in blue. They represented Dagelet Island and the Liancourt Rocks.[38] The message was clear — those specks of rock in the middle of the Sea of Japan are *NOT* Japanese. They are sacred Korean soil just as hallowed as all the other rocks and dirt that make up the mainland. And furthermore, it is *NOT* the Sea of Japan, it is the "East Sea." Whether or not there is a dispute about which of the two Koreas gets to claim the rocks was, at the moment, not being revealed. They were showing a unified front with their Southern cousins and reiterating yet again their joint territorial claims.

The Liancourt Rocks have been a particularly sore spot for the South Koreans in recent years. Despite the South Koreans maintaining a continuous armed presence on the rocks since the end of the Korean War, the Japanese claim ownership. The subsequent skirmishes have resulted in deaths, the capture of boats, the exchange of prisoners, and a very irritating Liancourt-Rocks-themed pop song on South Korean radio. The North Koreans have never had occasion to publicly take part in the dispute so it was interesting to see them jump in and make a statement on the floor of the May Day Stadium. South Koreans are particularly sensitive to all the islands, sandbars, shoals, reefs, atolls, specks, and spits in the waters surrounding their nation and can become openly emotional when discussing these locations.[39] For several years the two Koreas have now and again jointly participated in international sporting events. During those rare occasions when the bickering is set aside and the track suits are harmonized, the combined team participates not under the flag of either of the two nations, but under the recently created

During a performance of the Arirang Spectacular, costumed dancers create the image of the Korean peninsula as well as the islands of Quelpart, Dagelet, and the spot-lit Liancourt Rocks. Tens of thousands of school children sit in the stands behind the performance and create enormous and intricate images by flipping colored cards — in this case a depiction of traditional Korean filial piety.

Unification Flag: a simple blue silhouette of the Korean peninsula on a white background. Until 2006 the Unification Flag did not include Dagelet or the Liancourt Rocks. When that regrettable oversight was revealed, both Koreas marshaled their graphic design forces and jointly created a panel of expert cartographers, historians, and artists to address the problem. After much consultation two tiny blue dots were officially added to the Unification Flag — one for Dagelet and one for the Liancourt Rocks.

As the ninety-minute production came to a spectacular conclusion, the image of a united Korea was sufficient to bring thousands of North Koreans to their feet for a standing ovation. For the non–Koreans it was a terrific opportunity to stand up and stretch weary limbs. Reunification is a favored topic on both sides of the DMZ and is never without emotional undertones. The symbolism of reunification comes in many forms, but the most simplistic is the silhouette of the peninsula against a plain backdrop. Without need for words, that image strums on the collective heart strings and many of the evening's spectators would depart the stadium with moist eyes.

We were ushered through the nearby exit as the house lights went up and the entire stadium was vacated in a few brief minutes. Mr. Kim had been correct. People were streaming out at an unbelievably fast pace. Without parking lots filled with private cars and without nearby public transport, the proletariat simply walked through the stadium exits and then continued walking into the darkness.

The door of our van was closed behind us and Mr. Bae drove through the gloomy, empty streets. As we moved through the darkness, Mr. Kim the Younger stood at the front of the van and announced that we were heading to the hotel where we would check in, eat, and then as per the itinerary created by communist tour organizers, we would retire. That was the plan; there were no other options.

The *Yanggakdo* Hotel[40] is yet another of the fabled North Korean structures and monuments I had never laid eyes on, but with which I was already familiar. The stories that trickled back through the barbed wire of the DMZ would have us believe that the foyer of the huge hotel is festooned with plastic Christmas trees year round, that there is a giant sea turtle and full-grown sturgeon swimming in lobby aquariums, that the staff are all imported from China and no North Koreans actually work there, that there is a brothel and casino in the basement, and that the whole thing was constructed by the French who mysteriously removed all traces of Gallic snootiness when they departed. The rumors swirling around the hotel have evolved into greater and greater wackiness as time has gone by.

We entered the lobby of the towering hotel and like so many other buildings in that city it was immediately grandiose, and simultaneously austere, really big and very empty. Scattered around the lobby were the fabled Christmas trees. Bare of any ornamentation, the trees were tucked away in corners or on balconies and against large windows. A copse here, a coppice there, a grove against the concierge desk. All of them featured a thick coating of fine dust that suggested a more environmentally acceptable way of flocking.

To the side of the lobby sat the dim lobby bar, which prominently featured a fish tank acting as a dividing line between the bar and the rest of the immense lobby. A few pathetic fish meandered in dimness, and above them lumbered a full grown sea turtle turning tight little slow circles in a very cramped tank.

Mr. Kim the Younger rapidly completed the formalities at the check-in desk as we four foreigners stood and gawked in the middle of the expansive lobby. Twin portraits of the Great Leader and Dear Leader gazed at us from above the reception desk. All four of us maintained our own speed and direction, but all four of us slowly and silently rotated on our heels as we did 360° gawks. Mr. Kim had our passports and tickets and all official state paperwork documenting us as approved guests, so there wasn't anything for us to do. We weren't even asked to sign anything. After a very brief time at the counter, he turned to face us and said, "Let's go. You can leave your bags here while we go eat." Kim Il Sung's eyes followed us as we walked behind Mr. Kim the Younger

We had not eaten since the experimentation with Soylent Gray on the airplane and it was already past 9:00 P.M. The corpulent lifestyle of the bourgeoisie had not prepared us for the substantial gap between meals and our stomachs were making the decadent groaning sounds of the pampered elite. Down through the cement-gray basement labyrinth we went, following Mr. Kim without question.

Korean basements on each side of the DMZ are usually designed to allow for very low clearance. In fact, for a grain-fed Texan transversing the basement of the *Yanggakdo* Hotel required leaning forward at an angle to avoid a sudden cranial impact. The shorter Koreans could pass through the basement with room to spare, but most of the gangly foreign males were navigating with bent backs and cocked heads. The cramped basement design certainly didn't appear to have been the product of French architects.

We passed a dimly lit ten-pin bowling alley with a few customers, a darkened shoe repair room, a couple of shops behind closed and locked doors, and another bar. Then around a cement corner we turned and up a small cement hallway deep under the hotel we trudged into a tiny little empty dining room. It was shadowy and still when we waltzed in expecting food, but the aproned woman in the corner looked up at Mr. Kim with an expression that announced she was closed and she would not tolerate any attempt to get her to re-open.

Mr. Kim the Elder spoke quickly and quietly to the matronly woman. It was clear before he turned to address us that her decision was final, we would be going elsewhere to eat.

We walked deeper into the murky cement labyrinth to an unmarked door that opened in to a cramped little restaurant no larger than a bedroom. A uniformed young man and woman sat in the shadows quietly polishing cutlery and organizing crockery. It was late and they were almost ready to go home when we burst in on them with growling stomachs and big eyes.

Mr. Kim said a few kind words and smiled at them. He was just out of range to understand, but it was clear that we were running out of options and Mr. Kim had four hungry charges to feed, water and stable. He was determined to make it work and this time his body language announced as much.

We were unceremoniously shown the back dining room — a windowless basement cubicle with a fluorescent fixture in the center of the ceiling that gave off a weak bluish glow. There was just room enough to accommodate a doily on the table, a plastic clock, and a cheap lithograph of a waterfall hung on a nail near the door, and us. We quickly sat around the table and Mr. Kim the Elder explained that they hadn't been expecting us, but that they were happy to serve us despite the fact that just a moment before they were about to lock up and walk out. Actually he didn't say they had been about to lock up and walk out, but it was easy enough to read on their gaunt faces.

Mr. Kim the Younger was nowhere to be found and only later would I come to realize that his frequent disappearances were due to the need to step out and suck some nicotine into his system. In deference to guests, our Korean hosts almost always refrained from smoking in our presence, but that didn't diminish Mr. Kim's desire to spark up and during our visit he would often quietly step out and then later inconspicuously reappear reeking of stale cigarettes.

In true Korean fashion the meal commenced with an assortment of a dozen small dishes known as *panchan*. Pickled this, and steamed that, hard-boiled quail eggs, salted and dried fish, tofu, squid — the variety is usually wide and the diner can never be too sure what might be included. It is typical for the *panchan* to come in a never-ending stream of little porcelain bowls that allow a table full of diners to pick and choose at will. The entree eventually comes and is consumed along with the *panchan*. Long after the entree has been finished, it is not uncommon for diners to continue requesting and receiving more *panchan* until they have satisfied their hunger. The swinging door to the little room remained in a near-state of perpetual swing as the waitress came back again and again carrying trays filled with food and drinks.

Eating this food was a familiar experience for Wally and me due to long years in South Korea. Even Charles had made sufficient trips to both Koreas to keep pace. Alice, however, was struggling. She made a gallant effort with the chopsticks, and that isn't necessarily easy. Korean chopsticks come in many varieties, but the common restaurant variety is small and metal and for the unaccustomed they are frustratingly difficult to use. Eating a meal with knitting needles would be an easier assignment. I have never uncovered the logic of designing a chopstick so difficult to manipulate and have never once been given a satisfactory explanation. That conundrum is one of many that usually have discussions concluding with the words, "unique situation" or

"You can't understand," or the double-whammy, "You can't understand our unique situation."

Alice obviously couldn't understand the unique situation and was struggling mightily with the exasperating little utensils when she silently capitulated. Unlike everybody else in the region, the Koreans also make habitual use of spoons during meal time and this discovery came much to Alice's delight. She sat her sticks down with a metallic tinkle, and went at it with a spoon.

Coming to terms with chopsticks is only the first requirement of the Korean menu. Coming to terms with the menu is the second requirement. There are a number of adjectives that come to mind when contemplating Korean food. Pungent is frequently used. Also odoriferous and effluvious. Alice was a real trouper as she used her spoon to pick up a piece of dried and seasoned cuttlefish and managed a hesitant bite. Cuttlefish is in the squid family and is known in the West as the source of the cuttlebone — that white chunk of abrasive material any self-respecting parakeet has wired to its cage between the water dish and food tray. In the East they don't dwell on the cuttlebone — they see the cuttlefish as yet another source of food. After a few chews of the rubbery tentacle she enquired about what she had in her mouth.

"It's cuttlefish ... kind of like squid," Wally told her matter-of-factly.

Alice put on a brave face and said, "...like squid? Squid is calamari. I like calamari..." After a few more chews of the rubbery limb she said, "Actually this isn't *that* much like calamari. I don't think I care for this." And with that she concluded her experimentation with cuttlefish for the duration of our visit.

The food continued to come out of the kitchen until the waitress was given instruction to stop the flow. We ate to our heart's content, then Mr. Kim the Elder helped the four of us retrace our steps through the maze of bare passageways, the three foreign men stooping and hunchbacked until safely back in the grandiose lobby.

Mr. Kim went to the desk and retrieved our room keys, then handed them to an amiable uniformed bellboy. "Boy" didn't do him justice as his grizzled face displayed weathered crevasses and graying stubble. Unlike most smokers his nicotine stains didn't end at the fingertips — his entire being was deeply and luxuriously nicotine stained. He wore his nicotine like a coat of protective lacquer, and was obviously a veteran of the North Korean hospitality industry and a real soldier in the hotelier business. Like the Sky Comrades, he represented another layer of defense against the encroachment of foreign tourists. His rumpled uniform was frayed around the edges and his dark necktie was loosened enough to reveal a ring of grime around his dingy shirt collar. In the North Korean sense he had a plum job. He grunted in no discernable language and tossed our bags on to a cart, then walked off towards the elevators with the squeaking cart in tow.

The four of us stood momentarily before realizing that we were expected to follow. We scampered to catch up and arrived as the elevator door opened and he shuffled in.

At the twenty-eighth floor he grunted again and as the door opened in to a pitch-black hallway, he stepped off. The four of us chortled and followed. The darkness was already becoming a theme and lived up to the rumors. The seasoned bellboy slapped at an unseen place on the wall and a few weak fluorescent lights came on to reveal a long, dim undecorated corridor with dozens of identical doors leading into dozens of identical rooms, the wallpaper and carpet water-stained and peeling at the corners. Alice was shown her room, then Charles, then Wally and I were taken in to the third room where with a thump the bellboy dropped our bags in the corner, played at adjusting the drapes in a very unconvincing way, then turned and said in heavily accented throat-cancery English, "Give me tip."

It was obvious that that was the extent of his English ability and that he had worked long and hard to master those three words. He unceremoniously held out an open nicotine-coated palm and stood stock still while Wally fished out a wad of Chinese notes. In that instant the bellboy helped the flagging North Korean economy by drawing in a little more precious foreign currency. Every *Yuan* helps.

With the transaction completed he showed himself out and closed the door with a loud thud. It took only a few seconds to survey the room. Two single beds, an empty and unplugged refrigerator, a television that didn't work, and lamps equipped with very low wattage bulbs. Except for the brilliantly illuminated monuments to the Great Leader and the Dear Leader, all of Pyongyang is low wattage.

The bathroom was typical of virtually all other hotel bathrooms in the world except that under the sink the plumbing was completely exposed. A Gordian knot of copper pipes snaked up and down the wall, over to the shower, in to the toilet tank, to and from the sink. In any other hotel the pipes would have been concealed behind cabinetry, or buried in the walls. Looking at this amateurish attempt at plumbing it was obvious to me that the French had nothing to do with that aspect of construction and I doubted they were involved at all. Surely if the French had had a hand in putting up the *Yanggakdo* Hotel there would have been more of an effort to conceal the sloppy pipe work.[41] Wally and I ventured back through the dark corridor and found the elevator, then returned to the lobby where we had both seen a sign for postage stamps and e-mail. The woman behind the counter was nodding in her chair as we approached. In Korean Wally enquired about e-mail and the woman patiently explained a convoluted pricing system that was completely incomprehensible. It was incomprehensible not because of any language barriers, but because the concept of pricing for goods and services in the Worker's Paradise is completely lacking. With anxious wives waiting for confirmation of a safe arrival, we both decided to take the plunge and send short e-mails without concern for the wacky pricing structure. In quick, short shifts we sat and typed brief messages to let them know we had arrived safely. On hitting the send button the woman informed us that the charge was €6 ... for each of us. At about two lines each, that worked out to about the most expensive e-mail service anywhere on earth. If the North Koreans could corner a steady market at that rate, they could wash their hands of any illicit business deals and their economic troubles would be steadily alleviated.

Socialist tourism was taking a toll and both of us decided we'd had enough of the Worker's Paradise for one day and returned to the twenty-eighth floor and crept through the dark corridor back to our room where we each sprawled across a little single bed with a firm mattress. Soft mattresses are for the bourgeoisie. We lay awake for a short time and freely talked about the day despite the possibility that the room was bugged. Within moments the two of us were creating sufficient snoring to dissuade any eavesdropper from maintaining interest.

Day Two

Sunday, 29 April 2007

At sunrise we were awake and eager to get back out there and take in more of the Worker's Paradise. Well before the scheduled 6:15 wake-up call Wally was in the shower and I was perched in the open window looking out across a mist-shrouded cityscape. South of the DMZ they haven't lived up to the "Land of Morning Calm" nickname in a generation. The frantic pace of rapid industrialization wiped away the remnants of quiet, calm mornings decades ago. In the North, however, mornings really are calm — morbidly calm. Topple over dead and not get noticed for a week and a half calm. The calmness is so all-encompassing that it becomes surreal. Foreign visitors have reported standing at their hotel window and hearing the cry of a baby across the river deep in one of the distant neighborhoods. The magnitude of quiet is startling.

At a quarter after six in the morning on the one day of North Korea's one-day weekend virtually the entire city was still sleeping. Other than a few birds nothing was moving. There was no traffic — from twenty-eight floors up not a single moving vehicle was to be seen. The early morning delivery vehicles that would be crisscrossing the streets of other cities at that hour were all absent because in Pyongyang there are no early morning deliveries. There's nothing to be delivered. There were no city sounds to be heard. It was as if it really were a back lot at a movie studio where none of the extras or stage hands had yet punched in.

The *Yanggakdo* Hotel sits on the northern tip of an island in the river and the view from our twenty eighth-floor window was hindered by the mist and little could be clearly seen other than the gray forms of riverside build-ings and long empty boulevards. Peering down it was pleasantly surprising to be able to look right through the *Taedong* River to the riverbed. The water was clear and fresh looking and completely unlike the *Han* River which passes through Seoul and carries with it the suspended weight of rapid industrial-ization. North Korea's industrial decline might have been damning for the

On a fog-shrouded sunrise in early spring, Pyongyang is silent and still. With a total lack of traffic and no background industrial noise, it is frequently possible to hear songbirds in the trees across the *Taedong* River. At 323 meters, the unfinished *Ryugyong* Hotel pyramid dominates the silent cityscape. Shortly after this photo was made crews started the process of covering the cement pyramid with a glass veneer.

economy, but it was fantastic for the ascetics. Though the *Taedong* River looked deceptively clean, it is likely to carry with it the toxins communist regimes so wantonly discard in the environment.

While Wally shaved I stepped out of the room and walked through the corridor to the opposite side of the building and looked through windows towards the south. At the base of the hotel is a diminutive par-three nine-hole golf course wedged in tightly between the hotel parking lot and the cavernous International Cinema Hall. A couple of golfers were up and at it, swinging their niblicks, cleeks, and mashies in the early morning silence. They were in clashing plaid/stripe/check/floral garments that could have pegged them as being from any number of style-inoculated origins, but my hunch was South Korea. The conspiracy theorists would have insisted that the golfers were just Chinese actors brought in with the actors and actresses playing the part of the hotel staff, but their garments screamed "South Korea!" in a shrill accented tone.

In the '90s a British acquaintance set up a Beijing-based business-consulting firm designed to facilitate intrepid punters willing to navigate the obstacles of joint venture investment in the Worker's Paradise. One of his tactics had been golf weekends in North Korea during which potential investors were flown in and allowed access to Pyongyang's golfing facilities between sessions of listening to the North Koreans pitch their investment potential. I looked down on this minuscule course and tried to picture portly cigar-chomping Western investors finding the *Yanggakdo* People's Revolutionary Golf Course adequate for their golfing needs. The fact that such an elitist sport would be deemed appropriate for the vulgus of the Worker's Paradise was awkward and uncomfortable. It was somehow not incongruous with the professed principles of the *Juche* ideology, but as a mere bellicose capitalist lackey I was incapable of rationalizing the otherwise obvious irony. The last place I had played golf was Sarajevo a few years after the war. The Bosnians had built a four-hole course and clubhouse where one could play the front two, then have a nice leisurely lunch before going back out for the back two. The North Korean nine-hole course was even more compact than the four-hole course in the hills over Sarajevo. Except for the lack of windmills, ramps, and a snow cone booth, it could have been a miniature golf course in Iowa.

The North Korean press has reported that Kim Jong Il routinely hits holes in one when he takes the time to play. Often he hits multiple holes in one during a single game. Maybe he perfected his ability to routinely hit holes in one on the little course under my window. One of the golfers in clashing plaid/stripe/check/floral motif whacked at a ball and drove it up the truncated fairway and I turned to go back to the room for a shower.

Wally was dressed, shaved, and answering the ringing telephone as I entered the room. He picked up the receiver and answered in Korean, then a slow smile crept across his clean shaven face and he glanced at me as the receiver was placed back in the cradle.

"That was odd," he said, pausing to build suspense. "The wake up call was in Chinese."

We looked at each other and chuckled. The enigma surrounding the *Yanggakdo* Hotel, and for that matter all of North Korea, was a never-ending fascination. Were the hotel staff members truly Chinese actors and actresses?

After a shower I came out and joined Wally at the open window where we both gazed down on the city, still silent in the mist. Just 200 kilometers to the southeast the city of Seoul was already jostling and elbowing and frantically searching for a precious parking spot, or racing towards a tee time in the foothills, or getting ready to go sit through a worship service with ten thousand fellow parishioners in one of the world's largest churches. Seoul was alive and pulsating while Pyongyang slept in exhaustion.

A rowboat made its way up the misty river and Pyongyang was so still and quiet that even from the twenty-eighth floor we could hear the oars thumping against the locks as the boaters steadily labored upstream. The great capital city of the Worker's Paradise, the capstone of *Juche* workmanship, the magnificent riparian metropolis, "where the Great Leader Kim Il

On the east bank of the Taedong River the *Juche* (or self-reliance) Tower, world's *second* tallest stone tower after Texas' San Jacinto Monument, stands above Pyongyang's morning mist. In the foreground the Taedong Bridge has yet to receive any morning traffic. In 1951 Max Desfor won the Pulitzer Prize for his photograph of this bridge titled "Flight of Refugees across Wrecked Bridge in Korea."

Sung lies in state and the Dear Leader Kim Jong Il carries out the duties of leading the nation," was having a sleep in.

The two of us made our way down to the lobby and passed the forest of plastic Christmas trees and the pitiable sea turtle still bumping against the glass walls of its undersized tank. Waiting on a long low cushion against the windows was Mr. Kim the Elder. He was perched there, perfect posture and patient expression, in the same attire as if he had been stationed in the lobby on guard all night. He stood and greeted us in a cheery tone despite the short night and early start. We agreed that he would stay at his strategically positioned cushion and wait for the other two to come down while Wally and I made a quick visit to the lobby bookshop.

The bookshop was all I had hoped it would be, and more. It is always a delight to peek at the official state line in Beijing, Hanoi, or Vientiane now that the vast majority of nations that experimented with communism have tossed it onto history's great ash heap as unworkable and impractical. The treasures one can find in those state-run bookshops are what keeps me going back again and again; five-year crop rotation plans, demographic information on traditional people-groups, coffee table books extolling the glamorous side of big cement monuments, and pictures of Marx, Lenin, Stalin, and Mao — all suitable for framing. State bookshops in communist nations still have on sale portraits of stalwart bulwarks of the communist pantheon like East Germany's Eric Hoenecker, Romania's Nicolae Ceauşescu, and Mongolia's Jambyn Batmönkh.

The lobby bookshop in the *Yanggakdo* Hotel didn't mess around with those lightweights. No need to waste time with the likes of Marx or Engels and their fluffy prose when the two greatest writers of all time happen to have been North Korean. Kim Il Sung and Kim Jong Il combined to write more books on more topics than anyone else in the history of the written word. Kim Il Sung was so staggeringly prolific that even a decade after his death the Pyongyang Foreign Language Publishing House was still struggling to get the backlog in print and into the hands of the eager masses. Between the two of them the Kims produced every sort of reference book one might require for the successful running of a nation, as well as poetry and philosophy, history, science, and applied mathematics. The bookshop had a wide sampling of many works by both Kims in a variety of languages because when the world's greatest writers write, their audience is global. That's why Kim Jong Il's detailed tomes on the *Juche* philosophy are available in not only Korean, but also English, French, Spanish, German, Arabic, Chinese, Japanese, and Esperanto.

The shop was brimming with volumes by both Kims, with pictorials, with coffee table books, and with the ubiquitous tracts that set the record straight on who actually started the Korean War. They also had videos and VCDs of the *Arirang* Mass Games, documentaries on the capture of the USS *Pueblo*, and of never-ending American war crimes (each more heinous than the last). There were also postcards with innocuous things like local birds and flowers and scenes of big cement monuments around Pyongyang and stamps. Plenty of stamps. Stamps showing the glorious Korean people in triumph over obstacles, adversity, and American imperialism. Most North Koreans would never have occasion to require postage stamps. Postage stamps are a natural byproduct of a society that doesn't have a problem with the free exchange of information or with sending for a mail order export commodity from a society that does. North Koreans simply don't have occasion to need stamps. The one and only reason North Korea continues to produce stamps is because they bring in a predictably steady trickle of hard currency from philatelic aficionados. Just as we started to become engrossed in the colorful spoils, Mr. Kim the Elder quietly called from the doorway where Charles and Alice were waiting.

Breakfast was served in a large banquette room just a few steps down the corridor from the bookshop. Going to meals in the *Yanggakdo* Hotel required guests to pass the bookshop going and coming and this was sufficient advertising. Each meal resulted in another item being added to the wish list. However, all of us first required coffee and it was to be found in the banquet hall.

Mr. Kim walked us to the doorway and stated with obvious pride that this banquet hall was a favorite among Japanese guests and then handed us over to the maître d'. It appeared that the North Koreans still considered the Japanese a barometer of all things hip. If Mr. Yakamoto looked on it as trendy, then that was the standard to which North Koreans aspired. With that thinking Mr. Kim had given the greatest endorsement he could give, a virtual Michelin three star rating.

Miss Paik, the maître d', held a clipboard tightly to her chest and asked Mr. Kim which group of foreigners we were. She wasn't in the mood to smile when she asked. For the duration of our stay at her hotel she wasn't in the mood to smile. Mr. Kim mumbled something to her, she glanced at her clipboard, then quickly pressed it against her chest again so nobody else could see. With that she indicated with quick gestures that we were to follow. Mr. Kim quietly vanished as we entered the hall for breakfast.

At one point Mr. Yakamoto must have told the Koreans that lime green was the in color because the furniture, fixtures, carpet and decorations had a lime green motif. It was a 1973 kind of a wake up and sing Broadway choruses sort of lime green. It was a lime green that looked well beyond the technical ability of the Korea Paint Exchange Centre. This looked like a shade developed under the direct guidance of the Dear Leader himself, like something that would have sucked up precious resources during the research and development stage. It would have taken farmers from the fields, miners from the mines, and students from the classroom until there were enough people lending a hand that this color conundrum was cracked and the working man's lime green was created for the masses.

One side of the banquet hall was covered in a gigantic mural depicting a stereotypical Korean scene: gushing waterfall, robust forests, and verdant glades. The opposite wall was covered floor to ceiling with mirrors. So the room appeared larger than it was, and surrounded by a retaining forest that corralled the restless lime green banqueting furniture. Scattered across the verdant glade, perched on the lime green furniture, were hungry foreigners with quizzical expressions. The vast majority was Caucasian, and of those most were European: their dark leather shoes and bad haircuts gave it away. A clutch of Chinese sat to one side and spoke English with Hong Kong and Singaporean accents. Beside them a table of French speakers welcomed an Australian with Gallic indifference, and in the distance a small table of assorted foreigners featured at least one or two Americans. They were obvious even from a distance because of the adjustable ball caps that they found necessary even inside the building, the glaringly white athletic shoes and socks, and robust waistline spilling towards the future.

Miss Paik the maître d' had checked us off her list, then returned to her station at the door. She was there to make sure no food was lost to charlatans just pretending to be foreign guests in North Korea. She dutifully managed her clipboard and stood in the breach against potential culinary pilfering by indolent foreigners. Like the Sky Comrade and Bellhop, she was yet another line of defense protecting the fatherland from touristic invasion. With the same stone-faced expression carried by the lovely young traffic wardens, Miss Paik kept the riffraff at bay and allowed in only guests authorized to be in North Korea. Because she was so busy keeping a lookout for unauthorized foreigners, she had no time to oversee the waitresses nor the needs of the authorized guests. Once we were past her rigorous clipboard screening, she was finished with us and we were in the hands of the waitresses.

The only problem was the waitresses weren't really there to wait on tables. That morning the kitchen staff had prepared a buffet. The waitresses stood around the perimeter of the hall in matching uniforms and looked blankly ahead as they daydreamed. They weren't required to seat guests, nor to serve food, nor to retrieve the used dishes. It wasn't clear what their function was, other than to stand around and look official among the lime green furniture.

After a few awkward moments of silence the four of us realized that unless we got ourselves up and got in to the spread of food, there would be no meal. So we got ourselves up and went to the buffet line.

The quantity of food was expansive. The buffet line was situated against one entire wall of the large banquet hall. There was traditional Korean breakfast fare (which is remarkably like the food served at any other time of day) as well as the Korean interpretation of non–Korean food. There were platters of beef, and sausages, and steamed vegetables, noodles, rice, rice gruel, rice porridge, and rice cakes. There were raw vegetables and fruit, bread and buns, and an assortment of steam tables with mysterious gelatinous things hiding in the steam under a layer of viscous sauce. I worked my way up the line and filled my plate with Korean food on the theory that Koreans are more than competent at preparing Korean food and one reduces the opportunity of disappointment (and incidence of choking) by avoiding their interpretation of non–Korean food.

I walked the entire length of the long buffet table and helped myself to anything I wanted and loaded onto my plate any quantity I desired — until it came to the eggs. The entire buffet was free of uniformed waitresses except at the egg station. Hovering over the steam table of scrambled eggs was a uniformed Korean woman with a metal serving spoon and schoolmarm expression ... yet another line of defense. As guests approached she scooped up a single scrambled egg and gently placed it on their plate. That was the state-approved allotment. Though the steam table was filled to capacity with eggs, the waitress was there to make sure only one was taken by each guest. I suspected that Miss Paik the maître d' had put her up to this.

I took my egg and was about to turn and retreat to the table when Charles appeared and was given his allotment. He looked down at his plate and back up at the waitress in Dickensian fashion and asked in English if he might have a second egg. It was obvious at that point that the Egg Warden did not speak English because her answer was in fluent pantomime. She was insistent that the limit was one egg per person and he should move along. That's what her pantomime announced to me, but to Charles she was just flapping her arms and making odd hand motions and flashing signs like a sixteen-year-old gang member in Compton. Charles repeated his request in a very kind voice and patiently held his ground. The Egg Warden shook her head and gazed off to the side in hopes that Charles would accept his fate and move on. He didn't. Unlike Oliver Twist he stood his ground and smiled, plate held up to receive the requested second egg. This was exactly the type of nefarious maneuver she had been trained to defend against.

In obvious agitation the Egg Warden peered at Charles, then glanced towards Miss Paik the maître d' to confirm that she was preoccupied. The Egg Warden shot her spoon in to the steam and came out with a second egg. In one fell swoop the spoon was twisted, the egg fell on the plate, and the Egg Warden turned away as if nothing had happened. Charles walked back to the table victorious, and the Egg Warden was able to rid herself of yet another pesky foreigner. Everybody happy.

Coffee is alien to the Korean menu. It has made a significant impact in the southern half of the peninsula where, in a single generation, people went from not having ever tasted it to seeking out specialty roast shops to buy a week's supply of beans which they grind at home. In between they passed through a ghastly stage during which they coveted jars of imported instant coffee, then they progressed to drinking thimble-sized cups of horrible instant coffee from vending machines, then eventually they mimicked a café culture and sat in coffee shops and sipped cups of instant coffee. It was a glorious awakening when South Korea started enjoying real coffee in those overpriced thimble-sized cups. Eventually a groundswell of South Koreans realized that instant coffee is neither instant nor is it coffee and on that day they joined the West in acquiring their coffee snobbery.

On the Northern half of the peninsula, however, the North Koreans are just now at the stage that jars of imported instant coffee are seen on the shelves of the hard currency stores. That's pretty much what they know of coffee. It is the drink of foreigners and it carries an aura of mystery, but they have probably never smelled a cup, much less tasted it. So into the *Yanggakdo* Hotel march a modest yet steady stream of foreigners every year and one of their expectations is a steaming cup of joe in the morning. To meet this demand Miss Paik the maître d' and her colleagues created a coffee table at the rear of the banquet hall. It had the feel of a cash bar at an office party — everyone wanted to go up and take advantage of what was on offer, but nobody wanted to be seen as too eager.

On seating myself and my plate of food at the round table for twenty, I looked up and saw that nobody had any coffee. That was when, across the hall, I spied the coffee table and the other guests standing around getting their caffeine fix. I excused myself and stood, and as I did, my tablemates had made the same observation and were standing at the same time to do the same thing.

We converged on the table as a group of Europeans were departing with full cups. The system was not obvious and the uniformed women behind the table did not stir as we stood in silence. They weren't waitresses because the women dealing with coffee had a uniform different from the others. They were special. They were members of the People's Coffee Battalion. They too represented a line of defense. They were defending one large jar of bitter Japanese instant coffee. The Coffee Battalion Girls finally snapped in to action when Wally said in Korean, "Excuse me, I'd like a cup of coffee."

They jumped and giggled and remarked that for a foreigner on the verge of barbarism he certainly had a decent command of Korean but with an odd accent and would he like sugar with that? We all got our allotment of bitter instant coffee and returned to our big empty table to eat.

As if on cue, just as we drained our little cups, Mr. Kim the Elder appeared in the doorway and cheerfully asked if we were ready to depart. He explained that we had an exciting full day ahead of us and that there had been a few changes in the itinerary.

In the lobby, surrounded by dust-covered Christmas trees, Mr. Kim the Elder was joined by the Younger and they revealed to us that we were scheduled to pay our respects at the *Kumsusan* Memorial Palace. Normally, Kim the Younger explained, *Kumsusan* Memorial Palace does not accommodate foreign visitors unless they are high ranking dignitaries, or it is a Sunday. Seeing as how it happened to be a Sunday, we were simply availing ourselves of the schedule and going in. At least that's how I saw it. Mr. Kim insisted that this was more than just coincidental scheduling, this was truly an honor. The likes of our band of freebooting usury merchants were never, ever, ever granted the permission necessary to enter *Kumsusan* Memorial Palace except on Sundays, so this was truly an unexpected honor and a special occasion. Even though it was a Sunday.

Though not listed on the original itinerary, the last-minute scheduling change was an obvious boon. It isn't every day one is allowed the pleasure of viewing a corpse of such significance.

Former US Secretary of State Madeleine Albright had gone to *Kumsusan* Memorial Palace on her official visit in 2000. It is often the first place where foreign dignitaries are taken after arrival in Pyongyang. They are whisked from the airport at high speed down empty roads and end up at *Kumsusan* Memorial Palace where they are whisked in and whisked out.

When it was built in 1976, it had been known as the *Kumsusan* Assembly Hall. Kim Il Sung eventually commandeered the complex for his primary Pyongyang residence and was sequestered there for many years. It remained shrouded in secrecy and hidden behind curtains of military protection through the eighties and into the nineties and little was known other than it was on the northwest side of the city and it was ridiculously immense. Then the Great Leader died in 1994 and the regime decided they needed an appropriate place in which his body could lie in state. With such a grandiose edifice of such ridiculous immensity at their disposal, they concluded that they had the perfect place and decided to allow his body to lay in state right there in the *Kumsusan* Assembly Hall.

It must have been on-the-spot guidance from the grieving Dear Leader that convinced them to take necessary steps to convert the *Kumsusan* Assembly Hall into the *Kumsusan* Memorial Palace, then arrange things so in true communist fashion the body could remain there for all eternity. Even in the midst of his mourning the Dear Leader instructed them to seal the windows and convert the interior to a space appropriate for the Great Leader's mummified remains to remain forever on display for the masses. After all, all the great ones had done it; Vladimir Lenin's body is still on display in Moscow, Ho Chi Minh's body is still on display in Hanoi, and Mao Zedong is still on display in Beijing.

This was to be our first stop of the day and a highlight of the trip. Our entourage followed Mr. Kim the Younger through the front entrance of the hotel and out under the portico where fifty guides, minders, and drivers loitered around in dark vinalon business attire and chain smoked as they waited for their foreign charges to emerge from their lime-green breakfast. We fumbled our way through the carcinogenic cloud and emerged in the parking lot where Mr. Bae already had the van purring in anticipation of our departure.

Just as we were about to step into the van, Mr. Kim the Elder pulled Charles aside and whispered discreetly into his ear. As soon as he was finished, Charles turned to me and quietly suggested I go back up to the room and change clothes because my wardrobe selection was not up to standard for such a solemn visit to such an auspicious place. I looked down at my new brown leather shoes, my belted khaki slacks, and knit shirt and pondered the international fashion *faux pas*. On closer inspection, the other men were wearing collared dress shirts — with tie. Not wanting to make waves, but concerned that I had not brought a collared dress shirt (and certainly not a tie) I quickly volunteered to take a cardigan out of my knapsack and slip it on over my offending shirt. I did so immediately and Mr. Kim gave an instant look of relief. Apparently this change was sufficient.

He said in a gentle voice, "That is OK, otherwise you look like a sports man," then smiled gently and took my arm to assist me in getting up the step of the van.

It was obvious that North Koreans take very seriously the viewing of the body and they would much prefer all men in dark jacket and tie, and all women in formal gowns. To accommodate unprepared foreign guests I had heard of tour groups swinging by hard currency department stores to allow foreigners to rush in and buy garments deemed acceptable for the viewing. In my case, at 200 centimeters and 130 kilograms, there would be no garment in all of North Korea I would be able to purchase off the rack and slip into. My genetics are influenced by the Texas tradition of eating copious amounts of beef starters, then beef entrées, followed by beef-themed desserts. We are of beefy stock. My cardigan was just adequate to grant me entrance, otherwise I fear I would have been forced to sit in the van with Mr. Bae and pore over the latest issue of the local papers while the others went in for the formal viewing. I was quietly relieved that a simple cotton cardigan was sufficiently formal. Searching for a quadruple extra large *vinalon* suit off the rack in the Men's Section of Pyongyang Department Store Number One at 8:00 A.M. didn't look like a win/win situation. I pulled the cardigan over my head and kept my mouth shut.

Mr. Bae drove the van out of the parking lot ahead of three dozen other vans and buses. Apparently all the other tourists were still inside grappling with the Egg Warden. We silently passed the golf course and saw it devoid of people. The plaid/stripe/check/floral festooned golfers had wrapped up their early morning round and were nowhere to be seen.

The van turned right and we crossed the *Yanggak* Bridge to the north. Next upstream was the *Taedong* Bridge, made famous in 1951 when Max Desfor was at the right place at the right time to snap the Pulitzer prize–winning "Flight of Refugees across Wrecked Bridge in Korea." The photo reveals hundreds of panicked Koreans slowly inching across the tangled support structure of the collapsed bridge as it dangles over the surface of the river. Though I saw it at a distance several times, we never crossed the rebuilt *Taedong* Bridge during our stay.

We passed the spotlessly clean and nearly deserted Pyongyang Railway Station and a smile crossed my face as I recalled a conversation many years earlier with a Seoul-based expat who had parlayed his brief adjunct position at Harvard into a steady consulting career. At the time he had just returned from an official visit to Pyongyang and stated with an air of authority that just as is the case with South Korea, in North Korea prostitution is centered on the areas immediately behind train stations. Surprised at his observation, I sought more information — as one does at a cocktail reception. Before the conversation could go any further, however, he announced he would not be interrogated and that no further questions about North Korea would be entertained. The pompous little man chomped a cigar and strode off in search of less inquisitive company, and I forever remembered his odd statement about North Korean train stations and North Korean working girls. Surveying the scene around Pyongyang Railway Station it was obvious that the adjunct hadn't had the slightest clue what he was rambling about. Even from the vantage point of a moving passenger van in the middle of a Sunday morning, it was painfully clear that the showpiece railway station in all its 1950s Comintern glory was not the place where streetwalkers were going to be leaning on lampposts — in front or in back.

The Pyongyang Railway Station was one of the many trophies in the collection of architectural mantelpieces designed to illustrate to the outside world that everything inside the Worker's Paradise is eternally perfect. A regime obsessed with having urban dwellers dedicate spare time to hand-sweeping wide esplanades to make sure they are always dust-free and ready for their Kodak Moment is not going to tolerate hookers in shacks behind the train station. If there is a red light district in Pyongyang, then it certainly isn't going to be where visiting foreigners would ever lay eyes on it. Pyongyang is an elaborate set in the real-time stage production of Kim Jong Il's epic cinematic masterpiece: *The* Juche *Idea Is Succeeding!* Prostitutes were not scripted into that movie.[1]

There had been a trickle of traffic the day before, but on this bright Sunday morning in April the streets of Pyongyang were completely silent and still. Mr. Kim the Younger explained that Sundays are reserved for electric vehicles and all petrol and diesel vehicles must sit idle that one day of the week. I pondered what I had just been told as our gasoline-powered van moved up *Sosong* Street towards the center of Pyongyang. Now and again a diesel-powered Mercedes-Benz limousine with tinted windows would zoom past. A few pedestrians walked on the pavement, but the electric trams and buses were nowhere to be seen. He went on to explain that tourists are exempt from the restriction and are free to explore Pyongyang at their will (under close scrutiny and non-stop supervision) in fossil-fuel-powered vehicles.

Even at that hour, a few of the shops had solitary customers standing at the counter. It was easy to see because the glass in each and every shop was unobstructed by advertising. Big clear draped picture windows allowed passersby to peer in and glimpse practically empty gray shelves. Shop after shop, it was always the same.

We drove through a city free from the hodgepodge of unfettered growth. Pyongyang is clearly a planned city and other than the steady flow of new monuments to the regime, the people on the planning committee hadn't come up with any new ideas in a decade. It was expansive, clean, and free from the visual confusion of advertising. Contrary to all of the reports about how intimidating and frightening the city was supposed to be, Pyongyang was thoroughly inviting in its simplicity. Long straight boulevards with ample sidewalks and intentionally spaced trees appealed to a desire for the orderly. The lack of obnoxious advertising appealed. The heavy dependence on public transport and the resulting lack of air pollution appealed. I had entered Pyongyang expecting to feel the overbearing evil of a totalitarian dictatorship manifest in the very urban layout because that's what other observers had reported, but I failed to see it. The overbearing evil of a totalitarian dictatorship manifest itself in other ways, but in urban planning the stark clean lines and orderly symmetry of gray cement planes broken by deliberately placed willows and sycamores had a certain surreal charm. It appealed. I find the wiggling, blinking, pulsating advertising and obnoxious noise polluting background music of capitalist cities much more offensive and socially worrisome than the communist minimalism that makes up Pyongyang's cityscape.

As we moved through the streets in comfort and convenience, I was fully aware that the common citizen on the other side of the window would inevitably never experience what I was experiencing. I had a full belly and was sprawled across a seat so as to take up enough room for three. Those citizens fortunate enough to be granted residence in Pyongyang were living the best life one could live in North Korea and they would never so much as ride down a street in a private vehicle in their own city. It is one thing to observe that the *Ryungyong* Hotel isn't at all frightening to look at, and the severe, barren cityscape really isn't any more severe, nor any more barren than an expensive and trendy Scandinavian dining room set; it is quite another to be a citizen and full-time resident.

Mr. Bae skillfully pulled the van against the curb at the corner of *Kaeson* and *Pipa* Streets. We stepped out in the shadow of a huge 92-meter stele straddling the entire width of four-laned *Pipa* Street. A couple of non-electric vehicles roared through the opening in the base of the stele and moved up *Pipa* Street with a sense of purpose. It was reminiscent of the old photographs from northern California featuring cars passing through tunnels bored right through the trunk of a giant Sequoia. Why did the road need to pass right through a tree? What idiot thought it would be better to hack a tunnel through the base of the tree rather than curve the road a little to the left? The same idiot decided to go to one of the broadest intersections in Pyongyang and select that exact spot for a 92-meter stele.

I squinted up at the inscription that ran the entire length of the central spire, from top to bottom in large bronze characters set into the stone blocks. Mr. Kim the Elder, standing just behind me said in a reverent voice, "This is the Tower of Immortality and the inscription says, 'The Great Leader Comrade Kim Il Sung Will Always Be with Us.'" He looked up at the inscription and beamed.

I smirked knowing that at the other end of *Pipa* Street was our destination; the *Kumsusan* Memorial Palace. We were headed there to gaze on the mummified remains of a very dead Kim Il Sung, yet just three kilometers away on the broad tree-lined street we stood in the shadow of a stone stele proclaiming that he was immortal. In fact, in 1998 North Korea declared Kim Il Sung Eternal President of the Republic, so even from the grave he is still the Lodestar leading the masses forward as they progress towards eternal single-minded victory over the hegemony of the oppressor class. Maybe there was something lost in the nuance of translation, but placing the Tower of Immortality at one end of the street and the mummified corpse at the other struck me as specious. This was obviously another of the unique situations I could not understand.

Wally was more interested in a sign he saw on the entrance of a nearby building and walked over to have a closer look. Mr. Kim the Younger kept his eyes trained on Wally the entire time he was away from our group. Nothing was said, and Mr. Kim didn't move at all, but it was obvious that Wally's unannounced departure had caught the attention of our minders.

He walked up to the first step at the entryway and took a photograph of the sign at the front of the building. Then he turned and walked back towards the group and said, "I've read about that place ... that's the new technology center. Kim Jong Il declared computers to be a worthy tool of the people, so they set that institute up to investigate computers."

Mr. Kim the Younger was openly relieved that Wally's independent foray into Pyongyang was so brief and innocent. He said, "That building is a place where technicians and the general public can exchange technological ideas about computers." It appeared that was the extent of his computer literacy.

A little further along the sidewalk was the Pyongyang Subway Museum. From where we stood Wally and I both saw the sign in Korean and immediately asked Mr. Kim the Younger if there was any chance of a visit. Koreaphiles have long debated the rumors surrounding the construction of the Pyongyang subway system and a quick visit to the official museum might shed some light on the various subway debates.

He smiled as he realized, yet again, that the barrier of language was not sufficient for this group and gave what would be one of his stock answers to unexpected requests for a detour, "...next time you visit Pyongyang..."

We were on a schedule and it appeared that Kim the Younger was determined to adhere to that schedule at all cost. We stepped back in to the van and Mr. Bae drove out *Pipa* Street towards the glorious mummified remains of the Great Leader.

Running along the north side of *Pipa* Street are tracks. Unlike all the other tracks in Pyongyang, these are not in the roadway, but over in a grassy reserve running parallel to the street. On the tracks run thin green trams[2] that used to ply the streets of Zürich. They are spotlessly clean and in pristine condition, and the Swissness of the trams somehow adds to the amusement-park feel of the city.

Every few minutes a green tram clattered down the tracks parallel to the road, filled to capacity with uniformed soldiers looking as scrubbed and pristine as the trams. They covered the seats, stood in the aisles, and strained to keep from being pushed out through open doorways.

Each and every soldier, in tram after tram, looked apprehensive. On a scale from sheepish to anxious, most of them were drifting up towards really big and pointy pins and needles. They were all steadily heading in the same direction as us — towards the glorious corpse.

The wide boulevard was completely empty as we passed *Kumsusan* Memorial Palace on the right and swerved into a u-turn. Mr. Bae deftly maneuvered the van across *Pipa* Street and into a side lane opposite the colos-

Unveiled in 1997 on the anniversary of the Great Leader's 1994 death, the Tower of Immortality straddles *Pipa* Street and proclaims, from top to bottom, "The Great Leader Comrade Kim Il Sung Will Always Be with Us." Ironically, the mummified and very mortal remains of the Great Leader Comrade lie on display about three kilometers further down the same street.

sal mausoleum. We had ventured only three kilometers from the bustling corner where the stele stood, but already it felt as if Pyongyang was ending and the countryside was commencing. The surroundings were eerily still and silent. The expansive *Pipa* Street, multiple lanes in each direction through the heart of the city, was strangely devoid of vehicles, bicycles, and pedestrians.

The van moved through a slow curve and ended up in a modest parking lot directly across the wide boulevard from the huge mausoleum. Along the side of the parking lot was a long covered open-air porch. Off to one side the Swiss trams unloaded their uniformed passengers, looped around and rattled away empty back towards the center of the city. We had a quarter of an hour before the doors were opened to visitors and already it was apparent that we weren't going to be viewing the corpse alone.

Very quickly the open-air porch started filling with identically uniformed young men who silently assumed their position in perfect symmetrical lines, reminiscent of the throngs who queued perfectly on the floor of May Day Stadium the night before.

As we sat inside the still van, Mr. Kim the Elder said, with a pleasant smile on his face, "You are very fortunate to be here today because foreign visitors are allowed into *Kumsusan* Memorial Palace only very rarely." Even as he said those words three more trams filled with uniformed soldiers emptied and added to the growing number standing at ease under the long porch.

Without announcement, Mr. Bae opened the driver's door and stepped out to stretch his legs. As if on cue, one by one the rest of us followed his lead and stepped onto the asphalt of the parking area. Without a single head moving, two thousand eight hundred and twenty sets of eyes turned to watch us from under the porch. Most of the soldiers would have never seen a non–Korean before that moment and to see three hefty white guys and a petite woman with orange hair grunt and groan their way out of a van onto the pavement must have been slightly unnerving and very memorable.

Big Russian-built Kamaz trucks rumbled into the parking area and unloaded yet more uniformed soldiers from their broad, flat beds. Though not necessarily designed for transporting troops, when stacked in tight proximity, one of those trucks can carry fifty-six scrubbed, anxious, uniformed KPA soldiers. I know because I counted as they got off.

With only minutes to go before the doors opened, the previously empty porch and parking area was teeming with several hundred uniformed soldiers and sailors who remained eerily silent, solemn, and motionless as they waited. They were about to be provided with an once-in-a-lifetime opportunity to view the sacred remains of *Juche* deity. For them this was an extraordinarily solemn and significant day that would be a cherished memory. They had no digital cameras, no mobile phones with photo capabilities, there were no souvenir stands selling commemorative trinkets. They would spend hours working through the queue for a few precious moments in the presence of the sacred corpse, then go away with nothing but a memory of the day. For a seventeen-year-old private in the North Korean People's Army this event would be pants-wetting stuff.

Charles lifted his camera and pointed a telephoto lens towards the soldier-laden rear of a Kamaz truck and started taking photos. I braced for the tongue-lashing from one of the Kims, or a furious reaction from the soldiers, but none came. The camera whined as rapid-fire shots were captured, and Charles happily aimed his telephoto lens at conscript after conscript. Mr. Kim the Younger contemplated a smoldering cigarette and glanced up to watch, but said nothing. It was as if the warning about taking photos of soldiers had expired and new regulations had been issued ... we just hadn't received the memo.

When not looking at the hefty foreigners, the large clock suspended from overhead was the focal point of thousands of eyes as all stood in hushed reverence. In silence we watched as the big black hand jerked its way from minute to minute to minute up towards the twelve. I looked over the hushed queues of teenage recruits, past thousands of olive drab hats, out at the equally silent and still *Pipa* Street. Across eight lanes of empty boulevard strolled a pair of pheasants, slowly perambulating in the morning sunshine. With each and every olive drab head locked in place with eyes forward on the minute hand, none of the soldiers saw the pheasants slowly strolling across the empty expanse of *Pipa* Street. On the broadest boulevard through the capital city a pair of pheasants silently strolled without the slightest risk of injury because there was not a single vehicle — coming or going.

A few foreigners, including a handful of South Koreans yammering with Seoul accents, gathered in groups near our van and a moment later, as the minute hand jerked its way to the twelve, Mr. Kim the Elder bounded forward and quietly said in a low voice, "Let us go now ... we should hurry!"

With that the small groups of foreigners in the parking lot shot forward behind their respective guides and confidently strode towards the doorway, while row after row after row of uniformed soldiers stood stock-still and waited for the command to advance.

Behind Mr. Kim the Elder we scurried under the porch and through the entrance of a passageway that led to a large set of steps. He bounded forward, taking two steps at a stride, and we hurried behind instinctively knowing that thousands of marching feet would be unleashed down the steps in a matter of moments. Mr. Kim the Younger brought up the rear and made sure any stragglers were driven forward towards the inevitable macabre encounter with the people's mummy.

The Kims worked themselves in to a dignified frenzy, never raising their voices nor losing their composure, but reduced to quick, jerky motions and frantic glances. The harried need to leapfrog past the soldiers was evident in the eyes of both Mr. Kims and they were feeding off each other's frenetic energy. Scampering forward, Mr. Kim the Elder was also looking back again and again to make sure we were keeping up. His bandy little legs were pumping hard to propel him in a brisk walk that stopped just short of a sprint up the passageway. His left arm pumped and his left hand cupped air as if swimming, a long expanse of white shirtsleeve extending well beyond dark *vinalon* jacket. As if paralyzed by a stroke, his right arm remained frozen against his side in a strangely stiff position that was supposed to create the illusion that he wasn't scampering, rather gently strolling with dignity. He could almost be heard whimpering in frantic haste as he fought his way forward through unseen obstacles — left arm pumping, right arm ramrod straight against his side. Mr. Kim the Younger matched pace in the rear and made sure our little group was as far out in front as possible before the invasion from the rear. The tempo of his shoes slapping against the stone steps increased as he abbreviated the distance of each stride from a graceful gallop to a series of frantic little steps that made shallow slapping sounds on the polished stone walkway.

The Kims hastily drove us deeper into the passageway; we rounded a corner and encountered a very long and very slow moving-sidewalk. As soon as Mr. Kim's feet made contact with the moving surface he froze, resulting in the four tourists piling up like an accordion being squeezed into high C.

In front of Mr. Kim the moving sidewalk was completely empty for two hundred meters, yet he stood his ground with hands firmly planted on each of the moving handrails. He formed a human barrier prohibiting us from doing anything other than joining him in silently standing still. North Korean moving-sidewalk etiquette, like the etiquette for the escalator at the subway station, is absolutely rigid on the walking option. So we stood still and allowed the sidewalk to move us forward at the preset pace, chests heaving as we caught our collective breath. Very quickly the numbers accumulated behind us as other bands of tourists accordianed up into high C's.

Our moving-sidewalk hugged the left wall all the way down the incredibly long and eerily silent passage. On the opposite wall was another moving-sidewalk running in the opposite direction. In between the two was a conventional marble-floored walkway that remained empty except for official-looking men with walkie-talkies strolling comfortably at a pace twice as fast.

They remained silent, somber, and alert, with radios ready should there be an urgent need to communicate with the people's Crowd Control Committee.

With Mr. Kim playing the part of the cork we silently crept along under all eight lanes of *Pipa* Street and into the vast subterranean portion of *Kumsusan* Memorial Palace. After a painfully long mobile wait, we came to the end of the moving sidewalk and Mr. Kim released his grip and stepped forward towards a bend in the passage. We followed, as did hundreds and hundreds of people behind us. Around the corner was another even longer moving-sidewalk. Each of us walked forward a few paces, and as our lead foot came down on the surface of the new moving-sidewalk we froze and did not move again until we had been noiselessly transported much deeper into the complex.

At the end of the kilometer-long moving-sidewalk, Mr. Kim ushered us into a giant cloak room. A dozen solemn women in traditional Korean attire waited behind a counter where they received the contents of everyone's pockets: cameras, pens, notebooks, GPS or Navigator, publishings of all kind, and all our killing devices, in exchange for a chit. Our possessions were whisked away for safekeeping.

From that point forward we were like the throngs of raw recruits in that for souvenirs we had to count on memory only — photographs of the holy of holies were out of the question. We moved deeper into the bowels of the building and saw first-hand that North Koreans have truly mastered the art of tunneling. The entire *Kumsusan* Memorial Palace complex sat on an extensive network of tunnels and we were entering what must have been a tiny fraction of the vast hidden network. The entrance to an elaborate termite mound of secret passageways teeming with uniformed soldiers could have easily been hidden in the gloom right in front of us.

Mr. Kim escorted us forward like so many lumbering farm animals being driven through dip tanks. The passageway narrowed to a tight space through which visitors had no choice but to walk across a patented North Korean shoe scrubbing apparatus. As automated self-contained shoe scrubbing apparati go, North Koreans are on the cutting edge. Unlike the clunky models familiar to us in the West, the North Koreans have invested generations into perfecting their technique. This has paid off because they now lead the planet in automated shoe scrubbing technology. Little bristles stood up on the surface of the moving contraption and smeared soapy water on anything that came in contact. Simply by walking across the surface of the machine our filthy soles were washed clean and made fit to enter into the presence of the sacred remains.

As soon as our shoes were sluiced, swabbed, rinsed, and dried, the herd was driven into the X-ray corral. Two large archaic-looking Soviet-style behemoth X-ray machines were positioned to simultaneously irradiate multitudes of visitors. As we approached it was clear that they were both sitting idle and unused and a uniformed guard with an irritated expression ushered us past with the nonchalant flip of a uniformed wrist. If anyone had wanted to shove an ice pick or crowbar down their pants and sneak it into the inner chambers of the mausoleum, that was the day to have done so because the imposing machines weren't even plugged in to a wall socket. We skipped through that stage of the process without slowing our pace.

Deeper into the complex we were led by Mr. Kim the Younger who reacted to it all as if he had seen it all many times before and had ushered many groups of bug-eyed tourists through these same bizarre stages. All through the complex we were sent ahead of long queues of uniformed soldiers, male and female, waiting for their moment in the presence of the Great Leader. Around another corner we entered a vestibule that housed a freight train–sized machine that took up the entire breadth of the room and went up several meters to the ceiling. The only way forward was to move through one of four openings in the machine's middle. As one walked through the passage, a series of very high-pressure blowers directed unbelievably powerful streams of air towards the head. Apparently the intent was to remove any specks of dust or dandruff that a visitor might inadvertently take in to the presence of the Great Leader, but in practical terms the blowers effectively rearranged all hairstyles and violently dislodged eyeglasses. Guests emerging from the blowers looked bemused and disheveled, but were confident that all traces of dandruff had been forcibly evicted.

It was at this point that Wally and I found ourselves side by side walking slowly deeper into the bowels of the building. For years we had speculated about how we would react if placed in the awkward situation of needing to bow before Kim Il Sung's giant statue. The conversations never came to a conclusion because there is no clear escape route, no gracious way to be excused, no acceptable way to avoid the requirement — anyone granted access to North Korea is going to know beforehand that they are expected by their hosts to bow to the image of Kim Il Sung. Neither of us foresaw ever actually being allowed to visit, so the conversations were all hypothetical.

Since the days of those conversations, Kim Il Sung had died; and in addition to bowing to the twenty-meter bronze statue, it was also expected that guests of the state would bow to the mummified corpse. For the average American this is an intolerable predicament — bow to a dead despot or face the unknown consequences of refusing to bow.

I glanced at Wally and said in a low mumble, "Have you decided how you are going to deal with bowing?"

After so many conversations about this very predicament over many years, each of them ending in stalemate, I was startled by the immediate assurance that he had a plan. Without turning his head or raising his voice, he mumbled, "I know one of the aides who was in the delegation with Madeleine Albright on the official visit in 2000. He said the North Koreans didn't announce where the American delegation was being taken, they just showed up here and were led through the hallways and all of a sudden they walked into a room and there they were standing in front of Kim Il Sung's body.

"Albright was furious, but she didn't flinch. She stood there a few seconds and looked at the body then she silently bowed like this."

And with that Wally tilted his head forward ever so slightly. The movement was almost imperceptible — so slight that it could have easily been missed. In fact his eyes moved more than his head as he reenacted her "bow." His back remained perfectly straight, hands to his sides, feet planted on the floor, and with a sudden unexpected nod his chin dropped a few millimeters and his eyes dropped to the floor. Then, just as suddenly his eyes were again focused straight ahead and his chin was back up at the upright and locked position.

Albright managed to adroitly maneuver between the Scylla of face saving and Charybdis of ass kissing. Though her official visit to the Democratic People's Republic of Korea in 2000 didn't produce all the outcomes the Clinton Administration had hoped for, it gave America "the Albright." For the duration of our visit, we would fall back on "the Albright" any time we were expected to kowtow.

Mr. Kim the Younger leaned in towards his four charges and said in a low voice, "When we view the body of the Great Leader, I will walk with you to his feet where we will bow. Then we will walk to his right side and we will bow, then we will pass his head without bowing and move to his left side where we will stop and bow before exiting the room." Then he confidently and quietly walked on through the passageway.

With as much warning as was given Madeleine Albright, we rounded a corner and found ourselves in a somber room illuminated in a rosy murk. Along the walls hung dark velvet drapes, and along those same walls behind velvet ropes waited scores of uniformed soldiers on tour with their appointed guides. At strategic points in the room, ceremonial guards in dress uniform stood at attention with very impressive nickel-plated-AK47s (with nickel plated bayonet affixed) strung across their chests. They all looked extremely forlorn.

Through hidden speakers a mournful dirge played. Later Mr. Kim the Younger would confirm that it was, in fact, *The Song of General Kim Il Sung*. The music was sufficient to stifle any remnant of happiness any visitor may have brought in with them. The melancholia induced by the despondent music was obvious on the faces of the soldiers awaiting their turn to bow. They all had lumps in their throats and tears about to well up in their eyes.

Kim the Younger flanked the four of us on the left, while Kim the Elder brought up the right. They strode forth to an invisible line across the foot of the bier and glanced to see that we followed suit. We toed the line and looked through a rounded glass cover at a shrunken, wizened little figure with a waxy face.

The Kims genuflected with pharisaical enthusiasm and the lumbering tourists did "the Albright" at the Great Leader's mummified feet. As the Kims led us a few steps to his right side, I checked my peripheral vision and felt my ears scanning for the sound of boots on the stone floor. I was convinced one of the armed guards would have noticed "the Albright" and deemed it an affront to the Great Leader, and by extension 1.1 million active troops, 4.7 million reservists, and 190 thousand paramilitary would also take offense. They are all armed, irritable and best left alone.

Much to my surprise and relief the only movement in the room was our little entourage circumnavigating the bier. The scores of soldiers, their guides, the nickel-plated guards, and the Kims appeared to have been lulled in to a state of despondency by the endless music and were so absorbed in their grief that their senses were dulled and our lack of respect had not fully registered. Or else they were satisfied with "the Albright" as a sufficient gesture of respect from imperialist psychopathological special-class running-dog toadies. Either that, or they hadn't noticed.

As we toed the line on his right side, I looked at his face. The embalming and mummification process has left Kim's countenance a wan and pallid remnant of the robust image he once presented. The waxy flesh revealed a slick sheen even in the dim rose-colored light of the inner sanctum. From his face my eyes drifted down to the base of his neck, just behind his right ear, to find that there was nothing there. This is significant because through much of his adult life Kim Il Sung had sported a tremendous grapefruit-sized wen just behind his right ear. It was the stuff of legends. It forced Kim to spend his adulthood making sure photographs were always from just the right angle to ensure concealment. Even now all the portraits and photos of the Great Leader are strategically composed to allow the right side of his head to be obscured. So long did Kim and his handlers work at concealing the existence of the growth, that now it is almost impossible to locate a photograph that reveals Kim's right ear. The campaign of concealment was so successful that now and again neophyte Koreaphiles enthusiastically deny the existence of the lump. It appears that part of the mummification process had been the post mortem cosmetic surgery to remove the offending mass and now in death, after decades of concealment, his neck was disappointingly bare.

We did "the Albright" towards the missing lump, then Mr. Kim the Younger walked us around past his head and to the left side where we again toed the imaginary line and gazed at the mummified remains, then gave him "the Albright" one final time. Mr. Kim the Younger ushered us through the back of the room, and as we walked away from the body we moved into the light and out of range of the music. The depressing effect of *The Song of General Kim Il Sung* was evident only after breaking free of its melodious hypnotic grip. Like *It's a Small World* with a dark twist, *The Song of General Kim Il Sung* got stuck in one's head in an endless loop of melancholy and dejection until long after the conclusion of the ride.

We had just passed through the North Korean holy of holies, but there was more to come. The Kims walked briskly through the wide corridors towards the next installment in the unfolding display and eagerly motioned for us to follow. Mr. Kim the Younger smiled pleasantly as he held open a door and said, "Let us now view a wax figure of Kim Il Sung. It is exactly his size and, in fact, they used one of his suits for the figure to make it even more authentic."

Then with wide eyes and airy voice he added, "It's like standing in the same room with him..."

The room had a variety of items along the walls, but it might as well have been empty except for the focal point against the back wall, for there in all its Tussaudesque kitsch stood a life-size figure wearing one of Kim Il Sung's old business suits and every eye in the room was instantly drawn towards the wax. It stood against a cyclotron painted to resemble some unspecified mountainous spot deemed dramatically majestic. The wax figure stood there beside a shrub and a dead tree with its back to the sky, looking into the room with a wise, knowing expression. The entire scene was bathed in a combination of pastel blue and pastel pink lighting and was much less dreary than the rose-tinted room of the sarcophagus.

It looked like one of those life-like dioramas in a natural history museum in which Neanderthal man stands barefoot with club in hand, draped in animal skins and joined by a dutiful Neanderthal woman similarly draped (and inevitably tending the fire, or using a stone to accomplish a domestic task, or suckling a Neanderthal whelp, or possibly simultaneously accomplishing all three). The wax figure's eyes followed us as we approached. Mr. Kim the

Younger instructed us to join him in bowing to the wax, and immediately started genuflecting towards the pastel-lit mannequin. Without a second thought I shot the dummy "the Albright" so quickly that my eyes were back on the smiling wax face before our guides had straightened their backs.

If the wax figure was Kim's actual size, then the propaganda had worked. I had the image of him being a barrel-chested hulk of a man, a head taller than his subjects. The years of carefully orchestrated and strategically angled photographs had created in my subconscious an image of Kim Il Sung that was larger than life. Now that I was standing right in front of this wax figure in his *virtualon* business suit, I realized what a runt he had been. There was no barrel-chest, nor chiseled jaw, no broad shoulders or manly gait. This was a tiny old man with pocket-sized features.

This wasn't the image of the founder of a totalitarian regime. This was more like the old guy in the projection booth at the local multiplex. The one who mumbles to himself and carries around week-old sections of the local newspaper filled with incoherent notes scribbled with a dull Number Two pencil. This was a guy called Eugene; this wasn't the People's Lodestar. It was all very deflating and I felt somehow cheated.

Mr. Kim the Younger drove us on. The eyes followed us as we left the pastel wax presence and entered a hall displaying awards, citations, and degrees conferred on Kim during his lifetime. He racked up a surprising number of doctorates for a kid who got no farther than Yulin Middle School.

Degree after degree, virtually all of them PhDs, lined the shelves of the hall and suggested a meritorious lifetime of intellectual and cultural pursuit. Scores of them were displayed in case after case. The conferring institutions were all located either behind the iron curtain (and had been granted while the curtain was still effectively dividing the world) or from deep in the Non-Aligned World (read "Third World"). They were on sheepskins, and parchment, and festooned with wax seals and gold leaf and resplendent with script so flowery that it made it difficult to decipher the language.

Then, in among all the honorary degrees conferred from the most prestigious institutions in the Marxist universe and the best-known schools in the Third World, there among all the ersatz academic credentials stood Kim Il Sung's honorary doctorate from the capitalist lickspittles. One cream colored vellum certificate stood among all the others as the only one from the United States. Kim received bogus academic credentials from institutions located all over the Comintern, but was snubbed by the universities of the West except for this single exception and the exception was not just from the West, but from a "university" in the United States.

When conjuring up universities in the Golden State, one often comes up with the UCLA Bruins, the USC Trojans, the San José State Spartans, and maybe even the Loyola Marymount Lions. One does not frequently come up with the Kensington Charlatons, but Kensington University of Glendale was the issuing institution for Kim Il Sung's honorary doctorate from America.[3] It stood there just as legitimate as the other worthless academic credentials from fawning admirers around the academic world.

In addition to the fake degrees, that part of *Kumsusan* Memorial Palace displayed a few knickknacks and gifts sent to Kim Il Sung. Included in the knickknacks were a handful of cars that Kim had utilized in life. They were all huge sedans or limousines and virtually all black. I stood beside a black armor-plated Mercedes-Benz 600SL (with 12-cylinder engine) and asked Mr. Kim the Younger if it might be possible to see the one on which Kim Il Sung's bier had been paraded through the streets of Pyongyang. At the time of his death, there had been published a number of photographs featuring a huge black limousine outfitted to carry Kim's coffin amid a sea of flowers affixed to its exterior. The photos showed the flower-laden limousine creeping through the streets of Pyongyang as the masses lined the roads and wailed in state-approved heartbroken anguish. In fact, there were so many flowers, that it wasn't easy to tell if the big black limousine was a Detroit-made Lincoln Continental or an old Soviet ZiL.[4] I have long clung to the dream that in a grand twist of fate Kim Il Sung took his final ride down *Pipa* Street laid out on an American-built limousine.

All I wanted was to wade through the limousines and get to the one that had acted as hearse. I just wanted to put the question to bed at last — was it a ZiL or was it a Lincoln Continental? The chances are overwhelming that it was a ZiL, but stranger things have happened in the Worker's Paradise and until conclusive evidence was produced I was holding on to my Detroit fantasy.

Mr. Kim the Younger was openly put off by my request. First of all, he explained, the cars on display were gifts to Kim Il Sung. Secondly, the car used in the funeral procession was not a gift ... it was the official state car used in funeral processions and tourists are not allowed to see state cars used in funeral processions.

That was that. The matter was not to be discussed further. I departed *Kumsusan* Memorial Palace with no conclusive evidence either way.

We had been given the great honor of viewing the mortal remains of the People's Guide, the Great Leader; the Matchless Patriot and Fatherland Hero; the Founder of the Down With Imperialism Union; The Unstoppable Guerilla Leader, The Partisan's Partisan, the Sun of the Korean People and all mankind, the Undefeatable Steel Commander, the Legendary Hero Sun of the Nation, the Father Marshal, the Foremost Leader of the International Communist Movement; the Genius for Theory and Practice of Management; the Storied Hero of the Battle of Pochonbo; Cresset of the Union, Successor of the Great Revolutionary Pursuit; the Greatest Hero of All Humanity. After a lifetime of longing for the honor, we had gazed on his loving countenance with our own unworthy eyes. What additional point on the itinerary could compare? The rest of the trip was to be a steady downhill slide.

We paused at the final stop on the circuit — a large room in which foreigners were provided hand-held devices with which to listen to a translated presentation as they moved around the display. The hundreds of uniformed North Korean soldiers, however, had the pleasure of standing at attention while they listened to a female docent in velvet dress do "the voice."

"The voice" is used any time a North Korean makes a public announcement. It is a quavering, emotion-drenched modulation of a normal speaking voice, but saturated with so much emotive passion that it sounds as if the speaker is just barely hanging onto self control and at any second they will crumble in to a writhing mass of blubbering remorse. Men use "the voice." Women use "the voice." They use it on local television. They use it on radio. They use it in propaganda videos. They use it in museums.

I had become familiar with "the voice" years earlier while residing in South Korea. In my possession at the time was a short-wave radio receiver and, at the time, I never got a straight answer to my question about the legality of possessing such a thing. So I kept my mouth shut and tuned in to North Korean broadcasts to get their take on world events and particularly their interpretation of South Korean news. They scheduled a few broadcasts in English (and Russian, and Chinese) at odd hours, but the highlight of my clandestine short-wave reception was tuning into their Korean language news service directed at the southern half of the peninsula and listening to "the voice."

As we entered the display area, I had to momentarily remove the black plastic hand-held device from my ear so I could listen to "the voice." From what I could gather, the guide was informing the soldiers about the tragic loss of their beloved leader and how bereft the entire nation, even the world, was at the time ... and still is. She stood in front of about fifty uniformed forlorn soldiers, hands clasped in front, eyes focused on some unseen spot beyond the soldiers as if she were standing in a suburban shopping mall in front of one of those Magic Eye posters from the early 90s attempting to see the hidden giraffe amid the squiggly lines. Her eyes grew large and unfocused while she searched for the hidden giraffe and quavered on and on about the tears of anguish cried by the people on that dark day in *Juche* 83.[5] She was so incredibly gloomy in her presentation that the toughened recruits looked ready to commence wailing on-the-spot. I caught more than one lower lip quivering. A few of them looked at the guide, but most of them hung their heads and looked forlornly at the floor.

We moved through the display and passed other guides with other groups of soldiers, all trying to spot the giraffe, all clasping their hands at their waists, and all using "the voice" to whip their audience into a quivering emotional mass before releasing them to the next guide at the next station. It was while I was taking in all of the presentations in "the voice" and straining to understand the heavily accented Korean that I heard a most curious voice in English whispering in my ear.

It was my handheld plastic audio commentary device and the man speaking to me had an accent that sounded as if he originally hailed from the Home Counties but had spent many years as a fishmonger in Bratislava, or volunteering as a laborer in a Latvian soap factory. There was something subtly Eastern European about his otherwise very English accent. As I listened he started doing an English language version of "the voice" and I could feel the hot tears welling up in his ducts as he described how devastated North Korea was, in fact how devastated the entire world was (including you and me), when Kim Il Sung was so cruelly taken from us. The words that caught my attention and pulled my focus from the quavering docents to the electronic voice on the device were, "...and the people of the world were so devastated at our Great Leader's death that they wept anguished tears that became crystal that, in turn, was transformed in to the very marble you now stand on..." I looked down at the floor. It looked like regular marble to me.

In silence we walked down a corridor together, each relishing the fact that they had actually been in the presence of the Eternal President of the Republic. He may have been dead, but he was still in office. As we stepped back on the moving sidewalk to begin the tortuously slow retreat out of the massive building, Mr. Kim the Younger stood at the head, and Mr. Kim the Elder brought up the rear. Both of them grabbed the moving handrails in vise-like grips to ensure our little entourage stood stock still as we were moved ever so slowly back towards the entrance.

As we dawdled along the moving sidewalk, our group encountered more uniformed soldiers and sailors standing against the opposite wall in brigade strength. Apparently the honor of riding on a moving sidewalk was not to be bestowed on them. It appeared that they would be expected to march into the bowels of the building. Ever so slowly we approached with tens of thousands of emotionless eyes glaring straight ahead. The muffled hum of the moving sidewalk was the only sound. At first it appeared as though the soldiers too were searching for the elusive giraffe, but now and again I caught one of them sneaking a rapid glance at the manicured and pampered philistines and I smiled when our eyes met.

Each and every soldier was precisely the same stocky build, modest height, scrubbed complexion and rigid stature. It was as if we were driving past a wheat field in Kansas where genetic modification ensured countless heads of grain of identical bulk, identical height, and identical coloring. Scanning the heads as they disappeared into the vanishing point, not a single one stood up even a fraction higher than the others. The Quartermaster had it easy — he needed to stock only one size of uniform, for in the Korean People's Army there is no deviation from the mean. Each and every conscript is an exact duplicate of the conscript to the left and the conscript to the right. Completely fungible and eternally interchangeable, three abreast, 500 deep, and not a single variation in any detail — each and every cog was an expertly created duplicate of the cogs that came before and after.

Just like the errant wheat grain that decides to produce a stalk just a bit higher than all the other conformist stalks, when I looked up the row and saw her it was just like looking across a huge field and spotting that one freak stalk. She was about the 200th woman in a queue of women three across and 500 deep. Of 1,500 young North Korean women all in identical uniforms with identical no-nonsense bobbed hair and identical ramrod straight stature, the gammerstang stood out as being about four centimeters off horizontal plumb. She was proportioned just like the rest and had coloring just like the rest. Her uniform was exactly the same shade of green, her insignia the exact same shade of red. But she stood out as the lone freak among so much genetic conformity. Four centimeters of difference might as well have been four kilometers of difference. Standing on the slow moving-sidewalk as it crept along at a snail's pace, it was easy to steal glances at this towering woman a full four centimeters taller than the other 1,499 women. As we passed I caught her stealing glances at me, equally the freak in her homogeneous nation. I smiled at her but she averted her eyes in timidity ... but 1,499 of her comrades simultaneously smirked.

Before taking the final moving-sidewalk under *Pipa* Street and back to the parking area, the Kims directed us through a side door that took us out onto the gigantic parade ground in front of *Kumsusan* Memorial Palace. Among other tidbits of information, Mr. Kim the Younger said that the paved parade ground was a hundred thousand square meters. I quietly drifted away as he continued listing the obligatory facts and figures.

The enormous *Kumsusan* Memorial Palace is the final resting place for the Great Leader, Kim Il Sung, Eternal President of the People's Republic. Before housing his mummified remains, it was known as the *Kumsusan* Assembly Hall. Koreaphile rumor has it that the people rose up and demanded that Kim Il Sung use the building as his Pyongyang residence ... so he did. Koreaphile rumor also suggests that the ducks, geese, and swans that swim in the moat in front of the palace are carefully constructed extraordinarily life-like robots

The April sun was just starting to warm the morning up and it felt good to soak up the rays after being deep inside the chilly mausoleum. Between the parade ground and *Pipa* Street is a moat that runs parallel to the street for half a kilometer across the front of the complex. As we stood in the sun, I watched swans and geese paddle around in the moat. Some Koreaphile conspiracy theorists hold that the waterfowl in the moat are ingenious and life-like North Korean robots — proof being that they swam only in clockwise circles. The North Koreans must have reprogrammed some of them because during my visit quite a few were capable of counterclockwise movements.

The expansive parade ground forms an enormous plaza in front of the huge building. Like so many of the structures and monuments in Pyongyang, the architects were able to play visual tricks with proportions and angles because there are no nearby normally proportioned structures to use as a benchmark. The *Kumsusan* Memorial Palace is gigantic to be sure, but because of its placement on the far edge of the cityscape and because of the enormous paved space directly in front, the impression is of being considerably larger. From the edge of the parade grounds the building takes up one's entire field of view, and the paved parade ground extends well beyond the point where peripheral vision blurs into obscurity. The sheer size of the complex appealed to the Texan in me.

Almost exactly twenty years earlier 19-year-old West German Mathias Rust flew a single-engine Cessna-172B Skyhawk from Hamburg and landed in Moscow's Red Square.[6] Incredibly, Red Square takes up only about a quarter of the space required for the parade ground in front of the North Korean palace-cum-mausoleum. Assuming he could maneuver past the air defense batteries, Rust could reenact the same stunt with a lot more room in Pyongyang. Standing next to the moat with the robot geese I could picture Rust's

Cessna dropping in for a gentle landing just under the large portrait of Kim
Il Sung mounted at the top of the palace. I'm sure the eyes would have followed Rust's plane as it taxied to a stop amid dozens of nickel-plated AK-
47s (nickel-plated bayonets affixed).

The North Koreans have long waxed eloquent about the building. Among
other more verbose things, a 1997 North Korean publication stated:

> ...the *Kumsusan* Memorial Palace was built to keep in state the great
> leader Comrade Kim Il Sung who decorated most brilliantly the annals
> of the 20th century as the gifted thinker and theoretician, prominent
> politician and iron-willed brilliant commander ... this is an event of great
> importance in Korea's history of 5,000 years. Its historical significance
> lies in the realization of the common cause of mankind for independ-
> ence. The *Kumsusan* Memorial Palace associated with the respected Com-
> rade Kim Jong Il's loyalty and filial devotion to the great leader Comrade
> Kim Il Sung and the people's warm hearts is the symbol of the dignity
> of Kim Il Sung's nation and its pride.[7]

On the horizon, just beside a bank of red flags was a hoarding proclaiming in giant red characters, "Let's Arm Ourselves More Thoroughly with the
Revolutionary Thought of the Great Leader Comrade Kim Il Sung!" Just
beyond that, off in the distance, the gray silhouette of the *Ryugyong* Hotel
was visible against the horizon.

I would have stood and gazed longer at the cement pyramid except that
my concentration was interrupted by Mancunian-accented English. I turned
to see a gaggle of young bleached blond men in their very early twenties standing near me in the sunshine. They weren't soaking up the rays as much as
posing and posturing in the rays. They were all wearing hip-hugging denim
trousers that would have exposed much more than I would have cared to see
had they not had their crumpled white dress shirts smartly tucked in all
around. One of them had a thick black leather belt with studs strung through
the loops on his trousers. His shirt cuffs were deliberately unbuttoned and
flapping in the breeze as he posed and postured with the rest of them. His
hair was a carefully tousled thatch of unkempt chaos, grown just long enough
to allow for sculpting.

They hung their thumbs in their waistlines and practiced looking nonchalant, then jerked their heads to flick the hair out of their eyes only to allow
it to slide back in to their eyes as soon as the flicking was accomplished. They
glanced coyly right and left to get a reading of their audience, then shifted
their weight and struck new poses.

So startled was I to see the lads away from the Manchester High Street
McDonalds, that I turned and looked to see where their schoolmaster might

have been, or a parent, or the girls they were preening to impress. But they were alone there in the hundred thousand square meter paved parade ground in front of *Kumsusan* Memorial Palace in Pyongyang. They had paid a great deal of money to come do their High Street posturing in a very unusual locale. It was as if they were the young male models for a fashion shoot, but got the location of the shoot horribly wrong, then decided to stick around and practice their routines anyway. There were no other poseurs to impress, there were no unattached young women to pick up, and there were no North Korean hipsters with which they could commune and they clearly were not arming themselves more thoroughly with the Great Leader comrade's revolutionary thought. They pouted for an invisible camera, then glanced away at the far horizon and sulked, then looked back at the invisible camera and winked. Of all the puzzling things I saw in North Korea, none was quite as puzzling as why those English punters had paid the same $1,000 a day I had paid to come prate, preen, and pose for invisible fans in Pyongyang.

I found Charles and Wally in the sun between the High Street poseurs and the robotic geese. Charles revealed that he had now notched up the superfecta of communist corpses. He had viewed Lenin in Moscow, Ho in Hanoi, and Mao in Beijing. Now he had seen Kim in Pyongyang; win, exacta, trifecta, superfecta. Wally and I too marveled at the feat — not many tourists can make that claim. We speculated about Fidel Castro; how much longer can he last? Will the Cubans follow suit and mummify his corpse, and if Charles sees it ... what comes after a superfecta? As we discussed these heady topics Mr. Kim the Elder gently reminded us that we had a schedule to follow and more things to see that morning.

We walked back towards the corridor with the Manchester poseurs strutting and flaunting and desperately straining to see if any of us would look at them. Once on the final leg of the moving-sidewalk, we crept under *Pipa* Street and emerged near the van where Mr. Bae was waiting. On the way back up *Pipa* Street towards the city, we encountered tram after tram loaded with uniformed soldiers going out for their moment in the mausoleum. They all looked forward in silence; resolute, somber, determined, and intimidated. This was a once-in-a-lifetime day for all of us.

On empty streets Mr. Bae retraced our path to the Tower of Immortality, then turned south on *Kaeson* Street and made a quick left across empty oncoming lanes into a narrow drive.

We had arrived at the *Chonsung* Revolutionary Museum and it appeared that we had it completely to ourselves. The museum compound is tucked in just behind *Moran* Hill and this realization bolstered my sense that Pyongyang truly is designed like an amusement park with entire neighborhoods craftily built up against the back side of a differently themed neighborhood, which backs up against yet another theme, and so on. All the monuments and museums and famous structures are placed in a compact area with strategically placed partitions and dividers providing a sense of urban vastness in what is really a small area.

The grounds were a little unkempt and the first crop of spring weeds was dominating the small lawn in front of the museum building. Standing on a paved walkway through the weeds was Miss Lee, our guide for the hour. She smiled expectantly as the van pulled up to the curb, then as we got out she spoke softly to Mr. Kim the Elder as he huddled with her just out of range.

Like the women at the mausoleum, Miss Lee wore a traditional style dress, but rather than silk it was made of thick velvet. Through most of the year a thick velvet floor-length dress would make sense. Minimally heated buildings in a Pyongyang winter would be made a bit more tolerable under a heavy velvet tent.

She had a quiet but steady voice and little crow's feet at each eye that crinkled when she smiled. Her black hair was business-like without being austere. She quickly sized up her foreign guests, then started her spiel in rapid-fire Korean. Wally listened intently and I strained to understand. Her accent and soft voice allowed me to pick up only every few words and before she had gone far, I already knew I had missed most of what she said. Charles glanced at the rest of the group with a bewildered expression, and Alice stopped her note taking to look up in confusion. Without fanfare, Mr. Kim the Younger stepped forward and started to translate and three of us relaxed and listened to the English. Wally kept listening intently to the Korean. Through the course of half a century the language on either side of the DMZ has been intentionally driven apart. As the years slip by the political wedge is driven deeper and deeper and the diverging linguistic paths stumble farther and father away from the common origin. Now something as simple as the way one writes one's name in the Latin alphabet has taken on political baggage — the Northerners capitalizing the initial letter of each of their three names, and their Southern counterparts capitalizing the first two then using a hyphen to connect the third name which is habitually left in lower case. Sometimes Southerners make things even more complex by flip-flopping family and given names and tossing in a comma for good measure. Not only naming conventions have drifted apart, words and the ideas they were designed to capture are now startlingly different on either side of the DMZ. Surveys of North Korean defectors in South Korea reveal that huge chunks of simple conversations are incomprehensible not only because of differing vocabulary, but also because the topics being discussed on either side of the DMZ are now so fundamentally different.

The guide told us, through Mr. Kim, that we were honored to be standing at the site of Kim Il Sung's underground bunker and command center during the Korean War. From early in 1951 through the armistice in 1953 Kim and his comrades had holed up here in caves and tunnels dug into an old quarry. This was the very spot where the invincible Kim had marshaled his forces and designed the startlingly brilliant sequence of events that lead to the triumphant armistice that ended the ruthless and unjustified provocation by the warmongering imperialist Americans.

At first she delivered this anti–American harangue in a normal speaking voice, but as the Korean tour guide blood flows directly into automatically shifted into "the voice." As her vocal chords rendered "the voice," her eyes moistened with emotion and her gaze froze on the horizon where she tried to focus on that illusive giraffe. I couldn't listen to Mr. Kim if she was speaking, and I couldn't understand the bulk of what she was saying, but because of "the voice" I was captivated. Her words quavered and she fought to steady herself, always on the verge of tears, as she reveled in the unbounded love the Great Leader had bestowed not only on the Korean people as a whole, but on her as an individual.... And it had happened right here under our feet in these damp, dark tunnels while the brutal and unnecessary American aerial bombardment went on month after month.

While Miss Lee used "the voice" to tell us of the virtuous rat hole escapades during the war, she started employing a hand gesture that I had until then only heard about. When I saw her do it the first time I had to bite my cheeks to keep from giggling. North Koreans have long used a particular hand gesture when speaking about the Kims. Though I had never seen it done, I was well aware of the physical expression because South Korean friends had joked about it for years. It was often employed when mocking Kim or his regime, or when belittling the North. It is often used by Northerners whenever the names of Kim Il Sung or Kim Jong Il are uttered. As the sacred name passes the speaker's lips, the speaker's open right palm is placed over the heart, while simultaneously the left arm raises the open left palm towards heaven in charismatic emotional rapture.

Miss Lee warbled along in "the voice," then lifted her palms in "the gesture," and the corner of her eye briefly become a little more sparkly — as if she had just managed to pull back the tears. Talking about Kim Il Sung is an extraordinarily emotional thing and she was impressive in the control and decorum displayed. A lesser woman would have dropped to her knees, rent her garments, and torn at her hair.

That was about when I thought I understood her to say something about the "blood sucking" American imperialists and their sneeringly despicable ways. I glanced at Wally, still concentrating on her accented delivery, and caught a very slight lifting at the corner of his mouth. He had heard it too.

She went on with her scripted tirade against the atrocities inflicted by the bourgeois aggressors, how they used the less-than-honorable tactic of aerial bombardment to turn the most beautiful city in the Orient, the pearl of the peninsula, into fields of rubble, how the Yankee war-mongers and their sycophantic puppet-state allies used the cowardly pretense of hiding behind the skirt of the so called United Nations[8] in order to aim their invidious weapons of hatred at the anything but belligerent civilians of Korea, of how the mighty civilians of the peace-loving Democratic People's Republic were marshaled behind the peerless leadership of the Great Leader General Kim Il Sung to gallantly stand alone[9] against the American-led invaders intent on looting, robbery, pillage, and rape.

The righteous people of the North had their *casus belli* and the world stood behind them in their quest for justice and independence as they struggled out from under the yoke of Yankee imperialism.

We stood in the weed-infested garden and listened to the language become more flowery and jingoistic as Miss Lee used "the voice" and "the gesture" like a Southern preacher waving a leather-bound Bible from behind the pulpit. The translation Mr. Kim the Younger provided was bowdlerized on the fly by omitting the direct references to the United States and softening some of the state-sponsored rhetoric. Rather than "blood-sucking imperialist warmongers" he simplified it to "invaders." Instead of using her "unprovoked and unwarranted aerial bombardment campaign against unarmed civilians," in English he said "bombing raid."

She ushered us out of the weedy garden and in through the front door of the modest museum building. On the walls were enlarged photos and maps, reproductions of documents, and illustrations that chronicled the events of the era. Everything on the walls was designed to justify the armed defense of North Korea after the American-initiated northward invasion across the 38th Parallel. Everything in sight was sympathetic to the Northern cause and reiterated the simple party line: The Americans started the war for no good reason, the North Koreans stood alone in defense of their noble land under the brave leadership of Kim Il Sung, the Americans were defeated through the righteous persistence of the people.

It would have been very fitting to place a large reproduction of Pablo Picasso's *Masacre en Corea* mounted right in the middle of the home grown justifications, but Miss Lee and her colleagues were either oblivious to the possibility of sympathetic views on the outside, or they didn't want to clutter the discussion with superfluous evidence. Beside the door was a small wooden box containing a dozen wooden dowels painted white with red tips. Without looking she reached down and retrieved one, then with it pointed to an enlarged black and white photo of Kim Il Sung seated before a microphone and informed us with "the voice" that the photo was taken on the very day the war broke out.

The black and white Kim sat at a table in a field uniform. Before him was a chrome covered microphone with a thick black cord running off the edge of the table. Kim more or slightly smirked into the camera and didn't look at all like a man concerned that his nation had just been invaded by the imperialists and their lackeys. He looked smug and resolute.

She moved down the wall and with her pointer showed us enlarged black and white photographs that revealed blurred images of the war. These images, she explained, were proof that the United States had escalated the fighting to an unprecedented biological war by dropping "typhoid bombs" and "cholera bombs" across the peninsula. She used her white pointer to direct our attention to a big black and white blow-up of an American F-86 Sabre screaming through the black and white sky over what may or may not have been Korea. She placed the red tip of the white pointer on the fuselage of the plane and used "the voice" to say in an odd-sounding Pyongyang accent, "The American aggressors scattered diseases with disease bombs dropped from these planes."

Enlarged black and white close ups of hand-written confession letters were prominently featured in the center of the wall. From within Chinese-run prisoner of war camps captured American pilots had signed letters of confession that detailed how they had peppered North Korea with biological bombardments Miss Lee tapped the photographs and explained that these confessions were proof of American guilt. What she didn't say, and probably didn't know, was that in 1952 the US Air Force brass told personnel that if they were taken prisoner they were free to confess to anything if it would make wartime imprisonment more bearable.

We entered the next room to see the next display of horrendous American military aggression, Mr. Kim the Elder walked beside me and quietly said in Korean, "She doesn't know you are Americans, Mr. Kim introduced you only as 'foreign guests' when we arrived." He thought it was hilarious. She was laying it on thick without knowing that we were the very imperialistic aggressors she was slandering.

We gathered around the next set of items on display and Miss Lee started her harangue again, pointer indicating American atrocities, vocal chords straining to maintain "the voice" and Mr. Kim the Younger struggling to continue translating a synopsis of her delivery without allowing himself to laugh.

The strain on his face grew as she became more and more effusive and finally he had to shut his eyes to concentrate on the task at hand.

Mr. Kim the Elder, with an equally broad grin, turned to Charles and said, "She's talking about YOU..." and shoved a playful finger towards him. Charles wasn't in on the joke. In bewilderment he turned first to me, and then to Wally, using his wide eyes to ask for an explanation. The Kims thought it was the funniest thing they had seen all day and giggled like schoolgirls. All the while Miss Lee continued to explain the significance of the images on the walls in "the voice."

The next room contained the plans for the rebuilding of Pyongyang. Miss Lee explained that even before the Americans had finished bombing the crap out of Pyongyang, Kim Il Sung started coming up with the grand design of the world's most wonderful city. After all, the slate was being wiped completely clean, so he would have plenty of leeway to dream up just about anything that could be constructed from cement. Modern-day Pyongyang was born in the subterranean planning rooms beneath our feet. In those dank, dark pits Kim had masterminded the entire cityscape in his limitless imagination, and then selected one Kim Jong Hui to draw up his designs.

There before us were the original drawings by Kim Jong Hui. On large sheets of yellowed paper, one could see the painstakingly precise lines of an architect turned urban planner. Crisp, even pencil lines laid out the broad boulevards and majestic gardens that make up modern-day Pyongyang. The Great Leader had dreamed big dreams for his beloved city and Kim Jong Hui patiently put them down on the sheets of paper that would become the reconstruction plans ... as soon as the bombardment came to an end.

The rendering technique of the plans looked strikingly similar to that used by Walter Burley Griffin when designing the layout for Canberra. Griffin raced to complete his drawings while in the middle of his 1911 honeymoon. Kim Jong Hui created his plans under pressure as well ... he had Kim Il Sung standing over his shoulder as he worked. It was obvious that the concept for both cities involved the creation of major geometric lines of sight that cut through the urban setting at calculated, precise angles; at the end of each line a monument or significant building was placed. The lines followed broad boulevards so the end result was a series of streets with a striking edifice at the distant terminus. Standing at one of the carefully designed spots on the map one could turn on one's heels and look down one boulevard at a monument, then a few degrees to the side look down a different boulevard at another monument.

In the end Canberra became a concocted city that people comfortably grew into. Pyongyang is just concocted. The people are only additional background props used to create a greater sense of realism.

Miss Lee took us into the tunnels and showed us the rooms in which the cadres waited out the bombardments. Like the Malinta Tunnel network on Corregidor, for a while the command center of the entire nation was housed in the underground facilities that snaked beneath the little North Korean hill. Offices, mess halls, hospitals, sleeping quarters, an entire community of dedicated cadres waited for the American bombs to stop in order to emerge and rebuild not only the flattened city of Pyongyang, but the entire destroyed nation.

Miss Lee showed us the very spot where Kim Il Sung's second in command, Vice Premier Kim Chaek, died of a heart attack in 1951.[10] She showed us the very spot where Foreign Minister Pak Hon Yong was caught coordinating the bombings with the American aggressors.[11] Kim's heart was broken twice during his underground stay, she explained, once because his friend and fellow laborer had died of a heart attack, and once because a man he though was a friend and fellow laborer was a back-stabbing capitalist-collaborating double-crossing running-dog quisling.

We emerged from the tunnels and walked through a beautiful little garden running around the base of the hill. We strolled along a well manicured path amongst budding magnolia trees and azaleas in bloom. The weedy entrance to the complex belied the fact that the well-tended garden was quietly tucked away at the back of the grounds. Miss Lee turned off "the voice" and spoke in normal tones about the flowers and birds as we strolled in the sun.

At the farthest extreme of the little looping path there stood a pool of crystal clear spring water in a tiny little stone grotto. Miss Lee asked if any of us would care to have a drink from the same spring the Great Leader once used. I couldn't resist. I grabbed a red plastic cup and ladled up the same cold refreshing water that had slaked the thirst of the Master Designers and Urban Architect back in the day.

We walked slowly back towards the van in a tight little group, chatting and laughing. Miss Lee reiterated her sincere thanks for our interest in the museum, which Mr. Kim the Younger translated into English. We returned thanks and started preparing to step back in to the van for the next point on the itinerary. Just before we departed, Mr. Kim the Younger smirked and said in hushed Korean, "Our guests are from America, so this is a special opportunity for them."

Without hesitation Miss Lee smiled and nodded slightly as she said, "Yes, a wonderful opportunity for them."

Mr. Bae sat behind his big aviator glasses and confidently drove us back into the heart of Pyongyang through empty streets. There were a few more pedestrians out, but the roadways were still almost completely empty. We went south on *Kaeson* past the Arch of Triumph and as we passed beneath it Mr. Kim the Younger said, "We will return here later, but now we have other sites to visit."

All heads turned to gaze up at the huge, heavy squared mass of cement and stone carefully placed within the urban archipelago of tributes to Kim strewn across the Pyongyang skyline. In stark contrast to the very similar arch in Paris, the Pyongyang arch looked abandoned and forlorn with not a single pedestrian anywhere near.

Along the roadway were permanently placed cement billboards designed to showcase big, colorful propaganda posters featuring dazzlingly predictable socialist realism artwork. Time and again the dome of the US Capitol building was depicted as being crushed by clenched North Korean fists, or shattered by incoming North Korean missiles, or pierced by the bayonets of advancing North Korean infantry. The iron-willed Koreans were shown with chiseled jaws clenched and righteous brow furrowed as they advanced against the imperialists. Not only soldiers, but intellectuals, and factory workers, and stevedores, and butchers, and farm hands ... they all had the same serious

A propaganda billboard in central Pyongyang featuring five unrelated yet equally bellicose messages. Other than the single exception of a few advertisements for a locally assembled automobile, all billboards in North Korea are for propaganda of one form or another. These five signs proclaim the same jingoistic and aggressive militaristic sentiments found plastered across the North Korean landscape.

expression as they chased down the cowering and effeminate tow-headed American conscripts in their ill-fitting and threadbare uniforms. Always the artwork was accompanied by bold slogans with rock-solid exclamation points indicating that these slogans packed more umph than those old slogans that ground to a conclusion with a meek little period.

Mr. Bae kept us moving at a steady, modest pace and the van passed under the *Chollima* statue as the road drifted towards the river and became *Sungri* Street. We were back in the heart of the city and within a cluster of the most notable buildings and monuments, yet there was virtually no traffic on the roads and only a few lonely pedestrians were out walking along the empty boulevards. In a city of over two million inhabitants, it never stopped striking me as odd that the numbers were never right — too few buses, too few electric trams, too few people on the streets in rush hour. On the one day of a one-day weekend I expected to see more people out taking advantage of the

The *Kaeson* ("Triumphant Return") Cinema, featuring the domestic productions from the Korea Feature Film Studio which are not designed to entertain so much as to guide the proletariat in correct thought and virtuous ideals. Past films produced in North Korea featured American Army defectors Joe Dresnok and Charles Jenkins.

time off; after all, their city was filled with grandiose amenities and parks and plazas designed to be the envy of the world. Why weren't they out there taking advantage of them? Why didn't we see people coming out of shops with a week's worth of shopping in their arms? Why weren't kids kicking footballs or skipping rope or playing tag?

The van turned right up *Mansudae* Street and we stopped near a fountain featuring two dozen cement figures of young women frozen in gestures that might have been graceful and inviting except for the fact that I was already weary of looking at cement. From a shallow cement pool rose a cluster of cement women. Water was piped in and through the figures and then squirted out from strategically placed holes. We all stepped out of the van to admire the cement figures and their strategically concealed squirt holes and I knew immediately that this was an opportunity to drift away and get a peek at something not necessarily on the itinerary.

I drifted in the opposite direction as quickly as one can maintain the appearance of nonchalantly drifting while actually attempting to sneak off as quickly as possible. Not surprisingly Wally was not far away doing exactly the same thing. The cement fountain wasn't appealing enough to keep either of us interested for more than a moment. As Mr. Kim started explaining the facts and figures behind the sun-bleached cement women, Wally and I hustled away like a pair of schoolboys cutting class.

We didn't get far because we didn't need to go more than a few paces to feel that we had slipped the authoritative control of our minders, even if for just a few moments. The freedom was exhilarating. We walked through *Sungmin* and *Sungyong* Park, a tiny green space in among several significant monuments and buildings. Across from the obviously-named Department Store Number One, we stopped to look up at one of the many mosaics featuring the image of Kim Il Sung. This one was a simple image from the chest up, surrounded by magnolia blossoms. He had distinguished salt and pepper hair and turned strategically to hide his right ear and provide plausible deniability for the secret goiter. Beneath his radiant face were a string of familiar Korean words that repeated a recurring theme across many of the monuments and buildings we would see, "The Great Leader Comrade Kim Il Sung Will Always Be with Us."

Behind the mural stood a building of about ten stories and across the roof was a red rectangular sign with white characters proclaiming "We Are Happy." I found that sentiment very unsettling. Why do the good citizens of Pyongyang need the Ministry of Love to generate such newspeak slogans? If it is a fact, then won't the citizenry already know that and show it on their faces? If you're happy and you know it clap your hands. If you don't know it

One of many propaganda billboards on the roadways of Pyongyang. Other than the single exception of a few advertisements for a locally assembled automobile, all billboards in North Korea depict state propaganda. Many, such as this image of the Great Leader Kim Il Sung, are elaborate images created with mosaic tiles and are left illuminated at night while much of the city goes without electricity. The caption below the image states, "The Great Leader Comrade Kim Il Sung Will Always Be with Us."

then an Orwellian state organ will inform you of the fact through illuminated signs mounted on tops of buildings. (But they don't produce sufficient electricity to turn the illumination on.)

A few pedestrians loitered around the small park, or walked through the park towards one of the buildings on its edge. A handful of children had emerged and were doing what children do in parks: scamper, cavort, and shout. But the scampering, cavorting, and shouting was all muted and controlled. They wore their Sunday best and were accompanied by serious-looking adults who held tight reins.

At one side of the small park a television camera crew was busy setting up equipment in preparation for filming. They were young Caucasians and their equipment was plastered with the oscilloscope waveform logo of the

On the edge of *Sungmin* and *Sungyong* Park in the middle of Pyongyang across from the unimaginatively-named Department Store Number One, a cement and tile mosaic billboard displays an image of the Eternal President of the Democratic People's Republic and proclaims, "The Great Leader Comrade Kim Il Sung Will Always Be with Us." The sign on the building in the rear reassures citizens that "We Are Happy."

Australian Broadcasting Corporation. The Australians had re-established diplomatic ties[12] with the North Koreans in May 2000 and their citizens therefore have a comparatively easier time gaining access to Pyongyang.

With a sense that we had experimented with freedom long enough, we turned and walked back towards the fountain and our waiting minders. We had always been within sight and were never actually out of calling range and that, coupled with the fact that two large white guys wouldn't get very far in North Korea without being noticed, probably allowed the Kims to shrug off our brief escape and simply wait for us to come back on our own.

As we inconspicuously mingled back in to our litle group, Mr. Kim the Elder was returning from purchasing a bouquet of flowers. A van, kitted out as a mobile florist, was strategically parked along the curb just up the road from the fountains. From inside a woman sold pre-arranged bouquets to tour groups who might be in need of a pre-arranged bouquet. Mr. Kim returned with the flowers and a grin. He had secured the two most beautiful flowers in North Korea — in fact, they are the most beautiful flowers in the world. Bundled togeter behind a sheet of clear plastic he clutched a spray of clashing hybrid pink orchids, and hybrid orange-red begonias. These are the co-national flowers of North Korea: the Kimilsungia and the Kimjong-ilia.

Along with the flowers we clambered back into the van and left the sun-blenched cement women and their concealed squirt holes to drive a short distance to the *Mansudae* Grand Monument. In fact it would have been easier to have walked from the fountain to the parking area beside the monument because it was only a few dozen meters, but foreigners walking in Pyongyang makes the North Korean hosts anxious, so Mr. Bae drove us in the van.

While in the van Mr. Kim the Elder explained that the Kimilsungia originated in Indonesia and was produced by Indonesian botanists because of their respect and admiration for the Great Leader. Likewise, Kimjongilia was developed in Japan because Japanese botanists were similarly in awe of Kim Jong Il. Together, he said, these flowers now grow in almost every country on earth and are a sign of the magnitude of the importance of the contribution the Kims have made to mankind.

As Mr. Bae cut the engine, and Mr. Kim the Elder opened the door, Mr. Kim the Younger explained that we were about to visit the *Mansudae* Grand Monument where we would pay our respects to the famous giant statue of Kim Il Sung. It was very important, he lectured, that while there we absolutely not mimic the pose depicted by the statue. I then waited for the instruction to not make any photographs in which any portion of the statue was cut off. I had seen that time and again in the various reports over the years. The North Koreans were supposedly adamant that 100 percent of the statue must be included in each and every photograph. He didn't. He was concerned only with the offense of mocking the statue's posture.

As a group we followed the somewhat concerned Mr. Kim the Younger through the manicured shrubs that led up to the front of the Korean Revolution Museum. We first came face-to-face with scores of sculpted figures caught in heroic pose. Extending out from either side of the museum building was a pair of sweeping wall-like sculptures featuring a long heaving queue of life-size brave North Koreans surging forward 30 meters against an unseen enemy. They stood against sculpted banners and flags that reached many meters in height and effectively formed a barrier, both visual and physical. Centered in front of the building, and between the enveloping arms created by the twin walls of sculpture, stood the twenty-meter-tall bronze image of

Kim Il Sung to which we were about to pay homage. First, however, I was captivated by the metallic figures of warring Koreans.

They were of the predictable socialist type. Mainly men, but more than a sprinkling of female comrades were lending a hand. They were all covered in the blue-green of verdigris — the patina lending a certain authenticity to the sculpture. All the men had expressions of resolute duty on their impassioned faces. Not many were standing fully erect, most were straining to lean forward into the fray. Each of them had metallic muscles rippling through their combat uniforms as evidence that malnutrition wasn't an issue for any of the models. Their forearms rivaled their thighs in muscular stumpiness, while their necks were all sinew and tendon. Those not wearing a KPA issue cap had taken the time to comb their neatly shorn heads of hair and shave before being dipped in bronze for eternity. They all had deeply furrowed brows because, obviously, defending the nation against invisible aggressors is serious business. There was an unseen gale-force wind blowing into their humorless faces as they struggled forward. The imaginary wind pressed their uniforms back against stout muscles. Taken individually, any of the figures could be stood beside a heaving woman and placed in front of a storm-swept gothic castle and the pair would make a typical cover for countless romantic paperbacks strategically placed next to the supermarket cash register. Each one of the male models surged forward into the gale with some sort of killing implement and a scowl. There was a war on, and they were busy winning it.

All the women looked stout and matronly with big, thick, socialist upper arms. Under their uniforms one could tell they had breeder's hips and breasts proportionately larger than any Korean woman on the peninsula. In the gale their metallic mammaries strained against metal pinafores. They were caught mid-battle in the sculpture, but it was obvious that as soon as they won the war they were going to grab one of the iron-willed iron men and go copulate for the fatherland so they could produce more little conscripts for Kim Il Sung's mighty army. If the sculpted men had been able to, they would have been ogling the women. The sculptor had taken inspiration from Frank Frazetta's illustrations and created images of women of an impossible combination — hardened überchick soldiers capable of major ass kicking while simultaneously voluptuously desirable. They carried wrenches and rifles and things that could kill, but always a slight hint of libidinous curves poked through the KPA uniforms. In the Worker's Paradise these metallic amazons with their hint of curvy thighs and pert breasts straining against passionless factory-girl uniforms was probably as close as one could get to pornography.

We walked as a group beside this wall of green metallic human figures

Flanking the *Mansudae* Grand Monument are two walls of sculpture featuring more than 200 figures locked in eternal class struggle. Among the figures are soldiers, factory workers, farmers, intellectuals and fishermen.

towards the end where we would round the corner and come face to face with the giant bronze statue of Kim. Two or three figures before the head of the long line of sculpted warriors there stood a clutch of men unlike all the others. The rest of the hundreds of metallic warriors were taking into battle implements as modern as a sculptor in 1972 North Korea could have imagined: rifles, pistols, foundry tongs, sledge hammers, channel locks, oversized bolt cutters, knives, and lots of sharp pointy things. They all raced towards the Southeast with concentration locked on the tools at hand ... except for a group of three figures near the head of the line.

A pair of stern yet effeminate blue-green uniformed conscripts who, on close inspection, were twin siblings, stood in the penultimate group of figures in the long queue going southeast with twin bugles pressed to twin lips. They stood side-by-side sounding the call to battle as their comrades in arms got down to the dirty work. Standing just below the bugling nancy boys was a soldier who had opted to resort to a more traditional form of warfare. He had tossed aside his helmet, discarded his carbine, and foregone his knife. He had reverted to skills lodged deep in the Korean psyche and acquired through countless generations participating in what is arguably the foundation of all martial arts on the peninsula. He had reached down to his feet and hoisted up above his head a large chunk of stone and as all the other warriors were racing off to the Southeast with guns and knives, he was about to heave his rock to the South in an obvious homage to the ancient and noble Korean tradition of the village rock fight.[13]

The traditional Korean sport of village rock fighting goes back to the misty dawn of the peninsula's history and pits the grown men of opposing villages against each other on either bank of a communal stream. The Japanese and Chinese civilizations to the East and West failed to explore this branch of sports evolution and I know of no similar noble social outing in their histories. This regal pastime provides a window into the mysterious Korean psyche and into the soul of the Korean individual. The beauty of Korean culture is displayed in an array of traditions, but in the rock fight the inner man is allowed out to wing chunks of jagged creek stone at the heads of neighbors without fear of post-fight reprisal. For five thousand years Mr. Kim has been allowed to pop Mr. Lee in the noggin with a rock hurled from across the stream and, assuming Mr. Kim is sufficiently nimble to avoid the return volley, there is no payback. Traditionally the winning village secured bragging rights for the following year, while blood-splattered competitors from both villages crawled away to tend serious head injury, broken bones, shattered teeth, gouged eyes, crushed fingers and toes, lacerations and abrasions. A nation that is a confirmed member of the exclusive nuclear club

As homage to the traditional Korean sport of village rock fighting, among the statues surging forward to confront the oppression of the masses is one rustic figure depicted heaving a large stone above his head in preparation of hurling it at an unseen adversary.

apparently still takes time out to enjoy a good old-fashioned rock fight now and again.

As we passed the prissy bugle boys and their rock-tossing colleague, Mr. Kim the Younger quietly reminded us yet again to refrain from the temptation to mimic the pose captured by Kim Il Sung as that was the height of ill-mannered and oafish behavior that no Korean would tolerate.

Then we rounded the head of the long sculpture, the foremost figure surging forward with weapon primed and leaning out in to the air, and there towering twenty meters above us was the enormous bronze image of the Great Leader standing resolutely on the crest of *Mansu* Hill looking out across Pyongyang towards the same unseen adversary in the Southeast that the scores of metal soldiers were about to attack.

At the giant feet of the statue was a collection of plastic-wrapped bouquets placed there in adoration. An old woman, back stooped from long years in the rice paddies, quietly moved around in 45-degree concentration — sweeping at non-existent dust with a little broom, and fastidiously adjusting and positioning the bouquets time and again. She was oblivious to visitors, her attention was on dust and flowers and basking in the glory of the statue and she kept her mouth shut.

Standing immediately in front of the giant plinth, and just behind the old woman and her broom, was a young couple in Sunday-go-to-meeting attire. In the arms of the man was a toddler in miniature Sunday best. Except for the crooked little woman, the little family had all of the enormous plaza at *Mansu* Hill to themselves. They quietly chatted and cooed and squealed with the child in an effort to force some sort of reaction. As we approached the young mother struck up the exact pose depicted by the statue: feet planted squarely on the ground, left hand resting on waist, right hand thrust open-palmed towards the city at the end of an outstretched arm. The woman mimicked the pose precisely and shifted back and forth to stay in the child's field of vision. When the toddler showed no interest in doing the same, the father gently took his little arms and tried to force him in to striking the same pose. Apparently oafish behavior is tolerated as long as it isn't foreign guests doing the oafing.

When the couple stopped their oafish behavior and moved off to the side, Mr. Kim the Younger asked who would have the magnificent honor of placing the flowers at the feet of the statue. Alice was standing nearest to him and had the flowers thrust into her hands before she had time to react.

Mr. Kim the Younger said quietly, "Approach the statue, lay the flowers among the others, and then bow to show your respect."

It appeared very much that Mr. Kim was eager to have yet another group of foreign visitors validate his system with the laying of the symbolic flowers at the feet of the monstrous image of Kim. I also suspected that the flowers were recycled. The van from which they were purchased very easily might have sold our very bouquet again a few hours later.

I cringed knowing that if I had been selected for the duty I would have struggled mightily to accomplish the assignment without somehow offending our hosts.

Alice performed beautifully. She walked solemnly up to the pile, carefully placed the plastic-covered bouquet of flowers in to the small Diana-like tribute against the plinth, gave a little bow, and then returned to our group. It was finished. I heaved an inward sigh of relief and then Mr. Kim the Younger said, "and now we will all bow."

Our little group of six took a few steps forward to an invisible line of which only the Kims were aware. We placed our toes along that line with a Kim at each end of the row acting as chaperone, then as if he had been looking forward to this opportunity to nonchalantly use a newly acquired English idiom, Mr. Kim the Younger said, "When in Rome, do as the Romans do..." and bowed deeply towards the giant bronze feet. I gave it "the Albright," but this time there was even less head motion. In fact, so little head motion that I'm not even sure if I could detect my own movement. I glanced around to see if the old flower woman or the young couple had seen. Thankfully, we were still alone — only our little group of six and the giant statue of Kim looking out with his big bronze eyes.

We loitered in the shadow of the seven-story statue and took photos (making sure we didn't mimic the pose or cut off any extremities in the process). Mr. Kim the Younger stepped aside to an appropriately respectable distance to pull out a cigarette and spark up. I looked admiringly at the huge bronze image and asked in an innocent voice, "Didn't this statue used to be gold?"

Unveiled in 1972 as a 60th birthday gift from the people to the Great Leader, the statue dominates the monuments of modern-day Pyongyang. It is strategically situated at the crest of *Mansu* Hill and allows the bronze eyes to gaze far across the river to the suburbs. They left it that way until 1977 when the dutiful citizens, needing to express even more admiration, covered the entire thing in gold leaf. It was only when Teng Hsiao-p'ing, who would later be known as Deng Xiaoping, expressed displeasure with such an ostentatious act (and hinted at severing China's steady stream of financial aid) that the Koreans sent crews up scaffolding to scrape the gold off and restore the more modest bronze finish. The North Koreans were humiliated, but desperately needed the charitable assistance from Red China.

Towering 20 meters above the plinth, the *Mansudae* Grand Monument was installed in 1972 to mark the Great Leader's 60th birthday and add yet another Kim monument to Pyongyang's already extensive collection.

In 1978 North Korean officials reluctantly removed the gold that coated this statue of the Great Leader after Teng Hsiao-p'ing (later known as Deng Xiaoping) reacted strongly at the extravagance while North Korea was accepting substantial aid from China.

Mr. Kim the Younger hesitated with a cough then answered, "Yes, in the early days it was covered in gold but that resulted in too much glare ... it was bad for photos and made it difficult when people tried to look a the statue late in the day, it was too shiny ... the gold was removed and the bronze finish restored." He took a long drag on his cigarette and looked, one eye squinted shut, and the other fixed on me with a harsh expression. He was serious. That was the end of that topic.

Just beyond the statue, down *Mansu* Hill on a paved walkway, is the *Chollima* Statue. Basically, *Chollima* is Pegasus, Pegasus is *Chollima*. Koreans on both sides of the 38th Parallel keep *Chollima* in their collective mythology, but neither takes kindly to a Westerner pointing out that we have the same creature in our mythology as well. The cousins on the North have taken things a bit further by gussying the winged horse up into an ideological symbol of the Kim regime. North of the border the horse represents work ethic far surpassing the call of duty, productivity above the goal, accomplishment beyond expectation, but more succinctly the *Chollima* Movement captured the traditional Korean *bbali-bbali*[14] philosophy. Immediately after the war the North Koreans frantically raced to rebuild a devastated infrastructure and the *Chollima* Movement suited the needs of the nation well because it encouraged the frenetic, frantic, breathless, jittery high-speed *bbali-bblai* labor the regime demanded. Kim Il Sung needed the rubble quickly hauled away and heavy industry created from scratch. He had a lot of manual labor and not much of anything else, so he had the laborers whipped into a frantic blur of motion as they grabbed shovels and picks and wheelbarrows and went at it hammer and tong month, after month, after month, after month.

The *Chollima* Movement started in 1958 and has never really concluded. North Koreans have been all elbows and knees as they go at it with frenzied abandon. They dug out from under the rubble that way, they built the massive *Potong* River Improvement Project that way, they built the world's largest stadium that way, they built the West Sea Barrage that way. Though the North Koreans have changed the name and remodeled the outward face of successive production movements, they remain basically one continuous frantic push forward using the brute strength of the populace as the only substantial input. It has been one speed battle[15] after another for half a century and the people are worn out.

We stood on the hillside and looked out at the *Chollima* statue forever perched in a great leap from the crest of *Mansu* Hill towards the wooded knoll across the road. The North Koreans see this as a symbol of their own great leap forward. A pair of dutiful party members sits astride the horse; in front a male worker holding aloft the Korean Workers Party "red letter" in which

The *Chollima* statue has been frozen in mid–leap over Pyongyang since 1961. Literally translated, *Chollima* means "thousand ri horse" or a horse that can bound about 400 kilometers (or a little over 248 miles) in a single leap. Astride the winged-horse is a citizen-worker bringing to the people the red letter that informs them their production quotas need to be exceeded, and a peasant woman holding a sheaf of grain who appears to be just along for the ride.

the nation is informed that the previously set production goals are going to have to be surpassed, and behind him is a female peasant seated sidesaddle and cradling a large sheaf of rice stalks. The metallic man, woman, and horse all appear very resolute. A trickle of vehicles quietly passed on the almost deserted roadway below. Since the unveiling on the Great Leader's birthday in 1961 the winged horse has been perched there beside *Mansu* Hill, about to sail over multi-lane *Chilsongmun* Street, and never once had it seen a traffic jam.

Turning to walk back to the waiting van, I heard in my head the refrain from my childhood, "Oh winged horse of marble white, take me on a magic flight," and knew that in a nation of twenty-three million inhabitants, other than my fellow foreign visitors, within the sovereign territory of the People's Democratic Republic of Korea, there would not be a single other person who would have seen a single episode of a single 1960s cartoon to know the catch phrases of my childhood. Mr. Kim the Elder and I were approximately of the same generation, but while I was sprawled across the den floor watching after-school cartoons in the mid 60s, he was busy knotting his red kerchief, practicing the Young Pioneer salute and singing the *Internationale*. Mr. Kim was orphaned by the war and raised by the state from his earliest years. The state instilled in him the clear understanding that all good things eminate from Kim Il Sung — including television and television signals. Through Kim Il Sung's munificence the North Koreans started broadcasting television signals in 1963, but not many people had access to a receiver and most people were too preoccupied with their local speed battle to have time to sit down and take in an episode of *Luna the White Stallion* while drinking Tang and munching on Saltines.

Mr. Bae headed west across the city and we passed one after another of Pyongyang's immaculately bare multi-story cement high-rises. Down each side street there were also immaculately bare buildings but they ended just around each corner. Beyond the false front of neatly arranged modern buildings on the wide boulevards were a maze of more traditional narrow streets with crude low-level dwellings haphazardly scattered as if the little alleyways and lanes had organically emerged where the dwellings weren't. Foreigners almost never have the opportunity to see the rabbit warrens of hovels and shacks behind the immaculately bare multi-story cement high-rises. From no tourist vantage point can one look down in to a neighborhood and see an un-approved view. Foreign guests are to be impressed with the copious quantity of immaculately bare multi-story cement high rises, foreign guests are not to be shown the soft underbelly of the capital. In this case, the soft underbelly encompasses a huge percentage of the available housing.

Like the sets in the movie studio, everything in Pyongyang was painstakingly designed to allow international guests to have a beautifully chimerical view from every angle. Nothing is left undone. The advance teams long ago went to every possible site on the tourist circuit and gazed in every direction to make sure not a single opportunity existed for the foreigners to lay eyes on the hovels. From those vantage points the advance teams took every possible path to the next vantage point and all along the path the same process was undertaken to ensure that under no circumstances would any foreign eye ever see a hovel, or a malnourished child, or a malnourished old woman picking weeds from a hillside for something to eat.

The state-approved face of Pyongyang is gorgeous. So much effort has gone into checking and rechecking that veneer of modernity and opulence that now it is no longer possible to detect the rabbit warrens that are within a stone's throw but completely out of sight. They are right around the corner, but nobody would ever know ... except for those pesky satellites that keep flying over.

Satellite imagery of Pyongyang shows the broad, grand boulevards and the tall, unadorned cement monsters. It shows the monuments and the stadiums and the towers and bridges and parks and all the communist eye candy designed for public consumption. It also shows what is right behind that thin veneer, the cramped little dingy ghettos, the piles of rubbish, the crumbling shacks, the check-by-jowl chock-a-block jam-packed deficiency of a system that is not working. The impoverished, inadequate, indignant catastrophe of the *Juche* Idea is not evident through the van window, but can clearly be seen from silent eyes in the sky. The system isn't working, it hasn't really ever worked.

Mr. Kim the Younger announced that we were taking a toilet break as the van swerved in to a small parking lot in front of a nondescript building. Other than the showpiece monuments, virtually all buildings in Pyongyang look nondescript. Even some of the substantial monuments are nondescript, so it becomes difficult to differentiate and distinguish. All that lovely cement in three dozen different shades of gray starts to blend together after a while.

Because none of us had been making noises about needing a toilet break, I assumed Mr. Kim had learned from experience that in our pre-approved itinerary this was a good time and a good location for the requisite stop.

I decided to just sit in the van and wait until he informed us that we had stopped at a Friendship Store and even if our bladders weren't in need of relief, we might want to step in and look at what was on offer. I had visited Friendship Stores in China before "socialism with Chinese characteristics" had been completely unleashed. The general theme was the paucity of products and incredibly ridiculous prices.

They call them Friendship Stores, but what they mean is, "This is a 'you're going to empty your wallet for crap you don't really want' shop." The Chinese transformed their Friendship Stores over time. First the prices came down, then the goods on the shelves became better quality and more abundant, then the variety increased, then they started accepting their own currency, then without much fanfare the armed guards at the door vanished and the great unwashed were allowed in ... but by that time everybody had had a bath and could drive their private car down to a hypermarket on the ring road to use their credit card to pay for "import" brands that were made in China anyway. By then it was no longer a big deal.

Stepping in to a Pyongyang Friendship store was like stepping back in time. The establishment was completely outfitted with light fixtures adequate to thoroughly illuminate the entire floor space, yet every single one of them was turned off. The store was illuminated by feeble rays of sunlight struggling down between the tall buildings. Not a single item was within reach of the customer as they were all safely displayed behind a counter. This required the shop assistants to interact with the customer and fetch the desired item for inspection when requested, which was rather difficult under the circumstances because both uniformed shop assistants were thoroughly entranced by a drama playing on one of the televisions.

A substantial amount of items were imported from socialist comrades in Red China: Pepsi, Pringles, Mars Bars. The world truly is a smaller place when the last bastion of unfettered communist dogma sells products from the premiere freebooting capitalist consumer-centered nation in the history of mankind and those products happen to be made under license at factories in Red China.

Though the shelves were full, the North Korean goods were few and far between. I wanted nothing more than to see the products of the Hamhung Disabled Soldiers' Plastic Daily Necessities Factory displayed for inspection — I wasn't in need of any fat-drenched, sugar-coated American snack food. There were numerous bottles of alcohol in various degrees of foulness, pepper paste, ginseng, dried seal penis in a can, dried fish, the ubiquitous local cigarettes, and a few cassette tapes featuring patriotic music as performed by the Korean People's Army Marching Band, the North Hamgyong Peasant's Collective Singing Troupe, and the Pochonbo Electronic Ensemble (locally famous for their light-hearted and upbeat ditty *Reunification Rainbow*). The rest of the offering appeared to be imported — almost exclusively from China.

From across the Yalu River and through their trading companies in Macau the North Koreans had brought in an assortment of electronic kitchen appliances, cutlery, and stemware. Additionally they had on sale cheap vinyl love seats oddly similar to those I had used on my visit to the North Korean Embassy in Bangkok years earlier. They also had chandeliers in case any friends wanted to come express their friendship through the purchase of such a fixture. The oddest thing in the entire collection of products (other than dried seal penis in a can) was an upright piano still fastened to the pallet on which it had been shipped from a factory in southern China. If I was a North Korean with foreign currency to blow, an upright piano would not be high on my list of desirable consumer items on which to blow it. The dried seal penis wasn't very appealing either, but maybe my tastes don't run along the same lines as a North Korean comrade with a satchel full of hard currency.

Wally engaged the shop assistants who giggled at his accented Korean. He brushed aside their bumpkinish amazement that someone lacking any input from the gene pool of the peninsula could master the language because, after all, everybody knows that language is a genetically influenced skill, and requested a large bottle of adder liquor from behind the counter.

Like many across East Asia, Koreans have long treasured adder liquor as the magic elixir that combines the best aspects of moonshine with the efficacious benefit of extreme sexual prowess. And, except for any stray chemicals that might find their way in the distillation process, or the preservation process of the snake, the stuff is completely natural (mostly). A few slugs of the concoction are enough to make the operation of heavy machinery ill advised, yet somehow the slurring, dribbling, stumbling imbiber is temporarily bestowed with throbbing stud-like abilities that turn him in to a modern Lothario while simultaneously attracting young, nubile women who are inexplicably desirous of what is on offer.

The product is prominently featured in apothecary shops, bars, souvenir stands, and at duty-free counters. As unusual as it might sound to Occidental ears, the Oriental mind needs no explanation as to why a bottle of moonshine with a snake in it is desirable. It's good for stamina. Up and down the peninsula, on each side of the dividing line, millions of dead snakes are suspended in bottles of local rot gut and placed prominently on display. They look out through dead, white snake eyes and beckon the impotent to come spend their cash on this sure-fire cure for celibacy. Saint Patrick rid Ireland of snakes, the libido is doing the job for Korea.

Wally picked up a bottle containing a large viper and grinned. It isn't every day that one has the opportunity to buy North Korean Adder Liquor. As he discussed price with the shop attendant, I took a closer look at a nearby bottle. The English blurb on the back label claimed that the snake was "venomous." I gave five extra points for knowing to distinguish between venomous and poisonous. The shelves behind the counter were filled with local fare,[16] but none of it struck my fancy enough to actually cough up the convertible currency.

Our van continued west through the city and I inspected Wally's bottle of booze. The snake was whole and intact with no sign of damage to the body. It must have gone in hissing, snapping and writhing in an attempt to get away only to then be drowned in North Korean rot gut. Not a very pleasant way to die.

On the *Polgol* Bridge we crossed the *Potong* River and turned in to the crowning achievement of North Korean cement artistry—*Kwongbok* Street.

The 100-meter-wide thoroughfare was whipped together in the late 80s to be ready for the 13th World Festival of Youth and Students. In short, the planners went out to the sparsely populated Southwest side of town and bulldozed a long flat expanse of ground, then brought in a bunch of cement and some shovels, and announced that there was yet another speed battle at which volunteers were required to donate labor and in no time at all the tried-and-true *bbali-bbali* philosophy had helped them slap together 25,000 new apartments.

The broad boulevard is a point of pride for the regime. As far as they are concerned, a drive down *Kwongbok* Street is evidence that North Korea is a modern, vibrant nation and the people have amenities as good (or better) than the rest of the world. This is, after all, the Worker's Paradise. The blocks of flats flank the dozen lanes in the shape of cylinders, folding screens, and staircases. The buildings aren't so much functional housing units for the masses as much as they are carefully placed ornaments designed as accessories to show off the expansive cement boulevard.

Mr. Kim the Younger rattled off facts and figures from the front, while Mr. Kim the Elder sat in the back and gazed through the window at the buildings with the glow of a proud parent. These fabulous cement structures had been built by his people, in his city, and showed the world the capability of his nation. This was his and he was full of pride.

We were informed that the entire boulevard had been constructed by the people in a matter of days, then the huge cement apartment buildings had been constructed in a matter of only a few more days, then the entire area was replanted with grass and trees in another couple of days, then tens of thousands of urban dwellers had the glorious privilege of moving over here to the Southeast side of the city to occupy one of the new flats ... and it took just a matter of days.

Time and again the Kims proudly boasted of the scant number of days it took to build a huge edifice, or turgid monument. In their minds it appeared this was a positive thing — this ability to rush forward with no plan, no skills, and no raw materials and through the sheer industriousness of the dedicated people and the on-the-spot guidance form one of the leaders a remarkably appropriate plan is developed on the fly, skills are mastered on the job, and lots of cement makes up for any other inputs that might be missing. *Bbali-bbali, bbali-bbali, bbali-bbali* ... through Western eyes I saw slipshod-slap-dash-careless work that started crumbling before the project was finished.

The 42-story buildings came and went, one after another, and Mr. Kim the Younger told us the apartments within ranged from 110 square meters up to 180 square meters. The families allotted these flats paid nothing for them because, as citizens, one of the many things the Dear Leader lovingly provided was free housing. These fortunate people got to live on *Kwongbok* Street in one of the cement flats in a cement tower. Just out of sight, in the cramped little alleyways that our eyes would never see, the less fortunate citizens put up with squalor in little crumbling shacks.

Mr. Kim didn't say so in his flowery presentation about *Kwongbok* Street, but there is an astonishing claim that none of those 42-story cement towers were outfitted with elevators. If one was fortunate enough to be assigned a flat on the 42nd floor, and if the claim was true, then one could plan on climbing 42 flights of stairs any time one came or went. Apparently elevators are not on the list of things the Dear Leader supplies to the masses.

At about the same time *Kwongbok* Street and its thousands of flats were being speed battled into existence, Seoul was more systematically building the athletes' village for the 1988 Olympics. Later, when the Olympians had departed, the athletes' village was converted to similarly coveted flats for the general populace. I visited a friend in those flats and found them functional and comfortable with only nominal signs of *bbali-bbali* workmanship. In an erroneous South Korean belief that it saved electricity the elevators had been clumsily jerry rigged to service only alternating floors, but at least they had elevators.

With a grin, I asked Mr. Kim the Younger if he could translate the square meters he spoke about into *pyong*— the archaic unit of measurement for floor space used in South Korea equal to 3.3058 square meters. South Koreans desperately cling to this anachronistic relic just like Americans cling to inches, pounds, and Fahrenheit. While the rest of the world has opted into a streamlined, logical and efficient system, the South Koreans and Americans have opted out. South Koreans conceptualize floor space only by the *pyong*, and the square meter has no relevance.[17]

Mr. Kim answered curtly and in a tone that indicated his disdain for me bringing up this embarrassing aspect of Korea's collective past, "We don't use *pyong* ... except maybe farmers who might still use it for agriculture."

He looked forward through the windshield, then after a short silence turned back and curtly said, "In reality we have no concept of the *pyong*."

In a not so subtle way he made sure it was clear that North Koreans are hip, with it, and in step with the 21st century, while their poor backward cousins down south are still using a system for measuring area that was developed back when folks on the peninsula were living in communal yurts, hunting with spears, and participating in village rock fights on a more frequent basis.

At the southern end of *Kwongbok* Street, we passed the *Mangyongdae* Amusement Park, then crossed an invisible line and suddenly we were back in the countryside. Immediately behind us was a wall of gray cement buildings and immediately in front of us old women were toiling in rice fields that went on for kilometers into the distance.

The road narrowed to two lanes, and then one and a half. Mr. Bae cautiously slowed down as the surface became rough and we wove our way through a maze of skull-sized stones scattered randomly on the surface. The road was being repaired. The repair team was comprised of local rustics heaving the stones into a patch in the roadbed. They obviously weren't engaged in a speed battle. Not only was there no mobile music brigade playing away on the shoulder, the people were slow and deliberate in their heaving. Like so many other citizens of paradise, they were obviously tired.

Mr. Bae carefully crept by the repair work as citizen-laborers stepped aside to let us pass. Their faces were just a meter from ours, separated only by the glass of the van window. They looked from under furrowed brows. They squinted to keep the dust out. One or two smiled, but mostly they just looked with expressionless eyes and waited for us to move along.

The narrow little cement road snaked off towards a modest hill standing in the middle of the fields. Mr. Kim the Elder announced that the name of the "mountain" was *Ryongak San*. The road meandered through the fields and climbed up the flank of the hill and Mr. Bae obviously intended to drive our van up that road. But he was in no hurry, and he wasn't taking any reckless chances. We puttered along on the empty little road and enjoyed the April sunshine and clean air.

I watched the fields being prepared for planting and the six of us had a congenial conversation about nothing in particular. Both Kims were at ease and open, each sprawled across seats that would have otherwise been occupied by three or four members of the proletariat. Five if they were really bony.

I turned to Mr. Kim the Elder and enquired, "What was it like here during the Cultural Revolution in China?"

Mr. Kim nodded and started formulating his answer. After peering into his memories he said, "I remember being up on the Chinese border area during that time. I remember looking out and seeing Chinese people strapped to plows ... they were plowing the fields with people, not animals. I remember looking at that and thinking, 'In Korea we have tractors to accomplish that job ... but in China all they have is manual labor!'"

We took turns probing their defenses with questions designed to touch on the hot topics without causing offense or overstepping bounds. After a few interesting exchanges about family life, how systems work, details about obtaining possessions, and military conscription (all questions put to the Koreans, not asked by them), I turned to Mr. Kim the Younger and asked if it might be possible to visit the house belonging to the grandfather of a friend. I explained that the house was east of Pyongyang, but not far from the city.

He leaned forward against the seat and calmly said, "I don't understand ... what would you like to do?"

So I explained, "I have a friend, and many years ago her grandfather was given a house by Kim Il Sung. I want to know if it might be possible to visit, since I'm a friend of his granddaughter."

The hum of the van's engine was all we heard for a few moments, then Mr. Kim the Younger's curiosity was piqued. He leaned forward and asked, "Who was it that received a house from Kim Il Sung as a gift! Only special people receive such gifts from Kim Il Sung or Kim Jong Il. It must have been a special person."

As nonchalantly as possible I revealed, "It was His Majesty King-Father Norodom Sihanouk of Cambodia."

Politics truly does make strange bedfellows. The very idea of a monarch being chummy with Kim Il Sung sounds like something created by second-rate television writers for a low-budget filler during the summer replacement season. But the friendship was real and the relationship spread across the decades. Highborn aristocracy meets the ultra radical bolshevist, reminiscent of an early Neil Simon play. Sihanouk and Kim had a mutual admiration that neither attempted to hide. While the 1960s stretched and altered the political landscape of Southeast Asia Sihanouk maneuvered and morphed and reinvented himself to suit the setting, while Kim's North Korea of the 1960s was busy entrenching itself in its own dogmatic ways (and busily concealing its growing goiter). The two appeared to have virtually nothing in common, yet they kept showing up in public together over the years. They became so chummy that when North Korea unexpectedly needed to play Australia in a pair of qualifying games in the lead-up to the 1966 World Cup Finals, Sihanouk invited the Koreans and Australians to take advantage of the neutral pitch at Phnom Penh's Olympic Stadium.[18]

Over the years Sihanouk found reason to visit Kim Il Sung numerous times and maybe Kim was tired of always having to put him up in the *Kumsusan* guest wing, or maybe Kim was embarrassed about the notoriously sorry state of hotels in Pyongyang. In 1974 Kim built the *Changsuwon* Palace a few kilometers east of Pyongyang and gave Sihanouk the keys.

Satellite shots reveal that it sits on the shore of an artificial lake and is surrounded by wooded hills. The hills are peppered with military installations of various types — including numerous surface-to-air missile batteries. Sihanouk never has to concern himself with crime in that neighborhood.

Though described as being designed in a traditional Korean style, shots from above reveal a building oddly reminiscent of the main complex at Angkor Wat. It has been reported that inside are forty rooms with an interior fashioned to resemble Kim Il Sung's own digs inside the then *Kumsusan* Assembly Hall.

Sihanouk came and went at will over the years, always knowing that he had access to a retreat in the Worker's Paradise whenever he chose to visit. He imposed exile on himself in early 2004 and did what he had done often over the previous thirty years — went to his house in Pyongyang. From above it looks like *Changsuwon* Palace wouldn't be a bad place to rest and recuperate after a lifetime of running things.[19] In October of 2004 he announced his abdication from the Cambodian throne.

For a season I navigated through the same Phnom Penh social circles as Her Royal Highness Princess Norodom Rattana Devi. I knew her as "NaNa," and she was the belle of every ball as well as Sihanouk's unmarried granddaughter. I ran into her at social functions and parties and now and again at the Elephant Bar of the Hotel Le Royal. The season was brief and I moved on. Years later I heard Princess NaNa had a royal wedding and lived happily ever after.

Maintaining my nonchalant tone I said, "Mr. Kim, I know King Sihanouk's granddaughter ... she's a friend of mine ... and King Sihanouk's place is just on the East side of the city."

His reaction was, like so many things in North Korea, not at all what I had expected. He was not impressed with my connection to the King of Cambodia (no matter how tenuous it might have been) and didn't even bother to acknowledge it. He didn't appear to make the connection that I was talking about a real live honest-to-goodness for-real princess. He furrowed his brow and looked askance.

"Why do you think it is acceptable for you to visit his home because you happen to know his granddaughter? Is this customary in your country? We have an itinerary to follow and no time for such things." With that Mr. Kim the Younger dismissed me, turned his attention to one of the other foreign guests and struck up a conversation about Korean cows.

Behind me Mr. Kim the Elder was speaking and I just caught the conclusion of what he said, but it struck me as significant for anyone attempting to understand the North Koreans. Just as I turned to face that conversation he concluded with "All problems in society come from Korea being divided."

I had not heard that sentiment in a long time. I used to hear it repeated in South Korea where the wound of national division was, for a long time, incapable of healing. The people of South Korea used to carry a lot of *han*[20] around with them over the division issue. Then in 1990 the two Yemens reunited on short notice and though nobody in South Korea was even aware that either Yemeni nation had existed, they had even more *han* because only Korea and Germany were left as divided nations. Then 134 days later the two Germanys reunited and only Korea remained as the last divided nation on the planet.[21]

Then the South Koreans sat up and paid very close attention to the process of reunification as experienced by the Germans. They suddenly realized that somebody had to pay for this incredibly expensive endeavor and as wealthy as West Germany was, it was still staggering to that economy. Then the South Koreans watched as the months rolled by and the cost of reunification continued to mount and the list of problems needing to be solved grew longer and more complex. It was a painful realization that at the time of Germany's reunification, South Korea was at a strikingly similar economic station in life as East Germany. If the vastly wealthier West Germans were struggling to pick up the tab for reunification, then South Korea was looking at a potential economic catastrophe in merging with a dysfunctional and derelict North Korea. At the tail end of 1990, then South Korean President Roh Tae-woo confidently predicted that by 1995 the two Koreas would also be reunited. By the time 1995 came around, a lot of taxpayers in South Korea had come to the startling realization that they didn't think they could necessarily afford reunification.

Since then South Koreans have continued to amass wealth and power and have climbed even higher up the ladder of national prestige. The younger generation appears considerably more pragmatic about the prospect of unification and have a pretty good sense that it is they who will bear the cost. They like their cars, and designer bags, million-dollar apartments, electronic gizmos, abundant electricity, and steady supply of food. Picking up the cost for twenty-two million needy cousins is no longer embraced as necessarily inevitable or absolutely desirable. For the first time since the war, it isn't uncommon to hear a little hesitancy in the collective voice of the people.

While South Koreans have grown sober and much more realistic in their views on reunification, the North Koreans appear to still cling to the emotion-based premise that the division of the peninsula is the root of all evil. If only the barbed wire across the DMZ were rolled up and the landmines dug up and defused, then the milk and honey would start flowing and the cornucopia of abundance would be realized at last. After all, Kim Il Sung said so.

Looking at Mr. Kim the Elder's eyes as he spoke it was obvious that he sincerely believed this to be true. Every problem, right down to the lack of canned peaches in light syrup on grocery shelves, was linked directly to the insidious dividing line ripping the fatherland in half. Additionally, by extension, the Americans are to blame. Therefore, if the Americans would just uncock their guns, pack up, and go home, then canned peaches in light syrup, heavy syrup, spring water, and six varieties of chocolate sauce would appear on the grocery shelves of North Korea. In addition to peaches, the North Koreans would have abundant electricity around the clock, and heat in the winter, and enough fuel for public transport to operate on Sundays, too.

Wally hesitantly and carefully phrased the question, "If Kim Jong Il was to go ... for example, and I hope this never happens, but if he had ill health and died ... what would happen to North Korea?"

Mr. Kim the Elder didn't hesitate when he answered firmly, "Our people have never thought about that thing. No such kind of planning by our people has ever transpired."

It took the Americans 171 years to figure out the current systematic plan for the succession to the Presidency,[22] so it is understandable if the North Koreans need a bit more time to get a contingency plan in place.

Mr. Bae brought the van to a stop near the crest of *Ryongak San*. Parked nearby was a large, empty, gray delivery truck.

Up a meandering path of cement steps we walked. To the side of the path was a stereotypical open-air cement pavilion with a stereotypical Korean-style roof fashioned from cement. Identical pavilions can be found on similar vantage points up and down the peninsula on either side of the DMZ and they draw Korean picnickers who march up hills with religious fervor just for the simple pleasure of eating lunch, taking in the view, then marching down again. Without saying anything we all gravitated towards the pavilion and climbed up its steps to take in the view.

Though there was a little haze, we had a clear view of the west flank of Pyongyang in the distance. It was easy to see where city stopped and countryside started because below us there were no suburbs, there were no strip malls and parking lots, no suburban megastores offering deep-deep discounts. There were just fields. For years a similar vista on the edge of Seoul would almost always feature a view heavy with brown-gray industrial pollution making it difficult to see much of anything.

The Pyongyang skyline was impressive, yet compact. The city is so strictly controlled that there is no opportunity for it to suffer the temptations of sprawl. The Great Leader, then later the Dear Leader, provided on-the-spot guidance that stupefied urban planners with simple brilliance and uncommon wisdom. The spatial balance and the grand symmetry are, in reality, beautiful. Looking down on the most thoroughly planned city on the planet it was clear that everything was just so. The people selected to live in that artificial setting know that they are special; that they serve a function for the regime, and most importantly that they are fungible. Somewhere down there the last surviving American defector, Joe Dresnok,[23] was lighting up another cigarette and baiting a fish hook as he lolled away the tail end of his adulthood in the Worker's Paradise. Dresnok spent the vast majority of his life acting out a part in the *Juche* play knowing that he was not ever going to depart paradise.

In the foreground of our view sat a smaller but equally isolated and forested hill. As we looked down on that hill, a plume of white smoke come up out of the trees. I asked in Korean if the smoke was from a forest fire.

Mr. Kim assured me in English, "What you see is just a cloud," but his darting eyes gave away the fact that he had yet to see the plume of smoke to which I was referring.

Wally perked up and said, "There it is ... it does look like smoke. Right there." And with that he pointed and Mr. Kim looked where Wally indicated.

Mr. Kim decided, "Oh, what you see is the smoke from picnickers like us. It is just average Korean citizens having a picnic!"

The spot was remote and looked difficult to access. Though it was Sunday and if they were going to picnic surely they would do it on this day, that location looked awfully remote. His explanation felt too conveniently pat, but there were many more pat answers to come.

With that Mr. Kim the Younger called to us from through the trees. Lunch was being served and we were wanted.

We sat on cement chairs at a cement table that had been set with plates, bowls, and cutlery. In front of us on the table was a small portable grill holding hot coals. Beside the grill was a platter piled high with meat ready for the cooking. Off to the side the crew from the big gray delivery truck was busy preparing our food.

We stuffed ourselves with grilled beef and vegetables. As the meat on the grill disappeared, a woman from the truck appeared with platter of skewered beef in hand and loaded the grill up again.

Through the meal we drank *Taedonggang* Beer, known for being the Dear Leader's favorite. It was good — good enough to compete internationally. In fact, it used to, sort of. In 2000 the North Koreans sent agents out to find a brewery suitable for making beer for the North Korean market. They came upon the recently closed Ushers Brewery in Trowbridge, Wiltshire, and liked what they saw. Since 1824 Ushers Brewery had turned out traditional English ales and bitters. At the turn of the century the North Koreans purchased the mothballed brewery for $2 million, dismantled it right down to the last copper pipe, and shipped it off to Pyongyang where it was painstakingly reassembled.[24] Now the same vats, kettles, pipes and spigots are used to produce *Taedonggang* Beer on the outskirts of Pyongyang. Tales of technical advancement through laborious reverse engineering have long found their way out of the communist realm, but the Koreans put their own special unique twist on the concept with their patented factory acquisition model.

While the foreign guests enjoyed the beer, the Koreans were already hitting the *soju*. I have never been a fan of *soju*. This stems from the fact that I came to know it in South Korea where, at the time, a handful of regional producers churned out what tasted like industrial cleaning solvents well past their use-by date. The aftereffect was a throat that felt like a cup of broken glass had just been swallowed. I learned to skillfully maneuver around social situations in which *soju* would be offered because it is better to completely avoid the offering than to vomit on the host's leg. Even worse was vomiting on the host's spouse's leg. I had not put *soju* to my lips in years when Mr. Kim the Elder poured a shot for me and lifted the tumbler towards my mouth.

Stranded on a remote North Korean mountaintop, surrounded by government-selected communists with sharp cooking implements in hand, after having surrendered my passport in a place where my nation does not have an embassy, a *soju* gaffe was the last thing I needed. I took the tumbler and placed it to my lips where I paused and allowed the fumes to waft up in to my olfactory receptors. Much to my astonishment my eyes did not water. I took one, tiny, apprehensive sip and my entire alimentary canal braced itself for a series of uncontrollable spasms. But the drop of *soju* sat quietly on my tongue without the slightest suggestion of civil disobedience.

Against better judgment and in spite of my teetotalling three-times-a-week Baptist heritage (which featured the common understanding that even though the Scriptures didn't state it, we could infer that if liquor were to ever touch one's lips it would be akin to progressing past the "You Must Be This High" sign on the rollercoaster to Hell), I swallowed. It was not at all like my memory of the *soju* on the Southern end of the peninsula. No essence of glass shards. No bouquet of industrial waste. No heady formaldehyde top note. I felt my alimentary canal stand at ease.

After a few more shots of *soju* all around, Wally raised his tumbler and proposed a toast to unification. I raised my *soju* and heartily repeated the toast in Korean — *Tongil!*— which in Korean means unification. Though the sentiment was appreciated, and they raised their tumblers in unison with the rest of us, it was clear that both Kims were uncomfortable with that particular toast. They were all for reunification, I know because they had both said so repeatedly, but real live honest-to-goodness for-real Koreans on both sides of the DMZ know there is only one acceptable toast ... they just can't agree on what it is. It is used for all occasions and there is no deviation from the mean. In North Korea one raises their glass and says, "*Mansei!*"[25] That is the only option. There is no menu of toasts from which to select some other variant. Kim Il Sung may have stripped away some of the outward signs of Confucianism in North Korea, but inwardly there was a silent acceptance that there is one correct place and one's place must fit within the rigid hierarchy of places. There is no room for deviation, much less experimentation. When one lifts a glass to make a toast, therefore, there is no room to come up with some wacky, spontaneous, off-the-cuff, impromptu heartfelt submission—not matter how timely or appropriate it might be. One lifts one's cup and says, "*mansei*," and one is satisfied in knowing the boat has not been rocked. Posta.

By lifting a tumbler of *soju* and toasting to the reunification of the peninsula Wally had rocked the boat and both Kims looked hesitant and uneasy. As much as they were all for the idea of *tongil*, they weren't comfortable talking about it during a toast. During a toast they were comfortable saying *mansei*. It would be like standing up at the Seventh Inning Stretch and singing *La Marseillaise*. When you stand up for the Seventh Inning Stretch you sing "Take Me Out to the Ball Game." Posta.

Maybe I was pushing my luck, but when my turn came around to offer a toast I lifted my glass and repeated what Wally had said in Korean: *Tongil!* It was met with silence. The Kims smiled and drank their *soju*, but they didn't join in the toast. It wasn't that I was unaware of their customary toast; it's just that I opted to do something different. Not Posta.

The meal was winding down, but I was still interested in a little more meat. Viewing the mummified remains of the founding father of a totalitarian communist state builds one's appetite. The woman who had been tending to our carnivorous requirements was off in the underbrush and preoccupied with her colleagues from the gray truck, so I reached into the platter with a pair of chopsticks and started tossing meat onto the grill. The sizzle of the meat acted like an alarm bell and she jumped up and dashed to our table. With deft flicks of the wrist she pulled the meat off the grill and placed it back on to the platter while muttering incomprehensible Korean insults under her breath. With body language clearly announcing her annoyance, she then loaded the grill with skewered beef.

Her colleagues from the gray truck, seated on the ground off to the side and out of the way, enquired in slurred tones about the problem.

She answered in a Korean whine, "He was helping himself to the duck!"

Her colleagues, clearly well into their ration of *soju*, exclaimed in Korean, "He was going for our duck!"

Not Posta.

Our meal at an end, Wally looked off at the horizon and smiled, then looked back at Mr. Kim the Elder and observed, "You guys need to reunify. You need to get together with the South and work out the issues, then just reunify. You'll face problems, but you need to just do it ... and I wish you the best."

Mr. Kim looked pleased with the sincerity and thanked Wally for his sentiments. The average North Korean is indoctrinated to believe that the average American has some vested interest in keeping the peninsula divided, so Wally's sentiment was unexpected and somewhat surprising to them. We stood and started moving towards the cement steps that would take us back to the van. As we did, I saw that the six or seven people from the gray truck were just sitting down in the dirt to prepare their own lunch. I went back to our table and retrieved the platter of duck and took it to them and said in Korean, "Do you like duck? We seem to have some extra..."

Without making eye contact the agitated woman sheepishly took the platter and offered mumbled thanks. As we walked down the hill, she used chopsticks to retrieve slices and lay them on the little grill that the workers had set up in the dust for themselves.

It was never clear what function the platter of duck served. Was it placed on our table in addition to the skewered beef to show us foreign guests how abundant things were at the Dear Leader's banqueting table? Were the workers scamming the system and holding back the duck that was intended for us in order to secretly eat it themselves? Was the duck off and was the woman simply protecting the foreign guests from scurvy or beri beri or whatever one contracts from rancid duck? Did the Kims conspire with the crew from the gray van to sell the excess duck on Pyongyang's fledgling black market? I suspect I will carry the mystery of the excess duck of *Ryongak San* to the grave.

The road downhill felt steeper than it had going up and that was probably attributable to the *soju*. Mr. Bae, who had had a few shots of *soju* as well, very carefully guided the van down the little narrow road — careful to the extent that on the otherwise rollercoaster roadway the ride was even and smooth.

We rounded a bend and made an unexpected stop. Mr. Kim the Younger announced that we had the option of a quick visit to the *Bopwan San* ... a temple which just happened to be a few meters up a path into the woods.

It sat against the hillside and was of the same design as many temples in the south — a tiny wooden structure just large enough to house a few relics, a statue, and some incense. Over the central doorway a traditionally styled sign proclaimed the temple name in Chinese characters — some of the very few Chinese characters still to be seen in North Korea. On the southern half of the peninsula Chinese characters are still strewn throughout society at random and are used to clarify and specify and other than being the bane of school students, aren't seen as intrusive foreign objects like they are in the North. Kim Il Sung long ago expunged Chinese characters from North Korea on the grounds that Korean characters are all a Korean requires to thoroughly and completely express themselves.

The elaborate designs and colorful painting under the eaves were exactly like similar temples across South Korea. Unlike those Southern temples, however, this one was completely covered in fresh paint. The Korea Paint Exchange Centre must feature a line of state-approved temple paint because somebody had gone to town on *Bopwan San*.

Mr. Kim the Younger jogged ahead as we strolled across a small courtyard of packed earth. He pressed against a closed doorway in the temple's side and spoke in hushed tones. A muffled voice from the inside replied to his enquiry, then Mr. Kim turned to us and said, "The resident monk is here and you may take photographs if you like."

There was a rustling of garments from in the little room, and out stepped the resident "monk."

He wore his robes like we had worn the costumes at the movie studio — on top of street clothes. Neatly pressed slacks poked out under the hem of the robe. He wore mirrored aviator glasses even larger than those worn by Mr. Bae and his fingers were heavily nicotine stained. He didn't carry himself like the monks I was familiar with in the South and he appeared preoccupied and fidgety like we had caught him as he was about to start a long tea break or depart for home. However, the thing that was most un-monklike was his beautifully coiffured pompadour. Rather than sporting the stubbled remnant of ritualistic head shaving he had a full head of lustrous jet-black hair combed up and back like Elvis in his hip-swiveling sequined prime.

He stepped out onto the little veranda across the front of the temple and leaned against a post like a diesel mechanic on a smoke break. All four cameras were immediately up and clicking photo after photo of this "monk" behind the mirrored aviator glasses. Like the churches we had seen the previous day, there was nothing about the little temple to suggest it was anything other than a state-sponsored sham.

The Kim regime has long suppressed religion within North Korea, yet allows a few showcase churches and temples to remain in existence as evidence of the nation's tolerance of citizens wishing to worship. *Bopwan San* is on the fringe of Pyongyang and allows visitors to see that Buddhist temples do, in fact, continue to exist and they are maintained by "monks" such as this stocking-footed individual in aviator glasses and street clothes under his robes.

As we walked back to the van, the "monk" continued to lean against the veranda post and stare into the near distance from behind the mirrors. He never opened his mouth to say a word, he just posed in his costume and allowed us to capture the scene with our digital cameras. As soon as we were gone, he would be on his way.

Mr. Kim the Younger pointed out a tree that was an impressive 1,600 years of age. It stood against the path leading back to the van, but none of us paid much attention to the antique tree — we were looking back over our shoulders at the pompadour, mirrored glasses and slacks peeking out from under the costume.

The journey back to Pyongyang took us past the road repair site a second time. The same weary people continued to manually rebuild the roadbed. A cluster of women squatted and methodically pounded rocks with hammers.

Charles lifted his camera and adjusted the lens as the van crept past. Just as he pressed the button, Mr. Kim the Younger raised his voice and firmly said, "Do not take any photos of the women working on the roadway because it will make them very angry!"

Two of the women looked up in to the window as we passed their little patch of reconstruction work. Both of them smiled huge, carefree smiles and started to quietly chuckle at the beefy white guy positioning his camera in the window. Charles pressed the button and took the photos of the women anyway. Everyone on both sides of the glass laughed. In defeat Kim looked into the distance the other way and pretended nothing had happened.

It appeared very much that our general gag order on certain photo opportunities was designed to prohibit us from capturing images that might be deemed unflattering. The soldiers hadn't appeared to mind and the road repair crew was tickled with the novelty of having a camera pointed at them. The stern warnings about upsetting the citizenry were, like so many things in North Korea, not entirely accurate. It wasn't the camera shy soldiers or the self-conscious laborers on a road crew we were protecting — it was Kim Jong Il's extended ego. Allowing the outside world to see images of the grandiose cement monuments is good; allowing them to see documentation that the crumbling infrastructure is maintained by squatting women with hammers is bad.

Despite flirting with the rules and collectively taking a number of "restricted" shots throughout our stay, none of our cameras were confiscated, neither Kim requested to see the photos on our memory sticks, and no additional warnings were given. Ultimately it was as if the two Kims were just as

labor-weary as the people in our photos and they just didn't have the energy
to pursue their obligation to chaperone.

Mr. Bae needed no instructions from either of the Kims on the way back
into Pyongyang. He had the routine down and needed no reminding of the
route he had driven scores of times before with other beefy foreign guests
pressed against the windows of the van. In North Korea the routine is very
firmly established ... all routines are very firmly established.

We pulled to a stop alongside the curb and spilled out onto the pavement in front of the *Mangyongdae* Revolutionary Site — the mythical birthplace of Kim Il Sung.

Just like Kim Jong Il, Kim Il Sung was not actually born where the Ministry of Truth would have us believe. They decided it would be doubleplus-
good to conveniently send the *Juche* pilgrims to the park-like fringe of
Pyongyang rather than to the less convenient *Chilgol* neighborhood where
he was most probably welcomed into the world. Pilgrims are shuttled in and
make a day of visiting the hallowed grounds on which the Great Leader was
born ... at least in the revised edition of the tale of his birth. A visit to the
manger scene on the edge of the capital is doable even when the lack of fuel
forces the pilgrims to hoof it all the way down *Kwangbok* Street for the privilege.

Mangyongdae is mysteriously similar to a life-size nativity one would see
in the front lawn of the local suburban church (each Saturday night through
advent, sundown to 9 P.M., hot chocolate and snacks available from the
Women's Missionary Union). The open-front buildings are obviously agrarian in nature with slanted, thatched rooflines that bespeak the state sanctioned credentials of a poor, honest lad with revolutionary sympathies. The
crowds are shuffled in and around and out with the assistance of prim, authoritative guides: all women, all wearing modest traditional dress, and all using
"the voice" to tell the story of their savior's birth and subsequent upbringing
right here in the manger scene.

Mr. Kim the Younger very clearly instructed us to avoid the mistake of
putting our feet up on the step in front of any of the structures. That would
be a social gaffe too horrible to fathom. With hundreds of local pilgrims
swarming around us in semi-religious fervor, it wasn't difficult to imagine what
they might do to a pudgy white guy who balanced a filthy shoe on the ledge
in front of a building while another foreign devil took photos. The retribu-
tion would be swift and final, and it would be meted out by stern men in
vinalon suits and prim women in sensible shoes.

The Ministry of Truth has long borrowed from the traditions of Christianity when creating the *Juche* back story: Kim Jong Il's birth heralded by a new star in the sky and by the descending of a heavenly dove, Kim Il Sung's birth in a manger and subsequent immortality. The propaganda department didn't find a way to convincingly work in three wise men bearing gold, frankincense, and myrrh, but they did create the legend of the bent pot.

Front and foremost in the collection of farming implements and rough accoutrements that testify to a humble beginning is a collection of three earthenware pots upturned on a plinth and carefully placed behind a little wood fence. While all three pots were homely, the third in line was so hideously flawed that it would not have been purchased even by a poor agrarian family (with or without revolutionary zeal). It looked as if something had gone horribly wrong in the kiln. The wall of the pot sagged to one side in such an exaggerated manner that the entire crumpled mistake looked completely malleable. Any self-respecting potter would have opened the kiln, seen that unsightly vessel, and written it off as a loss as it was tossed into the slag heap. Any poverty stricken peasant in the local bazaar would have dismissed the crumpled pot as nonfunctional and walked on to the next pot monger's stall. In the real world, the famous nonfunctional crumpled pot of *Mangyongdae* would never have survived. In North Korea, however, the famous crumpled pot of *Mangyongdae* is an integral part of the national foundation myth and average North Koreans stand in its presence and get teary-eyed and maudlin.

Our English-speaking guide used "the voice" to explain that the pot represents the humility and frugality of the Kim clan and was typical of their mean existence. This was proof, she explained, that the Kims were virtuous people. Other, more extravagant people would have sought an earthenware pot that was functional. The Kims, however, wore their useless and deformed earthenware pot like a badge of honor. It might not be good for much, but damn it, it was good enough for the Kims.

The Kims had embraced the famous crumpled pot of *Mangyongdae* long before it had been made famous. In a crafty maneuver reminiscent of Hester Prynne's reverse psychological ploy with the embroidering of the A, the Kim clan took the pot and elevated it to a position of familial pride. Everybody else got along with pots that could be used to contain things, but the frugal, self-denying, parsimonious, meager Kims had a pot that wouldn't hold a cup of tepid dog spit and they were chest thumpin' proud of it. Now the people of North Korea travel from near and far to get a look at this beautifully useless bent mass of terracotta. They stand there and weep because this is yet more proof that their home is the envy of the world, that their fearless iron-willed leader rose up from such honest and humble beginnings to become the

The famous crumpled pot of *Mangyongdae* remains a central ornament in the iconic Kim clan homestead. According to the official line, the Kim family displayed heroic virtue and enviable frugality by persevering in using the nonfunctional pot rather than replace it with a pot that worked.

The famous crumpled pot of *Mangyongdae*. Miraculously, the pot survived count-less bombing raids that turned most of Pyongyang into a pile of rubble.

greatest leader mankind has ever known, and that the treacherous American imperialists are guilty of starting the Korean War.

After three years of steady aerial bombardment, Pyongyang was reduced to a field of masonry rubble. Even the village of *Mangyongdae*, which at the time was well beyond the city's edge, was flattened. Not a shack remained, not a hut still stood ... except for the holy nativity scene the Kims called home. It was left unscathed. Not a single humble mud wall was cracked, not a stalk of golden thatch in the roof was upset. The hoes leaned against the door jam, the bucket sat on the stump. Even the famous crumpled pot of *Mangyongdae* managed to survive wave after wave after wave of American B-29 bombing runs. It truly was miraculous.

The clan moved into the now sacred accommodation in 1862. Kim Il Sung's great great grandfather, Kim Ung U, was the patriarch and showed the revolutionary zeal even then. More of great great granddad's state-sanctioned exploits would be revealed to us later.

The guide used "the gesture" to indicate certain farm implements of significance, and then used "the voice" to warble on about the Great Leader's virtuous upbringing. Again and again she repeated the line, "He led a twenty-year liberation struggle to a shining victory." I looked around at the North Korean pilgrims to my left and right, ten centimeters shorter than their stocky Southern cousins, emaciated and weary looking, incapable of ever turning on the radio and hearing the Beatles, prohibited from ever possessing a mobile phone, blocked from ever accessing e-mail, ignorant of Velcro, Frisbees, junk mail, and Ziploc bags, oblivious of orthodontics and lasic vision correction, never once in an entire lifetime tasting something as otherwise common as a banana, herded down the state-sanctioned path towards a state-sanctioned isolated future. Shining victory indeed.

We emerged from the nativity scene as hundreds of excitable new arrivals streamed in behind us. There is a small copse of trees near the entrance of the holy birthplace and as we walked past neither Mr. Kim the Elder nor Mr. Kim the Younger bothered to inform us that those trees had been ceremoniously presented to Kim Il Sung, one by one, by his fellow Comintern leaders and then planted in a sweeping socialist ecological gesture. I wanted to see the larch from Fidel Castro, the willow from Tito, smell the sweet scent of Hoenecker's pine, rest in the shade of Ceauşescu's maple, but we had an itinerary to keep. The Kims marched on.

Strolling up a paved path through a well-manicured garden, we reached the apex of the little hill to encounter another well-known image. It was one of the omnipresent mosaic billboards featuring one of the Kims doing something significant. In this case, a very young Kim Il Sung sat in the grass on that very spot in the early years of the last century and surveyed the land below with a knowing, albeit young and innocent, expression. Even though the boy in the mosaic was in modest peasant garb, he already had that authoritative look about him that suggested he surely would evolve into the people's guiding beacon. The young mosaic Kim was depicted seated on the ground taking a break from tending the family cow, his posture incredibly straight. While he took a quick break from herding the cattle, he had pulled out a revolutionary text to do a little impromptu studying. Young revolutionaries often take to book learnin'.

Around the back of the hill the path wound and eventually took us to yet another cement pavilion with a view. Someone had driven a large, expensive-looking Japanese four-wheel drive vehicle with diplomatic number plates up the pathway and parked it immediately behind the pavilion. Standing next to the vehicle with a broom and the indignant snarl of an inconvenienced people's street sweeper, a middle-aged Korean woman stood and screeched to anyone in the vicinity.

An intricate mosaic billboard on a hillside above *Mangyongdae*, on the edge of Pyongyang, marks the precise spot a young Kim Song Ju took family cows to graze. This image depicts Song Ju taking a break from shepherding to study revolutionary thought. He would later change his name to Kim Il Sung and return to Pyongyang to lead the people in a revolutionary struggle that would culminate in the building of the North Korean nation.

"Who does this car belong to!? Who does this car belong to?! Is this your car?! Hey, you! Did you bring this car up here?"

Her voice was grating and shrill because she obviously ruled the pavilion and its environs and some insolent fool had driven their car right up the footpath to the top of the hill where the Great Leader himself had played as a boy. The impertinence.

As Mr. Kim the Elder and I walked towards the pavilion, the broom lady looked at him with a fierce gaze and demanded through a cloud of kimchi-powered halitosis, "It was you! This is your car, isn't it!?"

Mr. Kim smiled and gently said, "No, we have just arrived. We did not bring this car. I'm just an ordinary person."

"You drove this car here! You brought the foreigners up here in the car!"

"No," he said in a very gentle tone, "we have just arrived. I am an ordinary person and am here just to enjoy the view."

"Liar! This is your car and it shouldn't be here! Who gave you the authority to drive up here?!"

The exchange went back and forth like that for several rounds with Mr. Kim the Elder maintaining his quiet, dignified demeanor and never feeling the need to raise his voice, which infuriated her. She leaned closer and turned up the volume demanding that he admit he had been responsible for illegally parking the car on her turf.

I hustled up to the pavilion and left poor Mr. Kim on his own with the screeching banshee. They stood face to face for several minutes while she unbridled her frustration. Job satisfaction among the sidewalk sweeping crews of Pyongyang is probably not real high.

In the pavilion I found Charles chatting in Spanish with a group of olive skinned picnickers. They were all animated and amiable and they went back and forth exchanging pleasantries and chit chat. After a while Charles rejoined our little group and revealed that they were a family of Cubans connected to their Embassy in Pyongyang. Like everyone else, they were here to enjoy the view and relax.

Charles shook his head and grinned as he translated their question into English for us, "How can four American tourists visit North Korea, but you aren't allowed to visit Cuba?" Good question.

To one side of the group of Cubans stood a teenaged boy who must have been the son. He looked like any well-heeled teen one might see in Miami, or Los Angeles, or Houston, except this kid lived in Pyongyang. What do foreign teenagers do for fun in Pyongyang? There are no shopping malls, no video arcades, no fast food restaurants, no pop music, no cable television, no video streaming, and no convenience stores flogging deep-fried sugarcoated morsels.

We descended the steps of the cement pavilion and the woman with the broom was still screeching at Mr. Kim who, in turn, just repeated that he was only an ordinary person there for the view. We stepped around the car and continued down the path towards our waiting van. When and if the Cuban diplomat ever pulled the keys out of his pocket and returned to his diplomatic vehicle he would face the kimchi-scented wrath of a frustrated North Korean street sweeper. Surely between communists they eventually came to a mutually acceptable arrangement.

The van purred as it traveled up empty boulevards free of the need to deal with other vehicles. Mr. Bae made the driving look easy because it was. With no other vehicles on the roadways, he could do anything he wanted without the silly inconvenience of defensive driving. Mr. Bae was actually extraordinarily offensive in his driving; he didn't look, he didn't yield, he didn't brake, he didn't pay any attention to the carefully painted stripes on the road. With nothing to confront but empty space, Mr. Bae could drive that way and maintain a remarkably smooth ride.

Sprawled across the seats in back we resumed our conversation with Mr. Kim the Younger as he was eager to help us understand the correct interpretation of all things North Korean (and several things from further a field as well).

"Take for example," he said knowingly, "chemical weapon attacks by the United States ... how can you deny that the US is guilty?"

Topics such as this came up time and again when speaking with young Mr. Kim and that is one of the reasons he was so endearing.

Wally said in even tones, "Logically, it isn't very likely that happened." Wally, being the academic from the West, was used to linear logic being sufficient to conclude such a discussion. Mr. Kim, however, came armed with the fundamentals of the *Juche* Idea and those fundamentals superseded anything Socrates might have cooked up. After all, what do the Greeks have on Kim Il Sung?

Mr. Kim smiled and recited a well-rehearsed retort. "You have been told stories. They are beautiful stories and they sound real and look real, but just like a Hollywood movie they are not real. For example the movie *Titanic*. It looked very real, but it was just a movie and wasn't real. That is what your understanding is like ... like a movie."

It was ironic that Mr. Kim had opted for the *Titanic* as the example. On April 15, 1912, Wallace Hartley stood on the deck and led the ship's orchestra through "Nearer, My God, to Thee"[26] and the RMS *Titanic* sank in the icy North Atlantic; halfway around the world at almost exactly the same moment the Great Leader was born to Kim Hyong Jik and Kang Pan Sok. They named their baby Kim Song Ju. Twenty three years later Song Ju would take the nom de guerre "Il Sung" and that is the name the world would know him by as he displayed otherworldly brilliance in guiding his people in creating the Worker's Paradise.

Mr. Bae displayed his terrific offensive driving skills as the van smoothly glided back into the city on deserted thoroughfares. We swerved onto a narrower street and the immaculate cement towers faded into the distance. For a very short stretch we traversed a diagonal shortcut across the map. It went from island of grandiose splendor to island of grandiose spender and in between we sailed a sea of modest urban neglect obviously not on the must-see list for foreigners.

We weren't being shown anything off-limits because as a North Korean allowed the special privilege of living in Pyongyang and working among foreigners Mr. Bae thoroughly understood the penalty for the mistake of making a wrong turn. We had not taken a wrong turn, we had just drifted across a section of town not on the A List for sightseers. The forbidden list contains all the little alleyways one can see only in satellite photos. If Mr. Bae were foolish enough to allow us to see those warrens of disheveled confusion tucked behind the gleaming cement towers, then he would pay dearly. As carefree and nonplused as each of the Kims appeared to be, in truth their job was to keep tabs on Mr. Bae and their fellow Kim to insure strict adherence to the state rules. They were all three in a position to play the part of informer. If Mr. Bae had turned up a street we were prohibited from seeing, something unpleasant would have been done immediately.

We passed modest apartment blocks that looked remarkably reminiscent to those in Seoul that had been constructed in the impoverished, struggling early 70s. They appeared to feature the same Spartan and cramped quarters, the same sloppy construction, the same chips and cracks and stains. Between Pyongyang of 2007 and Seoul of 1977 if one of the apartment buildings could be transported through space and time, either way, nobody would take notice. Except maybe the giant hole in the ground where the building was yanked out. People would notice that, but they wouldn't notice yet another crappy apartment building in a cluster of seventeen similarly crappy apartment buildings.

Just like Seoul in the Park Chung-hee Era, these five- and six-story blocks had been rapidly built with only rudimentary skills. The result was the same and like Seoul, Pyongyang was left with cramped living spaces that steadily crumbled with use. The otherwise green spaces around the buildings were stripped of even a single blade of grass and the exposed earth was packed hard. The pavement was crumbling at the same rate as the poorly constructed buildings so chunks of sidewalk washed ashore here and there like cement ice floes building up on the banks of an Arctic seashore.

A few people gathered in the dirt to talk and scuff their shoes. Not many vehicles ever passed that way — I could tell because as we drove by each and every one of the pedestrians stopped and turned to watch the van pass. Just as quickly as we entered the side street we turned and started moving down a broad picture-perfect and empty pre-authorized boulevard designed for international consumption. Our little foray through the crumbling ghetto came and went without acknowledgement.

The Korean Central History Museum sits to the side of the much-photographed Kim Il Sung Square. The now famous video footage of goose stepping soldiers is made from the same square. The images of tens of thousands of olive-clad soldiers kicking heavily booted feet up into perfectly synchronized and ridiculously exaggerated steps appears to be taken from atop the museum. The artillery pieces and tanks, and the *Taepodong* missiles strapped to flatbed trucks — all the Soviet-style parading in Pyongyang happens right outside the front door of the museum. From the roof of the museum the angle would be perfect for capturing the square and its throngs of expressionless uniformed cogs. From there the cameras would also be able to zoom in on the Dear Leader in his special luxury suite where he stands under that signature bouffant and behind Imelda Marcos sunshades to oversee state-sanctioned military muscle flexing. The roof of the Korean Central History Museum also offered the perfect angle from which to capture state-sanctioned gopher-free photos of his father. The rooftop vantage point would have allowed shots across the square that produced grand three-quarter images from the left and allowed his bulbous secret to remain hidden on the right.

Mr. Bae drove the van around and behind the massive buildings flanking the square and re-emerged at the front of the museum. Unlike any other major city in the world, in Pyongyang one has the ability to drive up and park right in front of all the most significant tourist attractions. There are no other cars competing for the premier parking spots — the premier parking spots are just sitting there empty, waiting for the foreign visitor to come park.

We fell out of the van and into position. Our little gaggle of tourism was proving to be the perfect size for the Worker's Paradise. With a ratio of two foreign guests per minder it allowed for a little more relaxation on the part of the Koreans. If our group had been comprised of a dozen or more wandering foreigners, then the Kims would have been forced to tighten the reins and enforce more stringent adherence to the rules. As it were, they appeared fairly relaxed and completely at ease allowing us to stray just a little, to flirt with the rules just a tiny bit, and to test the boundaries in minute ways. That relaxation was manifest in an arrangement that was never discussed but evolved over time — both Kims were willing to allow us to individually stray away from the guided tour as long as we remained in sight and within voice range. Like taking a vanload of seven-year-olds to the zoological gardens, they were comfortable with us exhibiting our independence within a tolerable range. That range wasn't very extensive and we didn't ever wander far, but when we walked thirty paces away from the group to inspect a plaque or photograph or a monument from a different angle, nothing was said. However, both Kims appeared to be perpetually cognizant of our comings and goings and they worked in silent tandem like Australian sheep dogs to ensure we were quietly outflanked and contained at every moment. Our independence, after all, was illusory. In addition to the two minders, our driver Mr.

Bae, the guides at each museum, and those mysterious lone pedestrians loitering in the shadows at virtually every stop were all part of the machine. They were all selected for their jobs on the basis of their ability to work within the system, and that required the ability to play by the North Korean rules. They were all watching us, they were all minders, they were all part of the elaborate North Korean system. Anyone deemed unfit to be exposed to foreigners would simply never have the ability to get anywhere near us. Simply by being in Pyongyang they were demonstrating that they were already vetted and approved.

I exercised some of my pretend-independence and stepped away from the group momentarily to look at the square. The buildings on either side of the majestic square were built in 1954 by dragooned North Korean soldiers and their Chinese comrades. It bore a striking resemblance to Seoul's drab, gray Japanese-era City Hall. At the end of the Korean War vast numbers of Chinese volunteers volunteered to stay on and lend a hand in rebuilding. One of the first projects they volunteered for was the construction of the buildings around the square. Few on the outside can agree on which ministries are housed in the buildings on either side of the square and like so many issues among Koreaphiles, the debate can be contentious and inflamed. I suspect that either of the Kims would have postulated a confident answer had I asked, but in fact they may not really know what goes on inside those mighty drab structures. The buildings stand in the gray stone socialist magnificence that dominated capital cities across the communist world in the 50s. They could be from Moscow, or Belgrade, or Budapest, or Sofia. The communist structures of that era are universal and interchangeable, all very dour, and all proclaiming "state."

In every direction from the square all the surrounding buildings are adorned with huge propaganda slogans mounted along the flat roofs. The towering red characters form aggressive looking sentences that run half the length of the buildings and every rooftop slogan ends with a defiant exclamation mark: "Devotedly Defending the Great Leader! Long Live the Democratic People's Republic of Korea! Let's Sound the Drum of the Military-First Revolution Even Louder! Long Live the Glorious Korean Labor Party! Long Live the Great Military-First Policy! Let us Rush Forward at the Speed of the Military-First Revolution!"

The same gray stone used to construct the buildings was used to pave the square. Everything was the same solemn, serious gray. The only break in an otherwise gray environment are the giant red characters, huge red party banners, large national flags, and the thousands of white markings daubed on the paving stones at regular intervals. At first glance they look like the work

The paved surface of Kim Il Sung Square is covered with tens of thousands of white marks used by participants in military parades to correctly position themselves. The elaborate displays of goose stepping soldiers are precisely rehearsed, and then precisely executed according to the subtle guide marks covering the entire square.

of ten thousand pigeons with irritable bowel syndrome, but on closer inspection they are the marks that guide the goose-stepping frog-marching KPA recruits when they strut through the square *en masse*. Discovering the carefully placed white marks felt like being let in on a secret.

The ministry building on the south side of the square features a pair of portraits perched high up on the façade; one of Karl Marx, the other of Vladimir Lenin. The portraits are so large that they stretch from the third to the fifth story. North Korea had been a faithful member and team player in the Cominturn in the early days and images of the communist stalwarts like Marx, Engels, Lenin, and Mao were publicly displayed for all to see, but the advent of *Juche* dictated that the people's revolutionary maintenance crews be issued orders to crawl up on scaffolding and remove portraits of the foreigners and replace them with state-approved images of Korea's homegrown savior Kim Il Sung. So the people's revolutionary maintenance crews went all over Pyongyang and all over the rest of North Korea steadily dismantling all signs of being a team player in the communist club. The new images, iconography, and slogans announced that North Korea was going it alone and all they needed was the brilliant leadership of Kim Il Sung to show them the way. After a few years portraits of the father were joined with portraits of the son in a subtle announcement that Kim Jong Il's leadership was also brilliant and the people were blessed to be living in the nation in which not only the best, most skilled leader in the history of mankind happened to live, but the other most skilled leader in the history of mankind was also around and could lend a hand. The good fortune of the North Korean people manifest itself in a variety of ways, the most public being the neverending display of the tandem Kims in state sanctioned portraits. The portrait of Marx and its matching portrait of Lenin on the ministry building at Kim Il Sung Square are the last outward acknowledgement of the time when North Korea played well with others on the Cominturn playground.

As a concession to the indigenous leadership, the images of Marx and Lenin are dwarfed by an enormous image of the flag of the Korean Workers Party towering over the center of the building, and across the breadth of the entire edifice, were the huge red Korean characters proclaiming, "Long Live the Glorious Korean Workers Party." The two Europeans gaze eternally across the square to the north where, along the top of a nearly identical gray ministry building huge red characters proclaim, "Long Live the Democratic People's Republic of Korea!" Out of the center of the slogan springs a huge North Korean flag permanently frozen in mid wave, and in the center of the building was hung a gigantic portrait of the Great Leader, more than twice the size of either Lenin or Marx, peering right back across the square at them with a very self-assured expression. Off to the side another stately gray building held up a rooftop sign that proclaimed, "Long Live the Revolutionary Thought of the Great Leader Comrade Kim Il Sung!" On other buildings still more North Korean slogans screamed down from the rooftops. It was clearly understood that this was his square — not Karl's or Vladimir's.

From the same perch on which they have rested since the 50s, Marx and Lenin silently watched as I backtracked to the entrance of the museum and joined the group just as the guide appeared from the shadows and commenced her introduction. Like the rest, she was clad in a flowing velvet dress and looked intent on correcting any misconceptions we might have.

Using "the voice," she explained to us that this museum contained the artifacts of ancient Korea going back to the very origins of the Korean people. On both sides of the DMZ Koreans agree that all Koreans can trace their origins back to the very first Korean: *Tangun*. Though officially acknowledged

One of the unnamed Ministry Buildings at Kim Il Sung Square. The portraits of Karl Marx and Vladimir Lenin on the exterior of the building are the only remaining public acknowledgment of a time when Pyongyang was squarely under the tutelage of Moscow. Tens of thousands of painted white marks on the surface of street and across the surface of the square guide the large numbers of goose-stepping Korea People's Army soldiers when they are on parade.

as the Korean foundation myth, that official acknowledgement is often reluctant. Reluctant because by definition a myth may or may not be true, yet everybody knows the story on *Tangun* is true. As the story goes, the god *Hwanung* came down from heaven and cavorted about on the un-peopled Korean peninsula, taking in the views, enjoying the fresh air, drinking from the clear brooks, and generally having a fine time. Then a she-bear and a tigress sauntered up to *Hwanung* and confessed that they both wanted to become human. Though it was his first visit to earth and we can therefore assume he had no prior experience in dealing with talking animals, *Hwanung* knew exactly what they had to do — he loaded them down with garlic and mugwort and sent them to a cave where they had to remain in darkness for 100 days and subsist only on the odoriferous provisions he had given them. The tigress got bored and left after a few days but the tenacious she-bear was bound and determined to persevere and she stuck it out to the bitter end. When she waddled out of the cave and into the sunlight she discovered that she had been transformed into a beautifully curvaceous woman called *Ungnyeo*. *Hwanung* caught sight of *Ungnyeo* and promptly took her by the hand, turned her around, and marched her back into the cave where they immediately consummated their relationship. A few months later she gave birth to a son they called *Tangun*. He would go on to found the Korean nation.

Koreans may be the only people on earth who sprang forth from admitted ursine abuse. They may also be the only people on earth who know precisely when it all happened. *Tangun* was born, as any Korean can tell you, in 2333 BC. Our guide stressed that Korea has a 5,000-year history and is therefore blessed with wisdom, grace, and maturity far beyond other younger nations.[27] The slack-jawed, glazed-eyed mantra of "five thousand years of history" is repeated incessantly north and south of the DMZ, no matter how erroneous.

We didn't go very far in to the museum before she pointed out a large photograph mounted on the wall. It was of the white ziggurat built over *Tangun*'s tomb. They had actually found the bones and everything. This wasn't a sham — it was the real deal. The North Koreans had unearthed *Tangun*'s 4,327-year-old remains in 1993, proving once and for all that Korea is older than Japan and that *Tangun* was a North Korean — not a South Korean. Rumor has it that the Great Leader was studying the design and providing guidance to the architects of the new ziggurat on the night he died. But there are dozens of claims about what the Great Leader was doing when he died — each one as speculative and undocumented as the next. Soon after Kim Il Sung's death the tomb was opened to the public just a bit farther down the road from Sihanouk's *Changsuwon* Palace.

The guide allowed us the rare privilege of entering not one, but three different plywood mock-ups of royal tombs. She beamed with pride as she spoke about the regal history associated with each as if we were standing not in little painted plywood cubicles but in the actual unearthed tombs. Someone had taken the time to carefully render cracks and blemishes in the painted stonework. There were even faux water stains. As she spoke she reverently touched the painted plywood with delicate little fingers and beamed.

She also pointed out other plywood and plaster mock-ups of ancient relics trapped behind the DMZ in the "American-controlled" half of the peninsula. The artifacts, she explained, were coveted by the Americans and that was one of the reasons for their dastardly and unjust attack and subsequent cruel occupation of the southern half of Korea. The Americans, she said, attempted to steal anything of cultural significance from Korea, then without changing her pace, pointed to a single modest photograph mounted on the museum wall and explained that it showed an original manuscript printed with movable type, which was a Korean invention.

Mr. Kim the Younger was steadily translating the stream of jingoism when Alice perked up and asked if our guide had said that Koreans invented movable type. In a reassuring demonstration of professionalism, Mr. Kim did not answer the question, rather he turned and translated Alice's query for the guide.

"Oh, yes," the guide replied in Korean and radiated pride, "movable type is a Korean creation. We invented it 200 years before your Gutenberg stole the idea."

With that she smiled and directed our attention again to the photograph mounted on the wall. That was the proof. No examples, no recreations, no further displays, just a photograph of a sheet of parchment with murky, indecipherable Korean type printed across it.

Alice was startled. Like most Westerners she had never been told that movable type had been invented in Asia long before Gutenberg got around to the idea. Whether the idea traveled the silk road to Europe and Gutenberg capitalized on it, or if Gutenberg had had an independent invention we will never know. However there is solid evidence that the concept of movable type was first used about 400 years before Gutenberg — in China. The Chinese were printing documents with movable type long before the Koreans, but I thought it best to ignore the anachronistic oversight.

The last exhibit before the souvenir shop was a scale model of a Korean turtle ship, or *kobukson*. The Turtle Ship was mentioned in ancient writings but no remains have ever been found. The debates over the turtle ship are heated and wearisome. Each pedantic facet is argued loud and long; were they actually ironclad as we know iron cladding? Did they have flame-throwing dragon's heads on the bow? Could Korean boatbuilding skill have created a wooden hull capable of carrying such an incredibly heavy iron roof without capsizing? Did the Koreans listen to stories from American missionaries in the late 1800s and simply incorporate their wild and wonderful tales of the Battle of Hampton Roads and the ironclad *Monitor* and *Merrimack* into Korean mythology? I long ago learned to smile and nod appreciatively when confronted with the topic of turtle ships. With no desire to step in to the fray I will happily agree with any and all opinions on the matter if it means I don't have to listen to anyone's long-winded impassioned argument about their particular turtle ship stance.

The turtle ship, like the invention of movable type, can be such an emotive topic that aficionados raise their voices and flail their appendages, flecks of foam at the corners of their mouths, while shouting down differing views. Natural curiosity draws one to such topics, but the mordant shouting pushes one away. Such is the dilemma of the Koreaphile.

I walked past the turtle ship model and around the corner into the cavernous and chilly souvenir shop. The large stone building was still holding the cold throughout the day even in late April and the pale blue fluorescent bulbs didn't add any warmth to the ambiance. The same hackneyed knick-knacks were neatly arranged by scientific classification; species, genus, family, order, class.... Books by the Kims and about the Kims, music cassettes featuring songs about the Kims and their glorious accomplishments, added liquor, cheesy post cards, wonderfully socialist postage stamps, wooden gew-gaws, and cigarettes. Carolus Linnaeus could walk in to any souvenir shop in Pyongyang and recognize his classification system in use. They were all carefully arranged in precisely the same way with the same products starting on the left and working through the spectrum of souvenirs until culminating with locally produced cigarettes on the right. Posta.

Wally gravitated towards the books, Alice to the postcards, and Charles to the stamps. Mr. Kim the Elder stood at the counter and admired the souvenir items with the tourists while Mr. Kim the Younger retreated to a chair to address certain nicotine needs. He graciously extended the pack towards me as I sat down, but simultaneously said, "I think Americans do not smoke, but you can have one if you like."

I informed him that the rumors were true: more and more Americans have prudently forgone tobacco. We have dramatically increased our consumption of refined cane sugar and trans fatty acids and we find it acceptable to wolf down massive quantities of genetically modified junk food dripping with chemical preservatives designed to extend shelf life beyond the far end of the standard actuarial tables, and we sit and watch giant screen television while the plaque on our artery walls thickens and congeals, and super sizing our fast food has forced us to super size our wardrobes ... but wisely we don't smoke.

Mr. Kim exhaled a carcinogenic blue-gray cloud and admitted that cigarettes were one of his only real pleasures. Leaning against the museum wall with ash quietly falling on his jacket, he said, "Most men in North Korea enjoy tobacco. We produce very good tobacco here and it is abundant."

As Mr. Kim took the last drag and snuffed his butt, Wally joined us and showed me the 1988 volume of the historical record of aggression against Korea. The Korean script filled every page with the damning evidence that Koreans were the victims time and again. Finds like that usually only happen in out of the way souvenir shops in North Korea.

Mr. Bae pulled away from the curb and we drove up yet another splendidly empty boulevard. A few meandering pedestrians were out, but the sidewalks were almost as quiet and empty as the roads. We passed a lone grandmother with a toddler strapped to her back in the traditional Korean fashion. She leaned forward with a rice paddy hunch and walked along the sidewalk while the child slept in drooling contentment against her warm shoulders. Koreaphile legend has long insisted that this form of traditional baby-hauling was outlawed in North Korea because of the peasant-like connotations, but there granny went up the broken sidewalk leaning in to her journey with vigor. This was the first child I had seen on the streets of Pyongyang. Like a shadowy metropolis in a Madeline L'Engle tale, the urban landscape was eerily devoid of children. They must have been there, behind curtains, sequestered in cement towers, in the protective custody of the state. I knew they must be there because we had seen thousands of them prancing around the floor of the stadium during the *Arirang* performance, but along the thoroughfares and in the parks, on the riverbanks, in the shops, and up the side streets there was never a sign of children.

The van meandered through more empty boulevards and we passed the sprawling compound of the Russian Embassy. For decades it had been a tit-for-tat competition between the two Koreas. The game was simple: establish diplomatic ties with a greater number of nations than the other Korea. As per the rules of the game the Korea with more embassies was more legitimate. For years the tally was predictably in line with allegiances on each side of the Cold War divide. South Korea had embassies in the United States and United Kingdom, while North Korea had the Soviet Union and Red China. South Korea had South Africa and Taiwan, North Korea had Bulgaria and Cuba. South Korea had the Vatican City, while North Korea had the Palestine Liberation Organization. But the South's drive to expand export markets for consumer electronics pushed their diplomats to establish embassies in what had previously been territory in the North Korean camp. The trump card was played in 1993 when long-time South Korean ally Taiwan was given marching orders and their diplomatic compound in central Seoul was unceremoniously handed over to the Red Chinese. By establishing diplomatic relations with the People's Republic of China, South Korea had pulled off a tactical flanking maneuver that landed them a billion new customers while simultaneously establishing formal diplomatic ties with North Korea's staunchest ally.

The game has evolved and now it is not uncommon to find the flags of both Koreas flying above diplomatic compounds in the same capital city.

Sometimes the missions are within close proximity in the same neighborhood.

Though it is no longer a tit-for-tat competition North Koreans have increased their tally in the diplomatic relations game. A short list of Western European nations and Australia have normalized relations in the recent past and all the new missions are assigned to *Munsudong*, a walled Pyongyang neighborhood known in the diplomatic community as, "the greenhouse." In the very early days, before the regime decided to wall the diplomats up in a nice, neat, controllable locale, the Soviets built a monstrous complex in the heart of the city. When the Soviet Union collapsed, the Russian Federation assumed occupancy of the same compound. They changed flags and changed the polished brass sign on the front door then just carried on — business as usual.

We rounded a bend at the front of the complex and drove down the side of the huge piece of Russian-owned real estate. Through a wrought iron fence we could see a set of tennis courts and to one side a cluster of Caucasian children playing — not tennis, just playing. In a social black hole like Pyongyang, the Russian kids must know the Cuban boy I had seen earlier. Maybe he gets invited to use the courts at the Russian Embassy. Maybe they go over to the Cuban Embassy and swipe cigars out of the Ambassador's humidor. Do these kids have any idea that Kim Jong Il built the Russian Orthodox Church of Life-Giving Trinity on the east side of the river? Do their parents make them go on days significant in the Orthodox calendar? In a place like Pyongyang having the opportunity to go do something wildly out of the state-sanctioned ordinary like attend a church service on the other side of the river might actually appeal to a Russian teen.

Rumors among Koreaphiles would have us believe that in 2002 Kim Jong Il returned from a very rare trip outside North Korea with the burning desire to have a Russian Orthodox Church in Pyongyang. Apparently the onion domes appealed to his inner man. After nearly 60 years of silence, church leaders in Russia were contacted by the Orthodox Committee of the Democratic People's Republic of Korea, of whom they had never before heard. When the Russian clergy expressed doubt that the Dear Leader would locate any surviving Koreans of the Orthodox faith, the Dear Leader is reported to have said, "Don't worry, we'll find some." Ultimately the committee sent North Korean students to an Orthodox Theological Seminary in Moscow for a crash course in how to be an Orthodox priest. *Feodor* Kim and *John* Ra — graduates of Moscow Theological Seminary — are now presiding over the Russian Orthodox Church of Life-Giving Trinity in Pyongyang.

While the Orthodox Church has had a continuous presence on the

Korean peninsula since 1897, for the past half-century it has been minute and limited to the southern half. When suddenly in 2006 the Holy Synod of the Russian Orthodox Church established the Parish of the Life-Giving Trinity in Pyongyang, Western journalists were skeptical. Where had the community of Orthodox believers been for two generations? Why were they suddenly coming to the surface now? What was the Dear Leader getting out of this? They suggested that it was a sham just like the Catholic and Protestant churches on the west side of the river.

The response was swift and stern. The Patriarch's public relations office in Moscow released statements explaining that it was the consecration ceremony, as covered by a publication put out by the Orthodox Church in Russia, that was picked up by the wire services of the world. It appears that the authors of that Russian publication were not able to fully describe the history of how the Orthodox church suddenly reappeared in North Korea because of limited print space. This is why, they explained, shortly afterwards ungrounded conclusions were drawn by secular journalists. They suggested that the church has had a presence all along and speculation about its demise under communism was premature. Simple as that — limited print space strikes again.

We crossed to the east side of the tranquil *Taedong* River and stopped along the curb, but Mr. Bae could have pulled to a stop in the middle of *Juche* Tower Avenue and it wouldn't have been a problem. The sun was beginning to set and the broad avenue was deserted ... as it had been all day, as it was every day. The few pedestrians who had been visible on the streets an hour before were now home for the evening.

None of us needed to be told where we were and what we were looking at. The *Juche* Tower is one of the iconic monuments that every Koreaphile knows. North Koreans frequently use the awkward transliteration, "Tower of *Juche* Idea." A more accurate translation might be "Tower of *Juche* Ideology," but hearing the Kims rattle off "*Juche* Idea" again and again added to the overall kitsch. It was built in 1982 on the riverbank directly across from Kim Il Sung Square, so when the Great Leader stood on the viewing platform to watch his thousands of uniformed troops goose step down the street, he need only glance up and across the river to the east and there stood his 70th birthday gift (from the adoring people, of course).

Mr. Kim the Younger recited the details by heart, "The Dear Leader Kim Jong Il lovingly designed it for his father. Including the base, it is 170 meters in height. In America the Washington Monument is only 169 meters tall! That means the *Juche* Tower is the tallest stone tower in the world! It contains 25,550 blocks,[28] one for each day of his life up until his 70th birthday.

The Tower of the *Juche* Idea was a gift from the adoring masses to Kim Il Sung on his 70th birthday in 1982 and stands on the banks of the *Taedong* River among dozens of other monuments to Kim, his philosophy, and the celebrated North Korean people.

The stone spire is four-sided for Korea's unique and distinct four seasons and has seventy dividers between layers of stone and each divider represents a year of his life. On top is a twenty-meter, forty-five-ton illuminated torch. The entire tower was built in thirty-five days and the finishing work was accomplished in only seventy-six days."

Like every other major monument, road, building, or bridge, it was built with traditional Korean *bbali-bbali* philosophy and workmanship. It is possible to take an elevator to the top of the tower, but knowing that they had built it in only thirty-five days I was quite happy when Mr. Kim the Elder said we would not be going up because guests were not being welcomed while we happened to be there. In truth, I suspect there was a power cut that left the elevator dark and useless.

On the back side of the tower, tucked into the base like a stone alcove, is a special nook where eighty-two little polished stone rectangles of uniform size are set into the wall of the tower. Mr. Kim the Elder explained that each stone was sent by admirers of the *Juche* Idea from all over the world. With that he beamed at the thought of the world's tired, the poor, the huddled masses, yearning to breathe free ... the wretched refuse of those teeming shores, the homeless, the tempest-tost, those hungry for the knowledge that only the *Juche* Idea can impart.

Sure enough, the stones were engraved with greetings and good wishes from around the world. From *Juche* Study Groups in Brazil, from Kimilsungism Societies in France, from *Juche* Cells in Africa, from China, Japan, Laos, and New Zealand there were fans who had somehow managed to get engraved stones (of precisely the correct uniform dimensions) to Pyongyang for inclusion in the tower's construction. Right in the middle was one that proclaimed in English:

LONG LIVE KIMILSUNGISM
New York Group for the Study of Kimilsungism
April 7, 1978, New York USA.

I couldn't help but picture two lonely vegans and a demented old socialist in a dank fifth-floor walk-up in Queens huddled around mimeographed pamphlets, a post card, and a North Korean flag drawn with crayons on cardboard proudly thumbtacked to the wall.

A few stones away was one from the International Action Center, U S of A. The name rang a bell but I couldn't recall where I had heard it. It was only weeks later, looking over notes from the trip, that I recalled the IAC as Ramsey Clark's social activist organization. Not only was he the 66th attorney general of the United States[29] and a fellow Texan, he was also known for

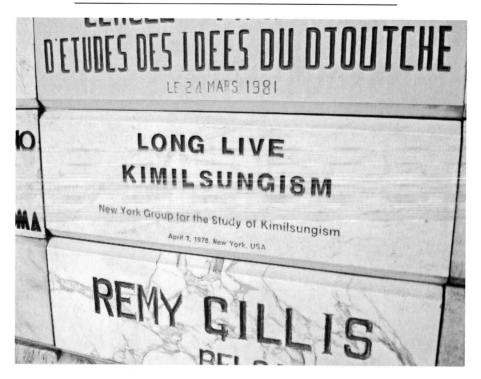

Within an alcove at the base of the Tower of the *Juche* Idea are 82 stone tiles sent from Kim Il Sung fan clubs and Juche Study Cells around the globe. Among those from the United States is one from Ramsey Clark's International Action Center and one from the New York Group for the Study of Kimilsungism. The tiles, though of different types of stone, are all of precisely uniform dimensions and were prepared and sent to Pyongyang at just the right time in the early months of 1982 for inclusion in the tower as it was being hastily built.

a career in the legal profession that included clients such as perennial US presidential candidate and convicted felon Lyndon Larouche, Branch Davidian leader David Koresh, accused Yugoslavian war criminals Radovan Karadžić and Slobodan Milošević, Nazi concentration camp commandant Karl Linnas, Staff Sergant and deserter Camilo Ernesto Mejía, Liberian strongman Charles Taylor, and Saddam Hussein. Looking at this list of clients, it's only fitting that Clark's group would make an effort to get a friendship stone sent to Pyongyang for inclusion on the tower.

At the base of the tower, on the riverside, is a thirty meter bronze sculpture of three resolute Koreans captured in the starkest of socialist realism as they gaze back across the river towards the viewing platform at Kim Il Sung Square. At the head of the three figures is the robust male factory worker hold-

The North Koreans boast that the Tower of the Juche Idea is the tallest stone-covered spire on the planet. While it is a meter taller than the Washington Monument, it falls short of Texas' San Jacinto Monument by 2.9 meters. The characters near the top of the tower proclaim "*Juche*," or self–reliance. In the foreground a bronze factory worker, peasant, and intellectual hold aloft a hammer, sickle, and calligraphy brush—representing the iconic logo of the Korean Worker's Party.

ing aloft a mighty Soviet-style hammer in his right hand. His trousers are neatly ironed and his hair is perfectly groomed. His expression is one of knowing determination. Behind him and to his left is a peasant woman holding up in a mighty right hand a large bronze sickle. She too looks into the future with a resolute expression. Both of them clutch books in their left hands, presumably books on the *Juche* Idea so when they get tired of hammering the anvil in the people's pig iron works or sickling the sheaves of abundant golden grain in the commune's back fields, they can take a quick break and bone up on a little more state-sanctioned political philosophy. Behind them is a third figure, the bronze image of an intellectual. You could tell he was supposed to be the intellectual because he was holding aloft an oversized calligraphy brush in his left hand and clutching a state-sanctioned book in his right. He was barrel-chested but poncy. He gazed forward out across the river towards the square with an expression that suggested maybe there were prurient thoughts clanging around in his hollow bronze head. While his colleagues hammered and sickled, the intellectual sat quietly and used his brush to draw frilly things and curlicues, to write the name *"Chul Su"* a hundred times with precise flourishes and whorls, and to doodle and sulk. There was good reason why the Russians drew the line at the hammer and sickle — their revolution didn't have room for effeminate dandies. There was work to be done and the workers were drawn from the factories and farms, not the salons and conservatories. Yet there he stood in bronze splendor, the *Juche* Philosopher's *Juche* Philosopher. Even though the figure must have weighed in at two tons, he was still light in his bronze loafers.

The three figures, like the figures in socialist realism statuary all over the world, leaned into a headwind and looked ready to confront the bourgeoisie enemies of the state. The embryonic form of the *Juche* philosophy was born in the mid 1950s when Kim Il Sung got fed up with Soviet icons, Soviet music, Soviet symbolism, and Soviet aspirations. North Koreans were preoccupied with everything Soviet and Kim had had enough. In short, the newfangled philosophy was one of national self-sufficiency. Rather than openly accepting the role as client state, the North Koreans stuck their collective necks out under the leadership of Kim Il Sung and decided to go it alone — at least on the surface, and at least for consumption at home. The timing was perfect because the growing Sino-Soviet rift allowed North Korea many opportunities to play the Russkies against the ChiComs while prancing around in the middle to the tune of national self-sufficiency. Not unlike the child of parents headed towards an acrimonious divorce, it doesn't take much imagination to find advantage in playing one bitter parent against the other.

Within ten years the regime had fleshed out the concept sufficiently that they started working on the back story and the supporting evidence. By the mid 1960s the North Koreans stopped bothering to translate the concept and reverted to the Romanized Korean *Juche* and suggested that the concept was so uniquely ingenious and indigenous that other languages were simply incapable of capturing the concept's essence in translation. For the audience at home this linguistic chauvinism was additional proof for what they already knew — their unique situation was the uniquest and their philosophy was so stinking cutting edge that other languages were incapable of even a rudimentary translation.

In the early /0s the *Juche* idea had been honed to such a fine point that it was obvious the time had come to allow it to completely replace Marxist/Leninist concepts in the constitution. Their long-time communist allies one by one gave up on communism and left the Comintern playground. North Korea had fewer and fewer playmates with which to play and the horrible inefficiencies of the North Korean system became more pronounced. For a state so hell-bent on self-sufficiency it must have come as a rude awakening when the wheels on the state machine started to wobble. In the '90s when the wheels finally fell off, the regime tap-danced around the fundamental issues, pointed a finger at the Yankee imperialists, suggested the Russians had abandoned the fraternity in a show of cowardice, noted the relentless cycle of draught and flood, and in a brilliant Orwellian flanking maneuver came up with the *Songun* Policy. Most pundits agree that *Songun* means simply "military first." In essence, the *Songun* Policy dictates that priority in resource distribution is granted to the military. On top of that, the regime now has a pampered, well-armed military to help convince the masses that *Juche* can work only if they get out there and give even more, go the extra kilometers, tighten the belt, sacrifice for the nation, and exceed production quotas. *Juche* may be in shambles and the people may be starving, but when *Songun* is tacked on to *Juche* it means the military has more liberty to knock heads and keep the populace in line and quiet. That allows *Juche* to continue leading the masses towards the great abyss without fear that the masses will rise up and attempt to alter the course.

Among all his other titles and accolades, Kim Jong Il is now also the *Songun* General — a coupling that allows him to draw strength and legitimacy from his connection to the military, while the military draws mirrored legitimacy from a continued close relationship with Kim.

The top of the *Juche* Tower is adorned with a huge leaded-glass flame that looks suspiciously reminiscent of the flame atop the torch held aloft by the Statue of Liberty.

While her torch welcomes all to the shores of New Jersey with a warm yellow-gold glow, the torch on the top of the *Juche* Tower is revolutionary red and the lights within the flame are wired to flicker in a very "realistic" way. At night, when the rest of Pyongyang is hidden in load-shedding darkness, a few significant monuments are illuminated to make sure the appropriate political statement is made without interpretation. The *Juche* Tower is one of them. From the window in the hotel the "realistic" flicker of the huge red glass flame stood out in an otherwise pitch-dark city.

I stood at the base of the tower and looked up at the flame, frozen mid-flicker, and admired the ridiculousness of it all. Mr. Kim the Younger came and acknowledged my admiration. He said, "It's very tall, isn't it?"

Mr. Kim the Younger was still under the impression that I was a run-of-the-mill regular American. He hadn't yet realized the truth of my Lone Star pedigree as I inhaled deeply and glanced down at his proud smile. He had no idea that I had grown up almost in the shadow of the San Jacinto Monument; a monument intentionally constructed, like the *Juche* Tower, to be just a little taller than the Washington Monument. While Mr. Kim prepared to reiterate the fact that his tower was a meter higher than the one in Washington, I hung my thumbs in to my belt loops and could feel General Sam Houston, Father of *my* nation, our *Songun* General, the most virtuous of all Texans, look down on me and smile.

"Mr. Kim, are you aware that in my country we have a stone tower taller than this one?" I inquired with all the subtlety of an irritated rattlesnake.

Mr. Kim smiled in his studied assurance and answered, "The *Juche* Tower is 170 meters. Your Washington Monument is only 169 meters ... somewhat shorter, I believe."

I smiled with the pleasure of victory even before the words could depart my mouth, "Mr. Kim, I am from Texas, and our War for Independence was fought near my childhood home. On that battlefield we have a stone monument that is 173 meters — taller than the Washington Monument, taller than the *Juche* Tower. It is the tallest stone tower in the world. In fact it used to be taller until we sucked all the oil out from under it and the land subsided."

This did not compute. His face remained that of the consummate state-approved guide with the steadfast assuredness that his regime had fed him facts and figures that simply could not be disputed, but his eyes darted quickly left and right and then up to the red glass torch and back to my face. His handlers had told him that most tourists wouldn't be American and wouldn't really know (or care) what the Washington Monument was. They also told him that the few American tourists that did show up inevitably wouldn't have a clue how tall the Washington Monument is, so he could rattle off the figures illustrating the North Korean tower and not expect any lip in return. They did not warn him that out there in the Western world are Texans who place exactly the same kind of significance on making sure their monument was just enough taller that they could boast in exactly the same way.

"You jest," he said, not too sure that I was.

"No, Mr. Kim, my nation was born at the foot of that monument, every schoolboy in Texas knows exactly how tall the San Jacinto Monument is."[30]

"You are not American?" he asked in genuine confusion.

He had collected my passport himself, he had seen the United States seal across its face. Then, before I could answer, Mr. Kim saw the obvious escape that would allow him to save face and also walk away without actually needing to concede anything. "When was your monument built?"

Obviously if my monument actually exists, then it must have been constructed after 1982 when the North Koreans completed the *Juche* Tower.

Unfortunately for Mr. Kim, the same chest thumping that appeals to North Koreans appeals to Texans. Every boy who grew up in Texas knows Jim Bowie, Davey Crockett, and John Wayne's deaths at the Alamo were avenged by General Sam Houston and his creepy eyes on 21 April 1836; San Jacinto Day. They probably told me the last time I was there, but after the bed wetting incident I couldn't remember when the monument was constructed. I made a guess and told him the centennial.[31]

I smiled the victor's smile and said, "Nineteen thirty six ... the hundredth anniversary of our victory over the Mexican imperialists."

He shook his head in complete disbelief and walked away into the long afternoon shadows while Wally looked on and chuckled. The North Koreans will never understand how much they have in common with Texans.

Again Mr. Bae drove us up empty boulevards and down equally empty thoroughfares. Other than the occasional Mercedes-Benz sedan with tinted glass, we had the streets of Pyongyang to ourselves. Pyongyang would be the perfect backdrop for an apocalyptic science fiction movie. The vast city remained almost completely empty of signs of habitation and as the sun dropped in to the horizon the few lone stragglers disappeared.

Yet the traffic wardens were on duty in the middle of each major intersection, pirouetting inside their perfectly rendered white circles of paint, flinging their baton up one street, then whipping it around to point down another. Their form-fitting dark uniform skirts were set off by the glistening white of socks and gloves. Each warden we passed was focused on the task at hand with laser beam attention to detail. Besides us there weren't any cars on the road — but if there had been the wardens would have been in the thick of things telling the drivers how to safely maneuver through the streets without a mishap or altercation. With the dainty little drill sergeants efficiently directing traffic, the civic authorities could continue to allow the traffic lights to remain switched off.

Every one of them looked like they had just come out of, were just going in to, or were perpetually suspended in the worst mood ever experienced in the history of human emotion. They all appeared capable of ripping off the head of the driver of any passing vehicle then nimbly shoving the entire cranial mass down the bloody stump hole before the vehicle could come to a complete stop. To say it appeared they were having a bad day was an under statement. It appeared they were having a bad life and they were looking for someone to unbridle their frustrations on ... preferably in a violently physical way.

It wasn't that the traffic wardens looked displeased to be doing their job — on the contrary they had one of the best jobs in the Worker's Paradise and as long as their looks and figure held up there was no reason to throw in the towel. Why would a beautiful young woman with a whistle and a baton chuck it all in to go repair roadbeds by hand with a bunch of wizened crones from the village? No, the wardens wore the menacing expression because it came with the job. They put it on when they slipped in to the uniform. It was as much a part of the required attire as the sensible shoes.

They all wore the same prim uniforms and carried the same bitchy moue, but as the afternoon sun slowly dropped and the glare increased, they all retrieved regime-issued sunshades and slipped them on under the rim of their hats. Unlike Mr. Bae and the "monk" they did not wear mirrored aviator glasses. That would have been a logical choice and might have offered the maximum UV-ray protection, but Kim Jong Il's battalion of attractive traffic wardens were issued something much more *haute couture*. They all had very stylish wrap-around frameless lavender sunshades of the type one might see on beautiful people lounging on the Mediterranean coast. They wore the trendy sunshades that don't look like they are capable of much shading from the sun. The type of sunshades that are constructed from virtually clear plastic and therefore the wearer has to go ahead and squint even after slipping them on. Each of the beautiful wardens scowled because their official job description required them to do so, and they squinted because their regime-issued lavender sunshades failed to fulfill their primary design task and announced for all the world to see that they had just come out of, were just going into, or were perpetually suspended in one of "those" moods.

There are tales of North Korean tour guides being convinced to allow a vanload of tourists to stop and step out on to the sidewalk in order to film this bizarre feature of the Pyongyang cityscape. Evidence that these tales are true comes in the form of dozens on dozens of photos of Pyongyang traffic wardens taken at exactly the same intersection from the same angle by different visitors through the years. Mr. Kim the Younger would not entertain the suggestion that we ask Mr. Bae to stop the van in order for us to set up shots of the lovely robots, but he had no objection to us lifting our cameras and shooting away as we passed their duty stations in the center of the street. Intersection after intersection Charles fired off a number of shots. The stern wardens occasionally caught a glimpse of Charles pointing a camera at them but never seemed to react. They maintained the standard-issue fierce *Juche* physiognomy at all times.

Then as if scripted we passed through a banal empty intersection Charles snapped a few shots of the warden assigned to that desolate spot, and as he lowered his camera she pirouetted and flicked her wrist to point the baton off in another direction, then in well rehearsed movements jerked her head with a mechanical fierceness and stole a menacing glimpse of Charles through her lavender shades.

He immediately grinned and offered a goofy, harmless wave and as our van pulled away, she pivoted on her sensible shoes, jerked her body into rigid alignment for the next set of gymnastic instructions, broke into a beaming open-mouthed smile, looked directly at Charles with a twinkle in her eye, then very quickly twiddled her white gloved fingers in a playful wave. For just that moment she was a beautiful, radiant woman unable to hold back the natural warmth and playfulness typical of youth. For that brief instant she was not only human, but accessible. Then with her regime-issued mean face she snapped to attention and fell back in to her syncopated gyrations in the middle of the empty street. All four foreigners sat grinning through the van's rear window as she faded into the distance.

For just that moment it was obvious that at least one of these Pyongyang background extras was a real, engaged, giggling human. Not too many years before that revelation a university-educated South Korean swore to me that North Koreans weren't completely human — just beneath their hair appear vestigial horns confirming a carpine, if not demonic, origin. He knew this to be true because he had served part of his time as a conscript on the DMZ where not him specifically but members of his unit encountered more than one emaciated KPA recruit with odd protrusions growing out of the skull. He promised.

A lasting memory from Pyongyang is of the swift, effortless passage through broad, empty boulevards and the eerie empty stillness that hung over the city as if in the grip of some silent epidemic. But there was no epidemic; there was only the isolation, both collective and individual, that came as the reward for the *Juche* Idea. The streets of Pyongyang are dark and empty, but thanks to *Juche* the darkness and emptiness are completely homegrown. They didn't need help from anybody to crawl into this predicament; they proudly achieved it on their own.

Mr. Bae drove us into the sinking darkness as Pyongyang was shuttered for the night. We arrived at a restaurant that appeared to be near the exclusive *Kwongbok* Street, but it was much too dark to recognize any landmarks. Though lights could be seen through open, screen-less windows, the Pyongyang streetscape was left in almost complete darkness. There were no working streetlights, no neon advertisements, no illuminated exteriors, just varying degrees of blackness. The city was just four nights away from a full moon, but clouds obscured any moonlight that would have helped out. And anyway, the light of a full moon would have felt like an unnecessarily wasteful gesture. The Dear Leader guided the people in the skill of producing light from electricity they generate, and they don't require assistance from the outside ... even from the moon. We ate a sumptuous meal without devoting too much energy to conversation. It had been a hard day of sightseeing and we were all famished.

The uniformed waitresses brought the usual assortment of *panchan* followed by grilled fish and grilled beef. The Kims sat at a table to our side and conversed between themselves in hushed tones and I couldn't help feeling like we were being evaluated. Wayward American capitalists in the Worker's Paradise on tourist visas for just the third time since the Yankee rascals had launched a sneak attack on the fatherland in 1950 surely must raise suspicion. As we ate, they peered over their uplifted bowls and averted their eyes when they were caught looking.

When we departed the restaurant, the neighborhood was pitch black and the streets were still without illumination. Other than the headlamps of the very few vehicles on the roads, the only light came from the murals of the Great Leader and/or Dear Leader, which were brilliantly lit at all cost, and from a few of the open screenless windows in the apartment blocks. Otherwise, Pyongyang was bathed in total darkness and we sat in silence as Mr. Bae drove us through deserted streets back to the *Yanggakdo* Hotel.

It was obvious that both Kims were tired at the end of our long day because when we arrived at the hotel, rather than usher us in and supervise us as they had the previous evening, they deposited us into the care of the dutiful and suspicious hotel staff, then swiftly withdrew to the waiting van and disappeared into the darkness.

This was the perfect opportunity to exercise our newfound freedom, and just like the primates held in the unbelievably lifelike surroundings of the new monkey habitat at the zoo, we were allowed to explore the facilities of the lifelike hotel at will and in complete independence. As long as we remained inside the hotel, we had complete freedom; therefore, Wally and I decided to go in search of the famed gambling den in the basement.

The casino at the *Yanggakdo* Hotel is another topic of heated debate among Koreaphiles. It exists; it doesn't exist. It is run by Chinese, and North Koreans are barred entry; it is run by North Koreans and is for the pleasure of Kim Jong Il's thuggish buddies. Profits from the casino keep the hotel open; the casino is a sham and no real money is used. The opportunity to wander into a North Korean casino and put some of these urban legends to bed was too alluring.

Down a spiral cement staircase in the hotel lobby we descended and sure enough, tucked in among a couple of restaurants and a spa, was a dwarf casino. It was just large enough to house about ten slot machines. From behind a desk in the back wall a thin young bespectacled croupier in tattered waistcoat peered at us silently with tiny, weak eyes. It was obvious that he was extraordinarily bored. Wally approached the desk and started rapidly speaking in Korean. The croupier looked at him sheepishly and responded in Chinese.

For the conspiracy theorists this would have been sufficient evidence to validate the Chinese actor theory. This lone acne-scarred and bespectacled croupier, dingy white shirt under an ill-fitting gold waistcoat that was spattered with greasy food stains, had been unable to respond to Wally's grammatically precise Korean. The more I looked at his facial features the more he looked Chinese — not Korean.

Wally pulled an American $5 note out of his wallet and slid it across the counter to the ChiCom croupier and from under the counter he pulled out a stack of twenty tokens for the slot machines and pushed them back with a grunt. I have never been attracted to gambling, but in the heat of the moment and under such immense peer pressure in the basement of a sequestered hotel on a guarded island in the middle of the capital city of the most isolated nation on earth, I pulled out two one-dollar notes and handed them to the ChiCom. Taking the eight tokens, I understood full well that I had just made a cash contribution to the regime of Kim Jong Il. The alcove containing the slot machines was reminiscent of the miniature casinos found on ferries that pass through international waters — painfully compact and impractical under any other circumstances. We appropriated all excess space in the alcove as we stood before the one-armed bandits. At eye level across the front of each slot machine, and in clear block letters in English, one line of capitalist text read: "Proudly Made in Nevada, USA."

Half the machines were out of order. They were fixed with laminated signs proclaiming as much in Chinese, English, and Portuguese. Macau's "Stanley" Ho Hung-sun was long ago reported to have been in cahoots with Kim Jong Il and was rumored to have invested in a Pyongyang casino. The US-made slot machines, the "out-of-order" notices in Portuguese, it was all falling into place. The Croupier wasn't a ChiCom, he was imported Macanese labor from one of Ho's casinos in the Macau Special Administrative Region. One conspiracy theory debunked, and one theory substantiated. I deposited one token after another, pulling the arm and watching the monotonous blur of symbols that to me were completely meaningless. In the end the eight tokens had disappeared into the bowels of the American-made machine and Kim and Ho split the two dollars in some pre-arranged contractually agreed portions and I was guilty of further supporting not only a corrupt regime, but also the vice of gambling. My heart raced.

Macau has long had ties to North Korea and in addition to legitimate diplomatic and business connections, the former Portuguese enclave has systematically been used as a conduit for money laundering and forgery, and as a legitimate and sometimes less than legitimate way to access the world's banking systems. It has also proven to be a valuable training ground for North Korean agents. Before being assigned the task of blowing up Korean Air flight 858 off the Burmese coast, the Mata Hari of North Korean espionage, Kim Hyun Hui, claimed to have been sent to Macau to pick up Cantonese language skills and to learn the rudiments of how humanity functions outside the restricted confines of the Worker's Paradise.

In 2005 the US Treasury Department blew the whistle on the Macau-based Banco Delta Asia and accused the institution of knowingly facilitating the North Koreans in laundering money; they also claimed that it had been going on for decades.[32] North Korea has maintained offices for various commercial entities in the enclave for years, the most infamous being the Zokwang Trading Company.[33] Like their British counterparts in Hong Kong, the Portuguese decided to dip deep into the colonial coffers and build an airport on reclaimed land just before repatriating the colony to the Chinese. When opened in 1995, one of the Macau International Airport's first tenants was none other than North Korea's Air *Koryo*. After the initial contact with the North Koreans in Bangkok, I made several more attempts at face-to-face meetings over the years. One of those attempts involved taking a taxi out to the new Macau airport just a few weeks after it opened, finding the Air *Koryo* office, then stumbling in unannounced and unwanted.

I knocked on the unmarked door, then let myself in, to the befuddlement of the North Korean Air *Koryo* staffer perched behind a desk reading a local newspaper. I explained in halting Korean that I was interested in catching one of the new direct flights from Macau to Pyongyang.

After a painfully long pause in which he looked at me in complete and total stupefaction, he said in accented English, "You already have a visa for North Korea?"

"No," I said with a confident smile. "I want to buy a ticket and arrange a visa. Can you help me out?"

Again he glared at me as the wheels in his brain spun round and round trying to make sense of this most extraordinary event. No amount of training could have helped a North Korean agent prepare for the possibility that a big sweaty white guy would one day walk in to the office for his operational front and in accented Korean ask to buy a round-trip economy-class ticket to the epicenter of cloak-and-dagger slickie boys. After what felt like an inordinately long time for him to formulate an answer, all the while the big white guy maintaining the goofy-yet-innocent grin, he looked down and silently picked up a ballpoint pen and a scrap of paper.

After writing a phone number on the paper he handed it to me and said, "When you return to Hong Kong call this number."

I thanked him and showed myself out of his secretive office. I had not told him I was going to Hong Kong, though I was ... I had a dinner date in Hong Kong with an old friend that very evening, but how did the North Korean know that? I boarded a ferry to Hong Kong and for the entire hour across the Pearl River estuary examined the scrap of paper which on one side had the phone number I was supposed to call, and on the other a series of random numbers and notes. None of it was decipherable, but all very mysterious.

As soon as the ferry docked, I was quickly stamped in to the territory at the immigration desk and went to the first pay phone I could locate, dropped a few coins in and dialed the number. After a brief pause a female voice answered in Cantonese. In English I said I was interested in visiting North Korea and wanted to know what steps would be required to secure the necessary visa.

In English with an unmistakably heavy North Korean accent the same voice asked, "Are you American?"

"No," I said, however, I didn't want to take the time to explain the whole complex and emotionally-charged Texas sovereignty thing so I added, "I'm Canadian."

She breathed deeply and I could sense that she was peering at me through the phone line just like her comrade in the brand new Macau International Airport had peered at me an hour earlier. Her handlers had not prepared her for this unexpected possibility. She excused herself and placed a hand over the receiver then had a rapid conversation with someone in the same room. It was impossible to make anything out — I couldn't even tell which language she was using.

Then her hand was removed and she said, "Please write down this number and call when you reach Macau...." She then rattled off the telephone number for the D.P.R.K.–Macau Travel Agency. She added, "North Korean visas cannot be obtained in Hong Kong except for Chinese citizens. All other passport holders must obtain their visas through our offices in Macau," and with that the phone unceremoniously went dead.

Only much later did the puzzle pieces come together to reveal that the D.P.R.K.–Macau Travel Agency was run by Wong Sing-wa who in 1990 had been appointed North Korea's unofficial representative in Macau. He was granted authorization to issue North Korean visas from the enclave and the entire operation was under the protective umbrella of the infamous Zokwang Trading Company. Wong Sing-wa and his long-time buddy "Stanley" Ho Hung-sun jointly invested in Pyongyang's *Yanggakdo* Hotel while it was still under construction. When it opened in 1995 it contained a massage parlor, a nightclub, the Macau Restaurant, and the casino in which we were standing.

Wally was on a roll and the blur of symbols had him up by a dozen tokens. I drifted towards the muffled sounds of gamblers. Around a corner was another small room with a couple of gaming tables and there I found a dozen Chinese yuppies watching their disposable income steadily drain in to the joint coffers of Wong Sing-wa, "Stanley" Ho Hung-sun, and Kim Jong Il. A sullen croupier stood over a Baccarat table, going through the motions as the gamblers quietly stood by with detached expressions. It was apparent that they were all struggling mightily with mobile telephone separation anxiety issues. The casino in the basement of the *Yanggakdo* Hotel carries none of the tense allure and certainly none of the classy sophistication suggested by James Bond films. The greasy-faced gamblers and disinterested croupier went at it as if they were doing so only because there was absolutely, positively nothing else to do.

Wally and I drifted out of the casino, collectively down by seven dollars. For both of us that was the extent of curiosity and the end of fun money. On the way back to the lobby we stooped under low-hanging concrete supports and moved around load-bearing cement columns that always seemed to find their way inconveniently into the middle of passageways.

The basement karaoke parlor was empty and sad with a lone uniformed attendant either waiting for the night's first customer, or counting down the hours until he could lock up and go home. He sat in the shadows and gazed into the distance, completely lost in state-sanctioned thought. The famed Macau Restaurant emitted the deep-fried aroma of Cantonese comfort food but was otherwise deserted. Other than the diminutive casino, the only other open establishment in the joint Wong-Ho-Kim subterranean pleasure complex was the spa. Koreaphiles long swore that the basement complex contained a massage parlor of questionable repute and different sources have reported over the years that the North Koreans have tried time and again to add prostitution to the list of money-making commercial ventures under state control.[41] I didn't see anything marked "massage parlor," but there was the spa and it was open. The vestibule contained three men, uniformed in white, leering at me from the shadows. I stepped around them to get at the list of services displayed on the counter, and as I did none of them budged. They didn't even look over their shoulders to see where I was going as I stepped over and around their outstretched legs. On scanning the list of garbled options I came to the final entry that helped me quickly determine that they had nothing on offer that I particularly needed: "Rub Down With Wet Towel €8." If this was the front door of a bawdy house, then they had done a wonderful job of disguise. The mental image of the three leering uniformed men, hair slicked back, cigarette ash tumbling down shirtfronts, manipulating my limbs while they administered wet towels was very, very unsettling. I stepped around and over their legs and they watched without moving as I silently departed. I suspect the customer satisfaction surveys come back with consistently low marks if those guys and their wet towels were all that was on offer.

Other visitors to the hotel have come out of North Korea and reported the entire menagerie of imported Chinese staff in the basement of the hotel are unceremoniously padlocked in at night. They have makeshift sleeping arrangements in corners and under tables. The next afternoon the padlocks are removed and hotel guests are allowed in — but the Chinese staff are not allowed out. This arrangement is enforced week after week after week until the contract period is completed and the subterranean servants are sent back to Red China — blinking and sporting an unnaturally pale complexion. At least that is the Koreaphile legend.

We deliberately passed by the lobby bookshop on the way back to the room and found it not only open, but staffed by the same bone-weary woman seated near the door fighting sleep with only moderate success. Tourists might not be able to visit the basement at 11:00 P.M. to pay for an illicit tryst with a stranger who maintains transaction-based morals, but they can stock up on regime-approved texts designed to explain the *Juche* Idea in expansive detail. And so we wandered in and started thumbing through the books and leaflets.

I picked up a flimsy 53-page tract entitled *Distortion of US Provocation of Korean War* and glanced at section headings such as *The Fake and the Camouflaged Offensive on the Eve of the War*, and *The "Story of the Attack from the North" Produced from the Pockets of Macarthur and Syngman Rhee*. As I examined the whacky little treatise with assertions pushing the logic envelope, I could feel a grin spread across my face. I had to resist the temptation to laugh at the infantile arguments. The reasoning put forth in the tract was well polished and painstakingly referenced emotional ranting, but emotional ranting nonetheless. I glanced up to find the woman at the door watching me from across the room. Our eyes met and a broad grin of contentment spread across her face. She saw my smile and just knew that I had started to see the *Juche* light. I was a potential convert to the cause; another lost lamb about to return to the fold.

It was strangely reminiscent of a visit to a Texas-based Ku Klux Klan bookshop in the mid 70s. The gap-toothed proprietress and her snuff-dipping man-partner leaned against the cash box and silently watched me meander through the shop and thumb through books and pamphlets from George Lincoln Rockwell, Nathan Bedford Forrest, and Lysander Spooner. To get a better look I held up a T-shirt festooned with the Rhodesian coat of arms and the slogan, "Rhodesia: it's Your War Too." With the shirt still aloft I glanced back at the register to see two racist rubes grinning at me, nodding, snuff-stained spittle sliding down their chins. Look Bubba! He's inspectin' the shirt! He un'erstands!

I took the meager little book to the counter and handed it to the woman. She grasped it with both hands and drew in a deep breath of satisfaction before reaching for the calculator and going through a meaningless series of calculations. In North Korea there is no sales tax, no VAT, no GST. She clattered away and checked her figures twice, then looked up and announced in halting, heavily accented English, "Six Euros."

In Korean I replied, "I don't have any Euros ... I'm not European. Will you accept dollars?"

Without answering she returned to her calculator and went through another complex series of calculations that she checked twice, then looked up and said in halting English, "Three dollars."

At the time the Euro was rapidly gaining value and the American dollar was floundering on the international currency market. I wasn't sure what the exchange rate should have been, but I knew that the quantity of dollars should have been significantly higher than the quantity of Euros required to purchase the little book.

I pulled out three notes and handed them to her and at that moment I saw a brief look in her eye that announced, "I don't know what the hell I'm doing." I briefly saw that look every time money changed hands. I saw that look every time a North Korean cashier suggested I give her fewer dollars than Euros.

By the end of my visit I concluded that none of them had the vaguest idea how to assign value to foreign currency. They knew the regime needed it and they knew that their job was to flog what North Korea had on offer in exchange for the much-desired foreign notes ... but that was about the extent of their understanding. The fact that a Euro was worth considerably more than a dollar had no apparent meaning. It was all monopoly money. Two green ones or six purple ones or a dozen of the ones with the picture of the pretty water buffalo and the yellow stripe ... they were all just strange notes from far away that the representative of the People's Cooperative Exchange Bureau came around and collected at the end of each day. Though she lost €4 on the exchange, she ended up with three of my foreign monies and I went back to the room at the end of the day with a new book. Everybody happy.

Day Three
Monday, 30 April 2007

Before the sun had crested the horizon, the Chinese-made phone was gobbling like an electric turkey. For the second day in a row Pyongyang was shrouded in early morning mist that made the city even quieter than its normal muffled state. Wally picked the phone up to hear the automated Chinese wake-up announcement and dropped the receiver back into the cradle without saying a word.

It was 6:30 and Pyongyang wasn't yet starting to rustle. Wally roused himself and went off towards the shower while I threw the window open and again looked out across the noiseless city from twenty-eight stories up. Unexpectedly, the telephone rang again. I picked it up and heard silence on the other end, then returned the receiver to the cradle. While I was in the shower the phone rang yet again. Wally picked it up and heard the same silence on the other end. It appeared that someone on the switchboard had been instructed to make absolutely sure the lazy bourgeoisie leisure-class visitors were awake.

In the lime green banquet hall we found Alice already seated at an empty table for twenty. She had also received mysteriously silent telephone calls that got her out of bed. Though Miss Paik, the maître d', had an almost empty banquet hall to work with, she would not be persuaded to allow us to sit together with Alice. Wally explained to her in Korean that we were part of the same group and we would prefer to sit together. Miss Paik quickly lowered the clipboard from her chest and glanced at the secret information, then looked across the hall at yet another empty table for twenty and said in clipped Pyongyang accented Korean, "Not possible, follow me."

We followed Miss Paik across the empty hall to the far side where she stood and waited until we were seated, then she turned and walked back to the door to await the next foreign guest. From across the empty hall Alice looked at us and shrugged.

Wally chuckled and got up out of his chair. As soon as he did it was obvious that he was going to reassign himself to sit with Alice at her empty table. However, as soon as he was standing, a uniformed waitress appeared and enquired in Korean if he needed assistance. Wally smiled and thanked her but said he was just going to join his friend across the hall to eat breakfast. With that the waitress shot a glance at Miss Paik, the maître d', and that was all the communication required — Miss Paik made a beeline for our table and demanded to know what was going on. Wally explained, "That woman over there is part of our tour group and I was just going to go sit together with her to eat breakfast."

"No," Miss Paik said in Korean as she checked her clipboard again. "Your seat is at this table. You have been allocated this space."

That was that. Alice was allocated a table for twenty in the far corner, we were allocated a table for twenty in the opposite corner. Between us were half a dozen identically empty tables. We were forty minutes early thanks to the automated phone calls and therefore the only guests to have arrived, but the allocation of tables had already been completed and we were bound to obey Miss Paik. After all, she may have been armed.

With Miss Paik forced to deal with us pesky foreigners, her duty station at the door was left unmanned and exposed. Charles breezed in to the banquet hall without going through the ritual of the clipboard and came directly to our table and seated himself. He greeted us with a smile. Suddenly a stream of foreign guests poured through the unmanned door and ever so slightly frazzled, Miss Paik rushed back to her station where she could wield the clipboard to its greatest advantage.

The stream of guests turned the empty lime green banquet hall into a fairly full lime green banquet hall in a matter of moments. The waitresses retreated through a door and returned to serve us where we sat. The buffet table was gone and with it went any semblance of choice. From behind closed doors at the rear of the hall they served bread, eggs, and a yogurt-like product in a drinking glass that is generally recognized among foreign visitors as something to be avoided. Though the South Koreans embraced milk two generations ago and now maneuver more comfortably among milk products, North Koreans remain lactose xenophobic. The yogurt-like product served as a testimony to their inexperience with milk. All across the lime green banquet hall the ever-so-slightly gray yogurt-like stuff went untouched. Coffee was quickly served at the table and there were many grimaces as the bitter reconstituted instant concoction was forced down. It was painful to know that we were having to grimace and squint to get the caffeine down, while at the same time a couple hundred kilometers to the south there were coffee snobs sipping delightfully complex orders at franchised coffee houses where people have learned to order things like a "three-quarter-decaf-quad-large-one-pump-whole-milk-one-pump-vanilla-one-pump-peppermint-stir-before-pouring-then-pour-120°-no-whip-Caramel-Macchiato," and the person behind the counter not only comprehends, but obeys. In the lime green banquet hall of the *Yanggakdo* Hotel, squinting-and-grimacing was the flavor of the day.

As the last of the bad instant coffee was drained, Mr. Kim the Elder appeared at our table. In addition to still being in the same dapper *whalon* attire he had worn since picking us up at the airport, he looked slightly rattled. He called Alice over so we would all be in the same table for his announcement.

With a serious expression and very concerned tone he said, "All foreigners are required to depart Pyongyang today, so there has been a change in itinerary ... we must go quickly."

With a sense of urgency verging on mild panic we all stood and quickly followed him out of the banquet hall. We exchanged a few quizzical looks, but mainly we just scurried through the hall behind Mr. Kim. Miss Paik, the maître d', stepped aside to allow us room to exit without ever lowering her precious clipboard.

At a brisk pace we followed Mr. Kim through the lobby and out the front door and out under the portico where the same fifty guides, minders, and drivers as the previous day loitered around in dark business attire and chain smoked. They watched us scurry towards the van with mild curiosity but did not show any sign of moving. When we got to the van Mr. Kim the Younger and Mr. Bae were there waiting with expressions of concern. They too were still wearing the same garments they had worn since picking us up at the airport.

With a solemn face and a lowered voice, Charles asked, "What's going on? Why do we have to get out of the city? Is there a problem?"

Mr. Kim the Elder replied, "We were not told why, but all foreigners are required to be out of Pyongyang today. We have no choice in the matter; we must go and we need to depart quickly." As he was speaking, the 50 drivers and minders under the portico were stamping out their cigarettes and hurriedly warming up their engines. Word was spreading quickly.

Mr. Bae had us rolling out of the parking lot before any other vehicle had moved and by the time we passed the proletariat golf course it was obvious that we were the first to depart. As we rolled along there was a modest attempt to bait one of the Kims into spilling the beans, but it soon became obvious that when they claimed they were not told why all foreigners had to get of Pyongyang — they were telling the truth. They simply didn't know.

Maybe a bomb threat? Maybe Kim Jong Il was out on his bicycle and the security detail didn't want to have to deal with foreigners? Maybe they were moving nuclear weapons through the city and didn't want prying eyes to see?

A subsequent search of the archives of the North Korean news agency revealed only two items that might have been cause for the complete evacuation of all foreign guests:

> Pyongyang, April 30 (KCNA)—General Secretary Kim Jong Il received a gift from Yadollah Tahernejad, first vice-president of the Central Council of the Iran Parties House, who is heading the delegation of the house on a visit to the DPRK. The gift was conveyed to Kim Yong Nam, president of the Presidium of the DPRK Supreme People's Assembly, on Monday by the first vice-president.
>
> Pyongyang, April 30 (KCNA) Kim Ki Nam, secretary of the Central Committee of the Workers' Party of Korea, met and had a talk with a delegation of the Workers' Party of Mexico led by Ricardo Cantu Garza, coordinator of its National Coordinating Committee, at the *Mansudae* Assembly Hall on Monday.

Maybe the combination of Iranian and Mexican delegations visiting simultaneously was sufficient enough to stretch North Korean resources thin. Maybe. It was all very sudden and mysterious. The Kims appeared to be as baffled as we were and had no more information than what they shared with us. The regime had simply decided that on that Monday the city of Pyongyang needed to be void of foreign visitors. In a place like that, no further explanation was required. We got in the van and moved out of the city as fast as Mr. Bae was willing to drive. (He was willing to drive at his rock steady fifty kilometers per hour).

We moved north through the city towards the *Pyongyang-Hyangsan* Expressway and Mr. Kim the Elder raised his voice so all could hear and said, "Unfortunately we will have to accommodate some changes in today's itinerary. Because we must get out of Pyongyang we will not be able to visit the University of Music. I am very sorry. However, since we must depart the city, we will be driving to Mount *Myohyang*."

This change was unfortunate because we had been scheduled to visit what was for me one of the highlights of the trip, the Cold War trophy USS *Pueblo*. The trade-off was the International Friendship Exhibition at Mount *Myohyang* where all of the state gifts, from elegant understated crystal bowls to stuffed crocodiles to gold-plated and diamond-studded AK47s, were on display as a testament to the world's admiration for the two Kims.

"Mr. Kim," I said with an edge of disappointment in my voice, "are you saying we will not be able to visit the *Pueblo*?"

"Well," he replied, "you need to make a decision about which stops on the itinerary you will omit."

In an embarrassingly short time the four of us had concluded that we were willing to forgo a visit to the Pyongyang Circus if we could squeeze in a visit to the USS *Pueblo*.

Charles, who had already seen a performance at the Pyongyang Circus, assured us that it would be, in many respects, a repeat of what we had seen at the *Arirang* Performance in May Day Stadium — just on a more modest scale. He announced our decision to the Kims and it was obvious both of them were a little startled and moderately disappointed. It was unclear if they wanted us to see the circus, or if they themselves wanted the chance to see the circus again — either way they were both slightly dazed at our surprising choice.

Mr. Kim the Younger said, "All right ... we will probably be able to stop by the *Pueblo* on our way back into Pyongyang, but it will be a very busy day."

After dreaming about it for years, it appeared at last we would visit the *Pueblo*. As an added attraction it looked like we might have the opportunity to see Madeleine Albright's infamous basketball at Mount *Myohyang*. The snap decision to push foreigners out of Pyongyang for the day was already looking serendipitous. Wally and I looked at each other across the van and exchanged the knowing nod of success. The *Pueblo* and the basketball — score.

The van continued heading north through the remarkably empty city. The odd shades of peeling pastel paint on the buildings was reminiscent of Tirana. Rather than brighten the place up, it amplified the faded shabbiness of it all. Again primary colors were nowhere to be seen. It was the first work-day of the week and in any other major city the rush hour would be under-way. In Pyongyang, however, the weary citizenry united in their struggle to roll over and catch a few more minutes of bourgeoisie shut-eye before return-ing to their assigned posts. Apparently Big Brother was still in bed, too.

Charles perked up as he recalled a question he'd wanted to ask, "What can you tell me about the new technology university?"

Mr. Kim the Younger lifted an eyebrow at Mr. Kim the Elder then asked Charles, "What university are you asking about?"

Charles looked at the ceiling of the van and slowly read off the words from the notes in his head, "The Pyongyang University of Science and Tech-nology."

Mr. Kim the Younger said emphatically, "There is no such university in Pyongyang ... are you sure about the name?" Before Charles could answer, the two Kims launched into a boisterous exchange in Korean in which they double-checked that neither had ever heard of any such university and that there is no way a foreigner would be able to know of such a thing without

North Koreans knowing of it first. After all, they reassured themselves, a university is a huge undertaking and it would have been all over the *Rodong Shinbun* and Kim Jong Il would have been out at the campus providing on-the-spot guidance at least once a term.

"No," Mr. Kim the Younger said nonchalantly in English as he sat back in his seat, "such a place does not exist in Pyongyang."

Charles pulled out a folded article he had carefully torn from a newspaper on his flight across the Pacific. It was a detailed piece about the new university and the potential to help North Korea make up for lost time in the area of technology development. It was to be a joint venture between the two Koreas with major funding coming from Evangelical groups in South Korea and the United States. It was all there in black and white with a photograph of the construction site filled with surveyor's stakes.

"Let me see that," Mr. Kim the Elder said curiously. Mr. Kim the Younger leaned over his shoulder and peered at the contraband clipping. Charles may have been guilty of trafficking in publishings of any kind.

In rapid Korean the Kims again exchanged reassurances between themselves that such a place simply could not exist ... and if it did, they would surely know of it.

Then Mr. Bae spoke for the first time in our visit. From behind big aviator lenses he looked in to the rear view mirror as he drove. "Mr. Kim ... I think I know that place," he said in two-pack-a-day Korean. "I live down there on the south side and I saw a new building going up. In fact, I was down there getting fuel for the van yesterday and saw it again. There was a sign and it said something about a university. Maybe this is the one they speak of? It's a new building site and it could be a university..."

Mr. Kim the Elder smiled and turned to the group in English and said, "Ah ... the driver says he knows the place ... he says it is a hospital."

We moved through the city and as we drove further north from the center the density of buildings did not thin. Then Pyongyang came to an abrupt end and the countryside immediately commenced, and at the same time we entered the *Pyongyang-Hyangsan* Expressway and Mr. Bae held the van at his rock steady fifty kilometers per hour.

Mr. Kim the Younger piped up and said, "The journey to Mount *Myohyang* is about two hours from Pyongyang, so sit back and relax and enjoy the scenery."

The *Pyongyang-Hyangsan* Expressway was reportedly constructed to facilitate transportation of goods to and from munitions factories up along the Chinese frontier. A spin-off benefit was that Mount *Myohyang* and its incredible beauty became accessible from Pyongyang for day trips. It stretches from Pyongyang's northern edge for 150 kilometers to the confluence of the *Chong-chon* and *Myohyang* rivers where it abruptly ends. For half an hour we drove north without encountering any other vehicles going in either direction. The four-lane highway was yet another grandiose cement monument constructed by the regime and it ran off to the horizon in well-maintained yet completely empty splendor.

The fields on either side of the Expressway were filled with men and women manually preparing for spring planting. Night soil was wrestled over the furrows in rickety wheelbarrows then spread by hand — literally. Clods of matted manure and straw were scooped up by hand and strewn across the barren field by people wearing manure-colored garments.

A few billboards came and went now and again — either a generic state-sanctioned propaganda message with accompanying socialist realism iconography, or for one of the new models from *Pyonghwa* Motors. All the reports touting North Korea's one and only billboard were long ago out of date. The North Koreans are moving down the slippery slope towards billboard blight that their southern cousins embraced decades ago.

The countryside continued to whirr past at a steady fifty kilometers per hour and we watched as group after group of tattered North Koreans worked their allotment of fields. Always in the background was a series of fluttering red banners or a jingoistic propaganda slogan along the horizon.

Earth-tone villages came and went. Each featured the same low mud buildings just far enough from the roadway to be beyond close inspection, but near enough to reveal that North Korean farming communities along the main north-south highway out of the capital city are very Spartan. As we moved further and further away from the city the colored corrugated roofing material was seen in fewer and fewer villages. Those villages even farther out of sight must have been on the bleak side of rustic. The propaganda slogans appeared as painted murals, as banners, in a Burma Shave–like series of signs staked across ridge lines, and in the form of huge Korean characters composed of carefully placed and whitewashed stones on barren hillsides: Long Live the Glorious Korean Labor Party, Long Live the Great Military-First Policy!, Devotedly Defending the Great Leader, Let's Sound the Drum of the Military-First Revolution Even Louder!, Let us Rush Forward at the Speed of the Military-First Revolution! And in an absurd testament to North Korea's penchant for denuded forests; Love Our Mountains and Forests.

Throughout the morning drive up the empty expressway the scene varied little: a cluster of earth-tone dwellings surrounded by worn-out fields being manually prepared for planting by worn-out people in worn-out clothes.

Taken from a vehicle moving up the *Pyongyang-Hyangsan* Expressway, this was the closest look our vanload of foreign visitors were granted of any of the agrarian collectives scattered across the countryside. From the car in the far distance villages could be glimpsed that were much rougher in appearance. Most of the fields were being manually prepared for planting on the day we passed through the area.

Encircling each cluster of houses in every direction were propaganda slogans to remind the people as they toiled in the dirt that they were the envy of the world and they had their peerless leader and his mummified father to thank for it. In other Third World nations there is often a society-wide layer of discarded plastic bags choking every trickle of stream, decorating every scrubby bush, and appearing at random in pinks and blues and yellows across a hungry landscape. Even in the impoverished Third World, there is enough affluence to allow for the random discarding of disposable plastic bags. Not in North Korea. The poverty in the countryside was so deep that North Koreans couldn't even afford to pollute their environment with cheap plastic bags.

Across South Korea, especially in the northern portion of the country, the hills and mountains are peppered with pre-dug trenches and strategically placed pillboxes, tank traps and helicopter landing pads on remote hilltops. From the vantage point of a city bus on a routine circuit across Seoul, it is possible to look up and see an empty pillbox waiting to be used, or a reinforced gun emplacement devoid of soldiers or guns but ready in an instant. They are so common that they are commonplace and residents no longer take notice. Even outside military installations, the countryside is military ready and should there be an invasion from the North the Southern defense forces would be able to quickly fall into position and start defending. If there is a Second Korean War, there will be no need for a Task Force Smith. For more than two hours on the *Pyongyang Hyangsan Expressway*, I looked for them. After so many years in Seoul I felt like I knew instinctively where to look; along ridgelines, at strategic junctions and in the rocks overlooking bridges and intersections. In two hours of countryside I spied just one lonely pillbox tucked away on a ridgeline overlooking the highway. It was identical to a pillbox on the Southern side of the DMZ and my eye instinctively caught the telltale perfectly rectangular slit of shadow in an otherwise natural landscape where perfect rectangles do not exist. That was it — one solitary empty pillbox. I used to see more while riding the bus to work in Seoul. Granted, the bulk of the pillboxes would be south of Pyongyang to the DMZ where the bulk of the soldiers and their accoutrements would be pre-positioned, but I expected to see considerably more preparation on the part of the world's third largest standing army.

Soon after the pillbox, to the east was a muted gray radome on the edge of some sort of North Korean military installation in the distance. It wasn't as if the North Korean military wasn't around; from the limited vantage point of the highway it appeared that in that central part of the country they just weren't dug in, at least not on the shoulder of the expressway. If they had been invaded in the past, one would think they would put more effort to preparing for similar aggression in the future.

A lone motorcycle, heading down the middle of the expressway in the wrong direction, rumbled past and Mr. Bae gently swerved the van around and back in to our lane as if nothing out of the ordinary had happened. As we drove away the motorcycle continued heading south down the middle of the northbound lane. Even though all the Koreans in our van had seen the motorcycle speeding down the wrong side of the divided highway, not a word was said. It was as if every trip up the expressway featured disoriented motorcyclists heading in the wrong direction and for them it was all mundane.

A curious structure loomed on the horizon and as we drew closer it was clear that the two-story building was surrounded by a packed dirt courtyard which was ringed in tall, spindly pines. All of us looked at the building in silence before someone turned to Mr. Kim the Elder and asked, "What is that building?"

Without hesitation Mr. Kim said, "That is a middle school." The immediacy of his answer and the matter-of-fact way in which he informed us created the impression that not only had the answer been scripted, but rehearsed.

Charles smiled and asked suspiciously, "Mr. Kim ... how do you know that is a middle school?"

Mr. Kim gave his trademarked slow and steady smile, and his eyes twinkled as he reassured us, "All middle schools look like that. They all have a play yard surrounded by pine trees. All over North Korea middle schools looks the same ... like that."

In the context of Kim Jong Il's *Juche* idea the suggestion that every single junior high school in every single commune, village, town and city looked exactly the same was not farfetched. In fact, in the North Korean setting it made sense. Why waste precious man-hours on alternate designs for a school building when the People's Committee on Revolutionary School House Construction has come up with a perfectly functional design that can be constructed at low cost to provide a school building?

Had we been close enough we could have confirmed his claim by checking to see if the requisite *Let Us Learn for Korea!* sign was mounted over the front door because each and every school in every corner of the nation mounts that motto over the front entrance. However, as we moved up the expressway at a steady fifty kilometers per hour, we were too far away.

Around the school the ragged commune members were busy in the fields. It was difficult to discern the ages of the laborers carrying buckets of manure and mud in to the brown, empty fields. They were all dressed in similar earthy colors from head to toe and they all performed the same basic task; haul a winter's worth of night soil out into the field by brute force, then spend the day spreading it evenly from the cart to the individual furrows. It was obvious that both men and women were clawing up clumps of dung and casting them in to the field, but it wasn't clear if it was a family affair. The laboring citizens were too far from the road to make out if the children were lending a hand.

Now and again, in the distance, yoked oxen could be seen doing some of the work. Once or twice on the trip north a tractor tore at the earth and turned up furrows, but for the most part the glorious chore of preparing the fields for spring planting was accomplished joyfully and cheerfully by the happy citizens who were thankful they had the privilege of living in the Worker's Paradise — the envy of the world. Ankle-deep in dirt, and elbow-deep in human shit one had to wonder if they really bought the "envy of the world" line. They all looked completely weary.

"Mr. Kim," I inquired, "isn't it a little early for the people to be preparing the fields? The weather is still cold at night and it will be some time before it is warm."

"The timing is right," he assured me. "The rains are coming and they have to get the fields ready before the rains come."

Rain, too much or too little, had been the scapegoat of the regime for almost a decade. If only the rains were normal then the people would prosper. If only the Yankee imperialists would stop their economic meddling and stand aside, then the mighty Korean people would see the rains return to normal and the cornucopia of abundance would once again proclaim Kim Jong Il's economic and agrarian brilliance.

The volume of manual labor in the fields on the day we passed was staggering, but it begged the question: what do they do during the labor-intensive times like harvest? So I asked.

Mr. Kim smiled because this was a topic that allowed him to, yet again, reveal to us the depth of unity across the North Korean society. It allowed him to provide a concrete example of how the people banded together to make sure they remained the envy of the world.

"During harvest time," he explained, "people from the cities volunteer to travel to the farms to help with labor. Students, soldiers, office people, everyone..."

It reminded me of tales of forced volunteerism in Burma where happy citizens are rounded up and volunteered for civic projects by men with deep frowns and big guns. "Mr. Kim, you mean the people have a choice? They don't have to volunteer or they have no choice in the matter and have to go?"

"No," he laughed, "people do it because they want to. I did when I was younger ... I did it many times and enjoyed it. I traveled to the farms and helped with whatever they were harvesting at the time."

I chuckled openly at him and asked again, "Mr. Kim ... you want me to believe that you and your colleagues left the city of your own will and traveled out to a farm to toil in the sun for three weeks ... every harvest season? Nobody made you do it, you just did it because you wanted to?"

"Of course! All of my friends were doing it, so I wanted to join along and travel to the countryside with them. It is called *Minbak*,[1] and it's a kind of exchange where city people assist the farmers. But these days the situation is different. Some cooperative farms don't really want the city people to come out and help because these days they are required to pay for the labor. The volunteers receive a receipt for the work and are later paid in rice. The cooperatives find this system too expensive and would rather not have the assistance just so they can avoid the cost."

Maybe this is the first sign of "socialism with Korean characteristics." If cooperatives in rural locations are authorized to tell the city slickers that they aren't wanted because they charge too much for their services, then maybe the economic ice is just starting to break. Rumors of a state-sanctioned flirtation with rudimentary capitalism have been slipping out under the barbed wire for several years: farmer's market right in the heart of Pyongyang, peasants being granted permission to barter, and whispered rumors of cooperatives establishing a market price for their crops and then selling it for cash ... all supposedly with the blessing of the regime.

Mr. Kim the Younger gazed contentedly out the side window as we crawled on through the middle of the nation. The earth-tone fields and earth-tone villages sprinkled with earth-tone peasants came and went along with their bright red propaganda messages. Charles pointed at one of the slogans and asked for a translation. Mr. Kim the Younger gave a languid smile and recited, "We have nothing to envy from the outside world."

The van hummed along the empty highway and we sat in collective silence for a while, but after it was obvious that the scenery wasn't going to change, I asked Mr. Kim the Elder if he recalled the Pyongyang International Sports and Cultural Festival for Peace in 1995.

The enthusiasm with which he smiled before launching into his answer revealed that not only did he remember, but he was a wrestling aficionado and understood the significance of the historic matches on those cool April evenings. "Oh, it was wonderful," he sighed. "There was Muhammad Ali, Ric Flair, Inoki, and Hirokidaji. Hirokidaji was given the idea of the tournament by Kim Il Sung himself! So he organized the event and invited the Americans to come ... and even the Americans came!" [2]

My understanding was that the Japanese wrestler Antonio Inoki had organized the event in the twilight of his sweaty career. At fifty-two years of age Inoki decided to draw his very successful wrestling career to a grand conclusion with the world's largest wrestling event. If one plans to hold the world's largest event, then one requires the world's largest stadium, so he arranged to stage the show at Pyongyang's May Day Stadium for a huge television audience in Japan. His professional mentor had been the late *Rikidozan*, father of professional wrestling in Japan. As any self-respecting North Korean wrestling fan will tell you, Rikidozan was only his ring name, his real name was Kim Sin Rak and he was actually North Korean. Staging the event in North Korea would provide opportunity to pay homage to his late mentor while simultaneously securing use of the world's largest stadium and the world's most wrestling-starved fans.

Mr. Kim reminisced about the wrestling for a while then drifted off in to silent memories of the two-night event and ended up looking off at the horizon with a broad smile on his face, eyes half closed. As far as he was concerned for those two days the attention of the globe was focused on the floor of May Day Stadium and all eyes were on North Korea as the galaxy's most important and prestigious professional wrestling event unfolded.[3]

As the Kims drifted towards sleep in the purring van, I told Charles and Allee about the Ric Flair propaganda leaflet. With quizzical expressions they asked for clarification and it was obvious that like most people they were unaware of North Korea's penchant for leaflet drops.

The North Koreans had it down to an art form. For decades, when the wind was blowing in the right direction, the North Koreans would launch balloons tethered to bundles of propaganda leaflets. Within the bundles were placed little explosive devices just powerful enough to harmlessly scatter the leaflets into the lower atmosphere. If the timing was just right, the cloud of propaganda drifted down on heavily populated areas of South Korea to spread tidings of good cheer. Then in 2000, subsequent to the face-to-face summit between the Dear Leader and Kim Dae-jung, both sides agreed to cease and desist with the government-backed leaflet barrage and the showers of propaganda leaflets came to a quiet end.

The leaflets were usually printed on slick paper and featured photographs of huge cement monuments, happy workers seated behind tables buckling under the weight of the cornucopia of abundance, peasants reaping bumper crops, and ubiquitous images of the Leaders both Dear and Great. They contained carefully worded messages to their compatriots in South Korea explaining how pleasant life north of the DMZ is and how they are welcome to join the loving family created by the Dear Leader if only they would renounce the Yankee-puppet government of the South and make their way to Pyongyang.

The North Koreans are so painfully unaware of the opulence South Koreans now enjoy that they did not recognize how unappealing their photographs of cement monuments and well-scrubbed peasants were. South Koreans capable of using their credit cards to go online and order exotic and expensive consumer products for immediate home delivery are not impressed by photos of stiff-looking uniformed North Koreans seated behind tables featuring pyramids of abundant ripe apples. The fighting has been over for half a century and while South Korea races down the path to social corpulence, North Korea is still necessarily preoccupied with having enough apples to go around. It is the preoccupation with the apples, and the stodgy fashions, and the boxy Soviet-style farm equipment, and the never ending parade of cement monuments and buildings that made the propaganda leaflets so collectable. The only problem is that it was illegal to possess them.

When I was a resident of South Korea, northern propaganda leaflets peppered southern lawns and parks and blew down cavernous city streets and landed in schoolyards and in trees and begged to be picked up and examined. They were little tiny windows to an otherwise closed society. Every time I leaned over to retrieve one a well-meaning South Korean would scold me. Apparently only the police had special authorization to pick them up and take them away because everybody else knew that to be caught with a North Korean leaflet was instant life-long imprisonment and probably torture — possibly to the point of death. At least that was the word on the street. So I spent years scampering about South Korea surreptitiously collecting as many as I could while everyone else stepped around them like stepping around the homeless. I squirreled them away in a secret hidden compartment behind a row of economic reference books and late at night, while the rest of Seoul was busy drinking *soju* or watching the ever-popular housewife singing contest on television, I would crouch in a dark corner of my little flat, pull out the illicit communist leaflets, and thumb through them again and again and again.

US Army Private First Class Joseph White was a collector of the leaflets too. He called them "odd testimonials to the joys of life under the communist regime." Eventually he defected to North Korea, and before dying under questionable circumstances, he was featured in his own propaganda leaflet that was strewn across the South Korean countryside in the early 1980s.

Though propaganda leaflets aren't very sophisticated, at one time both Koreas put enough stock in them to invest in extensive campaigns. While I was well positioned to see firsthand evidence of the annual barrage from the North, I was oblivious to the Southern leaflets coming from the South. They went at a different time of year when the winds were blowing north and they were inevitably launched from military bases abutting the DMZ. I had heard South Koreans obstinately deny that they would ever stoop to the dastardly practice of leaflet drops, but the proof is in the pudding and Wally carried the pudding around in his wallet for years.

It was a South Korean propaganda leaflet from the early '80s designed to travel north on a balloon and then flutter down in to the hands of some poor peasant or a disgruntled KPA conscript and entice them to trudge south. The leaflet was printed in anticipation of the 1988 Seoul Olympics. The lucky North Korean who found the leaflet was assured that it could be redeemed for free passes to the Olympic sporting events; all they had to do was make their way south in a country where internal movement is highly restricted,

cross over the most heavily armed strip of land on the planet without stepping on any of the 1.05 million antipersonnel and antitank mines on the
southern side of the DMZ, and then get past another 75,000 antipersonnel
mines in South Korean rear areas, navigate through the clogged roadways of
South Korea to Seoul without being noticed and reported by any dutiful
South Korean citizens, and show up at the entrance gate at *Chamshil* Stadium
on the precise morning of the event and hand over the leaflet at the turnstile
and expect the uniformed volunteer ticket taker to recognize the crumpled
propaganda leaflet as a legitimate entrance pass.

Even though there was no fine print stating that the offer was not good
in Alaska or Hawaii/must be 18 years of age to enter/no purchase necessary/
void where prohibited, and even though the leaflet had been printed with government funds as part of a government-funded campaign, it was highly doubtful that on that Saturday morning in September as the Olympic road show
was about to start up again with an elaborate Korea-themed Opening Ceremony, a volunteer ticket taker was going to look at the leaflet in the hands of
a disheveled KPA conscript, uniform in tatters, and say, "Hey, you made it!
Welcome to Seoul, cousin, enjoy the show!"

The purring of the van put Mr. Kim the Younger to sleep in the front
passenger seat and Mr. Bae's steady driving up the expansive empty expressway was quickly making the rest of us drowsy.

Wally asked about Kim Jong Il's trademark attire — that odd amalgama-
tion of military uniform and polyester leisure suit — and we were all awake
in anticipation of the answer. Mr. Kim the Elder smiled in such as way as to
indicate pleasure that his foreign guests were showing respectful interest in
the Dear Leader.

"It is called a *jamba*," he said, and four foreign hands raised foreign note
pads and jotted the word down in four different ways. "He always wears that
uniform; it is like his trademark!" Mr. Kim added.

Charles agreed that the style was interesting enough that he wouldn't
mind getting one if they were available for the rank and file.

Mr. Kim looked at his watch and then gazed at the horizon for a moment
before saying, "It is possible that we could stop by a tailor shop when we get
back to Pyongyang and you could be quickly fitted if you are really interested."

With that, Wally and I sat forward, interest piqued. To stroll the streets
of the Western world in a genuine North Korean–made Kim Jong Il–style
jamba would be pretty sweet. We all three quickly agreed that a visit to the
tailor late in the day would be well worth the effort. Charles was due to return

to North Korea with a second tour group a few days after our little group departed, so he would be well placed to pick up any tailoring that we had done. We were giddy with the prospect and Mr. Kim was delighted with our giddiness.

"Mr. Kim," I said, "does Kim Jong Il have his *jambas* made out of *vinalon*?" It occurred to me that if I had the option, I might as well go for the *vinalon* to make it even more thoroughly authentic.

"Excuse me?" he said as if he had never heard of North Korea's miracle fiber.

I repeated my question with careful attention to pronunciation.

"*Vinalon*?" he would ask, puzzled.

"*Vinalon*," I would repeat, carefully pronouncing each syllable, as a North Korean would say the word.

This exchange went back and forth a few times with Mr. Kim looking more and more perplexed and sucking more and more air through his closed teeth.

"*Vinalon* ... what is this *vinalon*?" he finally asked.

It was inconceivable to me that Mr. Kim would not know the glorious *juche* fiber, the people's textile, the miracle fabric from the North. Surely at least one of the Leaders, Great and/or Dear, has visited the February 8th People's *Vinalon* Factory in Sunchon to provide on-the-spot guidance. Something as significant as on-the-spot guidance would surely signify the importance of whatever was on-the-spot; in this case *vinalon*. It must have been my pronunciation I told myself, so I whipped out a notebook and clearly wrote the word in Korean. He took a look at my notebook, silently moved his lips as he formed the word with his mouth, and then slowly, silently shook his head.

"I do not know this thing, *vinalon*. Where did you hear of it?"

I was crestfallen. For years I had heard of the North Korean miracle fiber created from limestone. I had been told that the same versatile fiber was suitable for not only fashionable formal wear, but also canvas shoes, medium gauge marine rope, tablecloths and parachutes. It was the renaissance fabric, the ultimate wedding gift, the product that would eventually thrust North Korea to the top of the technological hill. With a half-life equal to polyurethane packing pellets, and durability far surpassing that of heavy-duty rain tarps, *vinalon* was the everyman of the fabric working world. I knew so because the propaganda leaflets had told me. They fluttered down on the streets of Seoul and landed right there on the sidewalk in front of the Gucci shop, and in the shrubbery next to the Burberry Outlet, and in the cramped parking lot beside the Prada Showroom. Sometimes they even drifted down on the front step of the Fendi shop.

"Mr. Kim, *vinalon* is one of the most famous products in North Korea. It is a cloth made from anthracite coal and limestone..." I said, but even as the words left my mouth I knew the conversation was finished. Either *vinalon* was not on the approved discussion topic list, or he genuinely didn't know about North Korea's greatest single achievement in the field of general haberdashery. I looked down at his jacket and could not tell if what I was looking at was *vinalon*, or a wool blend. My dream of departing North Korea in a tailored plastic trash bag was dashed.

The expressway paralleled the Chongchon River and provided for a slight change in scenery. In addition to the earth-tone cooperatives surrounded by earth-tone fields, now there was the addition of the clear running river. Along the banks were little earth-tone irrigation works that directed some of the water out into fields, and every now and again there were fish traps constructed from bamboo and planted into the riverbed like an aquatic corral. Occasionally we passed an earth-tone peasant or two squatting in the reeds along the shore with a fishing pole extended out over the surface of the water. Their modest bicycles were always somewhere near, leaning against a tree or standing up in the reeds.

Kilometer after kilometer we pressed on and the ubiquitous dirt-colored communes and villages passed again and again at a steady fifty kilometers per hour. I glanced back and discovered that, without warning, we had been joined by a long line of buses and vans filled with foreign tourists. The other drivers were all precisely matching Mr. Bae's steady fifty kilometers per hour and we moved up the expressway in an unchanging queue, content to roll along no faster and no slower than everybody else. We were steadily vacating Pyongyang *en masse* and in our wake we left behind a city devoid of any foreigner — a city in which the North Koreans had a full day to openly do whatever they wanted to do and the outside would never know.

In the Worker's Paradise one quickly learns that dramatic fanfares frequently indicate something of little interest and questionable significance is about to be revealed. Conversely, the significant often materializes out of thin air with no warning. So it was with a nondescript road sign beside the expressway that very clearly stated (in Korean) that we were quickly approaching the exit for *Yongbyon*.

Unless able to read Korean for themselves none of the foreigners in our growing convoy would have any clue that we were passing quite near North Korea's infamous nuclear reactors. Wally and I glanced at each other and as had happened multiple times on the visit, exchanged silent knowing grins.

Up and down the *Pyongyang-Hyangsan* Expressway one could see small collections of buildings that were identical to the buildings in all the other villages. The villages become more substantial and considerably more modern as one draws closer to the city.

Just a few kilometers off the expressway was the *Yongbyon* Nuclear Scientific Research Center — Kim Jong Il's ultimate trump card. It was work carried out at that secluded complex that had allowed North Korea, just six months prior, to join the nuclear club, and it was that complex that gave North Korea a very big bargaining chip at the international negotiation table.

Somewhere to our left, just behind the sad little denuded hills, was North Korea's Manhattan Project.

After a few kilometers of silence, Alice smiled and asked, "Mr. Kim ... can you explain what *juche* means?"

That was apparently on the approved topics list because Mr. Kim the Younger launched into a spirited description of the homegrown philosophy of self-sufficiency and self-reliance. He didn't get very far, however, before he had sidetracked himself into a detailed and prolonged explanation about how Kim Il Sung had come to power. He provided the majestic made-for-the-silver-screen epic tale of the pure-hearted lad with anti-imperialist tendencies and remarkable oratory skills, of how the lad made the heartbreaking decision to walk through the wild mountains alone at age thirteen to seek refuge in China where he educated himself (and in turn started educating his neighbors and colleagues) and marshaled a bunch of ruffians who became his band of guerilla fighters, and of how he cut one from the herd to become his wife, and how his fighters had single-handedly defeated the Japanese occupiers in 1945, and thus Kim Il Sung brought World War II to a conclusion and expelled the evil Japanese colonizers, and of how the Soviets had begged Kim Il Sung to triumphantly return to Pyongyang and establish the Worker's Paradise...

Wally sat quietly as long as he could, then could take no more. He politely challenged Mr. Kim's tale and pointed out the habitual North Korean inconstancies in the myth, and the anachronisms and chronological gaffes, and logical fallacies. He recited a truncated version of what Western scholars believe to be more accurate — Kim Il Sung was the nominal head of one of the weaker of five factions vying for power and through nefarious means and with a little help from well-placed associates, against all odds, he rose to the top.

As Wally concluded his version of Kim Il Sung's rise to power, Mr. Kim the Younger had nothing to say. He was curled in his seat feigning sleep. Obviously he had never encountered a tourist capable of reciting chapter and verse while steadily using propositional logic to dismantle the official myth. Mr. Kim the Elder gazed off at the horizon, oblivious to the conversation.

The home-grown *Juche* philosophy was a concept born in the nation's preadolescence when it was important to demonstrate to the other members of the Comintern that North Korea could grit its collective teeth, clench its collective jaw, and take care of its own. This created a Gilligan's Island–style isolation with all the hardships and absolutely none of the tropical pleasures. The indigenous scientific community played the role of the Professor and assumed responsibility for reverse-engineering tractors, inventing *vinalon*, and eventually building a nuclear bomb. The Korean diaspora in Japan returned to play Thurston Howell III and his wife "Lovey" by hauling sack-loads of hard currency to their new home and handing it over to the authorities and then using can openers made from coconuts and flimsy bamboo sewing machines like everybody else. The voluptuous Ginger was selected to be Pyongyang's traffic warden, while Gilligan and the Skipper were left to farm the cabbage, crawl down the hole and mine the coal, play the accordion and tuba during speed battles, and guard the frontier against imperialist aggression. If they were fortunate they would be granted permission to wed Mary Anne after their quotas had been exceeded. Gilligan and the Skipper were miserable farmers to begin with, but long periods of inclement weather, drought, and flood quickly emptied the homemade bamboo silos and warehouses. Eventually they arranged to receive food handouts on the sly while maintaining the ruse of *juche* self-sufficiency. Gilligan and the Skipper used the Professor's capacity to create nuclear weapons as the bargaining chip to get basic necessities delivered to the secret cove on the far side of the island when nobody was looking. From the outside the castaways appear ready to succumb to defeat, but somehow they keep finding enough bamboo and vines, sticks and coconut shells to lash together just enough makeshift commodities to keep stumbling forward with weekly sitcom predictability

The farther north we ventured on the expressway, the more starkly barren the hills became. The trees had long ago been felled for fuel or to make way for much-needed additional stepped rice paddies. The result was an almost treeless environment of browns and tans. Hill after hill was left almost completely denuded. The few trees that remained were scrubby and good for little. The Korea depicted in ancient paintings showed lush forests teaming with abundant wildlife, pristine rivers, sparkling mountains, and a vibrant people preoccupied with the finer aspects of culture. What I saw through the window of the van was a deforested near-moonscape populated by peasants who were almost indistinguishable from the dirt in which they toiled.

In a frontal assault on logic, the local authorities selected those same deforested hills on which to require peasants to lay out whitewashed stones on the barren, rutted ground to form four huge Korean characters that proclaimed the ironic message, "Love Our Mountains and Forests." It was as if the regime had made room for sarcastic irony.

Mr. Bae veered right and we exited the expressway towards the east. The long line of buses and vans filled with foreign guests followed down a narrow little side road. It was a good thing we had all exited because from our new vantage point it was clear that the expressway rose up on pylons as if preparing to enter the mountains immediately before us, but abruptly ended with the final section of the unfinished expressway hanging out in the air over the merging *Chongchon* and *Myohyang* rivers. It was as if the construction crew had worked until running out of cement and steel and had then gone home for lack of anything better to do. There had been no marking of any kind to indicate the expressway, in effect, became the ascending ramp for an Evel Knievel gorge-jumping stunt and as of yet there was no corresponding descending ramp in place on the other side.

Off the expressway, the van crept by a gaggle of earth-tone citizens man handling cross ties and rail tracks. It appeared that the assigned task was to manually reconstruct a washed-out railbed that ran parallel to the road. Similar to the peasant women who mended the road by hand, for tools these men had little more than crowbars, shovels, and straw hats. They looked tired and only marginally interested in the work at hand but didn't stop the slow, steady toiling as we crept past.

Mr. Bae carried on and the van crept beyond the construction site and onto a narrow road heading off towards the mountains in the east. He knew that even the slightest hesitation would mean losing his position at the head of the queue of vans and buses and every ten minutes we saved on arrival was ten minutes sooner we could commence the return journey to Pyongyang. For us it was a once-in-a-lifetime opportunity to peek at Kim Il Sung's subterranean trophy case; for Mr. Bae it was just another afternoon sitting in the parking lot re-reading state-sanctioned newspapers and chain smoking filterless cigarettes.

After a bend in the road, we were abruptly at the foot of the ominous International Friendship Museum. Surrounded by dramatic hills, the museum is a stereotypical Korean building of mock-traditional design with emphasis on carefully carved gray stone that not only dramatically adds to the weight, but also to the degree of importance placed on the structure. This wasn't just another mammoth cement monster, this was carefully crafted from stone — or at least it had a stone veneer over a cement-monster frame. The roof was of a traditional design borrowed from Korean temples and painted in the same painstaking detail with ornate, festive colors on the underside of the eaves. The massive, ornate building sat snugly beside the steep mountainside and looked somehow out of place — as if one of Kim Il Sung's trophy buildings from downtown Pyongyang had been absent-mindedly left behind in the mountains. The grandiose entrance to the enormous edifice was ill-suited to the setting.

But therein was the secret, the looming massive entrance was just that — an entrance — nothing more. Behind the huge steel doors was a labyrinth of tunnels that went deep into the heart of the mountain. The International Friendship Museum is housed in tunnels under the mountain, not in the elaborate building that serves as nothing more than an elaborate entrance. The ornate structure looming over us was just the housing for the blast-proof door designed to protect the collection from nuclear attack. The Great Leader knew that the imperialist running-dog Americans and their bellicose attitude meant his prized collection of diplomatic knickknacks was pre-programmed for a nuclear strike. In his infinite wisdom he decided to sink the valuable collection well out of reach of the meddling capitalists. It is, in fact, a bunker/museum and one Dutch visitor gave it the poetic name, *"De bunkermusea voor de internationale vriendschap."*

A Ceremonial Guard from the Korean People's Army stands watch on a wooden plinth at the entrance of the original wing of the International Friendship Exhibition at Mount _Myohyang._ The underground labyrinth is used to store thousands of state gifts that serve as a testament to the world's admiration for Kim Il Sung. A hundred meters away is the entrance to the new underground wing of the exhibition where tribute gifts for Kim Jong Il are housed.

Mr. Kim hustled us from the parked van towards the entrance. Already there were North Koreans in their Sunday-go-to-meeting finest gathering at the front door in preparation to swarm. They instinctively drifted to the side and allowed the foreign guests to enter first. Little did they know — every foreigner in Pyongyang had just arrived at the far end of the parking lot and was about to jump queue. From a different direction a gaggle of uniformed school students appeared, then the KPA in battalion strength. The numbers at the entrance were quickly escalating and Mr. Kim wanted us inside and in front.

Beside the ornate doors, on a small wooden platform, stood a member of the Korean People's Army in a ceremonial dress uniform. Like the platform, he was small and wooden. His eyes silently flicked around as he stole glances at the quickly growing crowd, but otherwise he was a statue of poise. His nickel-plated AK47 (with nickel-plated bayonet affixed) hung across his chest on a strap and was held in place by a gloved thumb through the strap.

Mr. Kim the Younger would have preferred for us to hurry through the doors and jump ahead of the quickly growing crowd, but he knew the routine. He stood with us and waited for the guide to arrive. Eventually she appeared in requisite flowing velvet and greeted us in a soft voice. Before anyone could respond, she turned to the closest tourist, who happened to be Charles, and said, "Look at the huge, massive doors that are the entrance of the museum." Mr. Kim translated her words.

The doors were truly massive. Each door was at least four meters tall and almost equally as wide. The pair of doors was set into stone-covered walls that appeared to be at least a meter and a half thick. As we stood waiting other groups joined us and admired the huge doors.

The guide smiled at Charles and said, "Go ahead ... try to open it." It appeared that her routine included pauses for admiring visitors to marvel at how incredibly large the doors were and how impossibly heavy they must be and, oh, no normal person could possibly possess the strength to force open such massive, substantial, hulking and unwieldy doors. She smiled and glanced around at the others in the group to gauge the reaction when Charles eventually squealed in confused delight like all the rest of them. Except Charles didn't squeal in confused delight. Charles had seen the routine before on a previous trip and when the guide invited him to open the door he reached up with one hand, grabbed the enormous handle, and threw the door open as if it were a veneered hollow-core closet door in a suburban tract house. Before his arm was completely extended, he was striding forth into the museum without uttering a word. Mr. Kim lit up in delight because by not playing into the guide's routine, Charles had jockeyed our little group back into the pole position.

The guide was left in the doorway explaining to no one in particular that the extraordinarily heavy doors could so easily be moved because the Great Leader had instructed the builders how to perfectly balance them so that even a child could push them open despite weighing tons. Scores of visitors jostled past and entered the museum as if she wasn't even there. Mr. Kim hurriedly ushered us to a counter where smiling, glassy-eyed uniformed attendants relieved us of all photographic equipment and in return we were all provided a pair of enormous one-size-fits-all felt galoshes. Running down the wall of the vestibule was a series of padded benches and Mr. Kim the Younger urged us to sit on them and explained that we needed to hurry. There was urgency in his voice and the quickly growing queue at the camera-for-galoshes exchange counter explained why. Pyongyang had undergone a one-day banishment of all non–Koreans and the deported had all ended up on exactly the same sightseeing schedule. All of us quickly pulled the oversized galoshes over our shoes and stood to go.

Morning fog has yet to burn off in the *Mohyang* Mountains as the day's first visitors start to gather in front of the entrance to the International Friendship Exhibition at Mount *Myohyang*. The underground labyrinth is used to store thousands
of state gifts given to the Great Leader. The heavy doors are reportedly designed
to withstand a nuclear blast and protect the tributes for the enjoyment of any
post–nuclear survivors. The elaborate building is little more than a façade for
the entrance to the underground treasure trove.

I was as excited as I had been since my arrival in the Worker's Paradise.
Seeing the huge statue of Kim at *Mansudae*, standing under the piddly (by
Texas standards) *Juche* Tower, and riding in a metro system that may or may
not be Potemkin in nature were all fun, but stepping into a subterranean
nuclear bomb-proof bunker filled with communist knickknacks, nonaligned
bric-a-brac, and the famed basketball from Madeleine Albright was surely the
high point of the trip and certainly a pivotal point in my life. I know because
the guide informed me of the fact.

As Mr. Kim translated, she said, "Welcome to the International Friendship Museum. This will be the high point in your trip, and for some people
this is a pivotal point in life."

She led the group towards a wall where a map of the world tallied the gifts that had piled up during Kim Il Sung's lifetime. According to the information on the map, within the bowels of the museum were 221,411 gifts from 179 nations.[4] Then the guide recited what I had seen written again and again in the accounts of visitors who had gone before me. She said, "Last week an English tourist was here and he calculated that 221,411 gifts would be a gift every day for four hundred years!"

She beamed in revealing this nugget of clear miscalculation and paused to take in our reaction to such an interesting tidbit. I had seen it time and again, a tourist of some Western nation other than the US marvels at the vast outpouring of gifts from admiring fans and does a quick mental calculation to reveal to the guide the rate of gifts per day. If a foreign visitor said it, then it must be accurate, and if a foreign tourist said something accurate about the Great Leader, then it bears repeating.

Before we were allowed to progress down into the collection the guide explained that we were to be given the honor of showing our respects to the dearly departed yet omnipresent President for Eternity, Kim Il Sung, and with that we stepped around a corner and came face to face, yet again, the image of the eternally deceased President for Eternity. This time it was a gleaming white marble statue. By this time everyone knew the drill and we required no additional instructions. The guide glided up silently to an unmarked spot in front and slightly to the side, we queued up along an invisible line with Kim the Elder on our right flank and Kim the Younger on the left. The Koreans bowed deeply towards the statue and paused. While they were down in their nadir we were still up at our collective apex flicking a quick "Albright" towards the stone mannequin.

After the obligatory bows, while still in the presence of the statue, we were invited to take in some of the overflow gifts that were displayed right there. Josip Broz Tito had once presented Kim Il Sung with a gold cigarette case hand crafted in Yugoslavia and there in a display case it sat. On the wall was an AK47 from the Popular Liberation Movement of Angola in Zambia. President of the Council of State and President of the Council of Ministers of Cuba Fidel Castro sent a pitcher and cups carved from stone and there in a display case they waited. A painting presented to Kim Il Sung by his pal Sihanouk showed Southeast Asia being swept clean of US imperialists as the fists of China, Laos, Cuba, Vietnam, and North Korea jointly hammered a hapless US soldier into submission.

Many of the gifts were meticulously labeled with full titles and names; others were garbled to the point of creating more questions than answers. One item had an adjoining card with the description, "A gift from the son of Samdeck Norodom Sihanouk, Head of State of Cambodia on 30 June 1970," without bothering to indicate which one of his nine or ten sons it might have been or if the son or the father had been head of state. A stuffed crane from Billy Graham was presented during a 1992 visit and the card stated, "From the religious leader of the United States."

Madeleine Albright had presented Kim Il Sung a silver bowl and it sat modestly behind glass and under light. As I looked it was more than I could take and I asked Mr. Kim the Younger if at some point we would be seeing the famed basketball.

"I believe," he said indignantly about the incredibly cheesy gift, "the basketball to which you refer was presented to the Dear Leader Kim Jong Il—not the Great Leader Kim Il Sung. Therefore we will be seeing that item in the other collection."

The surge of adrenaline made my freebooting mercenary heart race with giddiness. I had traveled all the way to North Korea to pay homage to Madeleine's basketball and now it appeared that my wish was about to be granted.

Turning to depart the statuary room, I saw in a low glass case the famed stuffed crocodile presented by the Sandinistas National Leadership of the Liberation Front of Nicaragua. This terribly tacky gift gets mentioned more than almost any other of the thousands of items on display. The modest stuffed croc is standing on hind legs while balancing a wooden tray of wooden cups with its forelegs. It is of an artistic standard that would appeal to a certain segment of the populace. That segment has bad taste. The Nicaraguan crocodile could be placed in an American truck stop gift counter among the velvet Elvis hangings, the pet rocks, and the bawdy coffee mugs and it wouldn't stand out. However, the frowziness of the gift is not why it gets so many mentions from journalists and tourists. It is so frequently referenced because personal cameras are prohibited and there are only a few state-approved photos of items in the exhibit and the most memorable is of the erect crocodile. The same photo of the erect croc graces the pages of countless locally produced guides and picture books, as if the staff of the Pyongyang Foreign Language Printing House have an obsessive preoccupation with the Nicaraguan crocodile. The same photo appears again and again and again. It is also because many visitors descend no further into the underground collection. After viewing the crocodile they are ushered to the door and sent down the road to the next stop on the North Korean itinerary. So they go back and write about the crocodile in ignorance that deeper in the tunnels are chintzier, shinier, gaudier gifts of such colossal tackiness that the modest little crocodile is almost instantly forgettable. Mr. Kim gazed appreciatively at the dead reptile and said, "This is a crocodile from Nicaragua..." then he instructed us to follow, and as we exited the crocodile room we turned left and went towards the motherlode rather than right and towards Mr. Bae and his van. The adrenaline kept pumping.

The floodgates opened and the gifts came at us fast and furious. I had only the basketball on my mind, but the dazzling array of kitsch was astounding. We had taken just a few guided steps in to the first display room, and already the rhinestone-encrusted gewgaws, gold-plated doodads, vibrating gizmos, shiny handsels, and hand-carved trinkets were spectacularly overwhelming. When Friedrich Engels coined the concept of false consciousness, he was imagining Kim Il Sung's treasure trove.

The long dark tunnels had been converted into immensely long and completely dark rooms finished in marble and granite. They were filled with display cases and glass fronted cupboards into which a lifetime of state gifts were crammed. The cases were well-lit and the items of interest were presented in dazzling brightness in an otherwise murky setting. The effect was marvelous. As we entered each display room the guide flipped a switch to turn the display lights on. All the switches were on timers and it appeared that the idea was to speed visitors up and usher them along at a more rapid rate; if the light goes out then the loitering visitor hustles on ahead into the next room. But in fact quite consistently the opposite happened, we would be three-quarters of the way through a room and the lights would all go off with a clank at which we would all freeze in our tracks for fear of knocking something over in the darkness. The guide would gallop back to her starting point and flip the timer again, then canter back to the other end of the room to eventually guide us on. This was our routine and it was used in each of the dozens of long dark rooms we passed through. Rather than speeding up our progression, the routine with the lights allowed us to linger a little longer in each room.

The guide announced that we had entered the room that housed the collection of gifts from Chinese admirers. Not only gifts of state were there to be seen, but also gifts from trading firms in Hong Kong and capitalist ventures in the new China. Ornate silver goblets, sad ivory lamp stands, jade sailing ships large enough to fill a two-car garage, vintage audio equipment from the era when Chinese producers were playing catch-up, tapestries, cigarette lighters, decanters, and mugs.

As we exited the room, mounted beside the doorway was a large needlepoint wall hanging presented from the Central Committee of the Communist Party of China on 15 August 1960. It was the full-size standing image of the 1960 version of the Great Leader. He was wearing formal attire and smiling as he looked to his left and exposed the right side of his neck. There in needlepoint, just starting to bulge over his stiff white collar, was the secret lump. It wasn't yet the bulging mass that it would become, but the Red Chinese had been true to the original and captured Kim's likeness right down to the wen. This was the one and only acknowledgment of Kim's subcutaneous friend in all of the images, statuary, iconography, mosaics, and photos in the Worker's Paradise. There it was, hanging on the wall of Aladdin's Cave, illuminated by recessed lighting; needle-pointed confirmation that the Great Leader had a Lodestar of his own hanging over his starched collar like a flesh-tone grapefruit. With a clank the lights went off and the secret goiter vanished into the darkness

Next came the room housing gifts from Japan. The guide's eyes danced as she told us facts and figures associated with the Japanese gifts. She took pains to make sure we understood that the one time colonial master of Korea was now paying tribute to the Kims and their unparalleled standing as visionaries and guiding lights. Most of the gifts were not so much from Japanese government officials as from heads of corporations and more often from ethnic Koreans in Japan. Like the Chinese, the Japanese tended to lean towards the extravagant and gaudy. Filigree and ornamentation was *de rigueur.*

The Southeast Asian room featured gifts presented from friends and allies like Ho Chi Minh, Noradom Sihanouk, and Kaysone Phomvihane. Prince Souphanouvong of Laos presented the Great Leader with a bracelet made of US warplane wreckage in 1970 and there it sat under a light. Mr. Kim the Elder and I admired the brass daggers and complex woodwork.

He said, "The items placed on a small piece of red carpet were presented by the heads of state, while those items on blue carpet were gifts from others."

Here and there were gifts on pieces of red carpet, but most were placed on scraps of blue.

We entered the next room and the lights came on as the guide announced that the gifts housed there were from Mongolia and Indonesia, the next room was devoted to tribute and booty from India. The volume was immense and it was apparent that taking it all in would be like attempting to view the entire collection at the Louvre, or the British Museum, or the Smithsonian.

The gifts kept coming. As we walked deeper and deeper in to the heart of the mountain the guide continued to fight with the lights; here a machine gun from the Revolutionary Guard of Iran, there a golden sword from Moammar Kadhafi, teapots, coffee urns, rhino horns from Somalia, cigarette cases, a pistol given by Erich Honecker, brandy snifters and shoes. A scruffy old bearskin was folded in a haphazard way and stacked against a wall. The guide explained that it was a gift from Nicolae Ceaușescu, who had hosted the Great Leader on an official visit to Romania. The guide adjusted her settings and went on in "the voice" to retell the tale of how the two, after a long day of statecraft, relaxed in one of Ceauşescu's homes and talked of bear hunting, in which they were both keenly interested. Ceauşescu, on discovering Kim's shared interest, instructed his staff to bring out three bearskins. The skins were laid on the floor before Kim and Ceauşescu instructed him to select the one he liked the best. Kim, being the modest and grateful guest, automatically went to the ugliest and shabbiest of the three and requested he be granted the honor of receiving it ... and there it sits to this day down a deep hole in the ground under Mount *Myohyang* in resplendent shabbiness. The guide beamed with pride as she finished the anecdote because this proved, yet again, that not only was their brilliant leader unparalleled in his diplomacy, but he was also humble to the point of being the standard of modesty, civility, and decorum on the international stage.

Looking at the moth-eaten bearskin I couldn't help but wonder if on the same visit Ceauşescu had taken up the case of Ali Lameda. The Venezuelan poet and committed communist had volunteered to go to Pyongyang to throw his lot in with the masses building the Worker's Paradise. He helped translate and edit the works of Kim Il Sung into Spanish and for his efforts he was summarily tossed into a North Korean prison. It was only the personal intercession of Nicolae Ceauşescu in 1974 that got him out after seven years of a twenty-year sentence.

Deeper in the labyrinth we saw that the crafty North Korean engineers managed to get two full-size train carriages deep into the museum. Two dozen rooms into the tunnels we came on the pair of carriages — one from Stalin and another from Mao. Beside the carriage from Stalin was a sign that claimed the entire carriage was bulletproofed by Stalin and then presented to Kim in Pyongyang as a gift in August of 1945, yet non–North Korean history books would have us believe Kim didn't actually return to Pyongyang until a month later. Maybe the carriage was there waiting when Kim got back. I peeked through a window of Stalin's carriage and discovered I was peering into the toilet. There against the wall was a porcelain commode situated so the Great Leader could watch the passing countryside as he vacated his bowels. I stepped around to Mao's vintage 1953 carriage and, at random, selected a window through which to peer. It just so happened to be the toilet. The porcelain fixture was of traditional Chinese design and to relieve oneself the user was required to squat over the opening in the floor. I could picture the Great Leader perched on the Soviet commode while he rattled up the rails towards some important rendezvous, but I could not visualize him squatting over a Chinese crapper in a rocking carriage as he attempted to maintain balance with that giant goiter always making him list to starboard.

The next room was a who's who of the old Soviet bloc. The walls were ringed with large photographic portraits of the Great Leader (always carefully positioned to hide the lump) greeting other leaders. Hugging, kissing, hand-shaking, back-patting, gift-exchanging, broad-smiling leaders from the Eastern Bloc, the Soviet Bloc, the Nonaligned Bloc and a few terrorists and revolutionaries thrown in for good measure. In addition to Eastern European communists from the sixties and seventies, there were portraits of men in crispy new formal attire who would have been more at home in camouflage or fatigues in Africa, Central Asia, or the Middle East where their personal insurrection was waiting. Fidel Castro paid Kim a visit in 1986 and their initial meeting was captured on film and plastered on the wall. Under the Castro photo was a display case containing a modest chess set presented to Kim in 1970 by the chairman of the Cuban Committee for Solidarity with South Vietnam ... a rather odd pairing.

The penultimate room contained gifts from Americans. In fact, to fill the room they had to include gifts from all of the Americas, but from the United States there was a pair of painfully empty cabinets. They weren't completely empty, but they certainly weren't jam-packed like the cabinets in the rooms for Indian or Chinese or Zambian gifts. As we entered, the guide struggled to get the lights to work and for a moment it appeared that we would not be seeing much, but she doubled up her fist and hit the plastic housing and with that the lights snapped on and the room was bright.

On 15 April 1982, Kim celebrated his seventieth birthday and his loving, weary subjects got together and decided to outdo themselves in the gift-giving department with three magnificent items: the *Juche* Tower, the Arch of Triumph, and a newly renovated 100,000-seat *Moranbong* Stadium which was rechristened Kim Il Sung Stadium for the occasion. Just ten days prior to the big celebrations, a delegation from the US Out of Korea Committee of Youth Against War and Fascism paid a visit and presented a silver cup and it now takes a prominent position among the tributary offerings from the United States. I couldn't help but speculate that there may have been at least a little membership cross-fertilization between the US Out of Korea Committee of Youth Against War and Fascism and the New York Group for the Study of Kimilsungism.

On 6 June 1994 former US President Jimmy Carter visited Kim in Pyongyang and gave a much-understated silver ashtray with his signature engraved. The small gift paled in comparison to an armored rail carriage or a shipment of endangered animal parts, but because it was from the former leader of the haughty-jawed belligerent war merchants, it got a spot alongside the silver cup from the US Out of Korea Committee of Youth Against

War and Fascism. A couple of weeks later, on 21 June 1994, someone from CNN dropped off a tasty little silver box festooned with the corporate logo. It sat there modestly among the smattering of booty from America and begged the question if Ted Turner had kowtowed, or if Mike Chinoy had been assigned the task. No matter who did the deed, the little silver box from Atlanta demonstrated that the brass at CNN understood how the game was played and what it took to assure access. Just seventeen days later the Great Leader would ascend to his position as Eternal President of the Republic and with his death the tiny trickle of gifts from the United States came to an end. The modest collection of cabinets with a few sparse items was all there would ever be.

We stepped in to the final room that displayed three big black Russian limousines: one presented in 1950 by Comrade Generalissimo Joseph Stalin, one presented in 1953 by Premier of the Soviet Union Georgy Malenkov, and one presented by Prime Minister Nikolai Bulganin in 1955. They were all huge and smacked of the brute fuel-indifferent design of Moscow more than a half-century ago. The same preoccupation that consumed me in *Kumsusan* Memorial Palace filled my capitalist head again. I wanted to see a Lincoln Town Car in the collection and I wanted evidence of North Korea's reluctant tip of the hat towards Detroit.

I sought out Mr. Kim the Younger and asked in a whisper, "Where is the car that was used during the funeral procession? Is it here?"

With near righteous indignation, Mr. Kim the Younger replied in crisp response, "That car would not be here in this collection because that car was not a gift to the Great Leader." And with that we mutually understood the topic was forever closed.

We shuffled back through the labyrinth in our oversized felt galoshes and I experienced the same tingly sensation I had on exiting Malacañang Palace where, twenty years earlier, I had rummaged through Imelda Marcos' extensive shoe collection. The sheer number of gifts stunned the visitor like a mullet being whacked across the head with an oar. Though there was certainly quality strewn in among the gifts, the emphasis was on unabashed mulletiferous quantity.

After exchanging our felt galoshes for cameras (and possession of GPS or Navigator, publishings of all kind and any killing device) the Kims herded us out through the front door and into the sunlight. I stood blinking in the mid-morning brightness and looked up the steep mountainside that started its dramatic near-vertical ascent just a few meters away. It was so close that I could have strolled over to inspect the wall-like mountainside in one of my unofficial demonstrations of touristic independence, and then stroll back to the group without raising the ire of either of the minders. Gazing up at the looming mountain, I knew that a few hundred meters above, well out of sight but easily within range, was a series of huge luxury villas clustered along the ridgeline to take advantage of the alpine setting. What was once the stuff of Koreaphile rumor is now confirmed with crystal-clear satellite images that reveal much more detail than the regime would prefer. The Great Leader and the Dear Leader each had a series of opulent palaces up there and it was entirely conceivable that they had elevators that provided direct vertical access to the bunkers we had just explored. The image of self-possessed little men sneaking down the tunnels late at night for one more frolic among the treasures made me chuckle. There was no logical reason to have gone to the trouble of sinking an elevator shaft from the villas on the ridgeline to the trinket collection below, but the Worker's Paradise has been granted a special dispensational edict allowing for the necessities of logic to be set aside until further notice. Lots of things in the Worker's Paradise defy logic.

Mr. Kim the Younger guided our little group around the side of the entrance and up a small set of stone steps where we were invited to enjoy the view from the back porch. The granite and marble porch was equipped with reclining wooden deckchairs designed to allow visitors to sit and take in the spectacularly magnificent, contrived scenery. It was as if a construction crew had been brought in to shape the mountains so they would look like a stereotypical Korean painting. There was no hint of the denuded brown vistas we had spent more than two hours traversing. This verdant little glade was amusement-park perfect. From the porch we looked into the dramatically vertical crotch between two peaks that rose so abruptly they looked unreal. Down the center of the scene cascaded a stream that ended in a splashing waterfall at the base of a shadowy glen. Up the steep sides of each mountain were trees in dense abundance and they were all displaying the light, airy colors of early spring. Just enough sunlight found its way down between the mountain walls and through the trees to dapple the glen and leave the pool of water in a murky, green shadow. In an ode to not being capable of leaving well enough alone, one not-very-lifelike cement fawn stood in the grass midway between the waterfall and the porch and, through crudely painted and disproportionately large eyes, stared blankly into the shadowy trees.

Standing on the porch admiring the cement fawn, Mr. Kim the Younger pulled from his jacket a packet of cigarettes and started the ritual of tapping, twisting, fondling and lighting.

After the familiar exhale that announced a smoker was once again momentarily satisfied, Mr. Kim said, "With gifts from all over the world to honor President Kim Il Sung, it is just like traveling around the world when visiting this museum."

This line has been reported so frequently by journalists, diplomats and visitors that when he said it I had to stop myself from laughing at the predictability. Just like the apocryphal tale of the foreign visitor with inadequate math skills, this hackneyed throwaway line is obviously on the Ministry of Love's approved list of talking points.

It is sad to think that Mr. Kim, who inevitably will never step foot outside North Korea, might actually believe the line he had been fed. Looking at a stack of rhino horns in the museum was just as good as standing on an African savannah watching the last remaining crash of rhinos, looking at a gold-plated sword from Libya was the same as visiting Tripoli and hanging out with the locals, seeing a jade sailing ship the size of a Buick was equal to actually visiting Hong Kong. No need for all the fuss and bother of following in Tony and Maureen Wheeler's footsteps on the well-beaten tourist track when one can visit this collection conveniently buried in a hole in the ground. He is one of the privileged few who had reason to visit the collection again and again and again, so it was just like Mr. Kim has filled a passport with stamps from all his exotic travels. Just exactly the same.

The view from the porch was to be enjoyed for only a limited time because, just like all the other stops along our route, there was a souvenir shop to visit and it just happened to be conveniently located right behind the porch. Mr. Kim the Younger carefully placed his cigarette butt in an ashtray and suggested we move on to the souvenirs. Just as with the shops before, the souvenirs were arranged in precisely the same way with the same products starting on the left and working through the official North Korean souvenir spectrum until culminating with cigarettes on the right. In between, they had all the same crude trinkets, tobacco, and booze. Among the bottles of alcohol were an assortment of adder and ginseng liquor, but also bottles of murky medicinal-looking concoctions with labels printed only in Korean. Those mysterious labels claimed that the contents were derived from extract of tiger bone, or generous portions of bear bile.

Off to the side, completely outside the normal sequence of souvenirs found in all the other shops, was a pair of odd-looking wooden slippers. They featured carved wooden nodes on the sole obviously designed to hurt. I picked up a pair and was examining the craftsmanship and admiring the odd design when a uniformed clerk teetered past and uttered one hesitant, frightened word in English: "shoes." As soon as the word was out of her mouth she bolted through an open door and hid in the stockroom.

Mr. Kim the Elder directed us back to the grandiose entrance, then we strolled away from the Great Leader's bunker museum a couple of hundred meters down the gentle incline towards the small parking lot. Our pace slowed to a near standstill as we came to the vehicles and the Kims chatted with the guide. When I saw our waiting van, my heart sank. We had not yet seen Madeleine's basketball. We had traveled all that way and it appeared that the opportunity to take the final steps on my sacred hegira would not come to pass. In rapid Korean Mr. Kim the Elder was discussing logistics with Mr. Kim the Younger. I initially understood him to say that we had to hurry back to Pyongyang, but after a few more sentences it gradually became clear that they both wanted to hurry through the Kim Jong Il collection so we could beat the crowd to lunch, and with that we walked past the van and on up to a newer, less ornate entrance to the Dear Leader's collection of tribute booty. The adrenaline gland once again got a good squeeze.

Just like his father's, the Dear Leader's was a building entrance connected not to a building, but to the mountain. The front doors opened to the maze

The new wing of the International Friendship Exhibition at Mount *Myohyang*. When Kim Il Sung died in 1994 the stream of tribute gifts was diverted to Kim Jong Il and his expanding collection required a home. The entrance to Kim Jong Il's wing is a short stroll from the entrance to his late father's wing and houses a steadily growing quantity of tribute gifts from all over the world, including a basketball presented to Kim Jong Il by US Secretary of State Madeleine Albright.

of tunnels into which his mounds of tribute were rat-holed behind blast-proof doors. Somewhere in that hole was Madeleine Albright's basketball and we were walking towards it. My pulse increased.

The guide stopped us at the front door and in the same innocently dramatic manner in which she had attempted to set Charles up at the Great Leader's door, she motioned for us to step back and watch. With that, she extended an index finger and pushed a button, then as the huge blast doors were pulled back on a track, she glanced at our faces to take in our startled reactions. Apparently she was unaware that through the '70s and into the '80s the patented Genie Automatic Garage Door Picker-Upper had been installed on every single garage in North America, and we were all thoroughly unimpressed that the same 40-year-old technology had been applied to Junior's front door.

As we stepped inside the subterranean foyer, she explained that in 1995 it was suddenly obvious that the Dear Leader required his own display space for tributary spoils, so from 1996 through 1998 the North Koreans used their highly advanced tunneling skills to further honeycomb the mountain with passageways, chambers, vaults, and lots of secret places that the average tourist will never see. As they put the finishing touches on the new Kim Jong Il portion of the exhibition, the truckloads of gifts started pouring in. Perfect timing — all this despite the Yankee imperialist economic blockade. She explained that the Dear Leader had motivated the workers to finish his tribute tunnels even as the blood-sucking capitalist leeches attempted their nefarious tricks. As per usual, the Dear Leader outsmarted the fumbling Yankees.

We exchanged our shoes, cameras, and killing devices for huge felt galoshes and commenced spelunking. The Dear Leader's collection was housed deeper into the heart of the mountain than his father's, and it required walking down a set of long passages before arriving at the display rooms. At intervals along the passages were backlit photographs of exotic animals. The guide explained that loving admirers from all over the globe had sent Kim Jong Il dromedaries and giraffes and gnus and lesser dwarf gibbons of lower Sumatra and the photographs documented all those exotic and efficacious gifts. The Dear Leader had all the live gifts herded together and driven out to the Pyongyang Central Zoo[5] where privileged citizens were occasionally granted permission to visit.

As the guide moved deeper down the passageway, I veered over to one of the backlit photos to steal a closer look. The zebra in the photograph had been placed there among the trees in a ham-fisted doctoring operation reminiscent of Leon Trotsky being airbrushed out of existence by clumsy Soviet photo historians. The zebra was obviously lifted from some other source and dropped into the background by an unsophisticated technician. Thirty paces down the passageway the backlit photo of a llama was equally as unconvincing with razored edges around the animal's silhouette revealing light from a different source than that which hit the trees in the background. The long passageway was filled with backlit photographs of exotic animals at regular intervals and each and every one of the photos had been crudely doctored to place the animal in the Pyongyang zoo.

At last we arrived at the end of the passageway and there on the wall was mounted a map that tallied the gifts by geographic origin. Unlike the map in the Great Leader's collection, the Dear Leader's map was electronic. The guide explained that the rate of intake was so furious that the map required an adjustment the intake counter. Sometimes, she learned, the numbers changed while visitors were inside the exhibit! She proudly pointed to the counter, tiny 1960s-era incandescent bulbs forming each number, and read to us the figures on display. Friends and fans in 164 countries had, so far, supplied 55,431 gifts to the Dear Leader.

The guide marveled that despite the belligerent Americans and their back-stabbing tactics used in an unending attempt to dislodge the foundation of Korean stability with nuclear threats, cholera and typhoid bombs, an illegal economic blockade, and malicious slander in the world's press, the people of the world continued to send a steady stream of gifts in defiance of imperialist opposition.

In just thirteen years since the Great Leader's death, the Dear Leader had already amassed a quarter of his tribute. At that rate he would equal his father's take in the year 2046, at the age of 105 or 106 — depending on which version of his birth account is used. Since the Dear Leader has already been proven to be the people's supreme guiding template in physio-extracurricular sport forms and the Olympic-class champion in an array of competitive sports, coupled with the marvelous genetic superiority inherited from the finest stock of revolutionary breeding, it is not inconceivable that Yura will rake in more gifts than his father before he is mummified and placed on display.

From the twinkling map and booty-counter we were taken by the beaming guide into yet another room featuring a statue of Kim Il Sung. Though it was Kim Jong Il's collection, we were expected to first bow before the image of his father, the Great Leader. While they were genuflecting, I threw down an impatient Albright and turned towards the gifts.

Jimmy Carter had presented a small crystal bowl in 1994. On April Fool's Day 1992, "The American Religious Leader" had given the Dear Leader a porcelain globe surrounded by doves of peace. A Cuban delegation had presented a fine painting of a bald eagle surrounded by the universal prohibition sign, under which was the North Korean flag with a dove of peace. A delegation from Mozambique had provided beautifully carved woodwork. A representative of Chad handed over a letter opener and an ink stand.

As we moved from room to room battalions of uniformed soldiers anticipating their turn at the exhibits stood at ease in the passageways and waited until the foreign guests jumped the queue. Time and again we were met by a thousand expression-free eyes watching us without revealing any feeling. The timing of the lights was identical in the Dear Leader's wing and the guide resumed her trick of cantering back and forth to hit the light switch at the required time.

Unlike the Great Leader's collection, the Dear Leader's booty was arranged chronologically. From room to room one could gauge the state of North Korean relations by the types of gifts displayed. The early rooms housed gifts from the old Soviet bloc that the Dear Leader had received before his father's death, but as time went by one could read the changes like looking at an Antarctic ice core. The Soviet bloc collapsed and the grandiose gifts from long-time comrades dried up. The Great Leader died and the quantity of gifts to the Dear Leader increased. The Sunshine Policy was unleashed and the dominance of South Korean gifts skyrocketed. Like his father's collection, Kim Jong Il's collection was all about quantity. Case after case after case of every conceivable type of gift was on display.

In front of one cabinet I paused to admire a silver plate inscribed with "Camp David," the US Presidential retreat 100 kilometers north of Washington D.C. It was presented to Kim Jong Il while US President Bill Clinton was in office; however the plaque beside the gift revealed that not Bill, but Roger Clinton — the president's convicted-felon rock-and-roll-playing half-brother — had carried the gift to Pyongyang. The plaque stated simply, "Roger Clinton — Pop Singer of United States." How Roger managed to have in his possession on arrival in Pyongyang an object from the Camp David inventory remains one of the many Clinton Administration mysteries.

The guide stepped into the next room and her hand reached into the darkness and tripped the timer on the wall. With that the lights came up and the objects on display were thrust into artificial daylight. Immediately my eyes went to the glowing orange globe in the middle of the room. There before me, in all its officially licensed splendor, sat the infamous Madeleine Albright basketball. My pilgrimage was a success. Among Koreaphiles I had ascended to the special order of the orange orb and will forever have the final word in any discussion regarding any aspect of Korea, ancient or modern, for I have crawled through the belly of the mountain and feasted my eyes on Madeleine's ball. I am now content to die in peace.

The Wilson Indoor Outdoor Jet Tournament Edition basketball (serial number 026388763832) was mounted on a piece of wood that had been painted flat black. Across the top of the mounting was the United States national crest and below were the words, "Presented to His Excellency Kim Jong Il Chairman of the National Defense Commission and General Secretary of the Korean Workers Party of the Democratic People's Republic of Korea by Madeleine K. Albright, Secretary of State of the United States of America, October 2000."

At the time, in any discount sporting goods megastore, that ball retailed for about $29.99. At the same time, Madeleine Albright's official U.S. government *per diem* rates for Pyongyang were $190 for lodging, $12 for breakfast, $20 for lunch, $33 for dinner, and $16 for incidentals, for a total of $271 every day she was in town. Since she stayed at the *Paekhwawon* Guest House for Foreign Dignitaries and her hosts picked up the tab, then by US Federal regulation, she was not eligible to receive the $190 per night for lodging, but just two days worth of incidentals would have paid for the ball (plus tax). Another day of incidentals and a couple of skipped meals and she could have easily presented something a little less chintzy.

Granted, the ball did have a swirling black felt-tip smudge that was reputed to have been the autograph of Michael Jordan and, as those things go in sports memorabilia shops in suburban shopping malls, it was probably in the neighborhood of $500. Madeleine probably sent her intern out to the nearest shopping mall with an official State Department credit card and instructions to get something tasteful for the Dear Leader. The intern was obviously plugged into the intel chatter that suggests Kim Jong Il stays up late at night to watch NBA games through his top-secret satellite dishes attached to each of his dozens of top-secret villas. This commonly held belief has never been publicly substantiated, but those who subscribe to it do so with the same adamant fervor that used to be unbridled when insisting that he had a debilitating speech defect, or that his voice sounded as if he had just sucked down the contents of two helium balloons. They are usually the same people who can rattle off the precise number of video cassettes in the Dear Leader's movie collection and they inevitably know exactly which films are his favorites. Slasher movies and *The Sound of Music* are often cited as his bent.

So the intern came back with an autographed basketball. And Secretary of State Albright had her handlers sand down a piece of plywood and spray it with flat black paint. It was tossed into the luggage hold and off they went to meet the world's biggest top secret basketball fan.

This was either a diplomatic *faux pas* highlighting the complete and total ignorance of the Clinton Administration and the American penchant to treat all urban legends as credible until proven otherwise, or a brilliantly orchestrated diplomatic maneuver that allowed Secretary of State Albright to rationalize such an insultingly cheap gift while maintaining the straight face demanded by decorum.

"Here you go Junior, a nice new ball ... now run along and play while I chat with your Dad, we're busy here."

This too is one of the lingering Clinton Administration mysteries. From that point it was difficult to focus on any other objects in the room. Even as we moved forward through the collection my eyes kept returning to the illuminated orange ball against the darkness of the room. Others in the room were also drawn to Madeleine's ball by some unseen force of nature and a half dozen visitors stood quietly marvelling within the other-worldly orange glow. It stood out among the silver and gold, pearls and emeralds, craftsmanship, pomp, and circumstances like a very large sore orange thumb.

There was another ball in the room — a soccer ball presented to the Dear Leader by Edison Arantes do Nascimento in 2003. He signed it with his nickname, Pele. Pele's ball somehow lacked the significance of the one carried all the way from Pete's Sports Memorabilia Dungeon in Reston, or the Sweaty Jersey in Arlington, or the Cards, Caps, & More! in Fairfax. There was an addictively compelling appeal to the glaringly odd choice of gifts ... plus that, it had that officially licensed orange glow.

Mr. Kim the Elder joined me as we moved through the collection of objects sent during South Korea's Sunshine Policy Era. Big sound systems from Korean electronics conglomerates, television consoles featuring the technology of two generations ago, gold-plated mobile telephones, outdated computers, cameras, office equipment, and shiny black sedans on blocks and behind velvet ropes. Though cutting edge at the time, the South Korean gifts were already descending down the ice core sample.

On the wall in the middle of the jumble of South Korean treasure was a cheap battery-powered wall clock of the type one would receive when subscribing to a magazine, or signing up for a new savings account. It had been presented to Kim Jong Il by the then South Korean Unification Minister Park Jae-kyu, on 30 September 2000. Across the face of the clock was screen printed the photographic image of Kim Jong Il, Chairman of the National Defense Commission, Supreme Commander of the Korean People's Army, and General Secretary of the Workers' Party of Korea holding hands with Kim Dae-jung, fifteenth president of South Korea.

I had worked for Park Jae-kyu in a Seoul-based think tank long before he was appointed unification minister, and therefore, long, long before he toted the plastic clock up north to give to Kim Jong Il.

"Mr. Kim," I said pointing at the clock, "that was presented to the Dear Leader by my former boss, Minister Park Jae-kyu."

Mr. Kim the Elder glanced at me and smiled a gentle smile that could have announced either that he had no clue what I was babbling about, or that my name-dropping lacked any impact, or that in the presence of the Dear Leader's booty he was in a state of awe almost as significant as if the Dear Leader himself were wandering through the tunnels. Clearly Mr. Kim was not impressed that I had a connection to the former South Korean Unification Minister despite the fact that it was somewhat more substantial than my connection to Cambodian royalty.

The Dear Leader is still amassing his collection, so it is not yet as extensive as that of his father. There are some significant individual items on display, such as the $29.99 basketball from Madame Albright, but mulletiferous quantity is still given priority. Unfortunately for the Dear Leader, most of the world has abandoned communism as a failed experiment so there are significantly fewer likeminded rulers willing to exchange ridiculously extravagant gifts. From sixteen nations in 1980 to a paltry five left standing today. If one uses a purely command economy as the determining factor, then North Korea is arguably the last remaining true communist state in existence. Now Kim Jong Il must rely on South Korean and Chinese business tycoons wielding flashy gifts as an attempt to secure a business advantage. The likelihood of an armor-plated rail carriage being presented to the Dear Leader now appears faint, no matter what the commode style.

We concluded our visit and exchanged our felt galoshes and walked back through the nuclear blast doors into the sunlight. As a group we slowly strolled while the guide and Mr. Kim the Younger exchanged pleasantries. She enquired about life in the capital, and he congratulated her on being selected to reside in such a lovely locale. It was only as we were about to step in to the van that the Kims lowered the boom on the guide.

"Do you realize that these foreign guests are American?" Kim the Younger asked with a mischievous grin.

"Oh," she said with only the tiniest traces of reaction, "I would not have guessed American. Tell them," she said to Mr. Kim the Younger, "that I wish them good health and understanding between nations."

It required a considerable amount of resolve to translate her words without fleering in her face but he pulled it off with an acceptable level of civility.

Without making a sound, Mr. Kim the Elder turned his face away and shook with suppressed laughter. She had spent the prior hour and a half reciting the prescribed anti–American insults and epithets, and he thought it was absolutely hilarious that she was now confronted with this awkward revelation. Mr. Kim the Younger smirked openly and thanked her again and again for her excellent commentary and informative banter. Mr. Kim the Elder strained to keep from wetting his *vinalon* trousers in the process. Of course, we would have never known since *vinalon* has all the liquid-absorbing properties of a plastic trash bag.

She bowed at the waist as we pulled away and the Kims slapped their knees and guffawed heartily, almost falling to the floor of the van. When he caught his breath, Mr. Kim the Elder gasped in English, "She did not know you were American," and continued to cackle as we departed *de bunkermusea*.

Mr. Bae barely got the van up to speed before he started applying the brakes and turning into the entrance of the *Hyangsan* Hotel, hidden among tree-covered hills just out of sight of the entrances to the treasure tunnels. This 15-story cement pyramid is topped with yet another of North Korea's frequently inoperable revolving restaurants. It is known as the premiere hotel outside Pyongyang and had recently been used to facilitate foreign and local officials dealing with nuclear issues. The surroundings are reportedly crisscrossed with walking trails through pristine forests and along crystal-clear streams. However, the most acclaimed aspect of the hotel is the tawdry lobby.

Two see-through elevator shafts formed the backdrop against which an artificial knoll was created. From the crest of the little knoll a little dry streambed fell through a maze of artificial stones and plastic plants to an artificial pool below. Beside the pool, in among the faded plastic moss and dusty plastic ferns, stood a pair of deer, one buck and one doe. The cement buck stood erect and looked towards the entrance of the hotel with antlers held high. His cement companion was caught in an eternal drink from the little pool. The crude paint job rendered both full-grown deer with dozens of white fawn spots on their cement backs. The waterfall and deer are renowned for the fact that someone behind the scenes is responsible for flipping the switch that turns the waterfall on just as guests walk through the front door. The whole wonderful brummagem display is made even more special because the behind-the-scenes person who flips the waterfall on stands there at the switch so they can also turn it off just as soon as the guests have moved on.

We walked through the front entrance and there before us was the knoll and the deer. Mr. Kim the Elder walked towards the other side of the lobby with purpose and Mr. Kim the Younger brought up the rear to make sure we kept pace. The waterfall wasn't switched on until we were almost to the opposite wall. With a roar the cascading stream fell at the feet of the cement deer and filled the lobby with a din of gurgling noise. We all glanced over our shoulders in the direction of the noise and as we took the first step to ascend the staircase towards the restaurant above, the din of noise abruptly ceased. The waterfall had unceremoniously been turned off and the lobby returned to near silence. The hotel staff never bothered to look up from what they were doing.

The restaurant on the mezzanine level was filled with empty tables set out and waiting for the onslaught of visitors. We still maintained a slight edge on all the other tourists in the other vans and buses and the Kims drove us onward in our tight schedule. They walked us to the table and ensured we were seated and that the sullen waitresses knew of our arrival, then they excused themselves and disappeared.

As was always the case, the food was abundant and we ate to our heart's content as we chatted and drank beer and cider and took in the unusual surroundings. In the background a large television played North Korean karaoke with the volume turned low and through the meal we were serenaded with tunes about the delights of living in a socialist paradise where apples are abundant and imperialist expansionism is kept in check through the diligent wakefulness of even the common farmer. The lyrics unfolded in Korean across the bottom of the huge Chinese-made television as the melody played in the background.

When we finished the meal all four of us eagerly retraced our steps back to the lobby where the dusty cement deer quietly stood beside the fading plastic ferns — the waterfall off and silent. The main doors of the hotel opened and dozens of foreign tourists streamed in and were guided towards the stairs and their waiting lunch. As the last of the new wave of foreigners started ascending the steps, the waterfall came to life and filled the lobby with the noise of splashing water for a few brief seconds, then when the new tourists had passed the waterfall was abruptly turned off.

Off to the side of the lobby was the souvenir section. It was created by some skillfully placed partitions that announced to everyone in the hotel that this wasn't just part of the lobby, this fenced off section was where one came to buy stuff. Like all the rest, the trinkets started on the left and worked through the spectrum of souvenirs until culminating with cigarettes on the right. In the middle was a rack of books authored by the Great Leader and the Dear Leader, as well as books authored by others but about the two leaders, and books detailing every aspect of the *Juche* Idea, and books on North Korean crop rotation cycles and other compelling topics. Wally gravitated towards the books, Alice searched for a suitable gift for a little girl, while Charles and I met at the stamp counter.

North Korean postage stamps aren't all angry and pugnacious, but most

are: stern soldiers leaning towards the viewer with bayonet fixed, angry fists
shaking at the sky, military hardware with the safety switch eternally in the
off position, and army issue steel-toe boots slamming down on the spindly
limbs of a pilfering Uncle Sam. There are fluffy dogs and butterflies and gem
stones and freight trains for the run-of-the-mill philatelic aficionados around
the world, but Charles and I were interested in the shaking fists and fixed bayonets.

The stamps were arrayed in two piles. The first pile was loose individuals and commemorative sets. The second pile was a mound of sheets of stamps;
seven by seven of the same angry fist shaking at the viewer, or seven by seven
of the same imposing rifle pointing right at the viewer's eye, or seven by seven
of a proudly North Korean nuclear missile preparing to spread atomic radi-
ation across a patch of the capitalist world (inevitably Washington D.C.).
Charles rifled through the stack and pulled out several sheets, then I picked
through the mound and found one particular stamp of interest that I knew,
in a seven by seven array mounted and framed, would be the perfect comple-
ment to my den. In blood red it depicts a KPA soldier pausing in his relentless advance forward to lift a rifle in one hand while with the other he offers
the open palm of encouragement to unseen comrades about to enter stamp-
left. His face is proud and resolute and with just one glance it was easy to tell
he had already crushed a couple dozen meddling imperialists and he is about
to crush a few more. The stamp was one of several issued in 2003[6] to mark
the 55th anniversary of the founding of the Democratic People's Republic of
Korea.

Though I have never been infected with the philatelic enthusiasm that
generates a Pavlovian response in some, I always appreciate a good stamp.
Especially a good stamp dripping with angry propaganda. With my desired
sheet in hand I returned to the box of loose stamps to pick out a few for
the requisite postcards back home. Postcarding is a dying art form and since
I knew my chances for sending postcards from North Korea would be limited to possibly one opportunity in my entire life, I decided to make the
effort.

A number of stamps stood out as fantastic examples of socialist realism
and the *Juche* Idea, many of them glorified the cement monuments that glorified the leaders, both Great and Dear, and several of them commemorated
significant dates in the North Korean calendar. The one that jumped out at
me with revolutionary fury featured the illustration of a grim KPA soldier
looking at the viewer, fixed bayonet off to the side. The stamp commemorated the Period of Joint Anti–United States Struggle, June 25–July 27 2005.
Most of us have never before been aware that the North Koreans set those

dates aside to recognize the Period of Joint Anti–United States Struggle, but here was the commemorative stamp to prove it. The alluring thing about the stamp was the tiny photographic montage across the bottom that featured North Korea's proudest moments of triumph over the United States; Bobby Wayne Hall standing before a downed US helicopter, Lloyd Bucher signing an admission of guilt after the *Pueblo* Incident, and the crew of the USS *Pueblo* marching with upraised hands of surrender, and a graveyard featuring what can be assumed to be American crosses. The KPA soldier points grimly at the Korean characters that proclaim, "American imperialist invaders, don't forget the lessons of history!" I grabbed a handful.

At the counter where the cashier waited, I laid my stamps out for her to see. The concept of market forces guiding us through the process of exchanging money for goods was dismissed as soon as I looked into her eyes. She had the vacuous look of sublime contentedness that comes from working in an assembly line. She was not required to communicate, nor to produce, nor to achieve. She need only stand in the hotel foyer when foreign tourists were in town and take their foreign currency in exchange for the items they clutched in their sweaty alien hands. In theory there is no competitive market in North Korea, so the bumbling foreigners must pay what the regime deems the souvenirs are worth. The assembly line had only one step; reach out and take money when a foreigner holds it out in their open palm. It may be three monies, or four monies, they may be big or small, sometimes they have pretty colors and sometimes they don't, but the more monies the better.

As was the case in all the souvenir shops, the prices tended to be marked in Euros on little slips of gray cardboard and placed against the items being sold. Sometimes the numbers appeared to correlate with the value of the item, sometimes they didn't. A stack of coffee table books featuring paintings of heroic citizens doubling their efforts to ensure the success of the nation, for example, sat under a little cardboard slip with the numeral 6 written on it. I assumed that translated in to the statement, "The books in this stack are €6 each." Then beside it would be a stack of postcards with a similar cardboard slip with a 3 scrawled on it. Did that indicate, "These postcards are €3 each"?

I looked into the vapid eyes of the cashier and asked in Korean, "How much is this sheet of stamps?" and held up the sheet of forty-nine identical stamps to make sure she understood exactly which stamps were in question. She looked at me with vacant eyes and, after a long pause, slowly and silently nodded.

I redoubled my efforts and attempted to put a Northern accent on my question, "Madam, can you tell me, how much are these stamps?" and with that she shot a glance at her colleague, giggled, then slowly and silently nodded.

I looked at her colleague and asked, "Can *you* tell me the price of these stamps?" to which the first woman again laughed and nodded. The second woman pulled out a large Chinese-made calculator and rapidly entered figures, subtracting unrelated sums, and double checking her calculations by entering and subtracting unrelated sets of numbers. After an inordinate amount of time the clattering keys were quieted and she said in heavily accented English, "Twelve Euro."

"I don't have Euro, I'm not European. Will you accept dollars?" I asked in my best Korean.

The second woman again picked up the Chinese-made calculator and started a lightning fast process of generating a number. She looked at the calculator, then glanced up at me and said only, "Eight dollars." She had no concept that the Euro was substantially stronger than the dollar or what that meant for the way our conversation should go. Like a re-run episode of the *Twilight Zone*, an almost identical scenario would be acted out each and every time I purchased something. The actors and actresses were different, but the props were the same and the conversations maddeningly identical.

The entire process was like playing "Store" in Mrs. Harm's 1966 Golfcrest Elementary School Kindergarten class. Mrs. Harms brought in a couple of refrigerator boxes and cut windows in them. The pretend shelves were loaded with empty cereal boxes and empty orange juice containers, empty oatmeal cylinders, and empty coffee cans. Before lunch on Thursdays one lucky student would get to act out the role of cashier from inside the box. All the other children had to loiter outside the box with their pretend money and wait their turn to stand at the window and tell the cashier which product they desired, then the cashier would "sell" it to them.

> MRS. HARMS: "Bubba, it's your turn."
> BUBBA: "Um..."
> MRS. HARMS: "Bubba, tell her what you want."
> BUBBA: "Um ... Milk."
> CINDY: slowly passing the empty milk carton through the hole in the refrigerator box, "Bubba, it costs nine monies."
> MRS. HARMS: "Bubba, give her the money."

Even as a five-year-old I was preoccupied with two thoughts: first; Cindy is kind of slow-witted; second, what are we accomplishing here? Let's go to lunch.

The North Korean cashiers appeared to be just like Cindy. They didn't yet have a concept of the value of currency and had only a rudimentary understanding of economic exchange. They knew there was the need to get some of my monies because the People's Committee Chairman had explained as much, but two monies was just as acceptable as fifteen monies or 238 monies or eleventy zillion monies. It didn't really matter because there were new monies going into the till and soon it would be lunch time. Everybody happy.

On inspecting my wallet I discovered the lowest denomination on hand was a US $20 note. I looked down at Andrew Jackson looking back at me from under bushy eyebrows and knew that Cindy and her socialist comrade were about to have a wrench thrown in to their works.

I handed the $20 note over and Cindy held it like a monkey with a shiny thing. Her eyes got very big very quickly and she pantomimed, to the accompaniment of guttural grunts, that she had no change. She wanted me to accept the $12 of change in the form of additional souvenirs.

I glanced around at the odder liquor and cigarettes and books on crop rotation and had that sinking feeling that I was about to be fleeced. However, before I could say anything, Cindy's colleague had found a US $10 note in her till and held it up to Cindy's accompanying grunts and gesticulations. In her best Marcel Marceau she let me know that if in lieu of change I would make up the difference in stamps, she would hand over the $10. So back to the stamp counter I went and two of Cindy's colleagues suggested a number of pointedly aggressive stamps strewn with propaganda, rhetoric, and lots of fixed bayonets. I pulled stamps out until I was told to stop. Everybody happy.

Charles, Alice, and I drifted towards Wally who was wrapping up his purchase of more books from Cindy's colleague at the book counter. We stood waiting under a sign that states in English:

> The book is a silent teacher and a companion in life. Young people should carry book with them at all times and read and read [sic] various good books zealously.— Kim Il Sung

Mr. Kim the Younger walked briskly from around a corner and found us all ready to depart. Without breaking stride he indicated we should fall in behind him so we could immediately commence the journey back to Pyongyang. As we passed through the foyer the waterfall erupted to life, but before we could walk through the main doorway it had already been turned off again.

The afternoon journey back to Pyongyang was simply the morning journey in reverse. Unlike the morning, however, it was difficult to keep eyes open as Mr. Bae held the van at precisely fifty kilometers an hour on the smooth, empty expressway. The steady hum of the engine made it even more difficult to stay awake.

After two hours, as Pyongyang neared, Mr. Kim the Elder roused himself and brought up the topic of having Kim Jong Il–style *jambas* tailored when we got back into town. It was obvious by the furrows in his brow that he was thinking about time and logistics. Charles and Wally were particularly keen on the option when Mr. Kim informed them that he calculated the total price of the fabric, measuring, and tailoring would be in the neighborhood of US $50. Quick calculations were made and Mr. Kim informed us that we might need to curtail our itinerary; he thought it could be done but suggested playing it by ear.

Not far from the city, on the northern edge near the Pyongyang Pig Factory, Mr. Bae was flagged by a uniformed policeman standing on the side of the expressway. He brought the van to a smooth stop and turned the engine off, then got out and walked back towards the policemen to enquire about his infraction. Mr. Kim the Elder quietly opened the door and joined Mr. Bae walking along the side of the empty and silent expressway. It was so quiet on the expressway that we could hear pebbles crunch under the soles of their shoes. With the engine off we sat silently in the van and listened to birds chirping in the trees. As they started discussing things with the uniformed policeman, Mr. Kim the Younger also got out in order to get a better view, but remained by the van.

The policeman carried a similar expression to that of the traffic wardens. It was the exact same truculent demeanor but with stubble. He calmly spoke with Mr. Bae who in turn wilted where he stood. His body language announced complete and total subjugation; slumped shoulders, wringing hands, scuffling feet, down-turned eyes.

It was all very mysterious because the expressway was clearly marked at 80 kilometers per hour and Mr. Bae had kept the van at a precise fifty all day and on the expansive empty roadway he simply positioned the van in the middle of the lane and remained there.

Mr. Bae and Mr. Kim the Elder quietly walked back to the van where they exchanged quick mumbled words with Mr. Kim the Younger as the three of them crawled back in.

Mr. Bae cranked the engine and used the indicator to carefully merge back in to the empty lane and continue our journey to Pyongyang. After a few moments of silence, from behind big inquisitive eyes, Charles asked what had happened.

Very hesitantly Mr. Kim the Younger said, "Well, it seems that the policeman signaled for us to stop, but we didn't manage to stop where he indicated so he was angry." And with that he quickly changed the topic.

We passed through the empty streets of the capital once again and ended up parked in the shadow of the Arch of Triumph. There is a striking resemblance to the arch in Paris, but by North Koreans this is brushed aside as mere coincidence. Towering 60 meters over *Kaeson* Street, the enormous stone monument memorializes, believe it or not, Kim Il Sung.

Because the traffic was so light Mr. Bae stopped the van closer to the center of the roadway than to the curb and as we piled out, we drifted all over the pavement while peering up at the three-tiered summit. The proportions are such that Pyongyang's Arch looks unnecessarily heavy. At sixty meters tall and fifty meters wide, it doesn't create a sense of loftiness, but a feeling of massive heaviness. The column on the left features "1925" at the top as a tribute to the year a thirteen-year-old Kim Song Ju packed up and left Korea to escape the repression of the Japanese colonizers. He walked north into China where he formed a band of like-minded guerilla fighters who, behind the matchless intellect of the Great Leader and through his ingenious iron-willed martial stratagems, eventually brought the Japanese to their knees and forced them, in 1945, to tuck their tails and escape back to Japan like the running dogs they are. In glorious triumph the Guerilla General returned to Pyongyang after a twenty-year hiatus. He returned with a new name; Kim Il Sung. The right column of the imposing arch has a large "1945" affixed to the top to memorialize his triumphant return.

Carved in stone across the top of the arch, directly over the four lanes of *Kaeson* Street, are the lyrics to the *Song of General Kim Il Sung*, the same dirge that played on an endless loop through hidden speakers in the viewing room of the *Kumsusan* Memorial Palace.

In a move more Kafkaesque than Orwellian, back in the early 80s Kim Jong Il decided to reduce the significance of North Korea's national anthem, *Aegukka*,[7] and inflate the importance of the *Song of General Kim Il Sung*. The lyrics of the national anthem remain largely unknown by the populace, but everybody can belt out the *Song of General Kim Il Sung* from start to finish and typically they do at the commencement of any public gathering. At the conclusion of the same gathering a song for Junior is sung — often the rousing ditty *No Motherland Without You*.[8] Across the arch were the lyrics to the song that is, for North Koreans, more patriotic than the national anthem.

> ...over Korea ever flourishing and free, so dear to all our hearts is our General's glorious name, our own beloved Kim Il Sung of undying fame...

According to the North Korean version of history, the dropping of two atomic bombs on Japan and subsequent conclusion of World War II don't factor in to the Japanese being driven from the Korean peninsula. It was the Mighty Lodestar and his band of merry men who swept down from the rugged northern mountains and skillfully turned the resources of the forest into weapons sufficient to overpower the otherwise better armed and technologically superior Japanese.

Mr. Kim the Younger looked up at the top of the arch through his sunglasses and announced to the group through a satisfied smile, "The Arch of Triumph. At sixty meters this is the tallest Arch of Triumph in the world."

He was correct the Arch of Triumph is nine meters taller than the *Arc de Triomphe* in Paris. But it certainly isn't the world's tallest arch. Up the road from *Arc de Triomphe*, in *La Défense*, is the *Grande Arche de la Fraternité* standing 110 meters, and in Saint Louis the Gateway Arch stands 192 meters above the banks of the Mississippi and is the tallest monument in the world but those aren't triumphal arches. Those are just your average run of the mill arches.

Mr. Kim the Younger commenced with the bestowal of disposable facts and figures: "The arch was constructed from more than 10,500 pieces of carved granite. It stands sixty meters tall and fifty meters wide, making it the largest Arch of Triumph in the world. Inside are many rooms and elevators which can carry guests up to observation platforms. One can see azaleas carved into the base..."

I drifted off to the side under the pretext of taking pictures, but in fact I was looking for any sign in the Arch of Triumph Square that would reveal that same square was once, long before Wade-Giles[9] gave way to Pinyin,[10] proudly called Mao Tse-tung Square. At the end of the Korean War when all those Chinese volunteers volunteered to stay on and lend a hand in rebuilding, some of them were assigned to moving the bombed out rubble aside and creating a large square surrounded by stately government buildings. The Great Leader named it in honor of the Great Helmsman as a sign of appreciation for the help. Western Historians claim as many as 700,000 Chinese entered the war on the Korean Peninsula, and tens of thousands remained behind as "volunteer" workers. Now, however, there is nothing left to suggest anybody ever helped out with anything. Time and again it was proudly announced that thanks to the peerless leadership they were so fortunate to have, North Koreans had pulled themselves up by their collective bootstraps. They are a self-reliant people and do not need assistance from the outside. But long ago, before history had been rewritten, on that very spot the Chinese had conducted a lot of the manual dirty work for their fraternal comrades.

Across the street from the arch was the *Kaeson* Revolutionary Site, the very spot on which the Great Leader stood and addressed the fawning populace on his triumphant return to the city on 14 October 1945. After defeating the Imperial Japanese Army, he came down out of the hills, slipped on a jacket and tie, and waltzed up to the microphone and delivered a speech so stirring that they are still talking about it. It was so stirring, in fact, that they carved the entire speech in stone and it sits there beside the spot for all to read. "...To contribute positively to the work of building the state, let those with strength give strength, let those with knowledge give knowledge, let those with money give money..."

The impromptu gathering of the masses and Kim's extemporaneous speech led to the spontaneous generation of the revolution right then and right there. The great Korean Socialist Revolution erupted forth by the sheer force of Kim's words and placed North Korea on the path towards eternal abundant prosperity. At least that's what the Koreans claim. The Russians tell a different tale. They claim that back when they were known as Soviets, they hustled Kim into Pyongyang and they orchestrated the gathering and they prepared and edited the speech Kim delivered, and when he, as a rough-hewn thirty-three-year-old political neophyte, delivered the address, the Soviets stood on the stage and flanked the trembling Kim on all sides as a sign of camaraderie and support. Photographs taken on the day attest to the Soviet claims, but in a fit of *Juche* idealism, the North Koreans airbrushed the Soviets out of official pictures. Now Kim stands alone at the podium and delivers the speech of a lifetime while the masses squirm at his feet in unbridled exuberance. That is the image depicted in the mosaic mural mounted at the site; a beaming Kim, alone before the people, explaining to them how it's going to be.

I strolled back towards the van just as Charles finished passing out a carton of deluxe Chinese cigarettes to both Kims and Mr. Bae. They all accepted their gift graciously, then quietly tucked them away inside the van. In the tiny fraternity of North Korean tour organizers, it is traditional to hand over a gift that is part tip, part gratuity, and part insurance policy to ensure the Korean handlers navigate as efficiently as possible through the bureaucratic maze. Seeing the unopened cartons being tucked away was a relief. The prospect of riding through the streets of Pyongyang in a van filled with carcinogenic ChiCom mundungus was not appealing.

From out of nowhere appeared an indignant middle-aged man in a huff. He spotted Mr. Bae as the driver and launched into him with a vociferous finger-wagging attack.

"Who authorized you to park in the middle of the street? What are other passing vehicles supposed to do?! Are you just in from the village!?"

On and on he grumbled, a stream of complaints coming one after another, while Mr. Bae stood frozen beside the van. At the same time Mr. Kim the Elder silently opened the sliding door and motioned for us to quickly take our seats. As soon as our wide Occidental bottoms made contact with the surface of their respective seats, Mr. Bae instinctively knew and churned out the appropriate effusive apology as he backed towards the driver's door. He was still mouthing apologetic words through the windshield as he turned the key and stepped on the accelerator. Mr. Kim the Elder giggled like a school girl as we drove away.

Mr. Bae drove the van back into the epicenter of Pyongyang, Kim Il Sung Square. In a circuitous fashion he wove around behind buildings and through narrow passages and brought the van to a stop near the crest of a small hill. Down below was the expansive Kim Il Sung Square hemmed in by gray stone ministry buildings of the Socialist Classicism school.

We had arrived at the Grand People's Study House which had been unveiled in 1982 as an odd capstone at the top of the square. While the boxy gray ministry buildings below could have been plucked from central Moscow during the height of the Cold War, the Grand People's Study House is an enormous green-roofed stone and cement structure that unashamedly pays homage to traditional Korean architecture. The upturned corners of the green roof emphasized the building's Asianness and contrasted nicely with the stodgy old Soviet-style buildings flanking the rest of Kim Il Sung Square.

Mr. Kim the Younger cleared his throat and resumed his role as docent. He looked up at the impressive structure and in an authoritative voice said, "Here we are at the Grand People's Study House. This is *not* a library. This is more than a library.... It is a place where people come and have access to books and periodicals and resources so they can study and learn."

Charles voiced the question we were all thinking, "You just described a library. This is a library?"

"No," Mr. Kim reassured us, "this is the Grand People's Study House and this is *not* a library."

For the duration of our time there we were told time and again that the Grand People's Study House was not to be confused with a library because it wasn't a library. It never became clear why the North Koreans felt the need to elaborate on this stance, but as if the statement had been underscored with a fluorescent green highlighter on the daily hand-out from the Ministry of Love, we were reminded again and again of what it wasn't.

Mr. Kim the Elder quietly walked over to a large heavy door and struggled to pull it open just enough to twist his rawboned frame through the opening. A few moments later he squirmed out again and walked back to the group to announce that we would be allowed inside, but that we would need to enter through a different door. This came as a quiet relief. Corpulent Occidentals squeezing through that crack would have been painful to watch.

We followed him across the front of the building and in so doing we could look down on the back of the viewing platform from which the Dear Leader observes parades that pass through the square. Many believe that it was originally designed as the mausoleum into which Kim Il Sung's body would have eventually been put on display, but plans changed and it continues to be used for the mummy-free viewing of parades. Just five days before our visit, Kim Jong Il had stood just below the spot on which we stood on the right side of the platform, where he took in the celebratory parade and testosterone-laden show of armed might to commemorate the seventy-fifth anniversary of the founding of the Korean People's Army. Five days before there had been half a million saber-rattling people in rapturous glee because they had been honored with the presence of the Dear Leader. They were packed in to the square shoulder to jowl in spit-shined splendor, but as we passed by five days later the huge square was completely deserted.

When we arrived at the main entrance, Mr. Kim the Elder ushered us into a large pillared room that, except for a huge statue of Kim Il Sung standing before a mural depicting Mount *Paekdu*, was empty. We all knew the drill. The Kims brought up the flanks, we all toed the imaginary line, the Kims genuflected while we shot a quick Albright towards the back of the room.

As we completed the formalities at the foot of the statue, an official in jacket and tie joined us. He introduced himself as Mr. Park and he sounded like he was a three-pack-a-day kind of comrade. Mr. Park spoke to us in English, and then asked in Korean if we would mind allowing Mr. Kim to translate due to his superior English abilities. With that Mr. Park launched in to a rapid synopsis of the requisite list of facts and figures.

The building is 100,000 square meters and has sufficient space to accommodate six thousand readers. It cost US $100 million to construct. The entire structure was thrown together using traditional *bbali-bbali* construction techniques in a mere twenty-one months to open on April Fool's Day in 1982.

As Mr. Park rattled off the tedium, Mr. Kim dutifully translated every word. I glanced down to see Mr. Park's hand fidgeting with something. On closer inspection it was a Glenfiddich key ring. After three full days of cement and agitprop, catching a glimpse of a colorful corporate logo was like peeking at pornography. It was bright and bold with the product name spread eagle in a voluptuous font that displayed just a hint of pert little serifs. The leggy consonants were set off by round, supple, curvy vowels that pouted playfully. The corporate logo was clearly contraband in the stark, gray socialist landscape. My heart missed a salacious beat and I looked up to see Mr. Park catch my glimpse and he immediately dropped the Glenfiddich key

The interior walls of the Grand People's Study House are adorned with numerous paintings and murals capturing important events in the North Korean version of history. In this painting, Kim Il Sung's great great grandfather Kim Ung U is depicted leading a band of righteous Koreans in the sinking of the *General Sherman*. North Korean and US historians agree on very, very little when it comes to the opposing accounts of that 1866 event. The caption presents the North Korean version of the incident in which the American ship was filled with loot-seeking pirates searching for the treasure contained in nearby ancient tombs.

ring into the *vinalon* abyss of his pocket. With no more than the lift of one eyebrow Mr. Park told me that the Glenfiddich keychain was not to be discussed.

We walked up a set of stairs to the mezzanine level where two dozen people were operating computerized card catalogues in a dim gloom. As we approached the lights were turned on and everything was suddenly illuminated in fluorescent splendor. Mr. Park paused and allowed our little group to gather, then he pointed at the rows of computer terminals and said in English, "Our card catalogue is completely computerized," apparently unaware that this was old news outside the Worker's Paradise. The setting could have been any high school library in the Western world with the lights turned off.

Mr. Park explained that universities in North Korea depend on the Grand People's Study House as a resource for their students. He recited names of universities in and around Pyongyang.

With that Wally asked if Mr. Park had ever heard of the South Korean-funded Pyongyang University of Science and Technology.

Mr. Park said, "Yes ... yes I have seen a car with that name on the side. I don't know about the university, but I have seen the car."

Mr. Kim the Elder was locked in concentration as he scrutinized a scrap of paper from his pocket and Mr. Kim the Younger had a sudden shoelace emergency that took him off to the sidelines. Neither of them were ever willing to acknowledge the Pyongyang University of Science and Technology actually existed.

We walked through the empty marbled corridors with our footsteps echoing off the cold walls. Now and again Mr. Park would open a door just a crack and peek in, then when he didn't find what he wanted to show us, turn away and keep walking. Finally, after several doors, he pulled one open

As in all other public places in North Korea, portraits of the Great Leader Kim Il Sung and the Dear Leader Kim Jong Il peer down with beatific expressions. This lecture hall within the People's Grand Study House is one of many designed to allow dutiful workers time off to return to the life of education at some point in mid-career. Lectures are conducted not only in Korean, but also Japanese, Chinese, Russian, and English.

to reveal a large room filled with lines of desks and chairs. On the desks were perched large television monitors and accompanying video-tape players. Two dozen well dressed and immaculately groomed North Koreans huddled individually in front of televisions — peering intently at the screens and listening through headphones.

Mr. Park explained that they were "studying." It was obvious that at least some of them were studying the same North Korean karaoke videos that we had studied in the restaurant at lunch.

We wound our way through the maze of corridors — all doors closed against the chill still lingering in the stone and cement building. Now and again muffled sounds could be heard behind the closed doors, but never enough to reveal what was going on inside. Once or twice preoccupied individuals passed by as they walked briskly towards a different part of the complex.

It appeared that we were strolling aimlessly through the complex, but Mr. Park was building up to something. As we walked he explained each specific subject had a reading room assigned to it and each reading room could comfortably seat hundreds of people. There was a room for Social Sciences, and a room for Technology, and another room dedicated to Literature. It certainly appeared that the North Koreans had simply used the Dewey Decimal System in assigning topics to rooms.

I interjected, "Mr. Park, how many topic-specific reading rooms are within the Grand People's Study House?"

"There are hundreds of rooms where one can study," he answered, not fully understanding what I was driving at.

"But for each major topic, such as Language, there is one main study room?"

"Yes!" he said, happy that I was so interested in the system.

Then before I could ask the obvious follow-on question, he answered it for me. He beamed and said, "There are twenty major topic rooms in the Grand People's Study House. There is one main room per major topic — we have ten of those rooms. We have two other topics that occupy the remaining ten rooms — the works of Kim Il Sung and the works of Kim Jong Il "

The Dewey Decimal System plus two.

Isaac Asimov almost accomplished the Herculean feat of publishing at least one book in each of the ten major Dewey Decimal categories.[11] In North Korean Library Science Kim Il Sung and Kim Jong Il not only published books in each of the ten major categories — they both had an additional category created for themselves. Melvil Dewey had no way of anticipating the need for an eleventh and twelfth category, but the ceaselessly amazing stream of brilliance that the Kims dutifully put to paper could not be bound to the pedestrian parameters of the established system. The North Koreans remedied the situation by revamping the system.

Mr. Park took us in to a large deserted study room and we gathered around an innocuous looking desk in a queue of many identical desks. With tremendous pride he said, "On one occasion the Dear Leader was visiting the Grand People's Study House and came to this room and observed the desks. Then he provided brilliant on-the-spot guidance! He said, 'All people are not the same height, so these desks should be adjustable, and with that he showed us how to alter the design of the desks which allowed them to adjust to the needs of the individual user.'" Mr. Kim the Younger nodded in approval while Mr. Kim the Elder actually reached out a tentative hand and reverently stroked the surface of the desk.

As we stepped back into the corridor, Mr. Park stopped and showed us a framed and red velvet-backed sign over the entrance to the room. The sign recorded the visits to that room by Kim Il Sung and Kim Jong Il. The dates were recorded in both the Juche system and the Gregorian calendar with a short description of the specific purpose of the visit. One would think that brilliant on-the-spot guidance would be reason enough.

Down the corridor some doors featured the velvet-backed signs and some did not. We stepped in to yet another large room with queues of desks occupied by teens in school uniforms. They all appeared to be quietly studying. Not one of them glanced up to see who had entered the room. Without bothering to lower his voice, Mr. Park announced that anyone seventeen years-of-age or older could freely enter the Grand People's Study House seven days a week between 8:00 A.M. and 8:00 P.M. The only exceptions were two days per month when the entire complex is closed for inventory. With a reported 30 million volumes in the racks taking inventory in two days would require a speed battle with at least a dozen accordion and tuba ensembles.

Our next stop was one of the highlights for many foreign guests to North Korea. For years visitors have described in clattering detail what we were about to see — a well-rehearsed demonstration of North Korean engineering brilliance.

Mr. Park walked us up to the lending counter which was oddly situated well away from the stacks in a dim little corner. A lone woman sat behind the desk looking blankly into the middle distance, obviously deep in a proletarian daydream. As we approached she came to her senses and clicked a button on her dated computer terminal and the screen switched to English. She turned to our little group and addressed us in Korean, which Mr. Kim the Younger translated.

She said, "With this advanced automated system any book the reader wants can be retrieved in moments," and before she could go on, Mr. Park mumbled something and her nimble fingers typed a few letters, then hit the return key. Seconds later there was a clatter and behind her a rubberized curtain parted to allow a tray on rollers to bounce its way down a wheeled conveyor belt. It came to a clanging stop right in front of her. In the tray was a big colorful American book: *Robots, Androids, and Animators; 12 Incredible Projects You Can Build,* by John Iovine.

The suggestion was that the wheeled conveyor system wound its way through the cavernous stacks behind the wall and in an ode to Rube Goldberg found the least efficient way of delivering a book from the shelf to the desk. However, the speed with which the transaction transpired suggested this was staged for our benefit and some accomplice behind the scenes had picked up a random English-language book and sent it rocketing down the track at the secret signal.

They were all very proud of their clattering delivery system and emphasized the fact that absolutely any book in the entire collection could be rocketed down the tracks from the hidden shelves ... any book at all. The system wasn't limited to just certain books ... any book could be called up and delivered ... any book in the entire collection. Any of them.

From other accounts some tour groups had stood at the same spot and been instructed to select a book that could be sent rocketing down the tracks for inspection. Previous tourists painfully suggested titles that could be called up: Orwell's *1984*? No ... any other suggestion? *Animal Farm*? No ... another suggestion? Adam Smith's *Wealth of Nations*? No ... another suggestion? Jonathan Swift's *Gulliver's Travels*? No ... it appeared that our little group instinctively knew that we needed to avoid that embarrassing trap and we simply moved on, content that if Iovine's *Robots, Androids, and Animators; 12 Incredible Projects You Can Build* was there ... other books were probably there as well.

Mr. Park walked us around the corner and down another long, frigid corridor. Here and there doorways were topped with the velveteen announcement that on-the-spot guidance had taken place within the room, and occasionally a piece of framed socialist realism provided artwork for the otherwise bare walls. We stopped at one point to pose in front of a familiar painting of the anti–Japanese heroine Comrade Kim Jung Suk, guerrilla extraordinaire, wife and consort of the Great Leader, and blessed sacred mother of the Dear Leader. The painting, titled *The Anti-Japanese Heroine Comrade Kim Jung Suk Protecting the Life of the Great Leader* was created in 1974 by a now forgotten North Korean artist. Since then the image has been recreated again and again and is one of the most readily recognized works of art in North Korea. It features a young smooth-skinned Jung Suk resplendent in pleated khaki uniform skirt, holding an equally young and earnest Kim Il Sung back as she dispatches an unseen Japanese colonizer with a pistol shot. The Japanese soldier is completely out of view, but you can tell by her expression that she capped him right between his beady little imperialistic eyes.

As he walked Mr. Park explained that at any given time there were 200 lecturers on duty to provide feedback in special Question and Answer Rooms. They were on call for the betterment of the general public, ready to delve in to their particular area of expertise.

Mr. Kim the Elder turned to Wally and jokingly suggested, "You have a PhD, you speak Korean, why don't you come get a job lecturing here?"

We all chuckled at the thought, then Wally asked, "Are there any foreign lecturers on staff?"

"Of course!" Mr. Park beamed, then opened the door to a large empty lecture theater and simultaneously maneuvered to a new subject while ushering us inside.

We walked as a group down to the stage where a large podium sat under framed portraits of the Great Leader and the Dear Leader. Mr. Kim the Elder laughingly suggested we pose for photographs while standing behind the microphone at the lectern. One by one we took turns climbing the steps and posing behind the lectern. With each new subject Mr. Kim suggested an arm uplifted in emphasis, a mouth open as if speaking, a gaze into the empty seats. Each time the camera clicked and the flash froze us in place on stage posed like a rabid orator driving home some salient point, Mr. Kim laughed until he was in tears.

Only much later did I stumble across journals about visits to North Korea in which were featured photographs of the same pose in the same theater. A little Peruvian woman, a tall Dutch man, a young Finn, A Pole, three Canadians, and many others. They all stood behind the same lectern, they all raised their hands as if driving home that exact same salient point, and they all looked as goofy as we had.

For Mr. Park one of the proudest points in the tour was when he threw open the door to a large room with scores of computers standing ready for use. He took on the glow of an expectant mother when he swept his outstretched arm through the air and announced that we were standing in one of many rooms in which ordinary citizens could have access to a computer. At first glance it was impressive — row after row of recent generation personal computers readily accessible to the rank and file. Mr. Park turned the near-

est computer on and it booted the Windows XP Professional operating system. I suspect Bill Gates has probably not ever received payment for any of
his software being used in North Korea. Mr. Park explained that though they
could not connect to the internet, within North Korea there is a very sophisticated intranet which allows users to have virtually the same experience. As
he spoke the computer booted Silivaccine 2005, a home-grown anti-virus
software not used anywhere except North Korea.

As the hard drive was scanned for viruses, Wally sat down in front of the
computer and asked, "Is there a problem with viruses among your comput
ers?"

Mr. Park smiled and, oblivious to the irony, proudly said, "No, in North
Korea the highly controlled access reduces the opportunity for a virus to be
introduced."

The most transformational aspect of computer application — easy and
instant communication with anyone anywhere — isn't allowed to exist in North
Korea. When North Koreans are allowed to sit down in front of a computer,
they can enter the regime-monitored intranet to look at the works of Kim
Jong Il, or review the news as per the state mouthpiece, or check crop rotation statistics from the '70s, but they can't chat with a friend, they can't peruse
a web page from the opposition party, they can't get scores from English Premier League games and they certainly can't follow a game live; they can't
receive a photo of their cousin in Pusan, and they definitely can't tap in to e-
commerce, and e-mail is out of the question. Of course this means they don't
have to deal with in-boxes filled with unsolicited spam from Nigerian scam
artists, so there is an upside.

When the virus scan was complete Wally clicked the mouse and was at
the portal for North Korea's intranet. The graphics were reminiscent of the
early days of the internet, before advertisers came, and other than the Korean
script it shared absolutely no resemblance with the wiggling, flashing, blinking, beeping, graphics-oversaturated web pages being hosted south of the
DMZ. We all stood behind and peered over his shoulder as he stumbled
around and translated what he uncovered; news items from the Korean Central News Agency, scholarly papers on the *Juche* Idea, details about Kim Jong
Il's comings and goings and all the valuable on-the-spot-guidance he had
meted out to the people ... and of course reports on crop rotation from around
the country. It was all very dry and predictable and not at all inviting. The Koreans looked on with tremendous pride. We saw firsthand that they had something just as good as, if not better than, that internet thing they had heard of.

As we continued the tour, Mr. Park explained that the 200 lecturers on
standby don't just man the help desk, they also stand behind lecterns and

deliver lectures on an array of topics in Korean, Russian, Chinese and English. The true disciple of the *Juche* Idea is eternally seeking to master more knowledge in order to lift the collectivist society even higher. To that end the Grand People's Study House welcomes specially selected day students who are granted permission to take up to six months off from their job to go further their education in full-time study. The less promising students aren't granted time off from work, but they are allowed to attend evening classes on their own time. With electricity in such short supply I found it hard to picture the Grand People's Study House open and illuminated in the evening.

In one of the music rooms we were shown yet more desks that had been converted to listening stations. Along the wall behind a counter were racks of open-reel and LP records in colorful sleeves — all of them North Korean. A few people were scattered around the room at random desks where they listened intently through headphones. Without warning Mr. Kim the Elder reached around one of the seated listeners and pulled the headphone jack out of a tape player. The room was filled with a cacophony of North Korean martial music and the dark-suited thirty-something man who had been minding his own business under the headphones looked up at Mr. Kim and blinked bewildered eyes. The walls shook and the furniture rattled to the strains of "We Will Man the Guard Posts to Protect Our Beloved Fatherland." When the headphones were plugged back in and the room returned to silence, among the capitalists there was a collective sigh of relief.

North Koreans are blessed with numerous and varied sources should they want to listen to some music. In addition to the selections presented on state-run radio and television, there are military bands, children's musical performance troupes, the People's Committee Encouragement Band and Vocal Chorale, the May First Nut and Bolt Foundry Charwomen's Choir, the Wounded Veterans Marching Brass Band, the Sinuiju Metropolitan Whistling Brigade, and if one is lucky there will be a speed battle going on so the accordion and tuba ensembles will be out in the neighborhood. With so much on offer at home, it is rare that a North Korean would need to listen to music from the outside world. However, should that need surface, the expansive Grand People's Study House has been stocked full of music from all over the world in countless styles and genres. And, according to Mr. Park, as long as they are 17-years-of-age or older, they can make their way from anywhere in the nation to the Grand People's Study House and, assuming they don't arrive on one of those two days a month when inventory is being taken, they can sit at a desk and discover the delights of foreign music.

Mr. Park was explaining this when Mr. Kim the Elder asked him in English, "Do you have any American music?"

Mr. Park walked towards a large cabinet and reached in with a satisfied grin. My money was on Miles Davis, George Gershwin, Buck Owens, Aaron Copeland, Chet Atkins, Simon and Garfunkel, or Benny Goodman; something seminally American. He fished around for what he was looking for. He popped a cassette tape in to a player and turned the volume knob up a few numbers and the room reverberated with the frantic sounds of a strained female voice. I had no idea who I was listening to, but it reminded me of any one of numerous anonymous performers given the task of singing the U.S. national anthem at a sporting event. Because the melody is difficult and the range greater than their ability, they use the shotgun approach and blast a cupful of random notes in the general direction of the correct one. That ballpark delivery is what came blasting out of the speakers. I picked up the plastic cassette cover and discovered that we were listening to Mariah Carey's Greatest Hits. Mariah Carey hadn't been on my list.

The spine of the cassette case had a hand scrawled " 미국 " ... "America." We stood to go and I passed the cabinet as Mr. Park replaced the cassette just as I moved past and had a clear view. Within the cabinet was a large wooden bin with a similar " 미국 " written on a large label. In the vast collection of the Grand People's Study House Mariah Carey's Greatest Hits stood alone as the solitary example of American music. They desperately need Benny Goodman, and Jimi Hendrix, Stevie Ray Vaughn and Jerry Jeff Walker, Patsy Cline and Roger Miller, Funkadelic AND Parliament, and Arthur Fiedler and his Boston Pops. They got Mariah Carey.

Mr. Park steered us towards the front door and we slowed to a stroll. Charles asked him what he had studied in university and when he revealed he had majored in literature the questions erupted. Had he read Steinbeck? No. Hemingway? No. Twain? No. Philip Roth ... Thomas Pynchon ... Danielle Steel? No, no, no. Mr. Park's painfully limited exposure to foreign literature wasn't a surprise. In a regime where e-mail is outlawed there's no way Danielle Steel is going to be permitted.

"Mr. Park, have you ever read Ma Kwang-su?" I asked as we strolled.

He paused and looked up with an astonished face said, "Yes ... yes I have. How do you know Ma Kwang-su?"

Ma had been a controversial South Korean author of the early '90s known for racy realism and open disregard and utter disdain for censorship. His work regularly featured salacious subject matter that did not settle well with certain parties, and when those certain parties rule the nation confrontation is inevitable. He was known by some as the D.H. Lawrence of Korea. He skirted the full wrath of those certain parties until he published *Chulgoun Sara*,[12] which contained passages about a young unmarried woman and her body parts and what she did with them and what her male acquaintances did with them in response. Ma was summarily tossed in jail and the book was officially banned as too prurient for respectable society. Banned books invite civil disobedience. I made a point of obtaining an illicit copy and struggled about a third of the way through the book before concluding that, A.) reading Korean for extended periods of time makes my head hurt, and B.) *Chulgoun Sara* wasn't a very interesting book to begin with.

I smiled at Mr. Park and said, "I read Ma's books while I was a student." That appeared to be sufficient for him because he smiled a knowing smile and nodded as if I had said the secret code words.

Outside, in the tiny parking lot beside the enormous building, we crawled in the van and started moving forward just as a late-model Japanese sedan pulled up in front of us to allow the passenger to get out. It was a middle-aged North Korean woman in sedate business attire. The door of the car was marked with the English word "taxi." It appeared that the "taxi" had hastily been written with bits of black electrical tape affixed to the car by someone not entirely familiar with the Latin alphabet.

"Mr. Kim," I said, "I have heard that there were no taxis in Pyongyang. That's a taxi ... right?"

Mr. Kim the Elder smiled as he glanced at the car through the van window. "Of course, that's a taxi. It has the word 'taxi' on the side, can't you see it?"

It looked as if the car might have been commandeered as a taxi and the word hastily affixed to the door before being sent out at just the right moment for foreign eyes to see it. There conspiracy theorists were going to love this.

I asked, "Who may use a taxi in Pyongyang?"

Mr. Kim nonchalantly replied, "Anyone may use a taxi.... We all do.... We just telephone them and they come to pick us up and take us where we are going."

In a nation where fuel is so scarce and vehicles so few, the concept of a fleet of taxis didn't comfortably fit. Yet there it was, temporarily parked right in front of us so that we had no choice but to notice it.

Mr. Bae twisted and turned through the showcase neighborhood. Then, around a sweeping bend in the road and we came face to face with scores of people queued up at the closed doors of a large building dressed out in stone. It was obvious that they were all silently waiting to get inside. The van moved a few meters beyond the patient citizens and came to a stop.

Mr. Kim the Younger announced that we had arrived at the *Rakwon* Department Store and we were free to step inside and buy anything we might require. I tumbled out of the van and looked back at the throngs gathered in front of the building across the road. Even as we stood there the queue grew longer as more people came to wait for the doors to open.

"Mr. Kim, what is that building and why are they gathering there?"

Mr. Kim beamed with pride when he informed me, "That is a health complex and they are there for health. All citizens can take advantage of such health facilities in North Korea."

It was *Changgwangwon*, the nation's finest "health complex." Inside were four levels of swimming pools and barbershops, beauty parlors, and most importantly, baths. The Korean public bath can be a luxurious respite. Segregated by gender, the traditional establishment allows fully grown adults the thrill of rediscovering the sheer, uninhibited joy children experience in the bathtub. Assuming the bather is capable of crawling into their own little personal space and concentrating on the soaking relaxation, it can be a wonderful experience. Otherwise the bather spends the entire time preoccupied with

At the end of a workday and in preparation for the next day's May Day festivities, citizens of Pyongyang wait for access to *Changgwangwon*, a large complex offering gyms, barbershops, beauty salons, and most importantly, public bathing facilities with hot water. It is speculated that even the homes of high ranking officials do not have access to hot water.

the fact that there are a whole lot of naked people and they are all lathered, slippery, and walking around really, really naked.

In South Korea the modern upper-end bath house should be thought of in terms of a spa where attention to detail and beautiful ambiance draw a steady stream of affluent customers who don't necessarily do much talking, at least on the male side of the dividing wall. In South Korea's fading past there was a time when the neighborhood bath house was a lot less like a spa and a lot more like the shower block at a state park. They were spartan and clean and customers went to them because they lacked the ability to take a bath at home. Back then the idea was to get in, get clean, and get out. Like Seoul three decades previous, one can speculate that bathing facilities with hot water are not frequently found in Pyongyang homes. We were not given the opportunity to go in and look, but I got the impression most of the people queued up at the door waiting for admittance in the late afternoon sun were there because *Changgwangwon* had hot water.

Across the street from the bathhouse, the *Rakwon* Department Store used to be the shop for diplomats and the regime's elite. It served the purpose of actually selling otherwise impossible-to-acquire items for hard currency. The Number One Department Store, on the other hand, was reportedly established simply to be able to demonstrate to foreign visitors that North Korea is sufficiently wealthy to provide consumer goods for sale to citizens. It has long been rumored to be a Potemkin department store with products permanently displayed and never actually sold. It appears that the two functions have been blurred and department stores of all description mix their permanent display with items that are actually sold. Like an amusement park where the General Store in Old West Town features snake oil, bolts of calico, hard tack, Dr. Johnson's Liver Pills, picks, shovels, prospecting pans and a rack of bumper stickers, T-shirts, key chains and miniature plastic license plates displayed in alphabetical order (Aaron, Amber, Ashley, Aubrey...), and anything that can be created through injection molding, the department store sat ready to accept visiting tourists. It all blends together and somehow we know instinctively that acne-riddled Old West guy in suspenders will sell us the stickers but the snake oil and liver pills are just for show.

Inside the two-level *Rakwon* Department Store we wandered the aisles and surveyed an odd assortment of packaged foods, ginseng, alcohol and hard candy. To one side were Japanese-made rice cookers, Chinese refrigerators and wide-screen televisions. Still no sign of anything from the Hamhung Disabled Soldiers' Plastic Daily Necessities Factory. With nothing of interest beckoning on the ground floor, we climbed the steps to the spacious upper level where there was more variety.

One can sling a lot of well-deserved and justifiable negative criticism at North Korea, but the North Koreans never force anyone to listen to Muzak and as I walked across the empty department store I was not subjected to any easy listening stylings, no syrupy piano renditions, no vapid variations on a theme. It was heavenly to not have to put up with someone else's bad taste in music. If I want bad music — I'll select it myself. In contrast, in Seoul any shopping experience is a full frontal aural assault designed to club the shopper over the head with sound, then use more pulsating sound waves to extract wads of cash from the shopper's pockets as they lay on the floor writhing in convulsions.

In 1995 there was a quick and very controlled influx of journalists admitted into North Korea to witness the International Sports and Cultural Festival for Peace. They were shown many of the same cement monuments I saw, and were shuttled around Pyongyang to see selected aspects of "everyday life in North Korea." The North Koreans were so unsophisticated that they did not comprehend the ability of the average Western journalist to see through the ruse. The North Korean "shoppers" were so unaccustomed to "shopping" that they walked away from the counter and left purchased goods with the cashier, or paid for items multiple times, or purchased items then personally returned them to their original place on the shelf before exiting the store. They were play acting with the snake oil, prospecting pans, and calico. I was on the lookout for these sorts of "shoppers" but for the most part the place was empty.

I drifted past the Chinese-made MP3 players towards the empty and pleasantly quiet men's department in search of *vinalon*. Though there would never be any off-the-rack garment on the entire peninsula large enough to fit me, I relished the sudden thought that I might be able to purchase a bolt of *vinalon* from the men's wear department. A matching jacket and trousers made out of limestone ... just think of the conversations one could have at a cocktail party. The conversation could lead to a series of short demonstrations. "Hey ... go ahead ... pour your cocktails into my pocket ... here; I'll even hold it open for you. See! It's completely impermeable ... it's *vinalon!*"

Off to the side was a sprinkling of mostly empty racks with jackets, shirts, and trousers meagerly displayed. As I stepped into the range of a uniformed shop attendant and was about to start speaking, she silently withdrew and vanished. I was left standing alone among the checked jackets.

I meandered across to the car accessories and tinned pet food section (opposite the fishing lure and sock department), and as I approached the uniformed woman quietly polishing the counter near the lures, she backed into the shadows and disappeared. The same thing happened in the women's shoe section — just as I got into range the attendant vanished.

I backtracked to the men's department again and mentally rehearsed my Korean, making sure to soften the Southern accent and change the vocabulary accordingly. As I passed the dress shirts, I opened my mouth and started to enquire just as she vanished around a corner and out of sight.

Every uniformed assistant I encountered magically vanished, in a splendid feint to the shadows. Like martial artists tumbling unexpectedly out of harm's way rather than confronting an adversary, each uniformed woman harnessed my forward motion to propel herself back into the shadows to avoid confrontation with a dreaded foreigner. As I passed they reemerged and continued dusting or polishing or sweeping. Determined to not have my one opportunity thwarted, I doubled back and passed through the Men's Wear Department again. In the end I accepted my defeat because it was obvious when I crossed each of their imaginary tripwires, and I could sense that each of them would automatically withdraw no matter how many times I passed. Each shop girl had a little territory of responsibility within which she stood guard. Each little territory had a pre-designated path of escape designed to be used when the little territory was invaded by foreign infiltrators. They weren't really there to sell the items on the shelves and racks and there was no reason for them to invest energy in dealing with a foreign intruder. I was allowed to observe, but I could not interact. Descending the steps I glanced up to see all of the uniformed attendants emerge from the shadows and return to their perfunctory duties in a tranquil customer-free environment. I departed never knowing if they stocked bolts of *vinalon* or how they would have reacted had I managed to find someone willing to allow me to enquire about it.

The next stop was the speciously named Victorious Fatherland Liberation War Museum, yet another enormous Soviet-era building that would have been just as at home in 1950s Moscow. Though North Korea came out of the war with a reduction in territory, and though they suffered significantly more casualties than their enemy, the Ministry of Love assures the people that they won. Western journalists habitually fall back on the hackneyed phrase, "technically still at war," when describing the two Koreas. In the North that phrase is unnecessary and unknown. The war was fought, the Great Leader led the valiant people through matchless brilliance to defeat the imperialist invaders, the fatherland was liberated, end of story.

A few days earlier I had taken a taxi across Beijing to the Military Museum of the Chinese People's Revolution (中国人民革命军事博物馆) in the Haidian District in hopes of getting the Chinese perspective on the War to Resist America and Aid Korea (抗美援朝). The museum is stuffed with exhibits and displays of much more than just the Chinese Revolution and at one time it housed an

At the entrance of the Victorious Fatherland Liberation War Museum in Pyongyang, this mural depicts a young, vibrant Kim Il Sung, the glorious Lodestar of the Masses, striding forth to lead the deliriously happy Korean people from every walk of life into the future.

extensive exhibit on the Korean War, but by the time I finally found the Korean exhibit room within the sprawling complex, all that was left were a half dozen rubber-slipper-wearing laborers scraping the walls in preparation for painting. The entire display had been dismantled and removed leaving no acknowledgement that China played a significant role in the outcome of events on the Korean peninsula. That wing of the museum building was so empty and cavernous that the voices of the laborers echoed as they chatted.

Unlike the Chinese, the North Koreans are still celebrating the victory. A female guide in a military-like uniform met us on the front steps and quickly ran through the obligatory facts and figures: opened in April of 1974 the museum is 52,000 square meters and contains more than eighty display rooms: the Dear Leader had visited the museum to provide on-the-spot guidance ... it all sounded like a variation of the same preamble.

With the prerequisites out of the way, she reached and grabbed a pointer from a box near the door and started quickly hitting the high points. Standing before a wall filled with large black and white photographs, she explained that the Americans had killed 149,000 people in the Southern half of the peninsula prior to the deceitful and insidious surprise attack on the North. The proof, she explained, was in documents revealing the cunning American plan, and the museum just happened to have photographs of those damning documents mounted and hung on the wall. So the North was morally obliged to avenge the ruthless murder of 149,000 innocent compatriots, but even if that had not been the case the Americans had instigated hostilities and invaded sovereign northern territory, thus the peace-loving citizenry had no choice but to take up arms. Fortunately for them, the greatest military strategist ever known to mankind happened to be available for duty.

The Great Leader, Kim Il Sung, single-handedly formed the Korean People's Army in 1932. Then in 1948, during the tense lull between the end of the Second World War and the start of the Korean War, he invited the Soviets to come down and assist against the provocations of the "Syngman Rhee puppet clique" and their American masters.

Again and again the Korean-speaking guide referred to South Korea's first President, Syngman Rhee, and pronounced his name not as a Korean would normally pronounce it, "E Seung Mon," but as he had Romanized it and as he encouraged Westerners to say it with name order altered, stress shifted, and pronunciation completely un–Korean. Her stern face and state-sanctioned diatribe were supposed to create a somber atmosphere, but every time she mentioned "Sing Man Reee" I had to suppress a giggle.

We followed our guide deeper into the museum and she continued to rattle off a synopsis of the North Korean version of the war: The Americans invaded the northern half of the peninsula so the valiant people's army of the north defended themselves, then, through the peerless stratagems of the Great Leader, the Americans were repulsed. Very quickly thereafter the cunning and deceitful imperialists were driven like dogs south towards the very tip of Korea. It was then that the treacherous Americans called on reinforcements from their imperialist military enclaves in Japan as well as various puppet states around the world that saw this as an opportunity to curry favor. Bolstered by millions and millions of imperialist mercenaries, hirelings, armed pirates, and freebooting profiteers, the Americans dashed north at the precise time that Kim Il Sung, coincidently, had ordered a temporary strategic retreat. The Americans and their arms-for-hire minions went as far as the border between Korea and Red China from where they bombed Chinese villages and killed innocent peace-loving Chinese peasants. For that reason the people of China volunteered in great number to avenge the deaths of their countrymen and to assist the noble Korean compatriots in their desire to be free of foreign tyranny. With their Chinese friends, the North Koreans pushed the American forces back to the Thirty-Eighth Parallel. From that position the Americans begged for a cessation of hostilities because they had no more strength to fight against the mighty vengeance of the Korean people.

As the gallant Koreans arrived at the Thirty-Eighth Parallel, we arrived at a set of theater seats where we were instructed to sit down and get ready for a heart-stirring presentation. Music started and a little curtain was pulled back and before us was a little diorama showing mountainous terrain bathed in moonlight. The recorded narration was so heavily accented that at times it didn't sound like English and it soon became difficult to follow except for the fact that it was being acted out in front of us.

A supply convoy carrying desperately needed ammunition was making a brave nighttime journey through a treacherous mountain pass in order to re-supply the gallant KPA soldiers holding back the imperialist advance. As the narrator skipped along through his half-intelligible monologue, scale-model olive green trucks with tiny illuminated headlamps strained up the side of a little mountain. We could hear the scale model engines groaning and the gears shifting as the ammunition trucks labored on through the night. Then, out of nowhere came a squadron of evil imperialistic attack planes that strafed the mountain road with invisible bullets. The sound effects were remarkably cartoon-like but rather than distracting the audience, they added to the surreal kitsch. We were treated to miniature airplanes on wires jerking their way over the diorama on gears that badly needed oil. Again and again waves of American fighter planes strafed the KPA convoy with little planes on wires flashing little lights and dropping little sparks of tracer rounds. The tiny tracer rounds rolled out the end of the little barrels and fell to the diorama directly below. It was all wonderfully cheesy.

The little convoy persevered and made it almost to their destination when the treacherous Americans bombed a small bridge that would have been the last leg in the arduous journey. Within a stone's throw of the front line, but cut off by the partially destroyed bridge, the convoy of vulnerable trucks waited in the moonlight, unable to deliver the ammunition to the tiny soldiers who were in such perilous need. Then, inspired by the teachings of the Great Leader and emboldened by their loathing of imperialistic treachery, the villagers from all over the mountainside marshaled themselves in the darkness, crawled under the broken bridge and used their own backs to support the broken bridgeworks. With the brave peasants holding the bridge up with their backs the convoy crept towards the front line and delivered the ammunition that helped eventually defeat the Americans.

The music swirled to a crescendo and the narrator turned all praise not to the peasants and their lumbago, but to the Great Leader who had inspired the selfless act. The lights came up and the curtain went down and our guide stifled a yawn.

A visit to the Victorious Fatherland Liberation War Museum would not be complete without perusing the war trophies captured from the great imperialist warmongers. Warehoused with as much pride as the Great Leader's collection of diplomatic tribute, the museum maintains a first-rate collection of tangled steel wreckage and bullet-riddled armaments. In the prolonged back and forth of the Korean War, both sides captured and surrendered the same real estate time and again. That provided ample opportunity for the KPA to pick up plenty of pieces of tanks and jeeps and half tracks. They also plundered US–issue helmets, rifles, artillery and mounted machine guns. Even captured canteens and mess kits were displayed with smug satisfaction. It was all there in twisted, crumpled, splintered repose.

To one side were the deformed remains of aircraft that had crashed or had been shot down by the valiant North Korean fighter pilots.[13] The guide stood in front of the remains of an F-86 Sabre fuselage, stubby remnants of wings suggesting that it had once soared through the sky, but otherwise looking heavy and earthbound. With her pointer she tapped the half-century-old rusting trophy and said, "These are the very planes that were used to drop germ bombs on Korean civilians. The Americans introduced typhoid, cholera, and tuberculosis by dropping germ bombs on villages. This is how the Korean people were first exposed to such maladies," she revealed.

"Until the Americans brought them, we did not know these diseases." Mr. Kim the Younger translated every word in to English to make sure we clearly understood that the US was guilty of biological warfare.

What appeared to be a crumpled F-51 Mustang fuselage sat in a heap beside the remains of the jet. Beside the pair of crumpled fuselages, bits and pieces of unidentifiable wreckage were neatly displayed on the floor behind ropes. Everything on display obviously went down fighting.

The last heap of wreckage in the room sat beside the exit door and was a recent addition to the collection. On 17 December 1994 Bobby Wayne Hall II piloted a OH-58A Kiowa Helicopter with Chief Warrant Officer David Hilemon at his side. They left Camp Page, which sits snug up against the DMZ, and flying north, somehow ended up mistakenly crossing into North Korean airspace and being brought down by a North Korean shoulder-fired *Hwasung-Chong* surface-to-air missile. Hilemon died in the crash, but Hall was kept as a prisoner by the North Koreans for thirteen days until on Christmas Day of that year he signed a forced confession of guilt. Five days later Hall was released, but the North Koreans kept the remains of the helicopter for their trophy case. While most Americans were never cognizant of the incident, other than the families of Hall and Hilemon, those who were aware probably long since forgot. For the North Koreans, however, this is an unforgettable proof of continued eternal US aggression against the DPRK.

On the wall was a black and white photograph of Hall standing among the wreckage with his hands raised in surrender to unseen KPA soldiers.

Wally turned to our guide and asked, "Did the Great Benevolent Songun General Kim Jong Il offer compassionate medical care to Bobby Wayne Hall while he was in custody?"

The guide took in the words and glared at Wally for a few moments, then said, "And now I will show you the final display."

With that she turned and walked briskly through the door with the tacit understanding that we were supposed to follow.

The drawing card for the Victorious Fatherland Liberation War Museum is what the North Koreans call the world's largest 360° panorama. We ascended a very long flight of steps in the center of the museum and emerged in the middle of a large cyclorama. On a tilted plane falling away from the viewer in all directions was a huge intricate diorama of the city of Taejon and its environs as they appeared on a July morning in 1950. Together the cyclorama and diorama seamlessly created a realistic miniature universe of chaotic defeated American troops limping south as quickly as they could limp, and immaculately clean and beautifully disciplined KPA forces liberating Taejon to the utter delight of the local citizenry.

The guide repeated several times that we were viewing the world's largest panorama. More than three dozen artists and craftsmen had worked on the painting for more than a year. It measures 132 meters in circumference and at the guide's insistence I peered at the canvas to see if I could detect a seam. She assured us that it was impossible to detect a seam because the craftsmen who created it had been so incredibly skilled in the construction. In fact they were the most skilled craftsmen in the world and they had built the cyclorama out of respect and admiration for the Great Leader. On not-too-close inspection one could make out the seams fairly easily.

At the flip of a switch the platform on which we were standing started a slow rotation so we could take in the miniature carnage caused by the scale-model marauding imperialists, and the righteous acts of courage and gallantry among the miniature liberating forces form the north.

As whole battalions of escaping cowardly Americans ran down the miniature dirt road towards a distant Pusan, just inside the little mud wall of a miniature peasant's simple but clean dwelling, a tiny little KPA officer presented a tiny little wizened old man with a framed portrait of the Great Leader Generalissimo Kim Il Sung. Though the tiny bullets were still flying around his head, the old man was too pleased by the portrait to pay them any mind.

Little olive green jeeps lay useless in little ditches, Lilliputian tanks sat in empty rice fields where itty-bitty KPA soldiers had taken them out with nothing more than rifles, superior intellect, and the moral high ground. It was a rout, and the dastardly Yankees had been taught a lesson by the pure-hearted forces of the north.

The liberation of Taejon was just one example of the relentless persistence of the heroic and honorable guardians against imperialist aggression. The guide beamed as she said, "In all villages across Korea when our army liberated the people we were warmly welcomed!" It was unclear if she was fully aware that today Taejon is a prosperous well-fed city of a million-and-a-half people deep inside capitalistic South Korea, or that at night Taejon has lights.

From the Victorious Fatherland Liberation War Museum on the corner of *Hasin* and *Hyoksin* Streets, Mr. Bae drove us due south through the heart of the city towards the most significant prizes in the national trophy case. The triumvirate sit near the *Chungson* Bridge on *Pyongchon-Kangan* Street and remain proof positive that the United States always has and always will have imperialistic designs on the Korean peninsula.

Mr. Bae brought the van to a stop at the curb and we opened the door directly in front of a towering stone monolith mounted on a huge plinth. Into the face of the enormous stone was carved the North Korean account of the 1866 sinking of the USS *General Sherman*. The Korean characters spilled down the face of the four-meter boulder, row after row of damning evidence right there in stone.

The North Korean version of events reveals the true motivation in the

Now permanently moored in the *Taedong* River in central Pyongyang, the USS *Pueblo* is North Korea's most significant war booty, though it has never been decommissioned by the US Navy. The North Koreans claim the *Pueblo* is moored at the precise location that the *General Sherman* was sunk by Kim Il Sung's great great grandfather in 1866. In fact, the North Koreans only started promoting the dubious story of the connection between the Kim regime and the sinking of the *General Sherman* in the 1980s. On the riverbank beside the *Pueblo* is displayed what appears to be a US Navy Near Term Mine Reconnaissance System, or NMRS. A little smaller than a conventional Mark 48 torpedo, it is designed to be deployed from a submarine through a conventional torpedo tube. After zigzagging around the coast the typical NMRS returns to the submarine and is brought on board through the same torpedo tube, then waiting technicians open it up and absorb all sorts of useful data.

incursion was rape, robbery, pillage, and plunder. The Americans sent their 187-ton blood-soaked schooner up the *Taedong* River looking to loot the treasure from ancient tombs. The aggressive Americans attacked the Korean peasants without provocation and, with superior firepower, would have inflicted severe casualties had it not been for the Great Leader's Great Great Grandfather Kim Ung U who marshaled the peasants and gave on-the-spot guidance regarding military strategy and the fundamentals in repulsing a naval invasion. Through his quick intellect and steady leadership the peasants defended themselves and in so doing also burned the ship to the waterline.

By day Kim Ung U tended the graves of wealthy capitalist landowners, by night he was a righteous revolutionary who raised his clenched fist in the face of imperialist aggressors. Just four years after moving to the neighborhood, Grandpa gathered some neighbors who grabbed some shovels, hoes, and pikes and rushed down to the riverbanks where they succeeded in sinking the *General Sherman*. Kim Ung U's central role in driving back the imperialist American ship was not revealed until the 1980s when the Ministry of Truth wove that thread into the historical tapestry. Up until that time they had recognized one Park Chun Gwon as the hero of the day, but the Park family no longer has claim to any riverside heroics because the Kim clan has subsumed the glory. Kim Il Sung's credentials as a revolutionary leader are, therefore, genetic. His family has been leading the pike-toting peasants into the fray for generations ... at least since the 1980s when the history books were altered.

The American version of events differs somewhat. They claim the ship was there on a trade mission looking to establish economic links. The crew sailed the ship up the *Taedong* River and encountered Koreans who eventually became belligerent. The *General Sherman* fired on the peasants in return. The Koreans managed to ignite the ship and as it burned to the waterline the visitors jumped into the river where they were all summarily hacked to death by their hosts.

Either way it was not a good end for the *General Sherman* or her crew. The only things remaining are a great deal of *han* and two cannons on display in the shadow of the stone monolith. However, for the past few decades the *General Sherman* Incident has been trumpeted as the desperately sought after back-story that connects Kim Ung U as the noble citizen-soldier to Kim Il Sung, thus establishing and reinforcing revolutionary credentials of the Great Leader, and later the Dear Leader.

Moored right where Kim Ung U put the "incident" in the *General Sherman* Incident is the most important of the three trophies, the USS *Pueblo*. In January 1968 the *Pueblo* departed Japan and, depending on which side of the story one believes, either did or did not cross from international waters into North Korean territorial waters. The Americans have consistently claimed the *Pueblo* came close but never actually crossed over. The North Koreans disagreed and sent a handful of sub chasers and torpedo boats, plus a couple of MiG-21s to confront the Americans. Within a very brief span of time the *Pueblo* had been captured, the crew whisked away to a secret prison camp, and Kim Il Sung had yet more proof that the Americans always had and always will harbor a deep desire to conquer and colonize the Korean peninsula.

Though Lyndon Johnson's script writers tried to stick with the story that the *Pueblo* was not a spy ship, and though poor Lyndon read the script as convincingly as he could, everybody on both sides of the incident knows that the *Pueblo* was designed to do just one thing — gather intelligence. The question is not whether or not the ship was a spy ship; the question is where was it?

For eleven months Commander Lloyd Bucher and eighty-two crewmen were beaten, tortured, paraded in front of the media, starved, housed in squalid conditions and placed in front of mock firing squads. Then, after Bucher signed a forced confession, the North Koreans abruptly took the entire crew to *Panmunjom*, where the Joint Security Area straddles the DMZ, and sent them one by one across the Bridge of No Return and back to friendly territory.

For almost three decades the *Pueblo* remained hidden in North Korea — a war prize too valuable to allow peering eyes to see. Then without fanfare it appeared as a tourist attraction and propaganda tool in the coastal city of Wonsan where Bulgarian diplomats, Soviet mine engineers, and Cuban dance troupes were invited to inspect the evidence and take snapshots. Soon after the outside world learned of the *Pueblo*'s location she was moved again — this time in a gutsy display of blatant defiance. By higher logic the *Pueblo* had to be towed from Wonsan on the east, through international waters around South Korea, and up to North Korea's West Coast to Nampo, then up the *Taedong* River to Pyongyang. This obviously would have provided ample opportunity for the United States to attempt recapturing the *Pueblo* as she sailed in international waters far out of the reach of North Korea's coastal defense forces. The United States Navy has never decommissioned the *Pueblo* and one would have to assume the US Navy wants her back.

The alternative was to cut the *Pueblo* up and haul her across the peninsula in sections, and then weld her back together in Pyongyang. I looked for any sign that this had happened and saw none. Whether the North Koreans are amazingly good at welding or they sailed the *Pueblo* around the Korean peninsula, she is moored in the river and is the greatest of all the trophies.

Now that the *Pueblo* is within range to be included on Pyongyang tourist

The personal possessions of Captain "Pete" Bucher and his crew, as they were found after the USS *Pueblo* was captured on 23 January 1968, remain on display in the *Pueblo*'s galley.

itineraries, the Bulgarian diplomats, Soviet mine engineers, and Cuban dance troupes have been joined by Australian school teachers, Dutch dental hygienists, Canadian farmers, and all sorts of dilettante from the expat community in Beijing who fly over on a lark. Once in a blue moon stray Americans show up and tour the *Pueblo*.

We were met in front of the gangway by a young woman in the military-like uniform that so many of the museum guides wore. Her English was impeccable and she appeared genuinely enthusiastic about her job.

Miss Cho welcomed us then went right into her well-practiced delivery. She pointed behind us at the monument to the *General Sherman* Incident and said, "The US Aggression Ship *Sherman* was guilty of killing people and looting all treasures. The crew demanded gold and silver from the people, but the Great Leader Kim Il Sung's great great grandfather led the citizens to rise up and sink the ship. Since then the history of aggression from Americans has not stopped."

She turned from the stone monument and walked up the gangway to the deck of the USS *Pueblo*. We followed her up the gangway to the deck and she gave a brief history of the ship.

She claimed, "It was built in 1932 as a cargo ship, but in 1966 the Americans refitted it as an Army spy ship but the imperialists disguised it as a civilian research ship. In 1968 it was captured by our gallant Navy as it trespassed into North Korean waters."[14]

Miss Cho guided our little group in to the cramped galley and we sat in the same molded fiberglass chairs at the same Formica-topped tables that Commander Bucher and his crew would have used. In the background a little generator hummed as it provided a trickle of electrical power.

After Cho hit a switch and as a small television blinked to life, she said, "Please watch this fifteen minute video.... It will explain everything." And with that we commenced a relentless fifteen-minute propaganda barrage in heavily accented English that not only explained the North Korean account of events, but provided evidence that US President Johnson was a belligerent reactionary seeking angles from which to launch his attack of cowardly disparagement on the peaceful people of Korea.

The narrator concluded the fact-filled dialogue by stating that, "The USS *Pueblo* trophy will testify to century after century of aggression of the US imperialists."

The house lights went up and Miss Cho took us around to the crypto room where shelves of machines that looked much like typewriters sat in virtually the same state as they had been in since early 1968. Many of them had "Top Secret" or "NOFORN" stenciled across faceplates. To one side a doorway and bulkhead were peppered with holes, rips, and tears where North Korean bullets had found their target. In case visitors had difficulty in identifying the bullet holes as bullet holes, the North Koreans had carefully encircled each with a band of helpful red paint. Seaman Duane Hodges had been shot and killed near the bulkhead — the single American casualty in the confrontation.

Opposite, top: Communication and eavesdropping equipment remain largely in place on the USS *Pueblo* almost 40 years after being captured by the North Koreans. Contrary to President Lyndon Johnson's claims at the time, in retrospect it appears obvious that the *Pueblo* was out doing what it was designed to do — gather intelligence. *Opposite, bottom:* Though President Johnson denied it at the time, the *Pueblo* was likely gathering intelligence. Even after nearly 40 years, the question is not what the *Pueblo* was doing, but rather where the *Pueblo* was. The North Koreans have always claimed it was in North Korean waters, while the United States has maintained the *Pueblo* never left international waters.

Like previous guides, Miss Cho substantiated her claims by quoting amusing things she had heard foreigners say. "Recently a Canadian visitor observed.... A German tourist said ... it was noted by a French guest..."

Any observation presented as an item of notable significance, as long as it wasn't said by one of the Kims, could be attributed to a passing foreign tourist for added weight. If one of the Kims said it then it goes without saying that it remains significant. Kims aside, English tourists appeared to be the most adept at coming up with quotable observations.

She concluded her tasks and meandered down the gangplank to the river-bank. While the rest of the group continued their exploration of the *Pueblo* I meandered after her. Standing in the shadow of the monument to the *General Sherman* Incident we made small talk about the weather; where I was from; and my impressions of North Korea. In her form-fitting militaryesque uniform she would have passed as a recruit at first glance.

"You have interesting shoes ... they aren't military issue, are they?" I asked in Korean with a smirk.

Standing on the banks of the *Taedong* River she giggled and glanced down at her black designer stiletto knock-offs with comically elongated toes. Within the hermetically sealed society of North Korea she had managed to acquire a pair of shoes that would have been stylish while standing on the banks of the Thames or the Seine.

"I was too busy to go home and change shoes before I came to work ... does it look funny?"

Compared to her sisters-in-arms at the other museums who had only the faintest spark of life left in their eyes, Miss Cho was alive and vibrant. They had succumbed to the mind-numbing drudgery of the *Juche* system, clad in the same olive drab outfit, they wore sensible shoes, tight low-maintenance hairdos, and expressions that suggested happiness and contentment were the domain of the capitalists. Miss Cho had not yet been sufficiently clubbed into emotional submission. The innocence of youth allowed her to find joy in daily existence and that joy bubbled forth in impractical-yet-stylish shoes, carefree hair, and a mischievous sparkle in the eye.

Before the conversation could progress further she was joined by a male colleague in similar faux military attire. He approached like a man returning to the bar only to discover in his absence a randy libertine had moved in on his date. He mumbled something and she frowned and excused herself. They walked back up the gangplank together and disappeared into the *Pueblo*.

The third trophy in the set is what the North Koreans claim is an "unmanned submarine." On 22 June 2004 the Koreans captured the small

One of the mounted guns on the deck of the *USS Pueblo* remains in place as it was on 23 January 1968 when the vessel was captured by the North Korean Navy. The gun was unloaded, unmanned, and unused during the incident.

black submersible snooping around off the coast near Hamhung. Today the "unmanned submarine" is housed in a low glass sarcophagus-like case on the quayside. The long black cylinder looks more like the Hollywood interpretation of a torpedo than anything else. With a double corkscrew propeller at one end, and a stubby sensor projecting out from the nose at the other, the entire craft is no more than three meters in length. Though it didn't attract as much attention in the Western media as when North Koreans were caught in 1996, and again in 1998, using a miniature submarine to insert agents on remote beaches of South Korea, the mysterious black cylinder was front-page news in North Korea. For the average North Korean day-tripper the long black cylinder is ominously sinister and significant as evidence of the continuing imperialist Yankee aggression.

In fact, it looks an awful lot like a gizmo the US Navy regularly deploys to assess coastal areas for potential mines. The Near Term Mine Reconnaissance System, or NMRS, is a little smaller than a conventional Mark 48 torpedo and is designed to be deployed from a submarine through a conventional torpedo tube. After zigzagging around the coast the typical NMRS returns to the submarine and is brought on board through the same torpedo tube, then waiting technicians open it up and absorb all sorts of useful data from the sensors and recorders. Reminiscent of Stalin being incapable of conceiving that the Berlin Airlift effectively sidestepped his blockade of that city, it appeared that among the North Koreans there was a lack of understanding that modern technology allows for something such as the NMRS to effectively spy without the need for submariners to hitch a ride. Even if the North Koreans failed to grasp the capability of the NMRS, assuming that's what the "unmanned submarine" really was, they understood very well that this evidence of aggression demanded redoubled efforts in remaining eternally vigilant at the nation's frontier.

The Dear Leader decided that the latest war trophy should be put on display alongside the *Pueblo* and the remains of the *General Sherman* to remind the good people of North Korea that the insatiable craving of the imperialists is nothing more than total domination and absolute control of the Korean peninsula. This 21st century trophy, placed beside the trophies from the 19th and 20th centuries, is proof positive that the aggression is clearly eternal. During our brief visit it became wearisome to hear again and again about the various pieces of evidence that proved American aggression, but the unenviable North Korean must endure the harangue their entire lifetime.

As our little group walked up the steps towards the van, it was easy to hear the boisterous conversations and raucous singing of a group of men, still clad in dark *vinalon* jackets and ties, seated in the dirt on the riverside among the trees and shrubs. It appeared that every one of them was in the process of smoking at least one cigarette, was about two-thirds of the way to snot-slinging drunk, and was following the rule of thumb that in the art of singing lack of ability can be compensated with sheer volume.

It was the shadowy end of the workday and the following day was May Day, a national holiday in a land with very few holidays. *Soju*-induced caterwauling is sanctioned by the state as an acceptable means for letting off steam only on specially designated occasions: May Day is one of them. All too soon the intoxicated comrades would be required to get up off the ground, brush the dirt from their impermeable *vinalon* trousers, and return to their position in the giant *Juche* machine. Maintaining equilibrium in the Worker's Paradise requires the regime to place a firm limit on caterwauling opportunities.

The sun set without interference from electric lighting and Pyongyang steadily sank into uniform inky shadows. Mr. Bae drove the van down a side street beside what must have been *Munsudong*. I knew because I could see the flags of various diplomatic compounds poking up from behind a very high wall that surrounded the entire neighborhood. As we came to a stop, I could see across the quiet boulevard and behind the wall the lone yellow star of the flag of the Socialist Republic of Vietnam — even their communist brethren were relegated to the walled compound diplomats have nicknamed "the green house."

We piled out and followed Mr. Kim the Elder through a doorway and up a flight of stairs into an empty dining room set up for more than a hundred patrons. We were the only guests and, until then, the waitresses had been entranced by the North Korean karaoke on the television in the corner of the room. They had obviously been studying.

Both Kims and Mr. Bae joined us at a table for eight and immediately the uniformed waitresses appeared with trays of *panchan* which they placed in front of us no sooner than our broad capitalist hips hit the hard, unpadded surface of the utilitarian chairs. The little porcelain bowls were placed in random order across the table and we all started picking at morsels and tidbits. As the first mouthful of starter was being swallowed, the waitresses came rushing back with trays heaped full of the entrée — Pyongyang *Naengmyun*.

Up and down the Korean peninsula there is a dreamy preoccupation with Pyongyang *Naengmyun* and it can make Koreans with absolutely no connection to the North nostalgic and sentimental. The name literally translates "cold noodles" and that's exactly what it is — a bowl of broth that has been allowed to go stone cold, some noodles that are equally cold, a few thin strips of frigid, fatty beef, a boiled egg that is near-frozen, and a few scraps of vegetables and an icicle for good measure. As much as I like most Korean food, I remain baffled with the fascination with Pyongyang *Naengmyun*. In the South it is touted as the perfect summertime food because in the sticky heat of August what better pick-me-up could one want than a bowl full of cold, congealed noodles and icy broth? In the North it is treasured as the food that made Pyongyang famous. Peking has its duck, Kiev has its chicken, Pyongyang has cold gloppy noodles. The thing even more exciting for Westerners is Pyongyang *Naengmyun* is eaten with chopsticks. South of the DMZ restaurateurs long ago decided to assist diners by having the waitress cut the noodles into more manageable lengths. To accomplish this they assigned their waitresses pairs of sewing scissors. They wear them in the pockets of their aprons and after placing big frigid bowls of Pyongyang *Naengmyun* on the table, they go around and use the scissors as if assisting a table full of children who need their *sketty* cut up in to more manageable spoon-sized units. They even cut up the noodles in the bowls placed before adult Koreans with complete dexterity in all ten digits. In South Korea Pyongyang *Naengmyun* is automatically scissored up whether one needs it or not.

Wally looked down at the frigid bowl of gelatinous noodles in icy broth and sighed. He looked up at the nearest waitress and asked in Korean, "Will you cut the *Naengmyun* for me?"

The waitress leaned towards Wally and replied in Korean, "Pardon me?"

"In restaurants in the South, "Wally explained, "the waitress uses scissors to cut up the noodles ... they walk around to each customer and use the scissors to cut the noodles, then it's easy for the customer to eat."

The waitress glanced up at her colleagues to make sure they had heard what Wally had said. They all giggled at the suggestion, stealing glances at each other while hiding their mouths behind empty hands.

Wally smiled and used his most polite Korean to reiterate, "I'm serious ... do you have any scissors to cut the noodles?"

And with that the waitress cackled and teetered away to a back room. Through the remainder of the meal we could hear laughter emanating from the kitchen each time the door was opened. Undoubtedly she and her colleagues spent the remainder of the night talking about the crazy request from the tourist with the funny accent.

By the time we had eaten our fill, the restaurant was packed with table after table of Chinese tourists slurping Pyongyang *Naengmyun* and screeching in delight. For the Chinese a quick visit across the border in North Korea is, in many ways, like stepping in to a historical reenactment of China in 1967. All draconian — all the time.

The pace slowed and the conversation tapered off and it was obvious that we were nearing the end of our final meal. In a gesture of friendship glasses were raised around our little table and because there was a momentary silence when nobody knew quite which salute to use, I proclaimed in a steady voice, "*Tongil!*" but immediately I could see in the eyes of the Koreans that this wish, no matter how heartfelt, could not be used as a toast. There is only one toasting word and "*Tongil*" wasn't it.

We walked as a group down the stairs and to the front door where Charles bumped into a British-born competitor in the North Korean tour industry. There aren't many travel firms dealing in tourism to North Korea and among those serving the tiny market the players often know each other very well. They stopped and chatted about the mysterious requirement to vacate the city for the day — the whole while maintaining a twinkle in the eye that suggested between them there was more communication left unsaid than said. However, he admitted being just as puzzled by the unexpected command to vacate the city. We had gone north to the International Friendship Exhibition at Mount *Myohyang* while the other group had been whisked south to the ancient city of *Kaesong*. Somehow the twinkle-eyed Brit managed to wrangle permis-

sion to stay behind sequestered alone in the hotel. After seeing Kaesong two
dozen times, he explained, he didn't feel like he needed to tag along to take
it in yet again. There are only so many angles from which to view the same
re-created rustic domiciles and picture-perfect re-created gardens. Being
allowed the luxury of staying behind and forgoing the stiff formality of
participation in the day's itinerary was unusually lenient. In the little *Juche*
universe to pull off something that decadent suggests significant behind-the-
scenes connections. He then revealed that the night before he had stumbled
down to the labyrinthine basement of the *Yanggakdo* Hotel where he found
himself at a golf driving range at 3:00 A.M. He was allowed to stand at an
opening in the side of the hotel and drive a bucket of golf balls, one-by-one,
into the *Taedong* River. This wasn't any ordinary running-dog capitalist, this
was a comrade of the people.

Soon we too were back at the *Yanggakdo* Hotel. At the front entrance the
Kims discharged us to the care of the hotel staff and assured us that they
would be back bright and early in the morning. It had been a long day and
they were eager to go unwind, so they didn't waste any time on unnecessary
pleasantries. Mr. Bae was driving the van off into the darkness before the
hotel doors closed behind us.

All four of us made a beeline to the little lobby bookshop where the
same bone-tired woman sat near the door manning the cash box on behalf of
the regime. It was obvious that we were all tired and nobody bothered to stifle
yawns as we circumnavigated the little shop. We picked through the stacks
and, among the four of us, came away with a substantial variety of books:
works by the Kims, works about the Kims, works influenced by Kim ideology, and coffee table books displaying vivid photographs of cement accomplishments under the guidance of the Kims.

In a moment of rapturous joy I picked up an English version of Kim
Jong Il's 1973 seminal work *On the Art of Cinema*. After years of fantasizing
about holding a copy of the book in my own hands, there in my grubby mitts
was a lime-green hardbound copy bursting with 332 pages of cinematographic
insights from the world's most brilliant cinematographer. The first 35 words
of the preface reached out and grabbed me by the wallet:

> This is the great age of *Juche*. The *Juche* age is a new historical era when
> the popular masses have emerged as masters of the world and are shap-
> ing their own destiny independently and creatively.[15]

At that point I didn't care how many monies Cindy wanted — it was sold.

I also found a paperback copy of *I Am a Korean,* the biography of the
father of Japanese professional wrestling North Korean–born Rikidozan.

While standing in the bookshop leafing through this classic tome, it was instantly obvious that it had originally been written in Korean, and then translated to English. Western place names and those of individuals were initially altered into Asian form, then during translation altered back into some semblance of Occidental pronunciation. The Los Angeles Civic Auditorium was thus rendered the "LA Shibik Auditorium" and the great American wrestler from the 1950s, Lou Thesz, was consistently referred to as "Rue Thez." Many other wrestlers mentioned were given indecipherable names and remain a mystery.[16] Though the book was not intended to be comical, I couldn't stop snickering as I thumbed through pages and read passages such as:

> Grabbing Destroyer's hair, he bumped his head against the iron post.
> Then he hit him by knees, legs, elbows, etc. But while facing Rkidozan,
> Destroyer watched for a chance. He kicked Rkidozan on the vulnerable
> spot from below. The latter crouched down holding his privates with both
> hands...[17]

Without a second thought that little paperback was added to the "must purchase" stack that was accumulating at my side.

Then in rapid succession I found books that I simply could not live without. One after another I picked up a once-in-a-lifetime find and knew that I needed to either purchase it on the spot or forever be denied the opportunity.

The little 53-page treatise titled *Distortion of US Provocation of Korean War*[18] laid out the facts and figures that once and for all prove that it was the imperialist aggressors from America who staged the surprise sneak attack in June of 1950 and started the war. After a lifetime of being told otherwise I felt a moral obligation to uncover the truth and that required purchasing the book.

Then the coffee table books beckoned, and the large colorful books filled with socialist realism artwork. It was all too much and on close inspection I was rationalizing the purchase of every book I browsed. Fortunately it was a "cash only" establishment or my bourgeois class credit card would have been abused. With all the willpower I could muster, I drew the line and drew the shopping foray to a conclusion.

But then I saw the postcards. Most of them were of objects in nature: famous Korean peaks, wildlife, waterfalls, *Poongsan* dogs, and lots of Pyongyang's cement monuments. None of those struck my fancy, but a particular postcard caught my eye, and I quickly rifled through the stack to make sure I had ten identical copies. The card featured an aerial view of what looked like an Air *Koryo* Ilyushin Il62 lumbering through a snow storm over Mount *Paekdu*. The cards featured a 3D effect created by a thick layer of textured plastic covering the image. It was reminiscent of the 3D baseball cards included in boxes of American breakfast cereal in the early 70s. Those cards frequently featured weak-batting utility players of marginal worth with names that were only vaguely familiar. Their images were blurred and indistinct due to the thick sheet of textured plastic. The ball players stood at the plate with bat slung over a shoulder and glared in to the camera with an expression so blurred that it could have been scorn or it could have been delight. By tilting the card kids were supposed to see the 3D effect of the batter swinging the bat at the viewer, but what the kids actually saw was a blurred image shift from an obfuscated ball player to a muddled, gauzy ball player. Due to their obvious low trading potential, these were the cards frequently clothes pinned to bicycle forks.

I gathered the books and cards and ferried them to the front counter. The weary woman at the door used a small calculator to tally the price of the books. In quick succession she checked her math three times, then with an assuring nod the calculator was turned so I could see the little gray screen. It had the numerals 6 and 3 silently waiting for my reaction.

Though it had been a long day and my patience was short, the continuing bizarreness of Korean street theater kept me engaged and willing to allow a little more line to be pulled off my reel.

Looking at the black 63 on the little gray display screen, I said in my most polite Korean, "Is that sixty-three Euros?"

The woman blinked and giggled.

Again I said in my most polite Korean, adjusted as best I could for the Northern accent, "Is that sixty-three Euros?"

She continued to look at me through wide eyes and forced a little unnatural giggle as the muscles in her cheeks relaxed and her smile faded. Koreans know instinctively that mastery of their tongue requires one to have a stake in the peninsula's gene pool and it is impossible for someone with the wrong genetics to possess the capacity to master the mystic tongue.

With one last burst I sighed and asked in a voice that hinted just a little that I was coming to the end of my tolerance, "Is that sixty-three Euros?"

"Yes ... Euros ... sixty-three Euros," she said as the lights came on in her eyes. Though clearly simian in intellect, the beast had been speaking Korean.

"I don't have Euros because I am not European. I have American dollars. Will you accept American dollars?" I asked.

"Certainly," she said with a smile, then reverted to her brain-dead glazed expression.

When it was obvious that she wasn't going to provide a conversion, I asked impatiently, "How much do I owe you in dollars?"

She looked deep into my eyes with a quizzical expression which quickly faded to pity. In a firm, motherly voice she repeated very slowly in Korean, "...sixty ... three..."

I counted out uniformly grimy American notes and handed them to her still unsure if she realized she was about to accept about two-thirds of what she had initially asked for. She played the slow-witted Cindy to my confused Bubba by counting the notes again, and then she slipped everything into a plastic sack and handed it over with a dazed smile. She had bagged sixty-three mummies for the Dear Leader. She had done her part.

Wally and I walked through the Christmas trees and past the sea turtle and sturgeons to the elevators and quietly went up to our room where we opened bottles of *Ryongsong Beer* and penned welcoming postcards. I carefully wrote gushing compliments about the beauty of North Korea and the wonderful hospitality of the nation, pointed out that I had arrived at last after so many years of dreaming about being fortunate enough to find favor with the North Korean authorities, provided a salutation and a flourish of a signature. I knew the contents of each card would need to pass the inspection of censors, so I kept my words brief and dripping with flattery. Then, on each card, I very clearly printed out the address in block letters openly displaying the fact that the postcards were intended for delivery to the United States of America.

With cards completed and addressed, we decided to get the task of posting them out of the way, so both Wally and I put our shoes back on and descended to the counter in the lobby from where we had composed our €6 e-mails on the first night. The same drowsy woman was there in a chair, head jerking each time she caught herself drifting to sleep. After rousing her I handed over the ten postcards and asked how much the postage would be to get them to the United States. She didn't flinch. She picked up her Chinese calculator and started the routine.

After a few moments of arduous mathematical calculations and a series of crafty double-checking maneuvers, she turned the calculator towards me and stated the price in Won. I was so shocked that I had to ask her to repeat herself.

"The postage is eighty-four Won for each card going to the United States," she said in crystal clear Korean.[19]

I rifled through the stamps she had on offer; flowers, puppies, birds, ceramic pots. I purchased the appropriate quantity of innocuous looking stamps from her and affixed the equivalent of eighty-four won worth to each card, then pulled out some of the extra bayonet and fist stamps I had accepted as change at the *Hyangsan* Hotel. I crowded as many pugnacious, aggressive, and overpoweringly red stamps as I could on each postcard. Missiles zoomed across the top of the card while North Korean boots crushed the US Capitol dome below. The KPA recruit on the left looked even more ferocious in his opposition to meddling imperialism than his counterpart on the right. I affixed quadruple the value that was required to get the cards across the Pacific, but I reasoned that this would probably be the final opportunity I'd have in this lifetime and I wanted them dripping with communist aggression.

I handed the cards over and she giggled at the hodgepodge of confusion across the face of each one. She told me it would take about a week for the cards to get to the US, so I returned to the room a happily content capitalist aggressor.[20] It took almost no time to fall into a deep sleep during which I dreamed of being a member of a group of North Korean people's volunteers hastily hand mixing low grade cement to be used in yet another monstrous monument to the regime, and to the side of the happy volunteer labor crew an accordion and tuba ensemble played *My Socialist Country Is the Envy of the World* in 2/2 time.

Departure

Tuesday, 1 May 2007

Dawn had broken on May Day, the biggest holiday in the shrinking communist universe, and just like every other day on our brief visit, Pyongyang was wrapped in a wet day. From the hotel window no bunting was visible, no marques had been set up, no streamers or Maypoles had been erected on the riverbanks. It was just the same cement-gray cityscape shrouded in fog and eerie silence.

We returned to the lime green banquet hall where Miss Paik stood on guard at the entrance. Miss Paik was the template for all the gallant North Korean women depicted in statues and paintings. Her stout farm-girl legs carried a torso as soft and inviting as a municipal fire hydrant and it was clear that she would have been more at home in the olive green fatigues of the Korean People's Army out on the front line where she could bag some capitalists. Her expression suggested we were going to find it much less painful to shut up and comply than to attempt to reason with her about where we sat in the empty hall.

On bandy farm-girl legs she walked us to our assigned table and we seated ourselves without conversing. Very quickly a pair of uniformed waitresses appeared and silently doled out bread rolls, eggs, and the experimental yogurt-like product. Breakfast was all very quiet and it was obvious that the frantic pace had taken a toll on our collective energy. Playing tourist is serious business.

Though the buffet line was gone, the coffee table was still there and the four uniformed members of the People's Coffee Battalion manning the table remained ready to serve up cups of bitter reconstituted instant coffee on request. I walked to the back of the hall and greeted the Battalion members in Korean. The three dull-eyed assistants didn't react, but the young woman who appeared to be in charge smiled and exchanged pleasantries in Korean.

All the way across the banquet hall as I navigated my way towards the coffee, I practiced again and again how I was going to construct my question, keeping in mind that North Koreans used a different word for milk, and the accent on the vowels was altered.

Looking the alpha waitress in the eye I said in my most pleasant May Day voice, "I would like coffee, but may I have two spoons of coffee and one of milk?"

She smiled broadly and said, "Oh! Your accent is fantastic! Where did you study our language?"

"I studied in school," I said matter-of-factly. "May I have two spoons of coffee and one of milk?"

"Yes, of course. Your pronunciation is wonderful! You are so easy to understand. I wish more visitors could speak our language. I hope you enjoy your stay in our country," and with that she handed me three steaming cups; two had a reconstituted spoonful of instant coffee each, and one had nothing but reconstituted coffee whitener. I thanked her and walked back to the breakfast table thrilled to possess Korean language skills sufficient to clearly enunciate precisely what I didn't want.

As I attempted to distribute the "milk" into the cups of "coffee," I looked up and saw, across the lime green expanse, a familiar face walking towards the coffee table. I watched as he requested and received exactly what he wanted, then turned and walked back across the hall towards his table.

Koreaphile and journalist Gainsley Bourke had been high on the list of most reviled foreigners in South Korea when, in the early '90s, he wrote a piece for an international news weekly that ended up being called "Slickie Boy at the Wheel." It focused on the meteoric economic rise in South Korea, and the fact that in many ways South Korean society was not adapting well to the newfound wealth. The general public south of the DMZ didn't appreciate having soiled laundry publicly aired by a non–Korean. It would have been bad enough had it been one of their own, but to have a foreigner with substantial insight reveal the same soiled linens was considerably more irritating. Then, several years later, after multiple trips north of the DMZ, he wrote a monumental thousand-page monster about the Kim Dynasty which he called *The Uniquer Uniqueness: North Korea the Special Needs Nation*. I was startled the North Koreans had granted him an entry visa after airing their dirty laundry as well.

Our group started moving towards the exit of the lime green banquet hall for the last time and I veered towards Bourke's table and greeted him. He was just commencing his tour as we were concluding ours. I exchanged pleasantries and confirmed that we had last crossed paths at the *Cam Chon—* Seoul's famed hole-in-the-wall tofu chowder house and long-time Friday night gathering place for resident expats, diplomats, dilatants, journalists, and those looking for a good feed before moving on to an alcohol-induced night of debauchery, depravity, and degeneracy in Seoul's *Itaewon* entertainment district. I praised his book and inquired if there were any more forthcoming, and he provided a polite and gracious response. He also told me the *Cam Chon* had sadly been shuttered. It was all very nice expat chit-chat that frequently stands in for real conversation as familiar faces pass like ships in the departure lounge.

The entire time we exchanged our expat pleasantries, Bourke's tablemate, a weathered European woman with wide darting eyes that suggested she wasn't completely with us in Pyongyang, looked on in awe that in such an unusual place one of her fellow tour mates had been recognized by a passerby. She maintained a deliriously surprised and pleased expression that hinted she was just about to start babbling effusively in rock-star adoration as I excused myself and skirted Miss Paik on my way out. Just as I turned to go, the graying European woman's dancing eyes darted towards Bourke and she inhaled as if preparing to commence a babbling outburst of psychotic Euro-babble. I strained my ear to see if she would ask Bourke for an autograph, but Miss Paik shooed me out of her way as she re-checked her clipboard to make sure everything was in order. My last glimpse was of Bourke's European tablemate launching into something that looked as if it was going to take quite a while.

Mr. Kim the Younger met us in the lobby wearing exactly the same garments he had worn every day of our visit. They did not appear rumpled, nor did they appear soiled. If the Kims' garments were indeed *vinalon*, then this was the type of testimonial endorsement the regime needed to take the miracle fiber to a worldwide level — four straight days of heavy-duty touring across North Korea and not a wrinkle or stain was visible. Maybe they were hosing down their outfits at night and wringing them dry before meeting us each morning, but I suspect they didn't need to. Garments made from limestone have mysteriously magical qualities that do away with the inconvenience of care and maintenance. I knew not acquiring a *vinalon* garment was going to be a lasting regret.

Mr. Kim the Elder joined us in the lobby near the Christmas trees to make sure we had all our belongings and were ready to depart. At the same time, Mr. Kim the Younger leaned over the reception desk and worked with the hotel staff to ensure we were crossed off the books and checked out. He surrendered our room keys and that was that. No money changed hands, no forms were signed, no documents exist that would confirm we had ever stayed in the *Yanggakdo* Hotel.[1]

We walked through the crowd of fifty drivers and guides standing at the hotel entrance in a cloud of fetid gray cigarette smoke and arrived at our van where Mr. Bae already had the engine running. Our handlers were obviously ready to be rid of their imperialist charges after sixty-three non-stop hours of chauffeuring, guiding, and correcting our misconceptions with the correct *Juche* interpretation. The van crossed the *Yanggak* Bridge as Pyongyang was starting to wake up and step outside into the regime-approved gray cement universe. Up the wide, empty tree-lined boulevards we moved, and the shroud of fog made sure the few solemn people on the streets moved in muffled silence. It was May Day and I had expected more. More noise, more commotion, more color, more smiles. But the same dark clad, weary people were emerging from the fog, walking, walking, always walking, and they didn't look very celebratory.

As the van moved through the heart of the city, more and more adults emerged from the fog — all in dark formal attire. They walked with purpose in the same general direction as if despite being an official holiday, the day's schedule was already established and quite full. Within the sovereign territory of North Korea, "holiday" apparently has a significantly different interpretation. The small groups of pedestrians making their way through the fog didn't look like they were out for a day of relaxation, picnicking, and fireworks. Their neckties and *vinalon* jackets and somber faces announced that there was something more formal in store for their May Day observance.

In much of the world May Day is filled with joy, wildflowers tucked into blonde hair, pastel streamers attached to poles in the village green, and an explosion of the blooming hues of spring. But in Pyongyang other than a hundred variations of cement gray, the *vinalon* outfits in black, charcoal, and navy, and bare trees, the only splash of color was a lone billboard for the Whistle car. The traditionally attired woman on the billboard smiled a broad, contented smile as she looked at me through the fog. Below her on the street none of the people were smiling — none of them would ever be able to afford a Whistle car. They walked.

At *Sunan* Airport it appeared that the entire guest list from the *Yanggakdo* Hotel was there to catch the same flight. Familiar faces that had been on the flight in, at the *Arirang* performance, at the International Friendship Exhibition, and all the other stops on our itinerary were now to be seated next to us on the same flight out.

The check-in process was painfully slow because everything was done by hand, however, Mr. Kim the Younger efficiently assigned himself to this task on our behalf and we were afforded the luxury of standing in a small circle chatting while off to the side he oversaw the formalities.

The check-in area was filled with North Koreans in every conceivable type of uniform — far outnumbering those of us in mufti. Men and women with stone faces moved around and did whatever it was that they were assigned to do. On 1 May 2007 *Sunan* Airport was scheduled to see two planes come and go. That was it. The capital city of the nation, hub of commerce and power for more than twenty million citizens, and all they required were two planes to fly in and fly out. By contrast, on the same day, more than 550 planes came and went from Seoul's international airport. None the less, *Sunan* airport was abuzz with the chaos of *bbali-bbali* preparations and the collective control knob seemed to be set at near-frantic. The majority of people in the room looked as if they were fighting a very real urge to reach out and jab their finger in to the lower back of the person in front just as a gentle encourage-ment to move it: *Bbali-bbali, bbali-bbali, bbali-bbali.*

Mr. Kim the Elder approached our little island of tranquility in the sea of check-in confusion and explained that because North Korea's Air *Koryo* is not part of the international agreements to which all other airlines adhere, our luggage could be checked only as far as Beijing, and if we were traveling beyond there, we would have to go through the step of claiming and recheck-ing baggage in China. Alice was scheduled for a continuous, grueling series of flights all the way back to a small city in the middle of America and was not pleased to discover that she would be required to start luggage check-in formalities as if from scratch when in China. The North Koreans, however, don't really need to join the system. The trickle of international visitors, though increasing, is still a trickle. Why bother signing an accord that, while providing benefits, creates new obligations and responsibility? Rather than getting tangled up in baggage issues — just foist the problem off on Red China and let passengers work it out when they land in Beijing.

Mr. Kim the Younger appeared with our boarding passes and distrib-uted them to us one by one, obviously pleased with himself for accomplish-ing the task with such efficiency.

Though they were just run-of-the-mill airline boarding passes with the airline logo, flight and seat number, and passenger name, all four of us paused and inspected the details to make sure they were correct. This close to being granted authorization to depart the Worker's Paradise, if something were to have gone wrong, it would have been unpleasant at the very least. A decade in solitary confinement for attempting to exit North Korea with an incorrect boarding pass would have been difficult to convincingly explain to my wife.

Mr. Kim the Younger took point, and Mr. Kim the Elder brought up the rear as we were walked through an inoperable X-ray machine. On the other side the mobile phones were returned to their respective owners and North Korea had, yet again, successfully assured itself that foreigners had not sent any illicit text messages nor had any clandestine phone calls while guests of the Dear Leader.

We stood again and waited in the middle of the chaos, surrounded by the frantic, jittery movements of North Koreans of every stripe. It became apparent that someone very florid was gesticulating just beyond our little group and, as if obeying his unspoken command, we broke ranks and made room for him to be engulfed into our protective Occidental circle. His body language had announced very loudly that he very much desired access to our little group. As soon as I looked up, I knew I recognized his face. With a flourish he handed out locally-made business cards featuring an archipelago of names followed by a string of titles:

Gustavo de Ambición del sapo de Demen Cia y Locura
Global Coordinator of the External Compatriots of Juche Korea,
Special Representative — Bureau for Social Interaction with Foreign Nations, and
Roving Unofficial Honorary DPRK Representative at Large

Gustavo was dressed in an exact replica of Kim Jong Il's tailored *jamba*. His body even mirrored the Dear Leader's — short and tubby. Had he worn a bouffant and Imelda Marcos sun shades, he could have passed as the Dear Leader on first glance. On the lapel of his tailored *jamba* was a Kim Il Sung pin. He was resplendent in his costume and he knew it.

Soon after diplomatic relations were established between Red China and South Korea in late 1992, a Chinese diplomat told me he had studied at Kim Il Sung University, then went on to represent his nation in the Red Chinese Embassy in Pyongyang. After thirteen years in North Korea he was given a lavish going-away party by North Korean friends. His one request, after all those years in the Worker's Paradise, was to be granted the honor of receiving a Kim Il Sung lapel pin.

His hosts firmly refused, saying, "That is not possible ... foreigners are never granted that privilege."

Charles openly admired Gustavo's *jamba* and asked where he got it. That was the cue Gustavo was waiting for. He took his position in front of the camera that only he could see, and started delivering a dramatic performance.

"Oh, jew like, no?" he said in an Argentinean stage whisper. "I can assist jew to get a *jamba*. I know the tailor who makes them for Kim Jong Il himself! She is my friend. Just tell her jew know Gustavo and she will make one for jew. Everyone in Pyongyang know Gustavo. She runs the tailor shop on the first floor of the *Yanggakdo* Hotel — jew can tell her jew are the friend of Gustavo and she will do fabulous workmanship, no? What hotel did jew stay?

Yanggakdo? Oh course! Ah, jew see, it is too late now for jew are departing. We are on the same plane, no?"

In Gustavo's magnetic tow was a mute sidekick, a young Asian man also in costume. His attire, however, was reminiscent of a Japanese boy's high school uniform — a stiff collared nautical ensemble in navy with Kim Il Sung badge proudly displayed above the heart. His mouth never spoke, but his eyes focused on Gustavo and said in fawning groupie fashion, "I love you."

After a breath he went on, "Jew will come again to Pyongyang, Jew will stay at the *Yanggakdo* Hotel. When jew do go to the tailor shop on the first floor and tell the tailor that Gustavo told jew to go and she will do to jew a beautiful job. Jew see, she knows Gustavo — Gustavo is her good friend. Everybody in Pyongyang know Gustavo! They adore Gustavo! She will impressed if jew tell her jew know Gustavo."

Wally leaned in to admire the Kim Il Sung lapel pin and asked Gustavo how he managed to get it.

"Oh!" he exclaimed with a dramatic flip of the wrist, "it is wonderful, no? It was awarded to me by the People's Committee. It was presented to me as a loyal friend of the D.P.R. Korea." He pronounced the letters as if they were words: Dee Pee Are Korea.

"They all know Gustavo, they all love Gustavo. Gustavo is the only foreigner to ever be awarded the Kim Il Sung lapel pin. It is an honor, it is a real honor. I can not tell you how rare an honor it is, but they all know Gustavo and they all love Gustavo, no?"

It was during that outburst of self-admiration that I recalled where I had seen his face — on the internet. An anonymous tourist to Pyongyang had filmed bits and pieces of their itinerary and placed it on the internet for anyone to download and watch. Part of the itinerary for that tour was a visit to the Joint Security Area which straddles the DMZ at the village of *Panmunjom*. It is possible for tourists to visit *Panmunjom* from either direction and, depending on which side of the line the tour guide is on, the tour is flavored to meet specific propaganda needs.

The Joint Security Area sits precisely on the border between North and South and is a hodgepodge of structures that are clustered together tightly in the little enclave of official neutrality. The actual dividing line is marked by a cement curb running right through the middle of the enclave, and on the line sit seven small hastily constructed buildings that look more like temporary classrooms at an overcrowded suburban elementary school than the venue for Cold War rivals to sit down and conduct face-to-face meetings. A few meters back from the line, on the Southern side, now sits an imposing structure that looms over the enclave. It is known as Freedom House. Before Freedom House was constructed in recent years the most imposing structure in the enclave sat on the Northern side; *Panmungak*.

International tourists on the Southern side have been guided by uniformed members of the US military for decades. These hulking young men are required to be taller than the average soldier, wear incredibly short hair, frequently reek of tobacco smoke, and are adept at delivering the scripted propaganda in a booming American-accented voices. One of the many points they have repeatedly made for decades is that *Panmungak* is nothing more than a shallow façade constructed, like everything else in North Korea, for appearance and nothing more.[2] "If you were to walk through the front door," they would boom in a thick Ohio, or Arkansas, or Georgian accent, "you would find yourself at the back door after only two to three paces! It ain't a real building, ladies and gen'lemen. What you are looking at is a sham." They would go on to explain how *Panmungak* was representative of the deceptive, shifting ways of the sneaking North Koreans and should be taken as a warning that they cannot be trusted.

In half a dozen visits to the Southern side of the JSA, it always struck me that these well-meaning nicotine-dependant soldiers had never once stopped to question the logic of their script. The American soldiers have been entrenched on the Southern side of the JSA without a break since 1953. In the pouring rain, in the driving snow, through the sticky summers, round the clock every single day for more than half a century America has had eyes watching the Northern half of the little enclave. Those eyes were watching when the Northern construction crew showed up and started building *Panmungak*. Inevitably they took pictures and filed reports. They could see clearly as the building took shape and came into being. They could see the surveyor's stakes; they could count the paces the construction crewmen took. They saw just how deep it actually was. Nonetheless guides on the Southern side go to great lengths to repeat the erroneous claim again and again — the building is a shallow sham.

In the video Gustavo stood on the steps of *Panmungak* glaring south towards the capitalists and snarled into a bullhorn, "If jew visit Panmunjom from the South the first thing the American and South Koreans will tell you is that this building is fake ... that this a decoration ... that we don't have money to build houses, and we are dying ... so this is a demonstration that the South Koreans lie!"

He concluded his rant by looking across the demarcation line at Freedom House and noticing, high atop the building on a viewing platform, uniformed soldiers standing in the shadows observing him.

He pointed an accusing finger at them for his fellow tourists on the

Northern side and screamed, "Look up there! The American Commander! They are the ones dividing the Korean peninsula and they put the South Koreans in front, just for a showcase for us. They also fly the United Nations flag when they are not authorized, the United Nations does not authorize this! It's a purely American decision, yes?

"This is very important, look up there the Colonels and Generals from the United States are waiting the division of the Korean peninsula. They are the guilty ones!"

From on top of Freedom House, on the southern side of the demarcation line, in the distance, the soldier that had worked Gustavo into a tizzy stood and silently watched. He was wearing the unmistakable uniform of a British paratrooper.

So here he was, the same Gustavo, effusively explaining how everyone in Pyongyang adored him. Among Koreaphiles stories about Gustavo abound — and none of them have pleasant endings. He is depicted as a slightly loony sycophant who does not flinch from the appearance of being nothing more than a toady for the regime. He has been called "party plaything" and "useful idiot." From Argentina he set up the international Kim Jong Il fan club, and then built a web site to promote it. He leads groups to North Korea, and while there remains in costume and in character for days on end. Somewhere along the way members of the press started giving him credibility and in one laughable outing a commentator for an American radio network interviewed him over the phone, and Gustavo, speaking on behalf of the North Korean government, assured listeners that North Koreans were peace-loving people and were conducting nuclear research only as a means to become self sufficient in electric power generation. He went on to say that North Korea had no desire to be involved in the production of nuclear arms because that would not meet the aims of such a peaceful nation. A few weeks later Kim Jong Il proudly detonated his first nuclear bomb.

There are stories of Gustavo's exploits in which he is almost always swaggering, usually playing the part of Party Bullyboy, and inevitably stepping in to protect the honor of the beloved Dear Leader. Inside North Korea, so the stories go, Gustavo is a Juche henchman and operates with impunity. Threats of physical violence from the pudgy little Argentine are taken seriously because the North Koreans step back and allow him room to maneuver whenever he decides to use thuggery to demonstrate his filial loyalty. In Argentina he's just another part-time taxi driver and occasional web page designer, but in North Korea he is Gustavo! Across East Asia on any given night at the bar of any Foreign Correspondent's Club someone nursing a beer has a Gustavo story and none of them have happy endings.

With demonstrative gesticulation, Gustavo and a growing audience moved up the steps toward the departure hall and I used the opportunity to quietly drift away.

In the departure hall were long counters stocked with duty-free items providing one last opportunity for tourists to support the regime with hard currency. Rows of large bottles contained coiled snakes with helpless, blank white eyes peering through alcohol. Stacks of sealed tin boxes contained North Korea's glorified white carrot — ginseng root. There were recordings of the Pochonbo Electronic Ensemble playing the happening sounds of today, and the KPA Third Brigade Vocal Infantrymen belting out praises for the Dear Leader in testosterone-laden baritone and bass. There were books by and about the Kims. There were a few cheesy postcards (but no stamps), and there were cigarettes. I kept my nose down and eyes averted lest Gustavo should make contact and draw me in with his regime-approved tractor beam.

Mr. Kim the Younger appeared from the wings and strode forth with marked purpose as he announced to our little group, "Please come with me." My heart skipped a beat.

We walked with him no more than three more paces before we all stopped at the end of a queue. At the head of the queue was the plywood booth concealing the uniformed immigration official who was prepared to stamp us out of the DPRK. Mr. Kim handed Charles his passport and documents and instructed him to step forward in the queue. He then handed passport and documents to Alice and solemnly instructed her to follow. He flipped open the next passport to make sure it was correct, then handed it to Wally. The last passport he handed to me.

As Charles stepped up to the immigration desk ahead of me, I turned to Mr. Kim and extended my hand.

"Mr. Kim, thank you for an exceptional time. It has been more wonderful than I could have imagined," I told him sincerely.

He smiled and said, "It was a pleasure to be your guide, I am happy you have been able to see my country and learn the truth."

With that I said, looking him sincerely in the eye, "Mr. Kim, I would like to make a contribution to the International Friendship Exhibition. I would like to show my respect for the Dear Leader by presenting a gift, and I would like to be able to give it to you and know that eventually it will find its way to him. Would that be acceptable?"

Mr. Kim furrowed his brow and said, "I'm not sure I understand ... you want to present a gift to Kim Jong Il?"

"Yes!" I said, "I want to give the gift to you and have you send it to him so it can be included in the International Friendship Exhibition."

Before he could react I reached into my bag and produced a Bootsy Collins compilation CD[3] and placed it in to Mr. Kim's hands. From the CD cover Bootsy looked back at Mr. Kim through exaggerated star-shaped rhinestone-studded glasses and leaned to the side as huge, dazzling teeth were exposed in a mischievous grin.

Mr. Kim looked blankly at the CD cover not quite knowing how to respond. He wasn't sure if my gesture was a subtle backhanded insult, or a genuine show of respect to the Dear Leader. Obviously he didn't know Bootsy Collins. How can anyone be insulted by fourteen groovalicious tracks of syncopated funk with the otherworldly sound of Bootsy's driving space bass? The tracks had been recorded back when musicians of that genre wore gravity-defying afros the size of high-altitude weather balloons and spangly sequined attire that announced there was a party going on and the entire planet was invited. Top hats, elaborate feathered headdresses, floor-length boas, novelty sunglasses, rhinestone-tipped walking sticks, ruffles, glitter, and platform shoes were all part and parcel of the sound that comes out of the speakers when playing Bootsy's music.

I bit my tongue to keep from laughing and said in a sincere tone, "Mr. Kim, if you would see that this gift is presented to the Dear Leader, I would be very honored."

He opened a sheaf of documents and slid the CD inside among his papers, then closed it and said, "Thank you for the ... gesture."

I will never know if Kim Jong Il received the CD, but there is a chance that in one of his many plush villas he poured himself a snifter full of aged French cognac, popped in the CD, leaned his bouffant back against a plush throw-pillow, and in the middle of the planet's most isolated nation made the fabled mothership connection.

The two Kims spoke in muffled tones as the queue edged ever closer to the immigration booth. I quickly leafed through my North Korean travel document for the first time and made a quick documentary photograph before it was surrendered and never seen again. With a small digital camera I took a single photograph, then quickly glanced around to see if any North Korean officials reacted to the flash. It appeared that either nobody noticed, or more likely nobody cared.

I glanced back at the Kims, both still wearing the exact same garments they had worn for the duration of our visit, and they both nodded and smiled. They had only a brief respite before having to pick up a group of Germans for virtually the same tour all over again. They were scheduled for five days with the Germans and their *vinalon* outfits certainly looked up to the task.

At the darkened immigration booth a hand snatched my passport and travel document then disappeared in to the gloom. I stood quietly waiting while below me, through the small slit, all I could make out was the top of an oversized Army hat. After a few moments of silence there was the familiar sound of papers being stamped, then my passport was placed on the counter and the hand disappeared once again into the murk of the plywood booth.

That was it. My passport contained no indication that I had ever stepped foot in the Worker's Paradise. It was as if the entire thing had been an undocumented escapade in a surreal Orwellian landscape ... which pretty much captures what it was. I turned back to wave at the Kims one last time but they were gone. It would have been a heart-warming wave between comrades, too.

In the final room before the stairs that lead to the tarmac, dozens of tourists loitered around waiting to board the plane. In the meantime a television blared in the corner and the North Koreans appeared satisfied that volume truly does make up for lack of content.

The counters and shelves were stocked with yet more adder liquor and cigarettes, ginseng root and postcards. Beside the exit door was the final corkboard of propaganda before departing the airport and departing the DPRK. On that corkboard were a pair of photographs showing a wheelchair-bound Ri In Mo meeting the Great Leader Comrade Kim Il Sung.

Ri had been caught south of the 38th Parallel at the end of the war and because he steadfastly refused to denounce communism, languished in a South Korean prison for more than four decades. With his health ailing and Kim Young-sam's Sunshine Policy needing some grist for the mill, Ri was wheeled north through *Panmunjom* and pushed across the line in to the all-embracing arms of the system to which he had been loyal through all the dark years of South Korean prison.

When he was finally repatriated in 1993, South Koreans were already starting to become somewhat cynical at the thought of reunification. Colleagues at the time joked that repatriating Ri would save Southerners the cost of room and board and by sending him back North when they did, the Southerners were going to save themselves the cost of his internment. Judging by the photos of the day Ri didn't appear long for this world. Illness and age had given him a bizarre demeanor.

He received a comrade's welcome and was the Red Star Hero of the Month in Pyongyang. This was a model citizen showing the entire world that

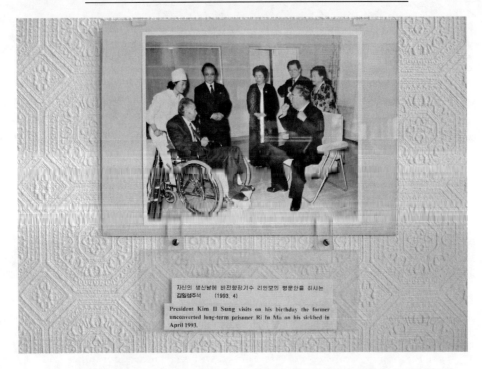

자신의 생신날에 비전향장기수 리인모의 병문안을 하시는
김일성주석   (1993. 4)

President Kim Il Sung visits on his birthday the former
unconverted long-term prisoner Ri In Mo on his sickbed in
April 1993.

On a corkboard positioned to be the last thing departing tourists see in North Korea, a photograph of unrepentant and repatriated former political prisoner Ri In Mo meeting the Great Leader a year before the Great Leader became the Eternal President. Ri's tale of 40 years in a South Korean jail was featured in a North Korean propaganda film and inadvertently confirmed to North Korean viewers that those imprisoned in the South were treated well enough to survive for that long.

his personal resolve illustrated that the Northern system was far superior to the corrupt system run by the puppet clique down South. The North Koreans hastily put together a documentary film to show the entire nation how resolute their loyal son had been. Only after the film had been distributed across North Korea did it become obvious that as an internal propaganda tool the film was a complete failure.

When the narrator used "the voice" to explain that Ri survived more than forty years in a South Korean prison and frequently went on hunger strikes to demonstrate his steadfast opposition to the corrupt and fraudulent Southern system, the North Korean viewers eventually recognized that if Ri had sufficient food to afford himself the luxury of a hunger strike, then food in the South must be pretty abundant ... and surviving just a couple of years in a North Korean jail was all anyone managed to do. Nobody in a Northern jail lasted any

The main terminal building at Pyongyang's Sunan Airport. The enormous portrait of the Great Leader Kim Il Sung features eyes that appear to follow the movement of planes as they taxi up and down the runways. The word on the left is "Pyongyang" in Korean script.

longer. Lee had done forty years in a Southern jail and was still kicking — thus many in the North concluded things down south must be pretty good.

I peered at the laminated photos of Lee and the Great Leader in a hospital room, mounted on blue cardboard and held to the wall with plastic clips. Caught on film in an animated moment, the Great Leader had his hands up like a boxer as he explained something important to Lee. In turn Lee helplessly leaned forward out of the wheelchair in a slow-motion slide towards the floor. The final piece of propaganda presented to foreign guests before departing the Worker's Paradise is confirmation that the South keeps their prisoners alive longer and in better health than the North. Tacked right beside the final exit door out of the country was a visual statement a little too subtle for the North Koreas authorities.[4]

The passengers on Air *Koryo* flight JS151 to Beijing were summoned to the plane and without fanfare we were herded down the steps and into a waiting bus that took us in a wide arc across a short distance to the plane. As was the case on the way into the Worker's Paradise, the ground staff who had assisted us to get on the bus were able to walk across to the plane and get in position to assist us getting off long before the bus clamored to a stop. What was probably started as a pretense to capacity and ability has long ago given way to the reality that it is all an elaborate façade. The ground staff sighed and looked blankly into the middle distance as they went through the motions of assisting passengers to get out of the bus and onto the steps leading to the plane.

The Great Leader, however, was looking directly at me. He didn't look at any of the other foreigners, just me. From atop the terminal building his portrait and those mysterious eyes followed me from the building to the plane and up the steps. The queue of passengers extended through the fuselage and out to the steps and as I stood on the top step waiting to move forward, I glanced again at the Great Leader Comrade Kim Il Sung—a big red "평양" to his right, and the Romanized equivalent "Pyongyang" to his left. His smile featured unbelievably dazzlingly white teeth, but his eyes were not smiling. His eyes were fixed directly on me as he sat up there on top of the terminal building watching until the door was securely locked shut to make sure I didn't try to pull any last minute capitalist shenanigans in the glorious paradise he had built. My sixty-six hour sojourn was over. His unwavering eyes peered relentlessly until our plane vanished over the horizon.

Epilogue

On arrival in Beijing I found a frazzled Charles in the crowd. He had been assigned a seat beside Gustavo and for the duration of the flight Gustavo had delivered a relentless stream of combative ranting and mindless panegyric jingoism. He was more than just a costumed fan-boy; Gustavo had been recruited into a cult.

With saucer-sized eyes Charles said with shaking head, "What a nut case. You should have heard some of the things he was saying ... at first it was unbelievable, and then it was just scary.

"He found out I have a travel company web page and it turns out he had seen it! He told me he and his friends were not pleased with the background section on the web page and suggested I might consider changing it! It's three paragraphs on how the North Koreans started the war! It was as if he was saying 'change it — or else!'..."

Alice appeared with her carry-on bag and chimed in, "I was seated in the row in front of you and I could hear everything he was saying. It was ... unsettling."

Charles added, "I don't think I want a *jamba*. If that idiot wears one, then I don't need one."

Wally, who had taken part in the conversation with Gustavo, said, "He's demented. That's a good reason to not wear a *jamba* ... looks like only demented people wear them," and with that the fleeting desire to acquire the signature Kim Jong Il costume was quenched.

We passed through immigration and re-entered the People's Republic of China as a group, but that was the final group activity. Charles exchanged pleasantries and hurriedly excused himself because he had another group of tourists arriving and he would be starting a repeat of almost the same tour of North Korea immediately. Alice found her way to the baggage claim area and, sure enough, the North Koreans had sent them an hour away to Beijing and no farther. She rechecked her bags and quickly boarded a long flight back across the Pacific. Wally and I had time to kill before our respective flights, so we both bought large cups of real coffee — the first coffee either of us had had in several days — and spent an hour reminiscing about our shared times in the capitals of both Koreas.

Despite what many Koreans on either side of the DMZ say, the Koreas are not one — not any more. They are two — two distinct nations, two distinct societies, two distinct cultures. There are lots of lingering similarities, but the days of two severed halves being able to fit comfortably back together are over. As the years go by they are not so much drifting apart as they are sailing in opposite directions at full steam. The *Juche* Idea has been very successful in isolating North Korea and giving the populace the jaw-clenching determination to succeed alone. The aloneness doesn't include South Korea. Likewise, the cousins on the South side of the DMZ have evolved into wealthy consumers preoccupied with issues that aren't even known or understood in the North. In many respects the average citizen on the streets of South Korea now has more in common with a pedestrian in Saskatchewan than in Pyongyang.

Wally checked in, we said our goodbyes, and he moved deeper into the airport to eventually board his flight to Seoul where he would attend a conference to discuss, among other things, aspects of North Korea. I had hours to kill before being allowed to check in for my flight to Bangkok, so I found the Sunbird Digital Relaxation Harbor and ordered a second cup of coffee and half an hour of internet time.

As I sent off quick e-mails alerting loved ones that I had made it out of one communist nation into another, I looked up to see Gustavo and his fawning sidekick docked at terminals on the far side of the harbor. They were conspicuously taking advantage of the internet that was not available in the Worker's Paradise and in so doing they had both opened the top of their costumes; Gustavo unzipped his *jamba* to reveal a white undershirt, and the sidekick unbuttoned and yanked open his stiff nautical collar. Both of them quietly slipped off and pocketed their Kim Il Sung lapel pins.

Several hours later I stood in a queue waiting to check in for a flight to Bangkok. Three queues away stood Gustavo and his friend.

Like the rest of the airport the business class lounge was cramped, soiled, and stuffy. Only two of five computers were functional and for the duration of a three-hour visit one was commandeered by a squirming Chinese lad engrossed in a mind-numbing video game, the other by an odoriferous, unshaven, swarthy man in white robes and headdress who spent the entire time scanning Arabic web pages, then glancing over his shoulder to see who might be observing him. Again and again other guests stood and silently waited for a turn at one of the computers. Again and again they eventually gave up and walked away. They would retreat to a chair, fan the damp air, and nibble peanuts and rice cakes and sip tepid Chinese soft drinks or flat beer. After a while Gustavo and his sailor-suited duenna stumbled in and attacked the complimentary beer like frat boys on a Friday night. I would have expected a committed communist like Gustavo to make a social statement by remaining outside among the proletariat in the seatless corridors, but apparently the lure of plush surroundings proved too seductive. His dedication to the masses was set aside until the final boarding call.

On arrival in Bangkok's massive new Suvarnabhumi Airport — a name the Thais insist on Romanizing with a handful of extra letters that aren't pronounced and missing a couple of letters that are — I walked down the exhaustingly long corridors towards very distant immigration desks. Gustavo and Co. rocketed past, obviously eager to get out there and start enjoying the capitalistic decadence of Bangkok. As he passed we made eye contact and he said with a smile, "Gustavo will find jew on the streets later tonight, no?"

Appendix I

Wrestling Results from the Pyongyang International Sports and Culture Festival for Peace

———— ∞ ————

DAY 1

Date: April 28, 1995
Attendance: 150,000

Bout 1— Yuji Nagata, the pride of Chiba, defeated Tokimitsu "Kendo Kashin" Ishizawa in a thrilling display of tactical genius and lightning-fast maneuvers in a brief 4:28.

Bout 2— Though now known as a professional golfer, Keiko "Bull" Nakano was a force to be reckoned with in Japanese Women's Wrestling. She joined All Japan Woman's Pro Wrestling 1985 Rookie of the Year Akira "Dangerous Queen" Hokuto to form a tag team that defeated the formidable pairing of Manami Toyota and Mariko Yoshida. Despite Yoshida's patented Spider Twist, Nakano pinned her in 8:34.

Bout 3— In 1984 he represented Japan at the Los Angeles Olympics, but by 1995 he was using his Northern Lights Suplex to win bouts with the most obstinate opponents. Hiro Hase pinned Canadian Chris "Wild Pegasus" Benoit in a dazzling 10:10.

Bout 4— Masa "Mister Black Jack" Chono teamed up with Hiro Saito, two-thirds of the famed Team Wolf, and used the Cradle Piledriver and Double Underhook Drop to wear down the masked Osamu "El Samurai" Matsuda and former sumo wrestler Tadao "Takanofuji" Yasuda. Chono pinned El Samurai after administering an Inverted Atomic Drop in 8:06.

Bout 5— American Charlie "Too Cold Scorpio" Scaggs defeated Shinjiro Ohtani in a quick 2:37. Despite Ohtani's Spiral Bomb and Cobra Clutch,

Scaggs had an arsenal of weapons including the Moonsault, the Shooting Star Press, and the trademarked Scorpio Twister I and Scorpio Twister II and in fewer than three minutes he had Ohtani bleeding like a stuck pig. The referee was forced to stop the match due to the excessive bleeding.

Bout 6— Kensuke "Masked Volcano" Sasaki needed a full 8:34 and a bag of tricks including his signature Strangle Hold Alpha, Strangle Hold Beta, and the Super Frankensteiner to eventually pin Jesse Ventura's one-time tag-team partner Masa Saito.

Bout 7— In the much anticipated International Wrestling Grand Prix World Heavyweight Title Match, Shinya "Shogun" Hashimoto pulled out all the stops and used every weapon in his arsenal, including his signature Running Leg Drop, the Bottom Rope Superplex, and the usually-lethal Triangle Lock in a twenty-minute extravaganza with the enormous American Scott Norton and his much feared Shoulderbreaker move. After an exhausting 20:00 time was called, the match was judged a draw, and Hashimoto retained the title.

DAY 2

Date: April 29, 1995
Attendance: 160,000

Bout 1— After achieving a tag-team victory on the first night, Hiro Saito returned on the second night and, despite his much-feared Guillotine Choke, managed to pin Yuji Nagata in 5:29.

Bout 2— American Eddy "Black Cat" Guerrero achieved initial fame in Mexico, but went on to fame in the United States and Japan with his patented Frog Splash and Three Amigos moves. He pinned Osamu "El Samurai" Matsuda in 4:56 to provide his second defeat in as many nights.

Bout 3— Canadian Chris "Wild Pegasus" Benoit came with more than sufficient moves to be a formidable threat to any wrestler. They included his infamous Gutwrench, the Crippler Crossfire, the Spinning Legtwist, the Sharpshooter, and the Crippler Crossface. That was sufficient to defeat American Charlie "Too Cold Scorpio" Scaggs in 6:22.

Bout 4— Despite the exhausting draw on the first night, American Scott Norton returned on the second night to join forces with Masa "Mister Black Jack" Chono in a tag team designed to defeat all comers. It took them only 8:40 to defeat the team of Akira Nogami and Takayuki Iizuka when Norton pinned Nogami.

Bout 5—American Michael "Road Warrior Hawk" Hegstrand was only half of the Road Warriors duo and was used to fighting as a team, but thanks to signature moves such as the Backhand Chop and the Hangman's Neckbreaker he needed only 2:21 to pin Tadao Yasuda.

Bout 6—American tag team heroes the Steiner Brothers, Rick and Scott Steiner, used namesake moves such as the Steiner Recliner and the Steiner Flatliner to defeat opponents Hiro Hase and Kensuke "Masked Volcano" Sasaki in 11:51 when younger brother Scott pinned Hase.

Bout 7—Akira "Dangerous Queen" Hokuto and Keiko "Bull" Nakano had been victorious tag-team partners the previous evening, but on the second night they were opponents in a hair-pulling, face-slapping, eye-gouging dual for the *Consejo Mundial de Lucha Libre* (CMLL) World Women's Heavyweight Title Match. After an exhausting 8:04, Hokuto pinned Nakano to retain her title.

Bout 8—In a match that would provide North Korea with images that would end up on propaganda leaflets strewn across South Korea, Japan's legendary Antonio Inoki, the same Inoki who had fought Muhammad Ali to a draw almost twenty years earlier, fought the equally legendary American Ric "Nature Boy" Flair in a match that lives on in the memory of 160,000 North Koreans as the day Rikidozan's disciple soundly spanked the blonde-haired Yankee imperialist on the floor of May Day stadium. The bout lasted a heart-stopping 14:52.

Appendix II

Foreigners Give Impressions of "Arirang"

———— ❧ ————

The North's Korean Central News agency provided this press release for the same Arirang performance seen by the author.

Pyongyang, April 28 2007 (KCNA)—The mass gymnastic and artistic performance "Arirang" is going on in Pyongyang, drawing a large number of spectators.

It was appreciated by the participants in the WHO Southeast Asian Regional Consultation on Strengthening Health Systems based on PHC Approach. They were unanimous in saying with deep emotion that such wonderful performance can never be seen in any other part of the world.

The performance "Arirang" is a great masterpiece, Tarun Seem, head of the Indian delegation, said, adding that he could came to know well about the meaning of the Korean song "Arirang" and the "Arirang" nation, watching the performance.

Sultana Khamum, director of the Regional Office for South-East Asia of the World Health Organization, said that the performance made him see how high the Korean people's wisdom, talent and sense of discipline are.

Mohammad Shahjahan, a member of the Indonesian delegation, said that it is great fortune of his to have enjoyed the performance, describing the performance as the best both in contents and level of creation.

Appendix III
Propaganda Slogans

American imperialist invaders, don't forget the lessons of history!

미세침략자놈은, 력사의 교훈을잊지만나!

Long Live the Glorious Juche Ideology!

위대한주체사상만세!

We Are One!

우리는하나!

Long live the peerless commander General Kim Jong Il who has established our country as one of the world's nuclear states!

세계적인핵보유국을일떠세우신절 세의령장김정일장군만세!

The Great Leader Comrade Kim Il Sung Will Always Be with Us

위대한수령김일성동지는영원히우리와함께신다

Let's Arm Ourselves More Thoroughly With the Revolutionary Thought of the Great Leader Comrade Kim Il Sung

위대한수령김일성동지혁명사상으로더욱철저히무장하자

We Are Happy

우리는행복해요

Long Live the Glorious Korean Workers Party

선군혁명의준마를다고질풍같이달리자!

Long Live the Democratic People's Republic of Korea!

조선민주주의인민공화국만세!

Long Live the Revolutionary Thought of the Great Leader Comrade Kim Il Sung!

위대한수령김일성동지혁명사상만세!

Long Live the Glorious Korean Labor Party

영광스러운조선로동당만세!

Long Live the Great Military-First Policy!

선배리!!!규제리께!

Devotedly Defending the Great Leader!

결사옹위!

Let's Sound the Drum of the Military-First Revolution Even Louder!

선군혁명의북소리더높이울리자!

Let us Rush Forward at the Speed of the Military-First Revolution!

선군혁명의준마를다고질풍같이달리자!

Let Us Learn for Korea!

조선을 위하여 배우자!

Love Our Mountains and Forests

산림애호

Long Live the Military-First Revolutionary Ideology!

선군혁명사상 만세!

The Great Kim Jong Il of the 21st Century

세기를위대한김정일!

You and I, together let's move forward to build a rich and powerful fatherland

너도나도떨쳐나부강조국건설하자

Chapter Notes

Arrival and Day 1

1. *Vinalon* is a North Korean synthetic fiber made largely from limestone. *Vinalon*'s inventor, the late Lee Sung Ki (리승기), is a national hero. The fabric created from *vinalon* fibers is lauded in the North Korean press as a miracle fabric and just one more weapon in the war against imperialism; however, non–North Koreans have reported it is somewhat akin to wearing a plastic garbage bag against the skin.

2. Rhodesian David Richardson and Englishmen Andrew Holloway and Michael Harrold were three of the early long-term native-speaking English language editors in Pyongyang. From their accounts it is obvious that their contribution was seen as useful and in their position seen by their employers as uniquely qualified. In contrast I spent many years being paid significant sums of money to edit English in Seoul and despite my status as a native speaker, on a regular basis my editing was dismissed as unnecessary and the final product reverted to the Konglish of the original author.

3. *Soju* (소주)—fire liquor. Never has a Korean to English transliteration been so accurate. Korea's national distilled beverage. Of such varying degrees of quality that it ranges from drinkable to offensive.

4. *Songun* (선군) is a purely North Korean concept from the early '90s that is difficult to capture in a simple English translation but is usually rendered as "military first."

5. Actually, the geographic Cheese Label fans count the points of integer degree intersections of latitude and longitude all over the planet. More than half of those points are in the ocean. The fanatics decided, for some unfathomable reason, that the points just off shore count as well. So on their list actually half of North Korea's points are offshore. Nine points are on dry North Korean ground, and nine would require an enthusiast to use some sort of flotation device and a waterproof camera. Hovering just off the coast of North Korea snapping photographs without meeting a grisly fate would be a tricky maneuver. I suspect it will be quite some time before any of the points on dry ground are visited, and even longer before any of those nine offshore points are bagged.

6. As of 22 March 2006 the European Union's European Comission has, through Commission Regulation (EC) No 474/2006 prohibited North Korean airplanes from getting anywhere near EU territory.

7. *Juche* (주체) is a homegrown ideology of self reliance that is one of the foundation blocks of the North Korean system. Also, since 1997, the North Koreans have forgone the Gregorian calendar and use their own "*Juche* Calendar" which commences from 15 April 1912 — the birth of the late Great Leader Kim Il Sung. Coincidentally, Kim Il Sung was born as the ill-fated *Titanic* was sinking.

8. The North Koreans refuse to stamp a passport from a nation with which they do not share diplomatic ties, such as the United States. Therefore, when a US passport holder is given a rare opportunity to visit North Korea as a tourist, they issue a special piece of paper on to which their official stamps are placed. That page remains with the passport at all times. On departing North Korea that page is surrendered and not a trace of North Korean officialdom remains to be seen in the pages of said passport.

9. *Rodong Shinbun* (로동신문), the official organ of the Korea Worker's Party, otherwise known as a newspaper.

10. *Hwiparam* (휘파람) is the Romanization of the word "whistle," thus the car is the "Whistle Car," which might be the most unusual and misguided name for a passenger automobile since the Daihatsu Naked or possibly the Honda Life Dunk. Of course there were other glorious naming failures such as

the Honda That's, the Isuzu Mysterious Utility, the Mitsubishi Delica Space Gear, the
Suzuki Cappucino, and the Toyota Deliboy.
However the worst possible name for an automobile was not created on the left side of
the Pacific, it came from Detroit; the GM
Impact.

11. Five months after we drove along the
flood control canal and listened to the glorious exploits of the heroic Kim and his mag-
nanimous leadership, Pyongyang experienced
unusually high amounts of rainfall and the
Potong River broke its banks and flooded that
part of the city. Hundreds of deaths were reported.

12. One of the many Koreaphile myths is
that bicycles are outlawed in Pyongyang. Apparently the importation of used bicycles
from Japan is outlawed, but the Tianjin Digital Bicycle Plant in Pyongyang produces 40
different models and churns out tens of thousands per year. At just under $30 a bike, most
people in Pyongyang can't afford them anyway ... but they exist.

13. Director Shin Sang-ok (신상옥) had
died at the age of 80 in a Seoul hospital almost exactly a year prior to my visit to the
studio. He produced more than 100 films in
North and South Korea, as well as the United
States where he was executive producer of *3
Ninjas: High Noon at Mega Mountain* (star-
ring Loni Anderson, Jim Verney, and Hulk
Hogan), recognized by some as one of the
worst films of all time. His widow, Actress
Choe Un-hui (최은희) is alive and in her early
80s at the time of writing. Long after the visit
it occurred to me that this studio might have
also been home to Prince Sihanouk of Cambodia while he made movies in exile during
the Pol Pot years, but that remains uncon-
firmed.

14. Known as Kenpachiro Satsuma and
also Kengo Nakayama, depending on the
film, he has donned rubber suits and stomped
scale model cities for three generations of
Godzilla fans.

15. There are other claims that he is an
ardent fan of the National Basketball Association and keeps up with games via clandestine satellite dishes, that he is a connoisseur
of cognac and maintains one of the largest
collections in the world, that he is a skilled
marksman and is a crack shot with pistols,
and that he bicycles through a labyrinth of secret tunnels under Pyongyang in an effort to
keep fit. Why attempt to substantiate any of
these claims when they are so fun?

16. I have seen reports of guides at the
studio giving very different figures. The most
impressive claim was 1,724 visits for on-the-
spot guidance and an additional 10,481 times
he didn't go himself, but sent specific instructions about various aspects of film production.

17. The State Book Shop in Vientiane
that provide an impressive and surprise — the official Cuban state response to the Elián
González international child custody battle
clearly presented in an easy to read English
language format complete with black and
white photographs of Havana's leading authorities on all things Elián. They made great
Christmas gifts for the cognoscenti.

18. Pyongyang's 1989 festival drew representation from 177 nations, while Seoul's
Olympics the year before had representation
from 159 nations. Pyongyang's festival drew
a reported 22,000 participants while the
Seoul Olympics drew only 8,391 athletes.
Though most of the world has never heard of
the World Festival of Youth and Students and
just about everyone is aware of the Olympic
Games, on the warm body tally sheet Pyongyang walked away the clear winner.

19. Both Kim Il Sung and Kim Jong Il
were known by different names at birth and
grew into the names we know only later in
life. Kim Il Sung was born Kim Sung Ju and
the story of how he came to be known otherwise is controversial and divisive. Kim Jong
Il was initially known as Yuri "Yura" Irsen-
ovich Kim in Vyatskoye, Siberia, where he
was born. Official North Korean accounts
have evolved over the years and no longer
agree with these claims.

20. Makers of "'*Taeyang*,' the new type
of innoxious anti-corrosive, anti-fouling
paint," that, according to *Foreign Trade*, comes
in black, white, red, green and grey.

21. It is so mesmerizing that in 2002 a
Finnish film maker released *Pyongyang Robo-
girl*, a four-minute short featuring nothing
but the hypnotic movements of those lovely
traffic wardens. I can't understand how anyone could watch for four minutes and feel
that they had enough.

22. Later we were told that the fare is
₩5, but that never had any meaning because

we were never provided the opportunity to buy local currency. We couldn't even see local currency. Even at currency exchange counters they did not have the local currency on offer to foreigners. The official exchange rate of $1 to ₩ 143 would put the fare at about 3.5¢ per ticket — a bargain at twice the price.

23. Reportedly titled *The Great Leader Kim Il Sung Among Workers.*

24. 3 예역원

25. Those stations were added to the Chollima Line as part of a line extension project in the late 80s. Prior to their existence, according to reports from that time, foreign guests were consistently shown *Kwangbok* and *Kongguk*— the final two stations on the nearby Hyoksin Line.

26. The appropriate translation and Romanization of the stadium name is often debated by Koreaphiles. They all have too much time on their hands. The literal translation of 릉라도 5 월 1 일경기장 is "Thick Patterned Silk and Thin Silk Island May First Stadium." Depending on the English language source the stadium is usually referred to as *Rungna* May Day Stadium, or simply May Day Stadium. When speaking English both Mr. Kims called it simply, "May Day Stadium." When speaking Korean they referred to it as "the stadium."

27. The North Koreans call it *Choson-ot* (조선옷), while the South Koreans call the same garment *Han-bok* (한복). Both can be simply translated "Korean clothes" but in Korean both names are politically charged.

28. Kim Hyun Hui (김현희), a.k.a. "Mayumi," was exceptionally photogenic and her newspaper images caught the eye of many a lonely South Korean bachelor. She received scores of marriage proposals even before she was released from protective custody.

29. Taking a cue from the US-led boycott (65 nations) of the 1980 Moscow Games, and the Soviet-led retaliatory boycott (14 nations) of the 1984 Los Angeles Games, the North Koreans cobbled together their own boycott (4 nations). Joining them in staying home in 1988 was Cuba, Ethiopia, and Nicaragua — perhaps the least impressive boycott since the Dutch, Spanish and Swiss stayed home in 1956.

30. The motto of the 13th World Festival of Youth and Students was "For Anti-Imperialist Solidarity, Peace and Friendship," while the Games of the XXIV Olympiad in Seoul used the unofficial motto, "Seoul to the World, the World to Seoul." I suspect the South Koreans sold more commemorative T-shirts with their motto blazoned across the chest than did the North Koreans.

31. Antonio Inoki is remembered in the West for his 1976 bout with Muhammad Ali during which he spent almost the entire fight lying on the mat kicking Ali's legs. Ali suffered blood clots in his legs as a result. Inoki later had a successful political career in Japan.

32. *Arirang* (아리랑) is a traditional Korean folk song popular on both sides of the DMZ. That is where all agreement ends. All other aspects of the song, its origin, its meaning, the correct lyrics, the order of the verses, and the cultural significance are up for debate. Usually the debate is contentious. Generally the topic causes strong emotion to bubble forth among Koreans and quavering voices and moist eyes are a prerequisite for any earnest discussion. While some argue that the name is onomatopoeic, others vociferously disagree and can explain the exact meaning of the word. Arirang is one of the many topics Koreans insist is beyond the comprehension of non–Koreans. In my experience any time a Korean explains Arirang to a non–Korean the explanation must be concluded with the reluctant phrase, "but you can't understand." The Mass Games in North Korea share the name with the song.

33. Non–North Korean historians would have us believe that Kim Jong Il was born almost a thousand kilometers to the North Northeast on the banks of the Amur River in a remote Siberian village called *Vyatskoye*. They would also have us believe that his birth happened a year earlier on 16 February 1941. His father, they claim, was there with the Soviet 88th Brigade when the future Dear Leader came into this world. In deference to their Soviet hosts, the Kims called their baby "Yura." At least, that's what the non–North Koreans would have you believe.

34. In the recent past North Korean officials guided the populace in decreasing dependence on livestock that required the input of feed and increased the emphasis on animals that could forage for themselves, such as goats and rabbits.

35. *Chamshil* (잠실) in Korean (from 蠶室 in Chinese) translates as "silkworm room."

36. The Koreans call the river "Amnok"

(압록강) and can be put off by English speakers using the name that became familiar due to the Korean War. Ironically the Korean name is derived from the same characters (鴨綠江) the Chinese use for the river. The meaning of the two names is precisely the same, the pronunciation just happens to be different.

37. The Koreans use the name *Cheju* (제주); however, since 1653 the old European name has been Quelpart. That island off the southern tip of the peninsula features a central mountain known in English as Mount Auckland and small coastal towns with old European names like Port Palm.

38. While among Koreans Dokdo Island long ago started going by "Ullung Do" (울릉도), the Liancourt Rocks and the name one opts to give them remain an incendiary topic in both Korea and Japan. It is wise for English speakers to remain neutral and use the name Europeans gave them in 1849.

39. This includes Socotra Rock, which the Koreans call "*Parang Do*" (파랑도). Tell a Korean that Parang Do belongs to China and expect a ruckus. It doesn't matter that even at low tide it is never above the surface of the ocean; it is claimed as sovereign Korean territory. Most non–Koreans would recognize Socotra Rock as part of the ocean floor.

40. Like many other buildings and monuments in Pyongyang, this one has a name that is debated among Koreaphiles. 양각도국제호텔 literally translates: Sheep Horn Island International Hotel.

41. Four months later I checked into a posh hotel in the swanky Latin Quarter of Paris and on entering the bathroom saw to my amazement a Gordian knot of copper pipes haphazardly left exposed under the basin identical to those in the *Yanggakdo* Hotel.

Day Two

1. Foreign residents of Pyongyang claim that in the 1980s Southeast Asian prostitutes were contracted to work out of the *Ansan* Club and capitalistic Joes could pay the regime a pimping fee to access the girls. Apparently the service ended when not enough customers could be found to make the endeavor financially viable. No money, no honey.

2. The Zürich 4/4 1b *Kurbeli* were decommissioned by the Zürich transit authority in May 1994. Soon after, the North Koreans paid a quarter of a million Swiss Francs for 18 of them. They were bundled up and shipped through the Netherlands in early 1995, then sent on to Nampo by ocean freighter. While the trams were en route, the North Koreans acquired and shipped sufficient rail for just over four kilometers of twin tracks.

3. Kensington University of Glendale was run from a shopfront in a little strip office complex on East Broadway just down from the Glendale Galleria. In November of 2003, on behalf of not only Hawaiians who might have "attended" Kensington but any other "graduate," the First Circuit Court of Hawaii slammed the gavel down on Alfred A. Calabro, President of Kensington University and instructed him to send letters out to former students informing them that on returning their worthless diploma he would refund all tuition and fees paid because KU never had been an accredited university.

4. A big black 1979 Lincoln Town Car looks astonishingly similar to a big black 1979 ZiL 4104, especially when a clear view of the car is hampered by a big coffin and a quarter ton of bouquets.

5. By the Gregorian calendar he died on 8 July 1994.

6. 28 May 1987 happened to be a holiday for Soviet Border Guards and may explain how such a gaffe could transpire. Nonetheless the stunt ended in the resignation of Soviet Defense Minister, Marshal Sergey Sokolov and Air Defense Commander-in-Chief, Aviation Marshal Alexander Koldunov. Another nine generals and 298 officers were dismissed from their positions because of the incident.

7. Korean Pictorial, Pyongyang Foreign Languages Publishing House, Juche 87.

8. The bourgeois-bloodsucker Americans brow-beat 15 toady-states into joining the anti-social United Nations puppet coalition: Australia, Belgium, Canada, Colombia, Ethiopia, France, Greece, Luxemburg, the Netherlands, New Zealand, the Philippines, South Africa, Thailand, Turkey, and the United Kingdom. They coerced an additional four toady-states into sending medical charlatans: Denmark, Italy, Norway, and Sweden. A total of 20 toady-states backed up the illegitimate troops of the Syngman Rhee clique.

9. The glorious North Koreans would have been annihilated had they not sought and received help from their communist comrades in arms. Joining the estimated 260,000 North Korean combatants were an estimated 780,000 Chinese "volunteers." Relatively recently it was confirmed that up to 25,000 Soviets participated as pilots and Air Force support staff.

10. So moved was Kim Il Sung by the unexpected death of Kim Chaek that he told the citizens of the coastal town of Songjin (신 핀) to rename their town Kimchaek (범 쾌). Nor surprisingly, they complied at once.

11. Recognized in the West as a trumped-up charge used by Kim Il Sung in one of many purges to remove challenge to his authority.

12. Australia and North Korea originally established diplomatic ties on 31 July 1974, but unexpectedly severed them after only 466 days on 8 November 1975. The reasons behind the severing of ties has never been completely explained by either side, but one can assume the reasons are "unique."

13. 돌싸움

14. *bbali-bbali* (빨리 빨리)—"hurry-hurry." One of the mantras of collective Korean consciousness.

15. Speed Battle (속도전), an organized frantic burst of activity that is, in reality, a desperate attempt at accomplishing unreachable production goals. While the *Chollima* Movement took North Korea forward at Mach 1, speed battles were quick bursts of afterburners designed to briefly hurdle the workers forward even faster. Classic photo opportunities during North Korean speed battles show crews of ditch diggers maintaining a ridiculous pace while accordion and tuba bands stand nearby and play encouraging music for their working pleasure.

16. **Pyongyang Liquor**: (120 proof) "Burning taste. It makes a clear distinction from other 'quaffable' liquors," **Sinyangsul Soju**: (80 proof) "A descent scent of a Korean soil floats in a mouth," **Pulrosul Adder Liquor**: (120 proof) "Tastes a bit fishy for its high alcohol concentration. Some find it unpleasant," **Morusul**: (32 proof) "Tastes of a red wine and leaves no inebriety."

17. Three months after asking Mr. Kim to convert to *pyong*, the South Korean government enacted a law that penalized merchants

₩500,000 for using old units of measurement such as the *pyong* in commercial transactions. Though South Korean law required the use of the metric system since 1961, it had never been completely enforced.

18. This graceful gesture on Sihanouk's part allowed the Australians and North Koreans, who had no diplomatic relations, to go ahead with the matches. With the unexpected cancellation of the 1963 Southeast Asian Peninsular Games, Phnom Penh had a new stadium with nothing to host, so Sihanouk instructed 25,000 fans on one side to cheer for the North Koreans, and the 25,000 fans on the opposite side to cheer for Australia. Two games were played in quick succession and the North Koreans won both the "home" and "away" game, then traveled to England for the finals.

19. Cambodia's King-Father Norodom Sihanouk wasn't just a monarch. He has been King of Cambodia twice, Sovereign Prince twice, Prime Minister twice, President once, and various positions in various governments in exile through the years.

20. Han (한) (from the Chinese character 恨): unrequited resentment.

21. Though things have changed since then, at the time many South Koreans were unwilling to concede that Ireland remains divided, Cyprus remains divided, China remains divided, and numerous nations across Africa were divided up and parceled out by Europeans and those divisions remain in place today. There was, and is, a collective need to recognize the uniqueness of Korea's division.

22. The Presidential Succession Act of 1947 queues up the replacements in the order of: Vice President, Speaker of the House, President Pro Tempore of the Senate, Secretaries of State, Treasury, Defense, the Attorney General, Secretaries of the Interior, Agriculture, Commerce, Labor, Health & Human Services, Housing & Urban Development, Transportation, Energy, Education, Veterans Affairs departments, and now Homeland Security. In North Korea they don't need a succession plan because the Great Leader Kim Il Sung is President for Eternity.

23. During lunchtime on the Liberation Day holiday, 15 August 1962, 21-year-old Private First Class Joe Dresnok ran north across the DMZ into the welcoming arms of Kim Il

Sung. Private Larry Abshier had gone up for the loving embrace four months earlier. Soon they would be joined by Corporal Jerry Parish and Sergeant Charles Jenkins for hugs all around. Eventually a fifth and sixth defector, Privates "Roy" Chung and Joe White headed to Pyongyang, but both died under mysterious circumstances and were not known by the older four. Today only Comrade Dresnok remains.

24. This isn't unusual in the Korean scheme of things. The first microwave oven production facility in South Korea was similarly created by purchasing the Amperex factory in Illmoh Island on Long Island. American producer of magnetrons — the key component in microwave ovens. The Koreans shipped the dismantled Amperex factory across the Pacific in pieces, reassembled the plant in Suwon, then proceeded to dominate the world microwave oven market.

25. *Konbae* (건배), to your health, is it south of the DMZ, but *Mansei* (만세) was used by those swilling booze north of the DMZ. The Korean equivalent of "*Bansai!*" in Japanese, or "*Viva!*" in Spanish. There is no exact English equivalent.

26. Survivors disagree as to whether the final song played was "Nearer, My God, to Thee" or "d'Automme."

27. If *Tangun* was born in 2333 B.C., and if the Korean nation commenced with *Tangun*, then Korea will not amass 5,000 years of history until 2666 A.D.

28. From and including his birth on Monday, 15 April 1912 to but not including his 70th birthday on Thursday, 15 April 1982 is 25,567 days. I speculate that either the Dear Leader's calculations didn't account for the Gregorian calendar's pesky leap years, or else he finished with 17 too many blocks and decided to just round the number off.

29. As difficult as it may be to believe today, for almost two years (10 March 1967 through 20 January 1969) Ramsey Clark was 7th in line for Presidential succession. During that period the entire *Pueblo* Incident came and went.

30. This was actually a lie. Every schoolboy in Texas is probably told how tall the San Jacinto Monument is, but then they go inside the museum and have General Sam Houston's eyes follow them around and they have no memory of how tall the thing is. Hundreds of thousands of little Texans piss their beds after having General Houston's eyes on them. This is a time-honored tradition. After that they don't tend to recall the monument's height nor the formula to convert from imperial to metric.

31. The construction of the San Jacinto Monument was another of the many Depression Era make-work projects under the auspices of the Public Works Administration. It was started on 21 April 1936 and dedicated on 21 April 1939 — exactly three years after the centennial.

32. United States Department of the Treasury Press Release JS 2720, *Treasury Designates Banco Delta Asia as Primary Money Laundering Concern under USA PATRIOT Act*, 15 September 2005.

33. Zokwang is not only infamous for alleged underworld business transactions and involvement in various unscrupulous deeds, it is also infamous for being Romanized with a Z. Koreans opted to do away with the Z sound when they dumped the △ from their script. The △ (known as the 반시옷) efficiently guided Koreans into producing the Z sound, but since their collective vote of no confidence, they come only as close a J or CH. The shadowy North Korean front company should, more accurately, be Jokwang or Chokwang.

34. At one time there was rumored to be a North Korean ship outfitted as a floating brothel that sailed the seas of the Orient and conducted business just inside international waters.

Day Three

1. *Minbak* (민박): South of the DMZ the same name is used for what is in effect a holiday pension. North of the DMZ it still captures a sense of mobile labor brigades leaving the comforts of the cement wonderland to breathe the fresh air of the countryside while helping to ensure the cornucopia of abundance is abundant.

2. After departing North Korea I looked for "Hirokidaji" and never found the name listed among the wrestlers of the event... and only much later did Charles reveal that he had been in attendance for the two-night spectacle in 1995.

3. In fact, on 28 April 1995 the world's

press was dominated by news that a tragic rush-hour explosion at the construction site of Taegu, South Korea's new subway system, sent school buses tumbling through the air and killed more than 100. On the 29th the reporters of the world were rushing to Kitchener, Ontario, to cover the unveiling of a 4,629-kilometer sausage — the world's longest.

4. After carefully triple checking the numbers in my notes, I departed North Korea and started combing through accounts from other visitors to North Korea after the death of the Great Leader (and thus after the new gifts stopped arriving). They had also carefully written down the numbers recited by the guides. None of the numbers matched.

5. The Great Leader decided that in the Worker's Paradise a zoo ought not feature any capitalistic creatures, so when it opened in Juche 47 it featured only Korean animals and those from Comintern nations. Since then the range had reportedly expanded to include a few critters from sympathetic non-communists.

6. Juche (주체) 92 by North Korean reckoning

7. 애국가.

8. 당신이없으면, 조국도 없다.

9. Romanization system for Chinese developed in the 1860s by Thomas Francis Wade, a British ambassador to China and Chinese scholar, and refined in the early 20th century by British Consul Herbert Allen Giles.

10. A Romanization system for Chinese developed by the Chinese in the late 1950s and foisted on English in 1979 when the ChiComs demanded that English print media use their system — thus the change from Peking to Beijing, and the change from Mao Tse-tung to Mao Zedong in written English. Users of other European languages laughed at the ChiComs and continue to Romanize as they please.

11. This is a contentious point between librarians and Asimov fans — did he or did he not publish in the 100s (Philosophy and Psychology)?

12. 즐거운 사라 "Happy Sara."

13. Nowhere in the museum did I see mention of the Soviet 64th Fighter Aviation Corps that participated in the war from November 1950. The Soviets shot down more than 1,300 aircraft of all types and lost only 345 of their own. Sixteen of the Soviet pilots made ace during the Korean War.

14. First launched in 1944 as a US Army

cargo ship, the Navy took possession in 1966 and outfitted her as an intelligence-gathering vessel a year later.

15. Kim Jong Il, *On the Art of Cinema, April 11, 1973*, 1989, p. 1.

16. Hured "Vampire" Brush, Batt Kachis, Jes "Mexican Elephant" Ordega, Gred "Ruffian of the Century" Togo, Gred "Man of Thick Forest" Antonio, Tany Mirth, and Ahre Laborok. Attempting to decipher the oddly phoneticized names is half the pleasure of reading the book.

17. Li, Ho In, *I Am a Korean: The Story of the World Professional Wrestling Champion Rikidozan*, Foreign Languages Publishing House, Pyongyang, 1989. p. 157.

18. Won, Myong Uk and Kim, Hak Chol, *Distortion of US Provocation of Korean War*, Foreign Languages Publishing House, Pyongyang, Juche 92 (2003).

19. At the official exchange rate that was about US 59¢.

20. Despite using four times as many stamps as required, the North Korean postcards never arrived at any of the ten American addresses to which they were sent.

Departure

1. Weeks later Wally discovered that one of the few Western diplomats stationed in Pyongyang had called the hotel attempting to find Wally so he could set up a meeting during his visit, but the front desk staff emphatically claimed that no guest with Wally's name had checked in.

2. Satellite images clearly show *Panmungak* to be at least 16 meters deep.

3. *Back in the Day: The Best of Bootsy*, by Bootsy Collins. Featuring such funk mainstays as "Mug Push," "Stretchin' Out (in a Rubber Band)," and "Psychoticbumpschool," a collection of possibly the most significant recordings to come out of 1970s America — funk or otherwise.

4. A little over a year after the photo was taken, the Great Leader was dead. A month after I stood there looking at the photo, the resolute patriot and hero of the fatherland who refused to buckle under the weight of the southern puppet clique, accepted the warm embrace of the Great Leader in *Juche* heaven.

Index

Numbers in *bold italic* indicate pages with photographs.